Shooting Movies Without Shooting Yourself in the Foot

Shooting Movies Without Shooting Yourself in the Foot

Becoming a Cinematographer

Jack Anderson

AMSTERDAM • BOSTON • HEIDELBERG • LONDON
NEW YORK • OXFORD • PARIS • SAN DIEGO
SAN FRANCISCO • SINGAPORE • SYDNEY • TOKYO

Focal Press is an imprint of Elsevier

Focal Press is an imprint of Elsevier
225 Wyman Street, Waltham, MA 02451, USA
The Boulevard, Langford Lane, Kidlington, Oxford, OX5 1GB, UK

Library of Congress Cataloging-in-Publication Data
Application submitted

British Library Cataloguing-in-Publication Data
A catalogue record for this book is available from the British Library.

ISBN: 978-0-240-81493-3

For information on all Focal Press publications
visit our website at www.elsevierdirect.com

11   12   13   14   5   4   3   2   1

Printed in the United States of America

Contents

PREFACE: WHAT IS A DIRECTOR OF PHOTOGRAPHY?...........................vii

ACKNOWLEDGMENTS xv

CHAPTER 1: Introduction 1

PART 1 • Realities: Preproduction

CHAPTER 2   What's First?...9
CHAPTER 3   We're Still Reading the Script....................................21
CHAPTER 4   A Few More Things to Think About...............................27
CHAPTER 5   The Shot List 31
CHAPTER 6   The Crew 37
CHAPTER 7   The Location 41
CHAPTER 8   Selecting a Camera...55
CHAPTER 9   Selecting Lenses...67
CHAPTER 10   Selecting Film StocK..77
CHAPTER 11   Selecting a Tripod and Head 83
CHAPTER 12   What Everyone Else Is Doing to Prepare........................89
CHAPTER 13   The Night Before 97

Part 2 • Realities: Production

CHAPTER 14   On Time and Ready to Shoot.......................................103
CHAPTER 15   First Day/First Shot 109
CHAPTER 16   Shooting Masters..117
CHAPTER 17   Close-Ups and Coverage 125
CHAPTER 18   Operating the Camera 141
CHAPTER 19   Still More Composition, or Follow the Money 159
CHAPTER 20   The Horror of the 180-Degree Line 169
CHAPTER 21   The Good, the Bad, and the Ugly (But Not Necessarily
              in That Order)..177
CHAPTER 22   Learning the Hardware..185
CHAPTER 23   Why We Light 189
CHAPTER 24   Exposure 195
CHAPTER 25   Exercise: Shooting Your Project on Film 215

v

Part 3 • Realities: Postproduction

CHAPTER 26 Postproduction: Timing and Transferring.........................225
CHAPTER 27 Postproduction: Putting Together a Reel 229

Part 4 • Technicalities

CHAPTER 28 Cameras: Black Boxes 235
CHAPTER 29 Lenses...245
CHAPTER 30 The Zen of Focusing..261
CHAPTER 31 The Magic of Filters 265
CHAPTER 32 Film...271
CHAPTER 33 Color Temperature...277
CHAPTER 34 Using and Handling Film Cameras and Lenses 279
CHAPTER 35 Using a Tripod and Head 297
CHAPTER 36 The Dolly Grip 301
CHAPTER 37 Laboratory and Postproduction Processes.......................303

APPENDIX 1: Cheat Sheets...309
APPENDIX 1.1 Introduction: Nonfilm Camera Checklists and
                       Cheat Sheets 311
APPENDIX 1.2 Simple Steps for Operating a Video Camera...................313
APPENDIX 1.3 PD 100 Cheat Sheet..317
APPENDIX 1.4 DCR-TRV15/17 Checklist/Cheat Sheet..........................319
APPENDIX 1.5 Preparation for In-Camera-Edited Shoots.......................321
APPENDIX 1.6 Tips for In-Camera-Edited Shoots.................................323
APPENDIX 1.7 Tips on Shooting When Scouting Locations 325

APPENDIX 2: Checklists 327
APPENDIX 2.1 DP Location Checklist 329
APPENDIX 2.2 Checklist for Movie on Film..331
APPENDIX 2.3 Camera Assistant Checklists 333

BIBLIOGRAPHY 337
INDEX 343

I think of the title *Director of Photography* the same way Robert Frost regarded the term *poet*: a "gift" word. It's not something you can just decide to call yourself—at least not if you want it to have any meaning. Director of Photography is a title someone else confers on you, "gifts" you with. It happens when you get hired to shoot a film, and your credit on that film is Director of Photography. We don't have to be so scrupulous about *cinematographer*. That's just describing the work done by the photographer of a movie.

The job of Director of Photography demands an ability to be creative and artistic while dealing with technical requirements, communication and organizational skills, budgeting, planning, and cost consciousness. As an artist, he or she is in charge of the entire visual component of a motion picture, and as a manager, he or she is responsible for directing a small army of technicians and craftspeople in working together to achieve an artistic vision.

The work begins with the script, which is always the final word for decisions before actually shooting and always the overall plan the entire team is working with. Reading and analyzing the script is part of the process of getting hired to shoot a film. The director will meet with me after I've read the script, and we'll have a discussion where I can present my ideas and impressions of the project and propose what approach I would suggest. It's the cinematographer's equivalent of an actor's audition. Of course, the director has already seen my reel and reviewed my credits, so this meeting can be crucial in landing the assignment. The director will also want to discuss how I would approach certain technical challenges, logistical problems, or budget constraints. I'm already investing a lot into the project before I've even gotten the job.

I read through the script several times. First, of course, I read for the story. Then I read to get a feel for the structure and for how long I think the film will be and how big the production will be. I know that for most films, one page equals one minute of finished film. But there are plenty of exceptions.

A dialogue-heavy film will move faster—maybe five pages to four minutes. On the other hand, a film with a lot of action will often take longer than a minute per page because the space it takes to describe action is usually short; it is the action itself that is long. The most famous 1/8 page (scripts are broken up into 1/8 pages for scheduling) is "The Allies Invade Normandy Beach." A half-hour of film later, we move on to the next 1/8 page. So my next task is to see how long I think the various parts of the script will take to shoot and if any special equipment (cranes, Steadicam, especially large lights, etc.) will be required.

Every crew member reads the script, and every crew member has to be on the lookout for special needs from his department. But the DP has to supervise all the other departments. Every aspect of the script, including those elements that are the responsibility of another department—location, period, time of year, and so forth—may affect the look of the film, and I am ultimately responsible for that look.

Meeting with the director, we discuss his interpretation of the script and his ideas for the visual style. Often we will refer to other films or to paintings or still photographs. This gives us a solid basis to communicate. We both have common visual references after exchanging our inspirational source. And since they are concrete items, they are more valuable than a generalized reference to "mysterious" or "romantic." What is mysterious to me may be merely dark to you, but with a common set of visual references, we can mean exactly the same thing by talking about "the motel scene in *Touch of Evil.*" When I have a pretty good idea of what the director wants, I begin work on my visual plan. I consider whether I want the film to be generally dark or light, if I want to give it a tone (warm, cool), if I want to use diffusion filters, what film stock I prefer, and what camera package I will order. I begin my breakdown of the script. This involves rereading the script, only this time trying to see in my mind's eye the finished film. Needless to say, it's just my imaginings. But I try to keep in the spirit of the director's wishes. I literally visualize every scene, and as I do this, I note down the way the scene in my mind is constructed of shots. When I'm through, I have a totally planned movie. Then I organize the shots, scene by scene, into a shooting order; this is the start of a shot list. It's now a list of shots in the (mentally) edited film. The shot list is the actual order of shooting, which is different from the shot order (by which I mean the edited film).

It's now time to meet again with the director. He has been working on a similar plan of designing shots and sequences. We compare notes. Most of the time, it's the director's ideas we will use. Sometimes directors will take suggestions from me or even incorporate into the shooting plan entire scenes the way I have designed them. Even if much of my work is not used, I have not been performing a pointless exercise. By doing this work, I have begun to see the film as a living piece. I am closer to the characters, I know the plot well, and I can use my ideas as improvisations on the set if necessary. This can be useful if the director's ideas don't work out or if we're running out of time to shoot. Most importantly, I have thought through the film, and I am more readily able to understand the director's concept by comparing it to mine. I have conceived a film; it's different from the director's conception. But by comparing my ideas to hers, I can see the reasons for her decisions. Without this preplanning, I might just be following her directions slavishly, and I would not be participating fully as an artist of visual storytelling. The shot list we have will be shared with the assistant director, who runs the set. He has to know how much and what kind of work we've planned so he can budget time during the shooting day. The AD is responsible for planning the entire schedule of the film (usually by making production boards—thank goodness we don't have to do that) and the schedule of each day.

It's up to the assistant director, me, and the director to make sure we've planned for enough work and we haven't been overambitious with our goals. On the set, the assistant director will use the shot list to make sure we get all the coverage we need and to use time effectively through the day so we actually shoot everything we've planned.

It's now time to take care of the business end of my work. I hire a crew and order camera, grip, and electric packages. I work with the production manager, the person in charge of day-to-day handling of money, to fit my ideas into his budget. Typically, the crew will be people I've worked with before. I know exactly how good they are and whether they are dependable. We all have a working relationship from previous films. This is why it is so important when you're just starting out to take any job on the set you can get or even work for free, just so people get to know you and see that you will do a good job. Every job is an audition for the next job.

Everything goes more smoothly when the crew knows one another. That way, everybody feels comfortable and can proceed to arriving at a mutually compatible way of working. I hire the camera operator, first camera assistant, key grip (head stagehand), gaffer (chief electrician), and often the dolly grip. The camera crew and the dolly crew make the shots, so it's important that I have the most skilled people I can get—people who can and will follow my directions. The key grip and the gaffer carry out my plan for lighting; they have to be in tune with my style of lighting and my way of working. The key grip and the gaffer usually hire their own crews with the same standards I use when hiring them.

Once we know in what medium we're shooting, I decide on the make and model of the camera. I order a number of accessories, and I let the assistant order the accessories she is comfortable with and needs to do the job. I'm very particular about lenses: They are the vital element in forming the picture. Different lenses have different personalities. Some are ultra-sharp, while others are gentle. Some have a bluish cast, some are orangish, and some are completely neutral. Sometimes I will order a set of lenses all from one manufacturer for consistency, and sometimes I order from several lines in order to have different lenses for special looks. I get both primes (fixed-focal-length lenses) and zooms, and I take care that they match fairly well in their look. I have to know how lenses behave, and I have to be familiar with many manufacturers' lines (Zeiss, Leitz, Cooke, Schneider, Canon, Fuji, etc.). I've acquired this knowledge through my years as an assistant, handling lenses for many different cinematographers, and through tests I have shot over the years as a DP.

I rarely order most of the grip and electrical equipment. Standard packages are available, and the key grip and the gaffer can get them and whatever equipment they know will help them to make this particular picture. And I will make a point of ordering specialized equipment, since I know what the script and the director require. I conceive of shots with specific equipment in mind. Again, working on many shows through the years, I have obtained a familiarity with the most common equipment and with much of the most esoteric filmmaking equipment available. I make a point of reading technical film publications and going to trade shows to keep up with the constant innovations in equipment and technology that are occurring in the film industry.

Meanwhile, I am also working with the production designer. Usually the production designer is hired even before the DP because a long lead time is needed to construct sets. I talk about the ideas the director and I have for a look or looks to the movie, and I work with the production designer to make sure his concepts can fit our plan. I have to be aware of his plans for putting in lighting, and I will often ask for practical lamps to be designed into the set so I can use them for illumination or for accents. I have to be aware of reflective surfaces—doors, windows, mirrors, pictures in frames—all of which tend to cause problems for the photography by being ugly or distracting. If there will be a lot of glass, I ask that it be removable or that windows be put on gimbals so they can be tilted to hide reflections.

As preproduction progresses, I scout locations with the director and the heads of several departments (always the gaffer and key grip, AD, location manager, production designer, sound mixer, and often others according to their interest and availability). When the locations are firmed up, I revisit them with my gaffer and key grip. We talk about anything that may cause problems, how to take advantage of certain locations, and what equipment we should order to deal with the characteristics of a specific place. You could, as I have done, find that the existing lighting of a large department store is ideal for the purposes of the film. So I will use it rather than bring in dozens of lights to create my own look. I save time, labor, and equipment rentals. Usually, of course, I will modify the existing lighting somewhat or enhance it in close-ups. But I want to take advantage of whatever the location gives me. I shoot location stills as a reminder to myself of the look of the locations.

And as production photography nears, I shoot a number of tests. I always test the emulsion of the film I'm using to make sure of its response to light. Although I have probably used the film stock many times before, I always want to be sure that there are no changes, and I need to know how the specific lab we are using will process and print my film. Going through this testing offers a chance to get to know the dailies timer at the lab, or the telecine operator. This person will be responsible for the look of the dailies. Dailies are the first time anyone—director, producer, actors—sees the quality of the DP's work on the project. I have to know that I can be sure of getting the result I want, so a system of communicating with the lab person is essential in making sure we're on the same page.

I also shoot tests of the principal actors. I need to know what kind of light flatters them or makes them look appropriate for their character. Faces vary vastly in their response to light: Some people look best in soft light, and others in hard. The angle—frontal, side, three-quarter—can change the audience's perception of the character. It's hard to maintain realism and at the same time light an actor in the way most flattering to him, but I can use my tests as guidelines, and I can plan camera setups to facilitate doing the lighting I want. Often I will shoot makeup, hair, and wardrobe tests both for the sake of those departments and to let me know if I will have any special challenges. Colors may not register as they do to the eye, patterns may be too busy or muddy, and prosthetic makeup always demands careful lighting to conceal it.

Now—at last—we're in production. Every day brings its own particular and unique character with specific work to do. But I'll talk about the usual routine. As soon as the assistant director calls, "We're in!" the actors come on the set and begin to rehearse. They've been to wardrobe and makeup and are in various states of photographic readiness. The camera assistant has put together the camera, and the dolly grip pushes in the dolly with the camera mounted on it. The director works with the actors while I observe, noting how they tend to place themselves on the set, whether they sit or stand, whether they tend to move toward walls and doorways. For me, walls—because there's always an ugly shadow from an actor near the wall—and doorways—because it's so hard to light them convincingly—are always red flags. If it doesn't disturb the overall blocking, I may suggest that the actors play in a slightly different area.

The director rehearses until he's happy with the blocking. Then there's a full rehearsal for the crew. When the actors stop in position, the second camera assistant lays marks at their feet; this is a memory aid for the stand-ins, who take the place of the actors while I am lighting. (The actors are off in makeup, hairdressing, or wardrobe, or they may be rehearsing.) The key grip and gaffer are watching to see how the lighting will be set and modified. The dolly grip and the operator are probably right next to me, looking for good spots to site the camera. Either during this rehearsal or during a "marking" rehearsal—in which the actors do their moves without emoting—the director and I will talk about how to shoot the scene, how many shots to break it up into, and where to put the camera for each shot. Of course, we have our plans and shot list, but often the actors will do something wonderful that changes our plans for the better, or the set or location might not accommodate exactly what we had in mind. We would like to stick to a plan, but usually it's more of a road map. It tells us where we're going to go, but it doesn't tell us what car we use or how fast we drive.

When everyone's satisfied, the director and actors leave the set, often to rehearse. Now I own the set, and everything that happens is aimed at getting ready for shooting. Usually this time is called "lighting the set" because that's the biggest job that takes place. It's my main work. But the camera crew is refining and rehearsing the shot. I will have shown the operator the shot I want and given a lens size to the assistant. If there's a moving camera, I will set the beginning and end of the shot so the grips can build a dolly track. I will check back with the camera crew to see if they have made any major changes—usually improvements, often just technical adjustments—and to make sure the shot looks like what I want.

I tell the gaffer what I want in terms of light. She and her electrical crew will place the lights. Sometimes the set is one we are returning to, and only a few adjustments are necessary. More often, it involves an entirely new set or location. I have to have in my mind what I want the scene to look like. I consider the time of day and the weather—or what is supposed to be the weather, which we will simulate (direct sun, cloudy skies with diffuse light, etc.). I always have an idea for the look, based on my discussions with the director and on my readings of the script. Let's say it's a day interior—inside someone's apartment. I decide whether this is a well-lit place where I can see everything, and I put light through all the windows, usually with large sources bounced onto cards so the light is diffuse and rich and fills the set. I will also use fill light, very indirect frontal light, to fill in the shadows. I will make sure that wherever an actor stops or has a dramatic moment—and therefore is likely to have a close-up—there is light waiting for him, justified by the set. If it's a day interior that is less bright—the character is depressed or is hiding something—I will bring light through the windows, but I will make it less diffuse so it doesn't reach into every corner. I will often put splashes of "sunlight"—light I have created—so I can keep the exposure dark while giving the illusion of daylight outside. I will keep the fill minimal; the shadows will have some detail, but they will be dark and foreboding.

So for every scene I have conceived a concept for the lighting. I know how I want it to look, and I know how to get it. Depending on the experience of my gaffer, I give more or less detailed directions. A good gaffer knows how to get any look just by my telling him. A less experienced one will need me to suggest which lamps to use and their general placement. Of course, I am working with the key grip simultaneously, since he's in charge of rigging the diffusion material I may need or putting up cards to bounce light into or putting up flags—black cloth on frames—to block the light from any areas where it's not wanted.

When we have the set lit, I check the setup of each lamp. Often I have to adjust it slightly for intensity, direction, or color. I will measure the main lamps to make sure I have a consistent exposure at the level I want. Sometimes I use a viewing glass—essentially a dark gray glass—to help me see where there are unwanted highlights or very dark shadows. I also use either a black-and-white professional Polaroid camera or a digital camera to take shots of the lighted scene. The print from the Polaroid system is very contrasty, so I can immediately see any trouble spots in the lighting. Its abstraction of black and white helps me imagine the two-dimensional picture. I also use a digital camera. I calibrate it to approximate the film or digital movie camera I'm using. The shots from the digital camera are much closer to the look of the film. They still have the advantage of being two-dimensional, as the film is, so I have a better idea of how it will look than from just eyeballing it.

Actually, by now I light mostly by eye. I have a lot of experience, and once I set my main (key) light, I can use it as a basis for setting and adjusting all my other lights. I still use an exposure meter for exact exposure, and I still use a visualizing device—the camera or viewing glass—to keep myself honest. It's likely—I think it's always true—that my eye will adjust to the level and the color on the set. (This is my entire eye-brain system, a subject too large to take up now.) So if I start with a very dark set, gradually it will seem normally lit to me. If I weren't careful, I would start making the light less and less to keep the look dark. Of course, pretty soon I'd have no light at all, and the film—or the chip—would get no exposure. So a mechanical device set to a predetermined standard will let me know that things are the same kind of dark all during the production day, even if they look "normal" to me.

When we are lit, the assistant director calls in the director and actors. There is one more rehearsal to make sure the lights we've set and the shot we've designed will work as we want them to. Then, after hair and makeup do last-minute touchups, we shoot.

This goes on day after day for the duration of the shoot. What may not be obvious is that there is always tension on the set. Everything is being done, literally, for the first time. So there's plenty of room for error and consequent embarrassment. One of my jobs is to keep an atmosphere of competence and goodwill on the set. I make a point of saying hello to everyone in the morning and having some small talk. During the day I'll do the same, taking a coffee break to talk with someone from, say, props. The director has the larger part of this job, but since I command the work of so many people, it's up to me to do what I can to keep relations on an even keel and to keep small irritations from spiraling out of control.

I view the dailies each day with the director and talk about what she likes and what she would like to see done differently. I have to keep a consistent look to the movie, so I can't be changing a lot every day. But I can make sure that whatever I do tends toward the director's wishes. It's possible that the editor—whose assistant assembles dailies—will see the need for a shot to cover something we've missed. There may be shots that won't match in the cutting, or we may face the necessity of doing reshoots (say, the actor is wearing a different-colored shirt in two shots in the same scene, though our problems are rarely that blatant).

After the film is edited and the picture locked, I work with the timer at the lab or the colorist at telecine to "time" the film. *Timing*, a term left over from earlier days, means adjusting the picture so that the color and density are correct for every shot and consistent within the scene. A great change can result from a small adjustment to the brightness of a lamp or the relative intensities of color. I go through the film shot-by-shot, often present with the director, to ensure that the finished film looks exactly as intended.

Timing is as important as preparatory discussions with the director when we decide on a look for the film. I have seen scenes shot in summer be manipulated in timing to look convincingly like a wintry landscape. That sort of extreme manipulation is unusual. But even small adjustments affect the audience's emotional response to the film. Every artistic or practical decision made has an impact on realizing the director's vision. I can change a shot from one that is bright and simply gives the audience information to one that is dark and creates a sense of mystery. I must keep in mind the entire emotional and narrative thrust of the film. The director has the final say, but I am the person who knows what the original intentions were, the one who knows exactly how the lighting was done to fulfill those intentions, and who can make or prevent changes that will alter the impact of the film. At the end of timing, I will approve the final answer print. The way it looks is the way all prints of the movie will look.

The question now is, how do you learn to do this? I've learned from all the cinematographers I've worked with. I've watched them like a hawk, and I've asked more questions than I should. I'll try to put you in my place. The next chapter tells you how.

Acknowledgments

Everybody needs a little help in this world. I hope this book is helpful to you. I have been very fortunate to have had lots of help from some very generous people, both in my filmmaking career and in writing this book.

I first learned the rudiments of filmmaking from Skip Landen, who ran the University film-making unit when I was a student at Cornell. Skip was a professional filmmaker who later became the head of Ithaca College's highly regarded film program. He was endlessly generous of his time and knowledge to all his students, many of whom went on to great success in Hollywood. I feel very lucky to have been one of the first of his many mentorees. I am sure there is a very special place in filmmaker heaven for Skip.

The man I hold most responsible for getting me from Ithaca, New York, to Hollywood, California, is Bruce Kawin. a writer of great books on film history and aesthetics. Without his encouragement and guidance this book would not exist. Bruce and I met in graduate school and have remained friends since. Bruce ventured to La-La land before I did, and it was at his urging that I made the move to Hollywood to attend the American Film Institute as a cinematography fellow.

It was at the AFI that I had the privilege of studying with a legendary teacher, Academy Award winning actress Nina Foch. She taught me about "Directing the Actor" and taught me about life. Also at the AFI, I learned professional cinematography from DP Howard Schwartz, ASC, who remained a mentor and a friend to me for many years until his death. George Dye, Sr., showed me my first professional camera—an ancient side-finder Mitchell BNC—and trained me to build and unbuild it with my eyes closed. He was the first man I knew who could estimate focus distances to the inch by eye.

In the course of my professional career, many people have been kind enough to take me under their wing as I progressed from assistant camera trainee through the ranks to Director of Photography.

Special thanks go to Joe Cosko, the best second camera assistant ever; Baird Steptoe, still a top camera assistant in the business; and Jack Tandberg, another great assistant, all of whom loosened me up and toughened me up at the same time.

Many thanks to DP Phil Schwartz who hired me for my first union 2nd assistant job back when he was a 1st assistant. Phil has been a loyal friend and associate throughout my career.

I owe all I know about cinematography to all the great DPs I have worked with, especially cinematographers Robby Müller, Gregg Heschong, and Bobby Byrne, ASC. I also want to thank John Dykstra, ASC, founder of Apogee and the wizard behind the original *Star Wars*, from whom I learned most of what I know about special effects photography.

Fellow crew members I have learned much from while working with them are 1st Assistant Henry Minski and Dolly Grip Basil Schmidt. As an assistant, I spent countless hours at Panavision and Otto Nemenz, prepping equipment. Both companies were generous with their technical assistance and were great at troubleshooting when problems would come up on the set. Thanks to everyone at those equipment houses who helped me. I want to give special mention to Bob Dunn, Larry Hezzlewood, and Phil Radin at Panavision, and Otto Nemenz, Alex Wengert, and Mark Gordon at Otto Nemenz.

I am also grateful to all the directors and producers with whom I've had the pleasure to work over the course of my career. Shout-outs to directors Joshua Beckett, inspiring and fun to work with; John Harper Philbin, master of the impossible; and Linda Hassani, always challenging artistically and personally.

For any success I have had as a teacher I thank Craig Smith, for six years the chair of the film department at California State University at Long Beach.

Putting together this book would have been impossible without my patient editor, Michele Cronin, and my amazing picture editor, Suzanne Danziger.

It will come as no surprise to anyone who knows me that I owe everything to my best friend Rose Ann Weinstein, my wife. From the first she has generously given me ideas and helped me structure the book. When I despaired of being able to go on, Rose Ann calmly guided me through what I needed to cover. We would often sit over breakfast, and she would ask questions that a novice cinematographer would want to know; I would make notes and work on answering them in my text. She read and reread my writing for clarity and pertinence. She managed to keep me from smothering the book in jargon, and made sure I explained every step clearly and in detail.

CHAPTER 1

Introduction

1

One way to learn cinematography is foolproof and effective, and it's worked for over 100 years. It's apprenticeship. No doubt it began with the first movies, but it unquestionably stems from no later than 1912 when D. W. Griffith brought his company to Hollywood to settle permanently and make movies. One of the people Griffith brought along was G. W. (Billy) Bitzer, his cameraman. Today, the person responsible for everything concerning the photography in movies—cinematography—is variously called the cinematographer or the director of photography (DP). In the early days and for many years after, the cinematographer was usually called the cameraman, or sometimes the first cameraman.

And, very specifically, it was always camera*man*. Women did not shoot feature movies until the 1970s. Certainly the first woman director of photography who was admitted to the Hollywood camera union, then called IATSE #659, was Brianne Murphy in 1977. She was also the first woman invited to join the American Society of Cinematographers, an honorary society and the oldest surviving organization in the film industry. Many female DPs, operators, and assistants are in the business now. Most terminology has finally changed to reflect that, although not always. The first woman admitted to the union as a camera assistant in 1976 was universally known as the "girl assistant cameraman." So please forgive me if I sometimes slip up and say "cameraman" when I am referring to the director of photography.

Getting back to Billy Bitzer, he began as an electrician and worked with Thomas Edison, who became a major producer when his employee W.K.L. Dickson perfected motion picture photography in 1889. Bitzer became a movie cameraman and eventually wound up at Biograph, one of the most important film production companies of the first decade of the 1900s. Biograph became a giant in the industry after D. W. Griffith started directing for them. Griffith quickly became the premier director in the world. So when Griffith became independent and moved to Hollywood, he took his company with him, including Bitzer, who had become the most prominent cameraman in the world and one of the best.

Shortly after the Griffith company arrived, Karl Brown, a young man in a theatrical family, managed to get Bitzer to hire him as his assistant. Bitzer may have had assistants in New York, but Brown is the first person I know of who was an official camera assistant. He learned from Bitzer and performed many duties not today associated with the camera assistant (e.g., shooting stills), but he did become the first professional assistant and set the pattern for the next 100 years.

Karl Brown began by carrying camera cases—still the first job for an assistant—and over the years he learned how to care for the camera, how to load, and how to photograph. He eventually became a top DP himself and a director of major Hollywood productions.

The pattern of apprenticeship is still unchanged: Start as a grunt, learn techniques, gradually get more responsibility, and move through more and more demanding and remunerative jobs until you finally advance to the highest position. It's still a wonderful way to learn. I got my start in camera work when I had the good fortune to be admitted to the Camera Assistant Training Program, a now defunct effort of the camera union (now the International Cinematographers Guild, Local #600, IATSE) and the AMPTP (Association of Motion Picture and Television Producers). The program assigned me first to Panavision (the manufacturer of the best movie cameras in the world) and then for two or three weeks at a time to various movies, TV shows, and commercials. I worked on *Pete's Dragon, Oh God!, The World's Greatest Lover,* and *One on One.* I learned from the crews of *Most Wanted* and *Charlie's Angels.* It was a fantastic experience.

One great aspect of this program was the chance to work with many crews with their different personalities and their different ways of getting the same job done. I could pick and choose from the many variant techniques of being an assistant and slowly build my own style of working. Of course, there's no one right way; a number of different approaches get the same work done in the same amount of time. You might notice that I refer occasionally to "industry standard"; this is an expression the crew uses to denote generally accepted procedures. Sometimes it's the best way to work, sometimes it's the only way, and sometimes it's just the cool way. And everyone on the crew knows it's vital to be cool.

And by the way, cool *is* important. It's not just a matter of social acceptability. If you're cool, you don't run, nobody ever waits for you, and your work appears smooth and effortless. It's a sign that you know what you're doing and that you've achieved mastery. Gaining the confidence of the people you work with—and work for—eases the day; everybody believes that the work is being done well, that the organized chaos of production is proceeding as efficiently and artistically as possible.

Okay, let's get back to my training program. Even though I entered the program with a film school education, I had little experience of the routine of a professional set and not much knowledge about the specialized jargon, the language of the crew. And I knew little specifically about how to load a camera, much less how to do the exalted work of framing and lighting. I learned by watching (and watching and watching). I asked questions, but soon discovered that while most people will be happy to share their knowledge with you, there is a limit to how much time they have to teach you while they're in the middle of shooting. So I learned it is better to watch carefully, pay attention, and see if I could figure out what the crew was doing and why. If you do that, you can ask questions selectively and not make a pest of yourself. It is unfortunate but true that much of what you learn comes from making mistakes. One of the purposes of this book is to share some of mine so you won't have to suffer as much embarrassment as I did while learning the ropes.

On my first day on the set as a trainee, I had been assigned to a TV miniseries, *How the West Was Won*. I was trying to remember who was who on the crew, and I was preparing my slate and camera report. (It seemed like a big thing to be trusted with, and I wanted to be perfect.) I leaned up against a big piece of equipment so I could write more easily. Suddenly, something hit me, my feet went out from under me, and I was looking up at the sky. A big guy leaned over me, reached out his hand, and said, "Let me help you up." Well, this was nice, especially after all the horror stories I'd heard about how rough crews were. He brushed me off and said, "No hard feelings." Hard feelings? I didn't understand. "But I want to make sure you remember this," he said. "See, that thing you're leaning against is a crane arm." Sure enough, I had been leaning against the Titan crane, which is the biggest crane available in the movie business. It is a truck with *ten* wheels and a pivoted arm that can counterweight up to 2,500 pounds, holds the camera at the far end, and can move silently up to 27 feet high. I wouldn't have believed *anything* could move it. And this nice guy who picked me up had knocked me down. "That crane arm has tons of mercury in it to balance it, and if you lean on it, you're going to unbalance it, and someone could get hurt. Remember that."

Chapman Titan crane.
Photo provided courtesy of Chapman/Leonard Equipment, Inc.

I certainly would remember. And I gradually learned that there's a lot of dangerous equipment on a set. But there are also experts who know how to use it properly and without danger to anyone. But a crane, while gigantic and apparently indestructible, can be lethally dangerous if it goes out of control. No one *ever* touches the crane arm except the grip who's working on it. (Grips are the jacks-of-all-trades of the movie industry. They are sort of analogous to stagehands, but they are craftspeople who do work ranging over a far greater area.) The worst case of a violation of crane etiquette is often an excitable director who rides the seat on the camera platform of the crane to see a shot, loves it, and excitedly jumps off before the grips can counterbalance the crane arm. More than one grip and cameraperson have been injured when the arm flies out of control, not to mention the cameras that have been catapulted through the air to land as million-dollar piles of junk.

So there's nothing quite like apprenticeship training. It might not seem terribly efficient—you have to work years to perfect your skills—but there's a lot to be said for having your ass on the line while you're learning. Unfortunately, not everyone can get an entry-level job working on a camera (or grip or electric) crew, where they can learn cinematography. So what else can you do? Another option is to enroll in a college course that allows you to work with professionals on a low-budget project. There aren't many of them, so you may have to go a bit afield to find one.

I was lucky enough to have this experience. One summer while I was attending film school at Cornell, I was given the opportunity to participate in a unique filmmaking project. My thesis advisor had gotten money from the university to bring Ed Emshwiller—a world-famous independent filmmaker from New York—to campus to make a film there using a student crew. I was on that crew, and the experiences of that summer transformed my life. That's when I knew I wanted to spend the rest of my life making movies.

Years later I was invited to Grand Valley State University to teach cinematography by supervising a student crew on a production financed by the school. Remembering how much the summer program at Cornell had meant to me, I was delighted to participate as the director of photography on this project. The director and actors were also professionals. Each student was assigned a specific job, and did that job for the entire production. Beyond learning technical skills, the students learned whether they liked the rigors and the culture of professional filmmaking, how to conduct themselves on a set, and practices, tools, and techniques they could use for making their own films.

Since then I've shot eight summer films with students: seven shorts and one feature. I knew that this opportunity could be really valuable for students, but the reality ended up surpassing all my expectations. The appreciation expressed by the students who went through this experience overwhelmed me. Many of these students are now in the film business, some locally (in Michigan) and some in Hollywood. Many have told me that what they learned about filmmaking on the set during their summer shoot prepared them better for working in the business than all their traditional classroom courses. So I advise you, if you can find a program like this, working with professionals, sign up now.

By now you're thinking, "Sure, it would be great to get on professional productions, but pigs will be flying over Hollywood before that happens. And how am I, a student at the University of Nowhere, supposed to find Hollywood professionals willing to spend a summer working with students?" That's a good question.

Realizing that few aspiring filmmakers will have these opportunities, I have written *Shooting Movies Without Shooting Yourself in the Foot: Becoming a Cinematographer* with the idea of simulating the apprenticeship experience as much as is possible in book form. This book should give you the means to learn the important things you need to know about cinematography: the importance of preproduction, the kind of equipment you'll need and how to work with it, how to use the equipment as an expressive tool, how to function and behave on the set, and how to avoid making the kinds of mistakes that will cost you your job and your future in filmmaking.

This is not a textbook. It is a guide through the process of shooting a film from the perspective of a director of photography and his or her crew. It covers technical and scientific details but only on a need-to-know basis. You'll be able to easily choose how much you want to delve into technical explanations, or you can skip them until you see the purpose of knowing all that (and I hope I can convince you that you do). And I won't be encyclopedic. My purpose is to focus on what the experience of being a DP or a member of a camera crew is really like in practical terms.

You will see that this book is divided into several sections. In the Realities section, I'll take you through preproduction, production, and postproduction. When we encounter highly technical subjects, I'll direct you to the Technicalities section, where you can immerse yourself in the hard-core science and how-to material. You get to choose when and how much you want to read about technical things. There is also a section of Checklists, Cheatsheets, and Datasheets, where I boil down processes and information I've presented in the rest of the book into quickly accessible and useful forms. These will be invaluable when you're actually working on a project.

You'll also see exercises that are designed to get you to express yourself with the tools of a working cinematographer. Sometimes you may not have access to all of the equipment we have in Hollywood, but I'll be giving you suggestions for ways to get around the access problem. You'll learn that it's important for a cinematographer to be resourceful. Many of the wonderful projects you work on may have very limited budgets. I've worked on mega-budget films, micro-budget films, and everything in between. Regardless of budget, every show I have ever worked on has had moments when sheer inventiveness—chewing gum and baling wire style—has been necessary. So don't feel deprived if you don't have fancy cameras, cranes, and lights. I will talk about the professional way to do things; most importantly, I'm going to lead you through a detailed approach you can adopt that will enable you to do professional work regardless of your resources.

Of course, artistic visual expression is why anyone is drawn to cinematography in the first place. But teaching someone to be creative is pretty much an impossible task. While I'll give it a try, what I know I absolutely *can* teach you is how to do everything necessary to make artistic expression possible. You need to have both technical and creative abilities to allow you to successfully realize a director's vision. A director of photography has to be a creative artist and the commander of an army at the same time. This book helps you learn how to do that.

I won't tell you what stories to shoot, but I will show you how to use your tools, introduce you to "industry standards," and share with you many of the tricks I know that make professional movies so good.

This book is intended to be a self-tutorial, an apprenticeship in a book. I can tell you how to do many things, and I can give you exercises to learn on your own. Each exercise is followed by a discussion of what you should have learned from doing it. Try to do the exercise without looking at the discussion first. That way you'll have the opportunity to learn what I set up the exercise for without knowing beforehand what the final intention is.

I am not foolish enough to think I can cover every situation that may arise. But I will talk about the mistakes everyone makes, and I will tell you some big ones I've been a part of. Remember: *You learn by making mistakes.* Both your mistakes and your solutions will stick with you. Not a day will go by that you won't learn *something*, and every member of the crew feels the same way.

So you have to improvise, and you have to make mistakes. The information and the exercises in this book will move you past the simple mistakes so you can learn on your own from the more interesting mistakes that only you will make. The book is organized to take you through the entire process of shooting a film, from reading the script to screening the final print. Each step builds on the previous one. I'm pretty sure each step is necessary, and I think you'll get the most out of doing all the exercises in order.

But I want you to play. The single most important thing for you to do is to shoot—anything and as much as you can. Don't forget that this is what you love doing. In his book *Outliers*, Malcolm Gladwell, commenting on why particular people achieve the greatest success, quotes neurologist Daniel Levitin: "Ten thousand hours of practice is required to achieve the level of mastery associated with being a world-class expert—in anything."[1] So let me start you out on your 10,000-hour adventure.

---

[1]Gladwell, Malcolm. *Outliers*, Little, Brown, New York, 2008, p. 40.

PART 1
Realities: Preproduction

CHAPTER 2
What's First?

John Wooden, the legendary basketball coach, made famous his admonition, "Failing to prepare is preparing to fail." This advice is as applicable to cinematography as it is to basketball or any other endeavor. Director Alfred Hitchcock took preplanning to such an extreme that for him the actual shooting of his movies became a very mechanical procedure. At the other end of the spectrum, shooting a movie with the freewheeling approach of an Altman or a Cassavetes takes no less preproduction planning because, interestingly enough, it takes a lot of preparation to be ready for improvisation on the set. All the tools and creative thought must already be at hand no matter which approach the director takes. So how, as the director of photography, do you do your preparation? It all starts with the script.

The script is the basis of everything that's going to be up on the screen. The writer has been bleeding into his keyboard for months or even years, the producer and director have committed to putting this story onto the screen, and somebody has put up the money to make it. So don't read the script with the eyes of a writer or director, thinking how you'd change the story or the dialogue. For you, as DP, the script is a blueprint and you're going to construct the building it describes.

The first time, just read it. Read it for the story as though you just want some entertainment. You'll find out pretty fast if you like it or not. If you're doing this as a job—I mean, getting paid—it really doesn't matter whether you like it or not. You're going to shoot it the best you can. If this is a labor of love (i.e., no pay), make sure you do love it. Now, in the documentary *Cinematographer Style*, Director of Photography Vittorio Storaro tells a story about quitting his first job. He felt that he and the director were not on the same page, so even though he was just starting out and had a wife and a kid at home, he quit. Okay, I believe him and I salute him. I don't know what his finances were like, but I commend him for sticking to his artistic guns. But if you are like me, and you have to work for a living, you'll be working on projects you well know are not intended to be great works of art.

Besides, there's an equally proud ideal held for many of us who work in the film business: You take every job offered, you do the best you can, and you don't quit. I think it speaks to professionalism and the duty of an artist in a commercial world. Yes, we all have to work to live. We can't be the arbiter of what the story is or of how appealing the script is. But we can—and we obligate ourselves to—do the very best, the most artistic, work we can in service of the vision of the writer, the director, and the producer.

Now, about the script. You probably read it at least once in the process of getting hired. If not, they just wanted to look at you and have a talk. They told you the story, and you convinced them you're the one to shoot it. Now you have to figure out what it is and how to do it. If you're about to read in preparation for an interview, think about this.

READING THE SCRIPT: WHO'S IN IT?

You've read the script once. Read it again. Make sure you get the characters clear in your mind. If the script is not well written, it may be a little hard to distinguish between characters; they don't seem to talk differently, and their motivations aren't very clear. Good writing makes the characters' identities clear and distinct. It will matter less if the actors who are cast bring their distinctive personas with them. If they have Brad Pitt playing against Dustin Hoffman, there won't be any problem with each character being distinctive. In any case, you want to have a feel for the characters and story so you can make sense when you're talking to the director. And the point of reading right now is to be able to engage with the director on his vision of the film. All further decisions will be based on an understanding of the director's vision. The director may or may not solicit *your* vision of the film. It pays to be careful of treading on the director's domain by putting forth too many of your own visionary ideas at this point in the process. There will be plenty of opportunity to contribute creatively as the project progresses. Directors will vary in how much of your personal vision they will tolerate.

The dialogue isn't the most important element for you—you're taking pictures, remember—but it often gives you the first inkling of who the characters are and how the plot goes. You'll be noting all the action in the script, and we'll get to that soon.

Back to the cast. You won't have anything to do with casting; that's the director's, producer's, and casting director's concern. But you may know who plays which part. If the actors are well known—say, Brad Pitt again—you will be imagining them in your mind as you read. More likely, the performers are "working" actors you've never met, probably never have seen. But the production office (there's always a production office) will have the glossies (8 × 10 photos of the actor with a bio and credit list on the back). You can take a look at the photos and begin to get an idea of what the actors look like.

Good. Look at them. Copy them or scan them, and take them with you. Actors' glossies famously never look much like them. Usually they're fantasies of how the actor would like to look, but they're a start. You will be spending a lot of time lighting and framing these people, so you might as well start thinking about what approach might best serve these actors. Do the actors fit the characters as you've visualized them? Do you think they need special makeup or hairdos or wardrobe to make them convincing? What can you do to make them look better? Imagine how light coming from one side or the other would change the feeling you get from the face. If the actress's face is washed out—overexposed—maybe that means you need to work on her complexion. There's a good chance she's got lines or blemishes on her skin, or she's not as youthful-appearing as she would like. That's makeup, of course, but it's also lighting. You, too, can overexpose. Often the actor will appear with a two-day beard stubble. I'm amazed that it's lasted in fashion a quarter century after *Miami Vice* premiered, but there you are. Will he be stubbly when you shoot him in *this* film or will he be clean-shaven? Check with the director about this. If it's a horror film, you can be pretty sure there are going to be facial and body prosthetics, but there might be special makeup effects even in dramas or comedies. Prosthetics require special lighting considerations. Generally the line between the prosthetics and skin has to be disguised. It may be invisible to the eye but evident on camera because the colors respond differently. This will take some time and some special lighting. And you'll have to remember to include time for tests of the prosthetic makeup.

By performing camera tests during preproduction, you'll have a chance to light the actors in all sorts of ways to work out the look that's best for them for this movie. We'll get to that later. But the earlier you can start thinking about any aspect of your work, the better. It's also nice to be able to put a name to a face so you know the actor's name when you meet him or her. (Folks really are impressed that you can remember names.) And you want to know early if there's a lot of cosmetic work you're going to have to do.

Take symmetry. Human beings are supposedly built bilaterally symmetrical—pretty much, you look the same in a mirror (with every characteristic reversed) as you do in the real world. But we're not perfectly symmetrical. Maybe you've noticed that we only have one heart and that it's not in the middle. Well, no one's face is perfectly symmetrical, although some come close. Usually those we regard as "classic" beauties are extremely symmetrical. But the rest of us are lopsided in varying degrees. In fact, the face you've confronted every morning for the last oh-so-many years is not the face the world sees. Try this: Look at a snapshot of yourself. If you're like most people, you don't like what you see. You say, "Oh, I take lousy pictures." Well, it may be you're just not photogenic. But that's probably not your fault. What's happened is that you're reversed. Take the picture with you into the bathroom and hold the picture up to the mirror next to your reflection in the mirror. It looks different, doesn't it? Now put the picture next to your face and look at its reflection in the mirror compared to the reflection of your face in the mirror. Now the two images look a lot closer, right?

I had a shock once. I was operating on a TV series and had gotten to know the actors, including the lead actress, really well. At one point I had to set up a shot for a close-up of the actress looking in a mirror. I got the camera in position, but when I looked through the viewfinder, I thought someone had taken her place. Her face was so asymmetrical that in this mirror image she became unrecognizable. Interestingly, she was less attractive in her reflection.

Mostly this asymmetry won't be a problem for you. But you've probably heard about actresses who have a "good side." That's a function of asymmetry. Claudette Colbert was famous in the 1930s for having "only" one good side. Look at any movie of hers (e.g., *It Happened One Night*), and you will seldom see the right side of her face. A situation this extreme is rare. But you want to be aware of the "good side" of an actor. Another example: I had a lead actress whose "parentheses" from her nose to her mouth were asymmetrical. One side was deep, and the other was shallow. No one would argue that she wasn't a beauty. But when photographed she looked lopsided. So I lit her to accentuate the shadow on the shallow side and to minimize it on the deep side. Thus, she looked more symmetrical—and more beautiful.

There are a lot of other strange things photography does to make people look bad or at least different. Thank goodness, it also smoothes out some problems, and there are always tricks we have to remedy the situation. We'll discuss this more when we get to lighting.

You want to concern yourself with other questions about the actors while you read the script. Have you got a big difference in height? Will actors who are of different heights have to be in a shot together (a problem faced and conquered in *Twins* with Danny de Vito and Arnold Schwarzenegger)? You want to think about what to do. You can often put the shorter actor on an apple box (a standard-size box we use, modeled on real apple boxes of a century ago; often called a man-maker). The actors don't have to be the same height, but they ought to be close enough so the frame isn't awkward. Of course, in a wide shot the audience will see the difference in height, so don't make them too close in a two shot.

What if an actress is pregnant? That's more of a concern for the producer. But I have worked with actresses whom we hid behind every possible piece of furniture on the set so we wouldn't see her belly with junior in it. Otherwise you're stuck with a lot of close-ups; besides unbalancing the film, it upsets all the other actors, who feel slighted when they aren't getting as many close-ups.

Thankfully, movies are becoming very multiethnic, so it is very common to encounter actors in scenes together with very different skin reflectivity. In the world of the cinematographer, the notion of racial differences, as some people put it, or differences in skin color are irrelevant. To me there's only one race—the human race—and it's got lots of skin tones from pale to dark. Every tone reflects light differently, and since we're recording reflected light on film or on a chip, it is more useful to think in terms of luminance (the measured reflectivity), not skin color or race. The cinematographer must be able to produce a balanced image even when there is a wide range of reflectivity among the people in the frame. Today any film negative and most professional electronic cameras can handle wide ranges of luminance. Twenty years ago, with less sensitive media, standard procedure would be to pump more light on the dark actors and, less often, take light off the light actors. This strategy was based on the widely accepted notion that one stop brighter than middle gray is "skin tone." Sure—if all the skin belongs to Northern Europeans or their descendants. We have the chance to shoot a wide array of beautiful skin, and I like to make sure the characters exist in all their rainbow splendor. Having said that, I, too, have had the occasion to light people with different skin tones differently. I once was shooting a feature whose lead was an African American. In a courtroom scene I had to shoot him sitting at a table next to the actress playing his lawyer; she was so light in tone as to be almost albino. While technically the film could accommodate the differences in luminance, the resulting image looked odd, as though the actress was overexposed. Instinctively a viewer's eye always goes directly to the brightest object in the frame, but the important person in the shot was the actor with the less luminous skin. I wanted the audience to be focused on this man. So I gently flagged off some of the ambient light hitting the actress, and I added slightly more light on the actor using a directed soft box. This approach gave him good eye light and filled in shadows on his face. That effect is a good idea with any actor. But also, by bringing his exposure up a little while bringing hers down, I could make the lighting balance in the shot better serve the purposes of the script and the story.

Finally, you may want to think about filtration. Photography, especially electronic, can emphasize lines or irregularities in a person's face. Usually these defects are more noticeable in older performers, but they can occur with actors of any age. Surprisingly, skin that appears smooth to the eye will often photograph blotchy, since film and chips are both more sensitive than the human eye to variations in the red spectrum (e.g., blood vessels near the skin). Makeup will handle a lot of this. But you may want to give a cosmetic diffusion (a filter on the lens) to some actors. You want to think about this early. You will have to do tests to determine the amount and kind of diffusion to use. And you will have to be conscious of maintaining consistency from one shot to another within a scene as the film cuts from the actor who needs the diffusion to one in the same scene who doesn't. You don't want to cut from a tack-sharp shot to one that looks like it was shot through a Kleenex.

DON'T WORRY, BE HAPPY: KEEPING TRACK OF IT ALL

So you're only in your second or third reading of the script, and you've already got all these worries. Don't panic. First of all, not every situation occurs in every film. Then, you're making notes—written or mental. I always write down my thoughts; otherwise, they tend to escape. And I recommend you do, too, as a way of organizing your thoughts and giving you something to refer to during the testing or shooting process. There's a lot of things to deal with. If you tried to keep them all in your mind, you'd get paralyzed. So make notes. Write on the script, or get a notebook for your ideas, or whatever works for you. I've often written notes on a tablet, a different page for each script page, and then put them in a notebook so the notes face the script page they concern. Another technique (I learned this from DP Rodney Taylor) is to use an artist's portfolio book. This is a loose-leaf book with plastic sleeves into which you can insert a picture or a piece of paper. One of the best I know is the Profolio made by Itoya. You can find it at most artist's supply and photographic stores or online. Insert the script pages inside the plastic sleeves. Write your comments on sticky notes, which will stick with tenacity to the plastic. Then, when the script revisions come, and they always will, you can simply remove the current page from the sleeve and slide in the new page. Since the sticky notes are attached to the sleeve and not the page, all your notes will still be in place.

Whatever system you use, be sure to keep notes from the very beginning, put your script in a notebook, and begin making your own production book. You'll have sections for camera, grip, electric, crew, and any other areas that concern you. Some things, like pictures of locations, you might never refer to again. Some, like your script notes, you may look at every day. At the end of the shoot, you have a nice memento and a lot of information you can use for the next show.

WHO KNOWS WHERE OR WHEN?

Okay, that covers story, characters, and some of the challenges casting may bring. Probably the very next thoughts you will have are about time and place. Time includes both the historical epoch your movie is set in, the period, and at what time of day or night each scene occurs. The big question is going to be, is this contemporary or is it historical? If it's contemporary, relax and have a beer. You can hardly go wrong. All the design, wardrobe, and props will naturally fall into what exists now. There's not much you have to do.

If it's historical, however, you've got some thinking to do. Which period? I just did a film set in the 1980s and 1990s; that's the recent past and involves a particular set of considerations. A different film set in the 1860s will call for other considerations.

Then there's place. What country? What part of that country? Urban or rural? And then there's time in a particular place. Some places are "behind the times." Another immediate concern is what kind of lighting sources were available in the specific time and place in your film. Does the story jump around in time and place? That's yet more you have to think about.

For a film set in the 1980s, most of the clothes and surroundings of today will pass. Although these details are largely the concerns of the art and prop departments, you, as a major force in the visualization of the film, can call attention to anachronistic faux pas. Cell phones didn't exist in the 1980s. Look out for streamlined cars; back then they were mostly boxy, and there were more American models. Are the clothing styles different? As a guy, I'm kind of insensitive to fashion, but I'm told there's a big difference at least in women's clothes.

And hairstyles! You want to make sure you know what the production designer considers important to define the period and what violates the fashions of the time. Many of us were alive in the 1980s and 1990s; that's a double-edged sword. On the one hand, we remember what a lot of things looked like, and we're not likely to allow an iPhone into the picture. On the other hand, when did laptop computers become the standard? When were they introduced? If you have to have a shot of a computer screen, when was Windows introduced?

As you suspect, the responsibility for getting most of these right is the Art Department's. But while you're reading the script, you want to look out for indications that there are things that can ruin the illusion of a particular time and place. And likewise look for anything that you as a DP can enhance to make the audience feel that they're in an earlier era.

Within the scene, time of day is very important to orient the audience to the progression of the story, to assure verisimilitude, and to set the mood. If you want to show a passage of time, you want to think about one scene as the night before and the next as the morning after. But the action takes place in the same room of the house. So now you're thinking of having to light for two different looks. Are you going to light the night scene for soft, romantic moonlight with maybe a hint of warm candlelight? Or are you going to light it with the glare of a streetlight and the pulsing of a neon sign? Each way sets a mood; you are now thinking about what's appropriate to the story. Likewise, is the morning the harsh glare of sunlight in the character's face, or is it soft, reflected morning light with glints of sun splashes?

Period imposes restrictions on practical lighting fixtures and to some extent on the movie lights you use. Of course, you don't want electric lights in a Civil War epic, just as it's not a good idea to have Roman centurions wearing wristwatches. But there are subtler differences. Compact fluorescent lamps are all over the world now, but you'd better make sure they're not in your picture if it's set before 2005. Fluorescent tubes themselves weren't in widespread use before the 1930s. The late 1800s will have gas light in town but kerosene lanterns in the country.

Now you're probably thinking, "Hey, this all has to do with props and art. What do I care?" Well, besides being responsible for everything in the frame, the kind of the light used in a particular era will affect the quality of light you use. If you have fluorescent lighting, as in the city room of the *Washington Post* for *All the President's Men*, you want to use a soft, even, almost shadowless look. (And Gordon Willis did this all with conventional incandescent movie lights; Kinoflos hadn't been invented yet.)

Look at one of the best recent examples of period lighting: Eduardo Serra's work in *Girl With A Pearl Earring*. Serra decided that the look of the film should be as close as possible to the spirit of the painting on which the story was based: Vermeer's *Girl With A Pearl Earring*. Since Vermeer had as his light only sunlight, candles, lanterns, and firelight, Serra decided to simulate those sources.

He succeeded brilliantly. It is hard to find any shots in the film in which there is any evident artificial light. Of course, he used artificial light just to be able to shoot. It is impractical to wait for the sunlight to be just right, and it is impossible to shoot a scene of any length and be able to depend on consistent natural light. The sun keeps moving. (I realize it is Earth that is moving, but, for our purposes, that damn sun keeps shining its light in different places and angles.) So in order to shoot economically and not wait for the sun, Serra had to recreate the look of sunlight. To take one example, in the light for Vermeer's studio he has most likely used very large HMI units projected through one or two layers of diffusion to give a bright, smooth light that is brightest at the window and falls off naturally as we get into the room. He chose HMIs for several possible reasons. First, their color is approximately the same color as daylight, so he can allow some actual daylight in the picture, and he's beginning with a color palette that matches his subject. And HMIs give more light for the same amount of electricity than the incandescent tungsten-filament lights with which we are all familiar. That lowers the number of lights he has to use, and it saves the producer money in paying for electricity. The use of large units allows him to cover a wide area; he can also keep them somewhat far away from the window so the light does not fall off too rapidly (this is a function of the inverse square law).[1] He can use fewer lamps, thus making his light appear to be from a single source (as we all know the sun is). He puts diffusion (translucent material that scatters and softens the light—not the same thing as a diffusion filter on the lens) between the lamps and the set so he suggests the soft, directionless north light most artists favored.

Granted, the film is called *Girl With A Pearl Earring*, but Serra has gotten his entire plan of lighting from looking at a painting and from reading the script. You will be trying to do the same every time you read a script; allow it to give up all its secrets

The script, of course, indicates time of day and whether you are outside (exterior) or inside a building (interior). Simply counting the pages for each gives you a start on determining the type of film stock to order (not a concern with digital, but if media are expensive, you may have to ration it just as you would film) and when and how much lighting and grip equipment you'll need. Count 1/8s of a page, and count day and night separately. So you'll have four totals: D/I, D/X, N/I, and N/X (that's day interior, day exterior, night interior, and night exterior). Probably all the D/Xs will be one type of film. These days, we usually

---

[1]An inverse-square law is a standby in physics. It says that any physical quantity—its strength—is inversely proportional to the distance from its source. Thus, light, responding to the inverse square law, falls off faster than we would think. And as the distance from the light is doubled, the intensity of the light is divided by four. So a light giving off 100 footcandles on the set when it's five feet away would give only 25 footcandles if it's moved to ten feet away.

   If you want to cut the footcandles in half, move the light away by a factor of the square root of 2 ($2 = 1.4$). So to cut the light in half, move it to 7 feet away ($1.4 \times 5 = 7$). And to double the light, move it in by a factor of .7 (the square root of $\frac{1}{2}$).

use a daylight-balanced film with a low ISO rating (more on film and ISO later). N/X will need a fast film. Will you light with tungsten or HMI? You may want to have a tungsten-balanced film, or you may opt for a daylight-balanced film. Right now, you've got your page counts to refer to, and you can make film stock decisions later. Or you'll be using a digital camera, and you'll still have to begin thinking how you will account for the different lighting conditions you'll encounter.

You will use different lighting instruments for day or night, interior or exterior. Most likely for day exterior you won't use lights; the sunlight is so bright that you would have to use very large lights to have any effect at all, and these lights are expensive (as are the power sources). For working outside during the day, you'll want to have more grip equipment (reflectors, bounce cards, frames with silk or other diffusion material). Working with the production manager and the assistant director, you may be able to schedule most of the days of exterior shooting together so that you can order the grip equipment you need only for those days. You can save money by returning the specialized equipment you needed for day exteriors when you're back shooting inside, and you can save more money by not renting interior lights for the days you're outside.

You will want to think of other equipment you will or won't need under a given circumstance. You may want certain filters for exteriors but not for interiors. Some lenses are practical only outside (because they don't let in enough light for interiors or they're too long to use inside).

And on a personal level, what about the weather? When you're outside, you want to make sure you have appropriate clothing: shorts, sunscreen, and insect repellent in the summer; long johns, heavy boots, and parkas in the winter. You want to look at the number of exteriors and interiors and consult with the AD about cover sets—the interiors you'll retreat to when the weather makes it impossible to shoot. If you have the luck to be shooting in southern California, you won't need too many cover sets; anywhere else, you'd better be prepared for a lot of bad weather.

And this brings us to the four seasons. When does your story take place? Each season has a distinct look, both the actual look of a time of year and our conventional representation of it. For summer you may want a warm, orangey look. You'll probably want to keep the look of bright sun, sharp shadows, and more than usual fill to give the sense of a season suffused with light. Fall can also be crisp, with bright sun and sharp shadows, but less fill light. This will persuade the audience that it's watching the year wind down. Gloomy fall will want desaturated color, clouds, wind, maybe rain or gusts of precipitation. You can control some of this with your lighting, but you'll want to coordinate with the special effects department to have big fans, bushels of leaves, and rainbirds to create your inclement weather. Winter is probably very cloudy; most of the color has left the world even if it's not covered with snow. There's a raw barrenness to it; you'll want to have mostly cloudy skies and a lot of gently backlit shots, with very little fill. Remember, the sun is hiding on the southern half of the world. If you have direct sun, it needs to be low in the sky and weak—again, very little fill. Spring is bright like summer but almost shadowless. The sun is bright, but it's through the sort of diffusion that mimics high clouds. There's a directionality to it, but the shadows are softer than the sharp shadows of summer. Like fall, spring is a time of winds and rain gusts.

Although it's not your official responsibility, you must be actively involved in scheduling to make sure you get every advantage of weather to help you create the sense of the different seasons. We'll talk more about creating illusions both inside and outside when we discuss lighting. We're only looking at the script now to figure out what we'll have to think about.

Remember, too, that the particular time of year you are in production imposes its own conditions. If you're shooting at night, summer nights are short but blessedly mild. You'll have a pleasant time, but you'll have to work fast to get your work done. You will have the advantage of prerigging lights and grip work in the daylight, and you must plan to take advantage of the time. Winter nights give you plenty of time to work, but it's cold—even in southern California—and your crew's efficiency goes downhill. Simple things happen, like batteries having a shorter life in cold weather, and this adds to expense and preparation.

Every bit of information you need to prepare for the conditions imposed by the real or apparent time of year should be in the script. When you read it carefully, you'll find the factors you need to take into account, and you'll have made notes to refer to in your meeting with the director, producer, and other department heads.

2A • FIRST EXERCISE: SHOOTING STILLS?

Yeah, I know. I'm the one who says stills are different from movies and that you might get into dangerous habits by shooting stills. But it's all photography, and like my dictum to learn still photography prior to becoming a cinematographer, there are concepts of visual expression you can learn from any form of image making.

Here's the assignment: Shoot a minimum of one image for each of the following eight conditions. Don't worry about what I mean by these terms; just shoot whatever they suggest to you.

1. Warm. Cool.
2. High contrast. Low contrast.
3. An everyday view of an object. An unfamiliar view of the same object.
4. Black and white (2 shots—yes, using color film or digital in color).

Trust me: There's a purpose to each pair of shots.

Now, before you get started, let's discuss a few practical considerations. In practical terms, when I first did this project, I suggested borrowing family's or friends' cameras or just buying an inexpensive disposable camera. We're not looking to get high-quality

2A • FIRST EXERCISE: SHOOTING STILLS?—CONT'D

professional-level photography right now. These days, almost everyone has a digital camera (or even a cell phone camera), and I'm happy for you to use any tool you can find. No matter what you use, it's a good idea to make prints. I like at least 4 × 6 inches. I know you can look at your pictures on your camera viewfinder, on your computer screen, or even on your giant TV, but I highly recommend making prints off your computer or having them made at the photo shop. Prints reinforce the two-dimensionality of the image, and allow a group of shots to be seen simultaneously, easily. I like to be able to see the photos, and I want to be able to move them around to contrast various approaches and to return easily to a previously viewed picture. So get prints made at the photo store or print them from your computer. Do it. You'll be happier.

2B • WHAT YOU SHOULD LEARN FROM THE STILL PHOTOGRAPH EXERCISE

So why are you doing this? The first answer is that it's fun. It had better be. If any of these exercises isn't fun, you're in the wrong field or you have the wrong book. The line on the set is "No one ever said it would be easy. They said it would be fun." And it is, but moviemaking is also a tough, demanding business. No one in his or her right mind goes into it for any reason but love. So love your work and have fun.

Now, what did each of the terms in the exercise mean to you? What did you think *warm* or *cool* meant? Is your warm image orangey and your cool image bluish (my first thought as a cinematographer)? Is it hot like fire or a sunny day or cool like the Arctic and the deep forest? Is it emotionally close and loving or cool and distanced? If you think of warm or cool as your "script" for this exercise, what you come up with will depend on your interpretation of your script.

Keep looking at the pictures. You will have emotional effects due to different colors; notice the ability of color to denote time of day—at this point, almost intuitively—and how these reactions might be used expressively. You will be leading your audience where you want them to go. One of your tools will be the color of your scenes and the various meanings that color gives to the audience.

In technical terms, the terms *warm* and *cool* refer to the visual look of the film. Taken that way, you should have the sense that red/orange/yellow are warm and green/blue/violet are cool. I want to introduce the concept of the nonhuman response of film to color. It's not intuitive, but it should become reflexive. You will soon realize that you have to be sensitive to the color temperature of light, and you have to control it to make your pictures look the way you want.

This brings us to the subject of color temperature and the necessity for white balance in digital and corrective filtration (either tinted glass on the lens or colored plastic on the lights) for film. White balance is the control for electronic photography that lets you

(Continued)

2B • WHAT YOU SHOULD LEARN FROM THE STILL PHOTOGRAPH EXERCISE—CONT'D

get the "right" color—not too blue and not too red, but just right. (Think Goldilocks.) But I'm not going to interrupt the fun with technical stuff. If you want to know more about the physics of color temperature, see Chapter 33 on color temperature.

What is contrast? There can be subject contrast: sharply defined areas of good and evil. There can be lighting contrast: harsh direct light brightly illuminating a part of the picture, throwing some parts into deep shadow. Some of my students come up with conceptual contrast: a shot of a person of color sitting with a white person or a police officer standing next to a homeless person. Low contrast for me tends to mean very even illumination of a subject or a subject that has a uniform color or tone. My original intent was for you to deal with differences in light, but, again, I'm interested in the variety of responses I have seen among beginning cinematographers. The use of lighting contrast is a constant; it's one of the most important tools of the cinematographer, and it's a decision that must be made for every scene, often for every shot.

The two different views of a familiar subject should show you the impact of changing camera viewpoint and position. One of my favorite sets of pictures produced for this exercise was two shots of a traffic light. The normal view, from eye level, showed a familiar street scene. For the unfamiliar view the photographer climbed to a balcony overlooking the street and shot straight down at the now much closer traffic light. The result was a beautiful abstract. Right away you can see the possibilities of making beautiful pictures simply by taking a different viewpoint. You can choose to reveal or hide information from the audience. You can decide how and when in a sequence to reveal information to the audience. These are your first lessons in composition; the familiar view may be just an eye-height, horizon-level snapshot. Almost always the unfamiliar view uses unusual points of view, odd angles, close-ups, or distant camera positions.

Finally, we have our "black-and-white" photos. I always love these pairs. I've gotten shots of zebra stripes at crosswalks and police cars. Sometimes there are monochrome interpretations of the subject; sometimes there are lighting situations so contrasty that even in color the lighted area is white and the shadow is a deep black. Like all the categories, this one overlaps. Black-and-white overlaps contrast, contrast overlaps warm/cool. Of course, a movie shot is rarely only one thing or another, and I am trying to get you to think of the many elements that make up your decisions while you're shooting.

CHAPTER 3
We're Still Reading the Script

You will very quickly decide what genre or style of story you're reading. Is it a comedy? Drama? Dramedy? Is it a genre film—horror, cops, even a Western? Is it *sui generis*: something that is its own thing, perhaps an original work of art? You will react differently, and you want the audience to react differently, too. You may want to clue them in from the very beginning with a particular look in the lighting or the framing.

You will want to ask the director how realistic the look should be. It's possible to convince an audience that they've seen a kind of neutral reality—without any camera "tricks"—while manipulating the image extensively. The late Conrad Hall, ASC, was a master of this look. In many of his films—particularly later ones like *Searching for Bobby Fisher* and *American Beauty*—the look of the film is, to the average audience, almost documentary. It's as though they just filmed wherever the camera just happened to be. But Connie Hall worked to give a convincing simulation of reality while manipulating the feelings of the audience. You and your director want to decide whether you want to go for apparent realism or you want a look that is more dramatic—in essence, artificial. If you're making a horror picture, the clichés are stark lighting, a lot of darkness, and a film shot almost entirely at night. Film noir is called "noir" (French for "black") because it's dark.

And then there are times when the time and setting require a look that contradicts the story and the action of the film. *Out of the Past*, shot by Nick Musuraca, ASC, is a film noir set largely in rural areas, not urban; often in daylight, little night; and often with very bright shots, not *noir*. The action and the dialogue are in contrast to the beautifully composed sylvan cinematography. In the beginning of the film, we are misled by the picturesque sunniness of a small town, only to be thrown into discomfort when bad people show up doing bad things and threatening our hero. As the film proceeds, the peaceful landscape becomes more menacing. We see more shadows in the trees, the darkness of late evening or early morning. Later, as the story moves to more urban locales, Musuraca conjures the urban claustrophobia of New York, the dark side of San Francisco's underworld, and the foreign ambience of Mexico. Returning to nature, our hero seeks refuge in the High Sierras, only to find that the surrounding beauty of the forest quickly becomes a death trap when the villains come after him.

You will notice pretty quickly whether your film will involve kids or animals. No matter how well-behaved they are, kids and animals mean that it will take more time to shoot. What will affect your photography is the way you have to work around them. If there are wild animals, you can only prepare in the most general terms. When the animals want to do something, they do it, and you'd better be ready to catch it. I worked on a Western in which we had a white buffalo. Well, buffalos don't come in white, so the trainer had to spray paint this very large animal. I'm sure he used water-soluble hairspray or something of the sort, and I'm sure the buffalo wasn't harmed. But no one told the buffalo that, and the beast was very unhappy about being an albino.

The buffalo was at one point quietly munching grass on one side of the set. The crew was busy setting up a shot. The grips had set up about ten reflectors—large boards covered with silver or lead foil to redirect the sunlight. It takes a grown man to handle the reflectors, and the most he can do is one at a time. Meanwhile, the buffalo decided that the grass looked tastier across the way, and he walked over to it. Of course, he was tethered with a rope, so as he ambled over, the rope knocked down every one of these large, heavy reflectors and stands. The crew scattered everywhere. I grabbed my camera and ran (I was an assistant and responsible for the camera), something I have done only once or twice in my career, since the camera weighs about 50 pounds with the tripod. The set looked as though a hurricane had scattered all of our heavy equipment like twigs. And the buffalo calmly ate grass. I learned that day what we mean when we say someone is buffaloed. I'm just happy the big guy only wanted to eat, not play. But we could do nothing to influence the animal, and it's pretty much the same with any animal you work with.

And it doesn't have to be wild animals that upset your plans. I worked several weeks on an old Disney movie, *The Cat from Outer Space*. We used real cats, cute little guys. One night we were shooting in an airplane hangar. The hangar substituted for a stage because we needed a big place for the spaceship models. We had a "hero" cat (the hero object or character is, in advertising and sometimes in movie parlance, the object of your attention) and a look-alike to sub for him. When the lighting was ready, the trainer brought out our star. The kitty star immediately ran off as fast as he could. Several minutes later, we heard our star meowing up in the rafters at the highest point of the roof where no one could reach him.

Well, no problem. We had another cat, and the trainer brought him out. You know what happened. So the crew of 80 sat around, drinking coffee and gossiping, on overtime, for eight or nine hours until the producers called it a day. I didn't go back on that unit, so I don't know if they ever got the shots. I think Uncle Walt had the right idea when he had animators draw the animals.

Besides the production trouble that animals give you, you have to work around them and their trainers. Usually you have to be quiet around animals, and they don't like quick moves. So you need to have a crew that can understand that and be sensitive to the animals' needs. You can't always set up your ideal shot. Often you have to use a long lens so you can stay at a safe distance from the animal (both safe for you and for the animal's nerves).

You've always got to be prepared for the most astonishing risks in this business. I got a call to work one day on a movie at Universal. It was called *Cat People*; I didn't know anything about it. The head of the camera department asked me, on the phone, if I had any problems with cats. At that moment I was petting my cute little black-and-white cat, Rocky, who had the sweetest disposition in the world. So I chuckled to myself and said, "No."

Then I got to the stage. The amazing Art Department geniuses at Universal had turned the sound stage into a replica of the African savannah. Yes, Africa. I started to get a bad feeling. I was right. This was no kitty cat from outer space; this was lions and tigers, oh my. In a dazed state of fear, I got the camera set up for the first shot. The director decided that the tiger should run directly at the camera and veer off at the last second. Once again, no one had explained this to puss. The trainer stood behind the camera with food. So the tiger made a beeline for it and ran right under the camera. I was saying my prayers as the cat ran straight at us, and I think my operator used up one of his own lives as the cat zoomed under the tripod, brushing his legs.

A little after that, the trainer had to go to one of the cats to do something. He handed me the food—a frying pan with a raw steak in it on the end of a ten-foot pole—and told me, "Let him have the meat if he wants it." No kidding. Did he really think I was going to argue with him? And, sure enough, one of the cats (did I mention there were several roaming the "savannah"?) came by for dinner. Very gently, almost daintily, he took his paw and flicked the meat off. I was just glad to have the proverbial ten-foot pole between us. Even at that distance it felt as if some monster was trying to tear off my shoulder. So think twice before working with animals, be prepared, and bring some clean underwear.

And then there are kids—a whole other kettle of fish. Of course, we love the little monsters, but your scheduling and approach have to change. First, children under 18 are limited in the hours they can work. It's different in each state, and varies by age. That's why 18-year-old actresses who look 12 are in great demand. They can work a full 12-hour day without breaking the law. Younger kids are limited to 8 hours or less. They have to have breaks for school or for recess. And if they're babies, they may be allowed as little as 30 seconds on set once the camera rolls.

Lots of crews think, "Oh, eight hours with talent! Swell, we get out early." *Au contraire, mon ami*. The laws are observed, and the kids work a short day. But that means you must get all your shooting done with them in the few hours allowed. So all the kids' coverage is shot first, irrespective of what the adults are doing. Then, when the kids go home, you have to relight the scenes with them and shoot the adult coverage—without the kids and without someone the actors can react to. Your lighting at 8 PM has to match what you did at 8 AM. You have to make sure eyelines match. The rest of the crew—props, script supervisor, for example—have to make sure everything matches despite the gap of time. It's not fun; people can get testy. So now what seemed a pleasant shoot has become a bitchy endurance test.

And don't think of breaking the law. Not only is that a bad idea as a moral principle, but you can put yourself in a world of hurt. There are probably not many people today who remember the *Twilight Zone* movie from the early 1980s. John Landis was directing a sequence that involved children, explosives, a helicopter, and night shooting. First off, you can't have kids around explosions and stunts, which a helicopter is. Second, you can't have young kids (these were under age eight) on the set at night—not at all, *ever*. So these very big Hollywood filmmakers just disregarded the law. And no one but the crew—and we don't gossip—would have known. Unfortunately, the explosions made the helicopter crash, and the spinning rotor decapitated the two kids (and veteran actor Vic Morrow). John Landis (*Animal House, Blues Brothers*) was never prosecuted, but he hasn't directed a major movie in over 25 years.

No, it doesn't have to be that bad. Neither animals nor children are an inevitable disaster. But you as DP have to be aware that pitfalls lie ahead; you have to use your experience to make things work. You won't keep the director from unwarranted optimism, but maybe you can buy a little extra time in the schedule.

The production manager and the assistant director are responsible for making up the production schedule and for allowing enough time to shoot while making as short a schedule as possible. You will be reading the script with an eye to schedule and budget as well. Every time you find that a special piece of equipment might be needed, you will want to make a note that this will be extra money out of the equipment budget. And you have to be sure that you can shoot the film in the allotted time.

Look for dialogue scenes with multiple characters. You will probably have to cover every actor in a single, two shot, and possibly over-the-shoulder, as well as the obligatory master. This can take a long time, particularly if the director is enamored of perfection in line reading. Besides the time used in coverage, you want to pay attention to the indicated movements of the actors. You may not know until you get on the set the real blocking of the actors, but you can anticipate occasions when they'll be moving around or times when they're sitting around a table. If they're moving, your lighting becomes more complex and time-consuming. Instead of what is essentially a portrait, you will have to be accounting for the position of every actor, and you will be working to avoid ugly shadows thrown when they move. If you have the room lit overall, and you can let the actors move at will, you may avoid the problem of relighting, but the director will probably want to see the actors' faces clearly at every point. And that's your job, again. And every close-up is likely to turn into a number of extra shots, since the actor will be different distances from you and facing differently in those positions.

And if you have a group just sitting at a table, you will have to light each side of the table separately. You will have to light the actors to look good while not throwing ugly shadows on the others around the table. All of this is your job, of course, but you must think about budgeting time to do a good job. Sometimes you can suggest alternative blocking; maybe the actor running all around the house can be confined to a smaller space. Maybe you can arrange the actors around the table so that you can easily light several with one setup. Any time you save helps the film, the director, and the producer. Don't be shy about pointing out the time you plan to save, because in the next breath you're going to have to ask for it back for another scene.

Remember, you're just reading the script for now—maybe for the second or third time—but you're not going into budget conferences yet. Just keep making notes. Before you have to engage in negotiations for more time and more equipment, you should be given a budget and tentative schedule by the production manager. You can tailor your requests to it. But it's always fungible. The production manager will be able to find space in the budget for an item you convince her you really need, so keep notes now to plan for your deals later.

This might be a good time to bring up a piece of vital advice: *Never say no*. Of course, you may at some point realize that the director's plan to recreate the Battle of Gettysburg in real time is impractical, but don't be negative. When someone asks you if you can do it or if the time and money allotted are enough, always say, "Sure." Don't elaborate. Don't promise the moon and the stars when you're unsure about delivering some sequins. But always be positive. The chances to say no or to be negative or simply to be realistic crop up all the time, starting from your first job interview. Deflect the question "How are you going to do it?" with pleasantries and "I'm sure it'll work out." Remember, the director wants what he or she wants, and the producer wants what he or she wants, and they're determined to get it. Don't throw a monkey wrench into their beautiful dreams.

I once interviewed for a job on what was described by the director as a "lesbian musical." (I'm not making this up.) During our first interview, he and the producer looked at my reel, talked about the business in general, and asked me some questions about how I would go about shooting the film. The interview lasted an hour, which is a long time. Usually I'm in and out in ten minutes, even if they like me. It was obvious that I had impressed them favorably. They gave me the script, and the director asked me to set up another interview in a week. At this point I was feeling pretty good. I read the script a few times, got a sense of how it could look, and prepared for the next meeting.

Now, I knew that the budget was around $150,000, which wasn't much even 15 years ago. I was set to shoot another feature soon; the budget for that one was $300,000, and we were scrambling to find ways to do a professional job with so little money. And this other picture didn't involve 16 musical numbers, some with up to 20 cast members. But I knew that I could get good production value and a good look without a big budget, so I went into the interview optimistic.

Again, we had a terrific time. We were becoming friends, and we were talking about shooting scenes as though I had the job. Then came the question: "If there's anything in the script that you think could cause us trouble, what would it be?"

Uh oh. I was not so green that I jumped in with "Well, trying to do a big musical for a budget that's too small for a music video might be a problem." No, I said, "I think it's a great script, and we'll make a terrific movie out of it."

The director persisted. "No, really, be honest with me. I know there's always something. I really want to be on an honest footing. We've got to trust each other if we're going to work together. So, really, what do you see that might be a problem?" So I decided to be truthful. I said something like "Well, it might be kind of hard work to shoot this music-and-dance number with 20 cowgirls in a western town, complete with a gunfight, in a 12-hour day."

Jeez, I almost got frostbite, the atmosphere chilled so fast. You may have guessed that I did not get hired. In an odd development, I met the director a few months later, and he invited me to his premiere. I went. I saw. I was stunned. The guy they hired had gotten a cardboard drawing of a western street—it would have looked bad on a theater stage—and he photographed the number in one shot. Well, that's one way of doing it. I would have been unhappy to do that, but I could have had a job and some much-needed cash. But no, I had to be honorable.

So don't do it. Stay positive. Always be a cheerleader for the film. Sure, they're dreaming. So is everyone who ever wanted to make a film. And you never know—they may figure out how to do it. Or they may get more money. Or things may change. You don't know everything, and you can't control everything. So be that upbeat guy they want on their picture, and never say no.

CHAPTER 4

A Few More Things to Think About

You're reading the script for maybe the third time. Get used to it because you're going to be reading it a lot more. At some point, you'll practically have it memorized. But this is a good thing because you'll be on the set and you'll have to talk with the director about what you're going to do, and I guarantee she'll have it memorized. And she'll be appalled when you don't remember every detail the same way she does.

Almost every movie, even one that is mostly two people talking, will have some action, stunts, or special effects. There are a few exceptions, such as *My Dinner With André* and the HBO series *In Treatment*. But pretty much everything else will involve more action. Even some of the simplest have had to have CGI shots to fill in backgrounds. Part of your job is to be aware of these needs. By and large, as DP you won't have to be responsible for creating them; that's what stunt coordinators and special effects supervisors are for. But you will be working intimately with them.

On the set, the director and stunt coordinator will usually work out the action. You're going to be the one shooting it. So make notes in the script every time a fight or any piece of action occurs. When it comes time to shoot, you need to make sure the shot is set up well: it has to be photographically interesting, match your personal aesthetics, and show the action and make it convincing to the audience without being dangerous to the actors. Stuntpeople will work with you to set up shots that will ensure excitement for the audience and safety for the actors. The bottom line is that no stunt is worth the life of a stunt performer or a member of the crew. I have been witness to a car stunt that went wrong and cost the life of the first AC and left the DP traumatized. I relive that horrible scene a lot, especially when I'm shooting any kind of dangerous action. So I can't emphasis enough the necessity for planning. Following are a few guidelines for the most common stunts.

Fights must be choreographed. You will want to avoid the improvised five-minute donnybrooks of some old Westerns; even the filmmakers then knew they were outrageously unreal and often unintentionally funny (*Rio Bravo*). So have a plan. After discussion with the director, break the action into elements. Don't rely on wide masters. Figure out how to shoot those elements in individual shots, keeping in mind how the editor will take these elements, find the rhythm, and assemble them into a synthesized whole.

For example, when there's a fistfight, the actors' or stuntpeople's blows don't actually strike their victim, but you want to make it look as though they are pummeling each other. So you shoot over the shoulder of the one throwing the punch. You can see his fist passing the victim's face. By using a slightly longer lens than normal (for 35 mm film and "super-35" sized chip cameras, a 75 mm or 100 mm lens; for super-16 mm film cameras, a 45 mm or 60 mm lens; for $^2/_3$-inch-sized chip cameras, a 30 mm or 45 mm; for ½-inch-sized chip cameras, a 24 mm or 40 mm lens), compressing the distance between them makes it appear that contact is made. Simultaneously, the second actor must react as though he's been hit. With sound added in post, it will be totally convincing.

There are several broad categories of effects. First off, what you'll mostly be concerned with are mechanical effects. Mechanical effects are fires, explosions, car crashes—anything that is staged in real time on the set or on location. Unless there's a large and elaborate second unit, the first unit DP will be shooting these scenes. On a limited budget, there's only one DP, so you're it.

The main issue with effects, and what you need to consider is that they take time. They're time-consuming to set up, there's a lot of safety provisions to be assured of, and it's difficult to rehearse them. So unless take one is perfect, you're faced with a long wait before you can do take two. Some of this should be addressed in the production manager's schedule. You can help by thinking of what scene with the actors can be shot at the same location while you're waiting for the effect to be set up. You and all the departments will be considering safety; this involves special equipment to be ordered and preparations to keep the crew safe.

This brings us to one of the most important concerns you'll have reading the script: What equipment is required to shoot this film? You will be going through the script now just for the purpose of determining what equipment you will need. At this point, don't hold back. Make a wish list of every piece of equipment you could possibly want. The production manager will be cutting down your list to fit his budget anyway, so give him a lot. Maybe he'll be embarrassed about trying to cut too many of your requests, and you'll actually get some of the wish list. Every member of the crew should be considering what equipment they may need to make the film. As a DP, you're not going to have to think about props or wardrobe specifically, but you will need to confer with those departments. You don't want to get to the set only to find that the pattern on the star's dress is too "busy" or the size of the floor lamp makes it hard to compose a shot. So make notes of where you think there's a likelihood of having to deal with other departments.

But back to the cinematographer's main areas of concern: camera, lighting, and grip equipment. On professional shoots, the camera assistant, gaffer (or his best boy), and key grip (or *his* best boy) will be consulting with the DP and then making equipment lists for their departments. The DP will be specifying any specialized equipment needed (e.g., a remote crane to do elaborate moves for a given scene). Some equipment is pretty much standard for any shoot. You will make notes of equipment you might want that will deviate from standard orders.[1]

For low-budget films, you may have inexperienced crews—for example, you may be faced with keys who have rarely or never ordered equipment. Unfortunately, this puts it all on you. Rental houses can help to an extent. There are various grip and electric packages (a five-ton truck, a ten-ton truck) that you can order that have all the equipment you need for a reasonable price. As the DP, you should familiarize yourself with these standard packages. Then you will be asking yourself questions: Do I need HMIs (yes, if you need to match or simulate daylight)? Will it make sense to rent Kinoflos (lightweight and compact, they take less power than conventional tungsten lights, but tend to be high-ticket items)? Do you want large frames and rags (nets, duveteen, silk, griffolyn) to manage exterior lighting? Do you want a dolly? Can you work with a doorway dolly, or should you have a crab dolly? Will you be using track or building a dance floor? Do you like to work with diffused or bounced light? Then make sure there will be a lot of material for bouncing and diffusing light. The amount of specialized grip and electric equipment, always large, has exploded as grips, electricians, and engineers have dreamed up new tools and have started to build them. It's impossible here to consider them all. Your best bet is reading books by Mike Uva,[2] and the various trade magazines and online news services.

Specialized camera equipment will include extra cameras for stunts or simultaneous coverage of shots, high-speed cameras for slow motion, very long or very short lenses, specific filters for a diffused look or a color tint to the picture, a Steadicam (which is almost a standard order on major films), and so on. Later, when we get to the set, I'll be talking about how to use all this equipment.

Now it's around the fourth reading, and you have a real familiarity with the material. It's at this point that I like to envision the movie in my head. From the first, I've been imagining characters and locations, and I've been thinking about how the movie would look. But now I literally try to see the entire film. I imagine it scene by scene, and I see it as a succession of shots cut together. It's as though I'm watching it on a "mindscreen." And as I'm imagining it, I'm making extensive notes. I note down every shot in detail: close-up or wide, single or master, what kind of lens (wide, medium, or tight), camera movement. Once I've gotten the whole scene laid out, I go back to my shot-by-shot

---

[1]Uva, Mike. *The Grip Book*, Fourth Edition, Focal Press, 2009.
[2]Besides Mike Uva's grip book, look for lists in Dave Elkins's book, *The Camera Assistant's Handbook*, Fifth Edition, Focal Press, 2009.

version of it and note which shots are repeated. For example, in a conversation between a man and a woman, I might go from a two-shot to a single of the man, then a single of the woman, then back to the single of the man, and back to the single of the woman. We shoot the entire scene on one person, then the entire scene on the other, and then intercut them. You're kind of deconstructing the scene you've imagined, breaking it down to all the individual setups that will be needed to construct the scene in the editing room.

I usually list the scenes in order of master, small master, two- or three-shots, over-the-shoulders, loose singles, and inserts. That's more or less the way they'll be shot, from wide to tight. Now this doesn't mean I'm going to shoot every one of these shots. That kind of mechanistic approach comes from a noncreative mentality, what we call providing "coverage." Any creative DP will only shoot those setups that are necessary to the scene as it has been conceived. So I might only shoot a fluid, moving master that covers the whole scene and then medium close shots of the principals that will be intercut with or come after the master. Whatever shots I've dreamed up for a particular scene, I look at the shot list and do what I like to call a "triage." I prioritize this way:

1. What shots must I absolutely have to make the scene?
2. What shots will be interesting and will contribute to the scene's clarity and artistry?
3. What shots would really be fun to have but are not vital and are probably too complex to get?

This kind of prioritizing will be going on every day on the set as the director, along with the DP and the AD, makes tough practical choices about what shots to eliminate when the shoot starts to get behind schedule. It will pay off then to have ranked your shots during the preproduction. That way you don't shoot a less essential shot first, only to find out later that the producer won't allow you time to shoot the more important stuff. When the shooting begins, we will have shot lists every day for the scenes planned for that day, and we will do our best to shoot everything listed in the time allowed for the scene. My list now is not a shot list; it's a way for me to begin thinking about the visual component of the film.

It can be a time-consuming process to envision an entire film. But it's worth it even if the director has different ideas. The merging of two different visions can cross-fertilize and produce a hybrid better than one idea alone. It also provides me with a stash of ideas to dig into when we get to the fourteenth hour of shooting, we're losing the light, and we've only got time for one more shot. I may be able to come up with an idea based on my early vision of the film. So you can see that no effort put into planning is ever really wasted.

So you've "seen" the film in your head and made notes of all the shots. Now you're ready to have a detailed discussion with the director.

CHAPTER 5
The Shot List

You have met with the director. You have figured out the look, the style, and the tone of the film, and you've analyzed scenes visualizing the shots as you see them in your head. Now it's time to create a shot list. A shot list is the list of precise shots you will make for a film. It's broken down scene by scene, and is usually in the order in which you intend to shoot irrespective of how it will be edited. Some directors bring in a storyboard artist to make sketches depicting, on paper, what they've imagined. If they are multitalented like director Terry Gilliam or Martin Scorsese, they may sketch out the whole film themselves. A storyboard (Figure 5.1) could provide some of the same information. But a storyboard is by definition the shots in edited order, and may repeat shots (as in alternating close-ups in a conversation) that are one shot, only cut up into pieces. Figure 5.2 shows a script page with a scene involving four people. Following is an illustration of a shot list for that scene:

DIXIE • SCRIPT NOTES • SHOT LIST 9

Thurs 6/28

9. REBELDOME D/X

O/S[1] Belinda over Bowie
O/S Bowie over Belinda
(Shoot Bowie from below, Belinda from above)
Med Wide for bump—+Frank & Eve
CU Belinda
CU Eve

So you will still need a shot list like this to know what you need to do on the set and to communicate to the rest of the crew, especially to the AD. At this point in your planning you will have determined whether you'll be shooting on sets

---

[1]O/S means over-the-shoulder. This list reproduces my notes, which contain jargon.

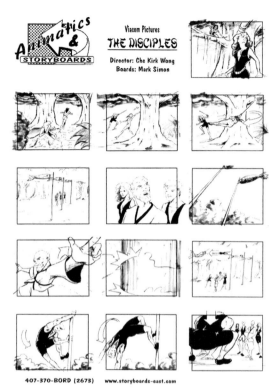

407-370-BORD (2673)   www.storyboards-east.com

FIGURE 5.1
A storyboard.
Reproduced with permission of Mark Simon from his book
Storyboards: Motion in Art. *Storyboards by Mark Simon on the*
movie The Disciples *(www.storyboards-east.com).*

```
EXT. REBELDOME - DAY

Belinda hands Bowie a camera and $5.

                    BELINDA
        Latasha says you need to buy film.

He takes her elbow.

                    BOWIE
        Stay away from my honey.

Belinda jerks away. Bowie smiles.

                    BOWIE
                  (continuing)
        Just joking.

                    BELINDA
        Not funny.

                    BOWIE
        I've got a surprise gift from you
        and me to Latasha. Let's go now
        and fetch it.

She isn't sure. Bowie gives her an uncomfortably tight hug.

                    BOWIE
                  (continuing)
        Come on!

As they turn to leave, Belinda bumps into Eve and FRANK
CHASE. Frank's late thirties, glasses, trim mustache. Eve and
Belinda seem to connect for a second.

                    BELINDA
        I'm so sorry.

                    EVE
        It was our fault, hon.

Belinda and Bowie continue. Eve checks her watch.

                    EVE
                  (continuing)
        We've got time to get a bite.
                  (a beat)
        I can only stay till half time.
```

FIGURE 5.2
A script page.
From the film To Live and Die in Dixie.
Reproduced with permission of GVSU Summer Film Project.

at a studio or at locations out in the field (Chapter 7) or a combination of the two. The more you know about where you'll be shooting, the more realistic and useful your shot list will be when you're in production.

You should talk through the whole script with the director to determine how the director sees the film; he or she may have very specific shots in mind or a feel for what her or she would like to see but not be interested or able to conceptualize each individual shot. A few directors may have no shots at all in mind and no interest in determining them in advance of shooting. These directors like to wing it.

Whatever the situation, you want to end up with a list of all the shots you plan to make for every scene. Now, you and the director may not always agree on exactly how to shoot a scene, but at this point the movie belongs to the director. It's the director who is going to be praised or blamed for the whole thing. She has to be able to do what will justify that responsibility and has to feel that you are there to be supportive, not to argue about opposing ideas. Use your creativity to support the director's vision. I don't mean you should be a lapdog, agreeing with everything the director says. You want to present your ideas as a means to enhance the director's vision, not to oppose it. This is where diplomacy comes in. You didn't think that was part of the DP's job description? Think again. Half of why a director hires you is for how you work together. No matter how talented you may be, no one wants to waste time trying to come to any agreement over how to shoot a scene.

In any case, regardless of the director's approach, it is useful for you as DP to have an actual shot list. How you come up with it will vary with each type of director I just mentioned. With the hands-on director you will spend considerable time together nailing down every shot. At the other extreme, with the director who has no ideas and not much interest in planning shots, you'll be designing all the shots. That doesn't mean you'll be directing the film. The work with the actors, the overall feel of the film, and the on-set decisions to modify, eliminate, or add shots will still be in the hands of the director.

Finally, and perhaps the toughest to work with, is the director who knows what he likes when he sees it but can't articulate it. Here's where your mind-reading abilities come into play. (Yes, mind reading is also in the DP's job description.) You will find that you have to read minds during your entire career, even while you are working your way up through the ranks, so you will have had plenty of practice when you finally become a DP. But it can be a minefield. Imagine the following conversation:

> **Director:** I want a … uh … you know … uhhhh….
> [Uncomfortable silence.]
> **You:** Something kind of noir?
> **Director:** No, sort of, but not really….

This kind of feedback isn't much help. But what you have to do is keep thinking about the script and keep trying to remember every single notion the director has expressed. Try to guess how he sees the movie, and suggest some approach. Be prepared for scorn and even abuse, but don't take it personally. It isn't. He's just lost in a dream. He may turn out to be a great director, just not a great communicator. With every suggestion, pay attention to what he says when he seems noncommittal or even slightly favorable. That's close to what he wants. You can build on that. And you can say to him, "That idea of *yours* for…." And he'll go for it. He doesn't remember who said what. So you can convince him that one of your guesses was his idea, and then you've got a place to begin. I know it all sounds cynically manipulative. Well, there's a lot of psychology in this business, and it's not all on the $200/hour couch.

An aside here: Some directors you work with will not have had as much experience shooting as you and your crew have. It's hard to get a film financed and produced. It's hard to get a job directing. And it takes a long time to complete and market a film. Smart and confident directors will welcome the chance to work with experienced people and will be happy to take suggestions. After all, if your ideas turn out well, the director will get all the credit. Other directors, especially first-timers, can be afraid they won't have the knowledge or power to exercise complete control. They are afraid someone will take the picture away from them. And they usually worry most about the DP, since on the set he or she is the one who seems most capable of doing everything the director is doing—and more.

Don't let yourself be caught in this trap. Always remind the director—and the producer—that it's their film. You're happy to be a part of it. You are excited to work on it. You love the script, and you are sure this will be a wonderful film. And you're thrilled to get a chance to work with—and for—the director. You shouldn't have to say flat out, "I'm not going to try to take over your film." But you may have to. Of course, sometimes you can't get past their paranoia, and you end up losing the job or getting fired before shooting even starts. That's show business. Just be sensitive to the vibes and be your collaborative best.

For example, I once was up for a job as DP on a low-budget horror film. I had just come off another film for the same company, where I was second unit DP. I was sure I'd have the job locked up because the director and producer of the horror film were the same director and producer I had just worked with. The three of us had worked together under trying conditions in the broiling heat of a desert, with a minimal crew, shooting action and stunts. We did a terrific job, worked together easily, and left the movie good friends. So naturally, when the director and producer got hired to do this horror picture, they wanted me to work on it with them.

I should mention that the director was new; the second unit we just finished was his first professional directing gig. Likewise for the producer, whose previous experience in the business was as an actress. No problem; they did a terrific job. Nevertheless, the production company assigned a supervising producer to the horror film project to make sure the budget and the company's interests were looked out for. And to do that the company picked a newly minted producer whose experience up until then was as a PA. (There's fast advancement in some companies.)

It turned out that the newbie supervising producer was worried that someone would realize he had no idea what he was doing, that he knew nothing and had no experience, and would end up taking the film away from him. And he didn't exactly like the camaraderie the three of us had built up. We might unite against him. Now he knew that the director and producer had little more experience than he had, so he didn't see them as a threat. But he took one look at my resume, and when he saw my 15 years of experience, it was as if I were wearing a big neon sign that said, "I've done it all and you know nothing. So don't tell me what to do." I will confess that for all my time in the business, before this occasion I couldn't have conceived of a situation where being skilled and experienced could work against you.

Anyway, he asked to see my reel. (See Chapter 27 for thoughts on putting together a reel.) He knew he couldn't say I wasn't qualified for the job, but he was determined to find some reason not to hire me that would seem reasonable to the company. He reviewed the reel I submitted, saw lots of exterior work (hey, it was second unit), and he said he was unsure about my ability to shoot interiors. So I put together another reel of interior work. Then he said he wasn't sure if I could shoot horror. I showed him the work I'd done on other horror films. He said this horror project had a lot of comedy, and he wasn't sure of my ability to shoot comedy. It was becoming amply clear by this time, if it hadn't been before, that he would say anything so he didn't have to hire me for this film.

What I learned from that experience is that you have to find a way, early on, even when you're being considered for a job, to communicate your respect for all the principals involved. You have to make it clear that you see yourself only as a specialist in your own area. You have no ambitions to run the show. It doesn't matter that the director and producer want you if some other power on the picture is afraid of you. You want to offer everything you have, all your ideas, all your abilities, all your enthusiasm. But make sure that from the start you present yourself as a nonthreatening team player, with no inclination to point out other people's lack of knowledge or experience. Again, *diplomacy*.

Now back to our shot list. If you're anything like me and most directors I've worked with, you'll have way too many shots. You'll have been given a shooting schedule for the entire film from the AD or the production manager, which you'll use to list all the shots you've planned for every scene scheduled for the entire show. And you'll end up with 30 or 40 shots listed for any single day. You might be able to make them all if you have very experienced personnel. But even so, this would be a killer schedule (it almost always looks like a killer schedule) that leaves no time for unforeseen circumstances—which will always come up—and offers no wiggle room for the director or actor to be creative or to improvise. This is when you want to do a final triage. The loss of a few shots has to be weighed against putting impossible pressure on the production. You don't want to be a slave to an unrealistic plan. When that happens, you are not shooting a movie; you are shooting a schedule. Audiences will not be impressed by that if the movie stinks.

When it's completed, make sure the AD has a copy of the shot list. A good AD will be able to estimate the time for each "setup." A setup is any one lighting arrangement that can be used to shoot any number of individual shots without making any major changes. The AD will devise an estimate of how much time can be allowed for the execution of each shot (a half hour for one shot, say, and one hour for another) and will institute deadlines to be met as the day progresses. The AD will keep on top of all this while you're shooting, keeping you apprised if you are falling behind schedule. The AD doesn't do this to annoy you but to ensure that you will not get to the end of the day and find that you can't get all the shots you and the director had planned on. And not getting those shots usually means not getting the shots at all. So it's better to eliminate shots as you're planning than have it done arbitrarily by running out of time. If by a miracle you end up having extra time on any particular day, you can go back to your original plan and pick up some of the shots you previously eliminated.

CHAPTER 6
The Crew

Let's start off planning for a film with a full professional crew. When you're working as a professional DP, your hiring responsibilities are for camera, grip, and electrical crews. The camera crew consists of the second camera assistant, the first camera assistant, and the camera operator in ascending order of status and authority. On shows using many cameras shooting simultaneously, there may also be a "loader." Usually loaders aren't necessary except on multiple camera or very physically difficult shows (like some hard-to-get-to locations where the camera equipment may be separated from the shooting company by miles). And on digital shows, the second assistant fulfills the functions of a loader, and there'll be a DIT (digital imaging technician).

The gaffer heads the electrical crew. Working under him or her are the "best boy" electrician and secondary electricians (sometimes referred to as lamp operators). Don't worry, when we get to the set, later in the book, I'll tell you all about what each of these crew members does, how he or she does it, and what the protocol will be on the set to ensure the smooth functioning of the group.

As DP you'll pick the gaffer you want but probably give her the job of hiring a best boy and the other electricians for the crew. The same goes for hiring the key grip, who will, in turn, hire the other grips. Very often you or your operator may want to determine who will be hired as the "dolly grip," since the dolly grip works so closely with the DP and operator.

Of course, the DP hires the camera operator, but I know many DPs who have the operator choose the assistant(s). There's a good argument for this: The operator works side-by-side with the assistant; he's more likely to know who the good assistants are, having more recently been an assistant himself; and it saves the DP trouble. I look at it differently. I figure I want the assistant to be my point man on the camera. He's the one who focuses—accurate focus is absolutely essential—and zooms, so he's helping to shape the look and feel of the shot. The assistant also checks out and prepares all the camera gear. He'll be the one saying what lens is acceptable. Lenses are the most vital element in forming the image, and I want someone who's critical about lens quality. I also want someone who is absurdly dedicated to perfection. That is the assistant's job requirement, and nothing less than perfection will do.

Then I will usually have the first assistant choose the second. The two assistants work together all the time, and the second is as much an assistant to the first as he is to the whole camera department. And here, too, the first is more likely to know the best seconds, having worked with more of them than the DP will have. Usually the first and second form a team, just as you try to form other teams among the crew: DP, operator, first and second assistants; operator, first assistant, dolly grip; DP, gaffer, key grip; gaffer and best boy electric; and key grip and best boy grip. Basic criteria for hiring are obvious: How much experience does the person have? Is the person good at his job? Have you seen her work? Have you seen any of the movies he's done? Have you worked with her and gotten along well? Most DPs work with the same people over and over again. It saves time and trouble. Because of this, getting a foothold into the film industry can be difficult, but good work and a good attitude will pay off. That's why, when you're just starting out, it's a good idea to take pretty much any job you can get. You'll have the chance to show that you can do the job, without fuss, and well. Every job is your audition for the next job.

The gaffer and the camera operator are the crew members the DP works most closely with. That's natural; on the set, the DP's main job is lighting and setting shots. Ideally, you should be on the same page for every scene, so you need a minimum of talk. The DP will have meetings with the gaffer before the shoot to discuss the "look" of the film, the approach to the lighting. You must have the same vocabulary; if you've been working in the business for a while, you will. You must share an aesthetic approach to the movie. It is essential that the terms you use mean the same thing to both of you. It's very easy to talk about a "shadowy" look, but what exactly does that mean? Do you want everything dark, both in the evening and during the daytime? Or do you just want backlight for every shot? Or do you mean no fill light? Talking beforehand and referring to specific pictures, movies, and photos will ensure that you two are talking about the same look all the time.

You must either have worked with the camera operator or have seen his work. The operator must be in tune completely with the DP; it's the operator's responsibility to know what the DP wants. But in hiring, the DP needs to get a good feel for the way the operator works. If the operator tends to make center-weighted compositions and the DP likes eccentric frames, the DP is never going to be happy with the operator. It is a sure thing that the operator will tend to revert to his normal composition reflex when an instinctual response is called for. The shot may be conventionally acceptable, but it won't be what the DP wants. Other points, such as proper headroom and precisely what the different shot descriptions (close-up, cowboy, etc.) mean can be worked out on the set.

Pretty much the same kinds of standards go for the key grip. I tend to think it's most important to have worked together before, so you don't have to start a new relationship and a new movie at the same time. Both the gaffer and the key will be the ones to choose their own best boys and crews. They know better than you do how good they are, and they know with whom they work best.

Now what I've just described is the ideal hiring situation. Reality can be a lot different. The DP may be hired onto a show to replace the previous DP who has left for another job or been fired. The rest of the crew may be staying on the shoot, so you have no choice but to work with this predetermined crew. Let's hope they all work well together, but you are definitely at a disadvantage in not having had planning time. You have to rely on the professionalism of everyone on the team, and most crews behave professionally.

Other times, you are hired onto a show early on, but you can't get your first choice of staff because they are already working on other shows with another DP. You have to be working all the time to be able to keep the same crew together on a consistent basis. This is usually more possible in TV, where you do a series, maybe work on other projects during hiatus, but come back to work on the show when it resumes production. On a successful show the team can stay together for years. This is less likely to happen in feature films, but a director like Clint Eastwood, who puts out a movie every year, can keep most of the same crew members with him for many, many years. That is why his set just hums along. Almost everyone knows one another and has perfected the way they work together. This is the ideal but very rare.

The main thing to remember is that the better your crew, the easier your job as DP will be. The performance of every member of the crew reflects on the DP. A great gaffer can execute the lighting the way you want it with very little supervision from you. Likewise, an operator who is really tuned in can anticipate what you want in framing and movement.

Many directors claim that casting is what makes or breaks a film and is the most important decision the director makes. Hiring your crew is the DP's equivalent to casting, and whom you hire is as important to you as the actors are to the director.

Let's talk about small, no-budget films. No matter how simple your film project, you need a crew. You may want to do every job and control every aspect of your movie yourself, but that is not possible. Admittedly, there have been some great artists of the cinema, like Stan Brakhage, who literally made their films single-handedly. But being a "total filmmaker" has significant limitations, and most films are made cooperatively by a group of skilled and talented people working together to achieve a single vision (the director's).

If you're just starting out, your crew will consist of just a few friends or school acquaintances who are just as movie-mad as you. Each of you is interested in everything, and you're all willing to do anything. Great! I love your enthusiasm. Now stop bouncing up and down, and let's get to the right way to run a set and a crew.

As a DP, it is your responsibility to put together a camera, grip, and electrical crew. If you have a small crew, even with only one crew member per department, you can still work well. One of the most important aspects of building a crew is to make sure each person has a specific job and that he or she has responsibility for that job only. Of course, you're going to have to help one another because sometimes equipment is too heavy or unwieldy or there's too much to do in one area (say, lighting) at a moment when another department (say, grip) isn't busy.

I can't emphasize enough how important it is that each crew member has a specific job assignment. First, each person knows what he is responsible for, so there's no possibility of "Oh, I thought Bob was doing that." You're the gaffer, and you are responsible for hanging and placing the lights and dealing with the electrical equipment. As the shooting progresses, you'll become more knowledgeable about the lighting equipment than anyone else on the set. And you'll be able to work faster, more efficiently, and more effectively with lighting than anyone else on the crew. Concomitant with this, you'll know how to care for each lamp and stand to make sure they don't break and that they're stored and travel well. You'll soon know when it pays to ask for help and when you don't need it. Of course, as you make more movies, the same person doesn't have to take the same job every time. In fact, at the beginner's stage, it's a good idea to migrate from job to job, to get an idea of what each department has to deal with and to see if each of you prefers one job to all the others.

CHAPTER 7
The Location

Okay, you're a little tired of reading the script. Who could blame you? So it's time to get out and stretch your legs. And ride around in a compact car with five other people, all over town, to neighborhoods you wouldn't go to on a bet, on either the hottest or coldest day of the year. And it's raining. This is what's known as location scouting.

Nonetheless, you have an idea of the kinds of settings you need for your story. Like so many movies, you're going to try to shoot on "practical" locations. Don't be misled. Practical doesn't mean that the locations work or that it makes sense to be there. The term is meant to differentiate already existing places from stages and sets. (Likewise, "practical lights" are simply nonmovie lights; they're either the built-in lights on a location—fluorescents in ceilings, say—or they're regular lamp fixtures on a set—anything, like a floor lamp, that appears on the screen as a source of light and as a prop.)

I really, really hope that your film has a location manager. The location manager's job is to know (or know how to find) almost every kind of place that is useful for movies. He or she will scout out a lot of places and see if there's a possibility of renting them for the film. He or she will whittle down the possibilities somewhat and then present pictures or video to the director, who then says, "Yes, no, no, no, yes, no, no," until the number of possible locations is reduced further.

If there's no location manager, the DP and the director will be the ones going all over hill and dale hunting for something that looks as if it might work. You may have some production people doing this scouting, but if you don't have a location manager or a production designer, you also don't have a lot of people in the production office. Since it matters most to them, the director and the DP get stuck doing the work. It's really not that much fun.

The thrill of checking out possibilities palls after visiting the tenth nice clapboard house that's just not right: it's too big or too small, it's a funky color, there's a gas station next door when the house is supposed to be in the country, the trees in front hide the entrance you have to use, it's on top of a picturesque hill that would kill the crew bringing up equipment every day, or it's perfect but they won't even think of letting a movie company in. God bless the location manager for taking care of all these problems—so you can have your own problems.

For a DP, there are some vital questions to be answered by the location scout. Always carry a compass, and not just for when the driver gets lost. No matter what the conditions of your shoot, you always want to know the compass point orientation of your location. I don't care if everything is interior and there are no windows in the place. Something is likely to come up ("Let's just get an establishing shot of the place"), and you'll need to know where the sun is so you can shoot in the most beautiful and revealing light. If the house faces west, say, and you want a richly illuminated look, you'll wait until late in the day to get the beautiful butterscotch of sunset. Or if you want it looking glamorous or mysterious, shoot in the morning for a dark front with an elegant-looking backlight. Or shoot during midday for a nondescript look.

And take a notebook and a camera. You'll need to make notes about a lot of factors for every location. You'll never remember all the details, and even if you did, you'd never remember which location has which characteristic. Take pictures so you can remember where you were and how it looked and so you can refer to a specific concrete image when you're discussing the location with the director or with the rest of the crew. The following are my Hot Tips for shooting location stills:

1. Take stills. If we like the place, we want to have something we can sit down and discuss.
2. You're also going to use video. Okay, there's a good chance your digital still camera will record some kind of video. That's even better. You can share with everybody on your own website (or just use Facebook). But do me a favor: *Think*.
3. Don't pan quickly. You will end up with strobing, an unwanted jittering effect that occurs when you move the camera so fast that the images appear like they've been captured discontinuously. (In other words, it's the same effect you get with a strobe light.) This happens because the position of an object on the screen changes radically from frame to frame. Try to simulate the pace of walking slowly around a space, frequently having your gaze come to rest on important details, then moving slowly on to the next focus of interest. If you pan, let the shot rest on something, then pan to the next pertinent thing, and so on.
4. Occasional close-ups are interesting, but mostly we're looking for wide shots.
5. Use a tripod. Get a small, lightweight tripod.
6. Okay, I have to be honest: Tripods are a royal pain in the ass. So use a monopod. It's like a single telescoping leg of a tripod. Buy one or borrow one or have the company rent one for you. A monopod is small and light, doesn't have to have a head (just a bolt to attach the camera), you can carry it like an umbrella, you can use it as a walking stick or a weapon,

and, most important, allows you to get steady shots. You may have image stabilization on your camera, but it's worse than useless if you pan or have camera moves. The stabilization program fights your panning, and the result is unpleasant.

7. Again, think. Don't shoot too much—although too much is better than too little. *Do* reprise areas—take us back to the first areas so we have our memories refreshed.

8. Make sure to capture a sense of the surrounding geography—adjacent buildings, surrounding streets, general neighborhood, streetlights, overhead electrical wires—anything that could be an asset or a problem.

9. Pay attention to windows and others sources of daylight; existing lighting (fluorescent, incandescent, mercury vapor, sodium, neon, other); and practical lights (e.g., desk lamps; size, possibility of moving, possibility of relamping).

10. Make sure you *know* the compass directions for each location. If you have video capability and can record sound, mention the direction you're facing for each shot so your crew can think about it.

11. You need to know parking areas, what floor any location is on, and—when you get serious about the location—a picture of the circuit breaker box for the building and a note where the box is located.

12. Make notes of any special problems or circumstances you notice.

In most cases, you can see why you want to know where east and west are. As I just said, if you're working on an exterior, the best-looking light is backlight or side light. In the morning, you want to face east, and in the afternoon, you want to face west. "When the sun is directly overhead, the light is at its ugliest. What I advise you to plan to do at that time, roughly from 10AM to 3PM, is to shoot close shots. You can use silk (probably on a large frame, like a 12'×12') overhead to soften and diffuse the sun. Then you can use reflectors and bounce cards to redirect the sun and get modeling on the faces. You keep the beauty of low-angle light all the way through the scene, and you've made use of all the time in the day for shooting." But you want to be able to say to the AD, "Schedule this scene in the morning and this other one in the afternoon," and so on so you can get the best light. You will also want to maintain the continuity of the look. If you start shooting a scene in backlight, you don't want it suddenly to be in frontlight just because the sun has moved. Schedule one part of the scene so you can face east (morning) and another part so you can face west (afternoon). Even though you may have shifted your actors 180 degrees, the scene will look continuous as long as you can make sense of the backgrounds and there's a bit of matching from shot to shot. It's more effective to have lighting continuity than spatial continuity. We can always create a new geography that doesn't exist in the real world by careful shooting and editing, and it will be convincing to the audience. A change of look to the film may not be noticed as a mistake, but the audience will know that something isn't quite right.

A good example is the movie *The Horse Whisperer*. Robert Redford and Kristin Scott Thomas have scenes set outside where they face each other and talk. Each of them is backlit by sunlight, and each has a soft front fill from reflected sunlight. Think about it for a second. If they're facing each other and each is backlit, there must be two suns. We're on an alien planet! But wait a second; it still looks great, and, more important, it looks right. As an audience we want to feel that a scene was shot in one place and at one time. Having the lighting look consistent from shot to shot gives that feeling. Again, it doesn't matter if it's not possible in the real world; we're making movies, and we're going for effect.

And if you're shooting interiors and you see out a window, you want to anticipate when the light coming from the outside will be best for your scene. So if you want to use the real sunlight coming in, make sure you can schedule the shoot to accommodate this.

You always want your location to be on the first floor. Otherwise, you're lugging loads of heavy equipment up the stairs. I've carried a 500-pound dolly up a 75-step staircase, and that may be why I have a bad back today. Forgetting that personal complaint, it's always a pain in the neck to get equipment up stairs, and it will take extra time, messing up your shooting schedule. I once had a courtroom location for a feature in which a large part of the action involved a trial. It was a beautiful room, perfect in almost every way. But it was on the second floor. Sure, there was an elevator, but it was small and slow, and we had to share it with the courthouse occupants, like judges who didn't like being kept waiting. During the early-morning hours or at night, we were fine. Any other time probably meant carrying the heavy stuff up the stairs. We used the courtroom, and we were happy to have it, but it meant running an extra 50 feet of thick, heavy electrical cable out the door and roping it to the fire escape to connect with the generator outside on the ground. And any communication with the crew down there had to be by radio or shouting—another inconvenience.

You want to have as short a run of cable to the generator as possible, not only to spare your crew the trouble of hauling it all but also because a long run can cause diminished electrical power—that is, voltage drop. You can consult references to ascertain the loss for different wire gauges and lengths of run. You can find this online or in many electrical reference books. I recommend *Set Lighting Technician's Handbook* by Harry Box[1] or *Lighting for TV and Film* by Gerald Millerson.[2]

And another problem with second-floor locations is having to figure out how to light from the outside. This is particularly a problem if you have a small room, and you want to simulate moonlight, sunlight, or a streetlight, and you can get that effect only by lighting from the outside. If you're on an upper floor, you'll need scaffolding ("risers") or very high and unwieldy lamp stands that could blow over in the wind (and have), or you'll end up having your light coming from too low an angle. This can lead to the "light from hell" look, when people are lit like monsters in a horror movie. However you deal with the placement of the lights, it will take added time for you to make it look good. So be adamant

---

[1]Box, Harry. *Set Lighting Technician's Handbook*, Fourth Edition, Focal Press, 2010.
[2]Millerson, Gerald. *Lighting for TV and Film*, Third Edition, Focal Press, 1999.

about getting a location on a ground-level floor. And when the director says, "Oh, but this room has the perfect look. I have to shoot here," you'll get to discover all the kluges and improvisations necessary to make the best of a bad situation. Plan ahead.

Let's get back to sources of light. You know the compass directions, and you've looked at windows, doors, skylights—any possible sources of daylight. You will be planning whether to use the daylight or block it out. Then, while you're in there, look up. Maybe there are built-in light sources. Most businesses and some rooms in residences have some sort of ceiling fixtures. These days it's often fluorescents, but they can be a problem because of the strange color temperature and the green spike in fluorescent light. (See Chapter 33 on color temperature for some background on this.) You'll have to decide between putting corrective filter material (minus-green gels) on every fixture, filtering your movie lights to match the fluorescents (plus-green gels), or turning off the fluorescents and not using them. Make notes about the possible need for gels. You really can't relamp fluorescents because the only color-correct fluorescents need a special ballast (transformer) to control them. And there's no way you're going to rewire an entire room. (By the way, I'm still assuming that you're keeping copious notes. If you're lucky, you'll have an assistant to whom you can say, "Write this down," and it'll be done. But I don't trust anyone else's notes; I know exactly what I need to remember, so I take my own.)

What if the existing lighting is tungsten—which is becoming rarer in the twenty-first century—or mercury vapor, or sodium vapor, or neon, or quartz-halogen, or something new like LEDs? I always carry a color meter so I can get a quick read on the color temperature of the lamps and an idea of what kind of filtration I will need to achieve the look I'm after. For a realistic natural look I'll want the lighting to appear as normal, white light. For more unconventional looks I might want to exploit the oddities of the existing light sources or further manipulate them in some way. In any case, knowing the color temperature allows you to achieve the look you want. Otherwise you may end up with some unpleasant surprises when you see how these lighting sources appear on the screen. Digital brings up the same problem (but let's call it an opportunity). Of course, you know you've had to white-balance your digital camera, but how will it react to mixed light sources? Digital tends to be less accepting of mixed light sources. So test it out.

I may be able to use the existing lights, either as the main light for the scene or the ambient light that I will supplement by lighting the actors. It's a lot faster and cheaper if I can use some of the existing lighting. Never compromise your work, but always look for ways to work faster and cheaper.

There are likely to be lamps—table lamps, desk lamps, floor lamps, and so forth—that you or the Art Department can easily move around. Again, some of these can be used to light the scene. I recall shooting a scene that took place in the small waiting room of a hospital. The lighting was overhead fluorescents, ugly as you can imagine. I filtered the fluorescents to make them appear the same color as tungsten lights, and I put some diffusion over them to spread the light and cut down its intensity. This provided a good ambient light; everything was softly, evenly lit, but at a low level—an ideal fill light. Then I got the prop master to scrounge up some table lamps; she even raided her own apartment to get them. We put high-wattage household bulbs in the table lamps and placed the lamps close to the actors in the scene. The practical lamps were now bright enough to light my main actors, and the fluorescents gave a presence to the rest of the set. This way I was able to impart a warmth and intimacy to the scene that otherwise would have looked sterile and sickly.

What I did there is something you always want to be prepared for. Carry a number of household bulbs of varying wattage—25 to 300—so you'll be able to replace the bulbs in practical fixtures with bulbs that give you exactly the amount of light you want where you want it.

You'll have to consider power for all these lights and for your movie lights. There may be sufficient power available using only the existing circuits at the location; that is, if the owner of the location will allow you to use it. Find the breaker box and check for the number and size of circuits. Households commonly have 15-amp or 20-amp circuits, with usually a larger circuit or two for an electric stove, air conditioners, or other power-hungry appliances. Businesses will usually have a lot of 20-amp circuits and several larger ones. You'll want to know what outlets and fixtures are controlled by each circuit. You would hope that the circuits would be labeled, and they may have been at one time. But by the time you get to them, they've faded to white, or the labels have fallen off, or they're torn, so all you can decipher is "rm." Sometimes the electrician who installed the box was originally training to become a doctor and his handwriting is illegible. Anyway, even if they're there, you can't always trust that the labeling is correct.

If you're still scouting several locations and haven't decided on one, just take a look at the box and make notes. Once you know you're definitely going to be shooting at a place, check what each circuit controls. Here's how: One person takes a test lamp (this can be a fancy electrician's tool or as simple as a work lamp with a plug) and goes to a room. He plugs the lamp into a socket in the wall. It should light up. Meanwhile, another person stands at the box and shuts off the breakers one at a time. The two people communicate by cell phone. When the test lamp goes off, the person at the box makes a note of the circuit and which room it services. The person in the house notes down on a room diagram which outlet was tested. Go around the room, plugging in the light and turning on light switches to see how many outlets are on that circuit. Write it down. If the light works on any other outlet, that's another circuit. Go back to turning off breakers to find which circuit any other live outlets are on. You should be able to do this fairly quickly, unless you have a whole house to check.

Common sense will do you no good here. There may well be several outlets in a room, but they are not necessarily separate circuits. It's likely that they're all on one circuit. But you could have a house like mine, apparently wired by a dyslexic drunk. The same circuit may go to the kitchen, my office, and part of the living room. So you want to be sure that all unnecessary appliances are unplugged when you shoot, or the lamp in the living room might blow out the circuit you're using in the bedroom.

"Yes, Jack," you say, "I'm checking the circuits and I'm making notes. But in the name of all that's holy, why am I doing this?" You are doing it because everything that uses electricity draws a certain amount of power. Circuits are made to carry a given maximum amount of power and no more. If you tried to draw more power, the circuit would become overloaded. It would heat up the wire to a combustible temperature and burn the place down. That's why we have breakers, switches designed to shut off the power when you exceed the allowed amount of electricity being drawn on a given circuit. You will be using lights that draw more power than most household or even business appliances. You want to be sure you don't blow a circuit, because that will disrupt filming and force someone to go to the deep, dark, spider-infested corner of the basement where the breaker box is located to switch the breaker back on.

Now pay attention. I'm going to tell you something that will save your life on the set and make you look like a genius. It's a formula: W = VA. Don't worry about what it means for now. Just memorize it. You'll notice that it looks like the abbreviation for West Virginia; just remember West Virginia, and you'll always remember this formula.

Here's what it means: W is watts, A is amps (amperes), and V is voltage. Watts is a measure of the power drawn by your device (a lamp), amps (amperes) is the amount of electricity flowing through the system we are describing, and volts is the force with which the electricity is pushed through the wires (it's like water pressure if you think of the wires as pipes and the electricity as water). This formula can be solved to tell you how much electricity (amps) your device is using and how close you are to overloading the circuit. You know the watts (you put up a lamp of a certain wattage—say, 1,000 watts). You know the voltage. (You didn't even realize that, did you? Well, in the United States, all line voltage is 120. Sometimes it's down to 110 or up to 125, but those are momentary fluctuations, and 120 is the standard.) So you can plug in the numbers: 1,000 = A × 120. Solving for A, we divide both sides by 120. 1,000 divided by 120 is 8.3333…. So each 1,000-watt lamp consumes 8.3 amps. If you've got a 20-amp circuit, you're safe putting two 1,000-watt lamps on that circuit, with 3.4 amps left over, enough for one 400-watt lamp.

But my advice is not to do that. Leave some room on the circuit. In fact, we build in safety room when we calculate. You noticed that when you divided 1,000 by 120, you had to get out a calculator or, worse, a pencil and paper, and it was a pain. How can you do all this math on the set? You can't. So we say that we are using 100 volts, not 120. *Voilà!* Suddenly it's easy to divide all those wattages by the voltage in your head. 1,000 divided by 100? That's 10! And you'll notice we say we're using 10 amps, more than the actual 8.3. The extra 1.7 amps we say we're using is our margin of safety. Now we can put two 1,000 W lamps on a 20-amp circuit. We say they use up 20 amps, and we're safe and contented. And you can forget about the math and just say for every 1,000 W lamp, you'll figure you're using 10 amps. We call this "paper amperage" as opposed to actual amps. Every electrician in the business knows this, and consequently, movie people rarely burn down buildings—except as a special effect or stunt.

Earlier I mentioned running cable to generators. If you are going to need high-wattage lamps, you will quickly surpass the capacity of the household or business circuits to handle them. So you will need an additional source of power, which is a generator. (We'll talk more about generators when we get on the set.) On your location scout, you will be looking for a good place to put the generator. You want it as close to the lights as possible so that the cable run is not too long (remember, you lose voltage on a long cable run—say, over 100 feet). But you want the generator to be far enough away that you can't hear it running. Or, more precisely, far enough that the sound recordist, "mixer," can't hear it when you're shooting. And be aware, these guys can hear grass growing. You may not notice the generator's hum, but the extremely sensitive microphones used to record dialogue hear everything in their area. So you have to keep the generator at a reasonable distance and, if possible, behind a soundproof barrier like a masonry wall. It's not always as easy as you might think to find just such a place.

And you never know what may happen with the generator or the household wiring. The script for a film I shot a few years ago in rural Michigan called for a lot of shooting at farmhouses. One of the locations was a ramshackle place owned by a septuagenarian lady who never missed her Friday night dance parties (or her gin, bless her).

But her house was about 100 years old, and the wiring was commensurate with its age. Of course, to have enough electrical power for even the smallest movie lamps, I ordered a generator. I didn't want to take any chances of faulty wiring burning down the house.

Our first day on the set found us in the sweet old lady's house, doing a flashback scene in which a man beats up his young son. Of course, there were first-day nerves all around, and of course, we had a kid on set. Kids tend to behave rather than act, so it's hard to get a performance instead of just behavior, and they're really intolerant of retakes, so you'd better get it the first time.

The action was to take place in the kitchen. My plan was to light the kitchen as a natural interior using tungsten lamps and film balanced for 3,200° K. I would let the bluish outdoors stay blue to keep the sober, almost sad intent of the script. Then I planted an uncorrected HMI (at around 6,000° K) outside, shooting through the window to blow out some of the action. By overexposing the light from the HMI, I could get a stylized look for the scene. The HMI light would seem like an extreme accidental splash of sunlight, even though the fields seen through the window would be only slightly bright, as though the sun was attacking the boy.

Since so many of the scenes with the grown son took place at night, I decided that the flashbacks with his younger self (all set during the day) should have an over-bright element to separate the look of the past from the present. I also used my favorite diffusion: an optical flat with a thin coating of Vaseline rubbed in one direction along a paper towel to give streaks of light. (An optical flat is just like a filter—same size, same optical glass, same strict manufacturing standards—but completely transparent. It's great for protecting the lens from explosions and mud and for making your own filters.)

We were all ready to shoot. The set was lit. The actors were ready. And suddenly the entire set went dark. Our generator had stopped. There was no time to figure out why. The child actor was there, and we had to get the shot.

While my gaffer raced out to work on the generator, I looked at the woebegone face of my director, and I knew I had to figure out a way to shoot—fast. Let's look at my lighting plan: I had a few small units—1 Ks and 2 Ks—inside to give a low-level light to the kitchen. I had left the window ungelled so it would be bluish and slightly overexposed. And I had my 4 K HMI outside to provide the effect light to (slightly) blow out the scene from the past.

Now, without a generator, I would have to rely on the power in the old house to run my lamps. My concern for overloading the house rose to a new level. Of course, the HMI was useless for now; that lamp would draw 40 amps, and more than one 1 K (10 amps) would probably blow out the house circuits. We checked, and the fuse box (which was an unpleasant surprise; I hadn't seen anything but circuit breakers in 40 years) suggested we had two 15-amp circuits.

I've spent a lot of time on big Hollywood productions, but I've also worked on many low-budget films. Here's where all those long hours at short pay began to pay off. When you can't afford expensive equipment, you have to be creative, and I've seen the most amazing jerry-rigs from my fellow crew members.

I had to shoot, I had to light, and I had only limited house power. What could I do? I know: W = VA! Cut down the wattage and use less power. I cut down the size of the lamps I would use to one-quarter the size of the ones I had planned. So where I had 1 Ks, I used some 250s, and I used a 100 W household bulb in a China ball for fill. By staying under 1,500 watts on any single circuit (remember, W = VA, W = 100×15 = 1,500 max watts available), I was safe from burning down the house, and the light from them was proportionate to what I had in my original setup. To get my "overexposure" effect, I used a Baby 1 K with half CTB (CTB is color temperature blue, a gel designed to convert tungsten light to approximately the color temperature of daylight)—brought inside the house—to simulate the HMI splash I originally had.

Of course, I had to shoot at a wider stop—all the way open at this point. Now I still had the window in the shot, and at the new stop it would blow out. We grabbed a couple of 4 × 4 grip doubles from the truck and clipped them up outside the window, and we were balanced. The window looked bright enough for day but dark enough to keep it moody and not blow out.

FIGURE 7.1
Flashback using small lamps. From *The Freezer Jesus*.
Reproduced with permission of GVSU Summer Film Project

Thank goodness, it all worked. We didn't burn down the house. My gaffer got the generator working for the rest of the day. The shot looks just as it did in my original concept. And I got an "Attaboy!" for getting the scene shot under impossible circumstances.

Things are different when you shoot on a stage. Among other things, you've got plenty of power and scaffolding so you can light from above. While it can be advantageous to light from above—no lights and stands cluttering the stage floor, for example—it can result in an artificial look. The look of many studio films and TV shows made up through the 1960s is probably attributable to the fact that almost everything was shot on stages. The light was very well controlled, and the conditions of control in the studios led to a "well-made" film look. There were always some films with studio scenes that were made to look as location-real as possible. But the aesthetic of raw reality didn't come into play until the Italian neo-realism of the late 1940s. With the eruption of the French new wave, starting in 1959, the preferred use of locations and of making studio sets look like locations spread throughout the world. Godard once famously remarked to his cameraman, Raoul Coutard, that his actress couldn't be expected to act a realistic bedroom scene on stage because all the bedrooms she had been in had ceilings. (Stage sets famously have no ceilings; that's how you can light from above. *Citizen Kane* attracted notice for, among other reasons, having ceilings on so many rooms. Of course, they were usually small frames covered with canvas on the parts of the set that might show the ceiling in the frame, leaving plenty of room for the lamps on the scaffolding above.)

It's quite possible to light and frame stage sets so they look extremely real, and plenty of not-so-good camerapeople have managed to make practical locations look phony. In the real world, the source of light in a room only sometimes comes from above. Often the light comes from a window or lamp at about the same level as the human beings. So don't fret too much about not being able to shoot on a stage. That comes with its own set of problems. I encourage you to glory in the use of locations and not feel deprived of shooting on stages.

So what else do you need to be aware of during your scout? You will have some vehicle(s) carrying your equipment: trucks, vans, or maybe your dad's SUV. You'll want to be able to park as close as possible to the shooting site to facilitate unloading and loading equipment and for access and storage of equipment in a safe, easily accessible place. Make sure there's a place for the equipment trucks to park close by, and if you have to reserve a place ("No Parking 7 AM–8 PM—Film Production" signs put up by the city), make sure the production manager takes care of it. You'll want to have a location with adequate parking for the cast and crew. On big shows, there will often be a parking lot up to a mile away from the location and regular shuttling vans to take everyone to and from the set. If you can't afford that, don't commit yourself to a location without thinking about parking. These questions are not really the job of the cinematographer, but if you keep them in mind, you'll help avoid choosing locations that will be a big headache for you and your crew. The work is hard enough without making it harder.

The production designer (or art director) will be with you on the scout. He or she will be making notes of structures and props that need to be changed or brought in. Try to look at the location through their eyes; there may be some things you would like them to do to the set, like putting up wall sconces temporarily to give you a justification for a lighting source in a specific area. Or you may need windows covered, window treatments made (blinds, shutters, curtains, drapes) to block out or filter external light sources. You may need something done to the floor to protect it from damage from camera, lighting, and grip equipment. Or you may want rugs or carpeting lifted so you can dolly on a hard, flat surface. But if a rug was photographed on the floor in the master, you'll want a remnant of it available so you can place it in the frame so it appears that the entire rug is there even though the big rug has been removed to clear the floor for a move.

And looking at the floor, ideally it should be smooth and level. If so, and if the show can possibly afford it, you will want to have a crab dolly on which you can keep the camera mounted most of the time. You want it not only as a way of making smooth moves but also as the working camera platform in preference to using a tripod. A tripod is a perfectly good camera support, but it's somewhat inconvenient to move. It's hard to set to a specific height, and it's got spikes on the end of the legs that can play havoc with nice floors. A dolly, on the other hand, with its balloon wheels on smooth bearings, is relatively easy to move and won't scar the floors. You can quickly raise or lower the camera to any height, fine-tuning your camera position to get just the right shot. I love the Fisher 11 and the Chapman Super Peewee; they're both very small dollies, easy to maneuver in tight spaces, and sized to go through almost any door. They're not too heavy in case they need to be lifted.

So we're looking for smooth, level floors. It's always possible to lay track (and both dollies ride on track with minimal adjustment), but you want it to be easy to make small adjustments quickly when you're setting up shots and shooting. And remember that laying track takes time, and time is money. So the presence of smooth floors and the choice of the right dolly really pay off.

Now all of this is a lot to remember when you go out to assess places to shoot. We've talked about many factors that influence the choice of location, and I suggest making a checklist to guide you through your evaluation of each location you visit. Your brain can get fried pretty fast in a day of scouting, and you'll never remember without notes. Lucky for you, I've already done it for you.

DP LOCATION CHECKLIST

- Take location stills.
- Note all sources of daylight.
- Make note of permanent existing lighting.
- Note all practical lights and the feasibility of adding practicals.
- Take note of the number and size (in amps) of circuits.
- Note the location of the breaker box (or, if you're really unlucky, the fuse box).
- On what floor of the building is your location situated? If it's not the ground floor, get a new location.
- Is the floor smooth and level?
- Measure the dimensions (in square feet, length and width) of the interior space and exterior spaces, if necessary.
- How long you would have to make a cable run from a generator?
- Where can you put the generator to shield the sound?
- How close to the site can you park the equipment trucks?
- Note the availability and safety of parking for the cast and crew.
- Note the availability of bathroom facilities for the cast and crew.
- Note how far the cast and crew will have to travel to get to the location.
- Determine compass orientation of the exterior of the structure.
- Determine compass point location of windows on the interior for exterior lighting sources.
- Note any changes to the set you will need the Art Department to take care of.
- Determine the need for any permits.
- Take note of any other special problems or circumstances.

As thoughtful as you will be when choosing locations, sometimes you just can't help a disaster. I was shooting a picture about an elderly man who lived his life alone and isolated watching TV all day. One day he sees a news story about another old man who was found dead in front of his television. Our "hero" dresses up in his best and goes out to be a part of the world outside. One instance after another, he suffers disappointment and heartbreak from the indifference or hostility of the people he runs into. Finally, while making his way home that night, he stops in front of a large apartment building. He looks up and sees, in each apartment window, only the flickering blue light of a TV set being watched by the lonely inhabitants within.

Well, we found what we needed in the building where our AD lived. It was a gentrified factory, so at the rear there was a blank brick wall pierced with uniformly sized and spaced windows floor after floor. Nothing could have said boring uniformity better. When we were doing the scout, we noticed railroad tracks behind the building, right where we would be shooting. Of course, we were concerned about this and checked with our AD. "Oh, no," he said, "the train only comes through at 6:00 in the morning. I know because it wakes me whenever it blows its whistle." Okay, that was fine, we figured. We were shooting during the summer, and at 6 AM the sun would be up, and we would be long gone from our night shoot.

So comes the night of the shoot. We get started lighting about 11 PM. We put lamps with flicker boxes in the windows of the apartments and set some lights on the exterior of the building and on our hero. I wanted to keep a sense of darkness, sadness, and despair, so I lit with uncorrected HMIs and used one 4 K backed off and flagged, a fair way down the track to the left. Then I put in a couple of small lights for a rim and frontal fill for when we move in to a close shot of our man.

FIGURE 7.2
Exterior building with train tracks frame still. From *Flickering Blue*. *Image courtesy xyz. Reproduced with permission of GVSU Summer Film Project*

Everything is set up, and we get a very good master. Of course, the director wants another, and we get ready to roll. As the AD is calling for quiet, suddenly my electricians are yelling, screaming my name, and hollering something incomprehensible. It sounded a little like "There's a train coming." And at the same time, they are scrambling down from the ladders and trying to move the big light that I had spent so much time placing and aiming.

Train? We don't have a train in this scene. I walked from the camera up to where the HMI was playing, just skimming the building, and—holy cow! There was another bright light—one I certainly hadn't set—coming at us from the other direction.

The train driver—I guess he was the engineer—was as surprised as we were when he saw a giant light facing him on the tracks, looking for all the world like another train headed straight for him. And there was no time to get the equipment off the tracks. The train stopped. It was only riding on a spur, not the main track.

If I learned anything from this experience, it's don't trust the folks who live or work in the building when you ask them questions about the place. Most people want to be helpful, and they'll give you some kind of answer. But if you have to know about the electricity, ask the house maintenance man or find an electrician. And if you want to know about traffic, call the police. Always go to an authority when you need an accurate answer to an important question—like train schedules.

Oh, I learned one other thing. When a crew is feeling tired, one foolproof way to make them work really fast, especially at three in the morning, is to have a freight train aim right for them.

CHAPTER 8
Selecting a Camera

It's time to start ordering equipment. This is where all the ideas and information you've been gathering come into play. And it is also where you come up against reality: the budget, the schedule, and the wishes and desires of the director, the producer, and even the star.

FILM OR DIGITAL? THAT IS THE QUESTION

One of the first questions that will come up (from production and/or from the director) is should we use film or digital? Sometimes it seems as though this choice is the only thing anyone talks about. And everyone has an opinion. I should say at the outset (let's call it full disclosure) that I love film. I began working with film, and I've always loved the look of film and the feel of film cameras. I love their nineteenth-century technology. I love the mechanical parts that I can see working. I like the arcana of film cameras. You may feel the same way.

And yet, you know what? That will have nothing to do with which medium or camera you will choose or the advice you will give to the producer or the director in considering that choice. This is a decision that will be made in concert with the principals according to your recommendations. You will not get to make this decision yourself. But you can advocate. It's up to you as director of photography to make sure the decision makers are fully informed. So be sure you know what you're talking about. There are lots of misconceptions flying around about both film and digital. And remember, no matter who makes the decision, *you'll* be stuck with making the picture look good. That said, film or digital?

If you're on a big-budget film—say, $40 million and up—money won't be a deciding factor, and you'll probably go with film. (Of course, there are exceptions: James Cameron needed digital for 3D and for effects for *Avatar*; George Lucas is likewise committed to digital effects and wants to have a digital original for easy compositing [*Star Wars I, II, III*]; and Michael Mann just likes digital [*Collateral, Public Enemies*]. But even with all the effects in his movies, Spielberg uses film.)

At the other end of the spectrum (budget under $1 million), you'll probably go digital to save money on film and processing. In the midground between those extremes—$1 million to $40 million—you've got some thinking to do. If you go with film, you've got everything going for you. Film's been used since the beginning of movies. The basic technology is over 100 years old, it's been tested beyond the need of testing, and it works. Film gives a beautiful picture. You can work in 35 mm, the standard for almost every Hollywood movie ever made. Or you can look at super-16 (a format developed in the 1970s but given a rebirth by camera and film companies in the 1990s). It's been proven as a practical format for theatrical exhibition by many films, such as Mike Figgis's *Leaving Las Vegas* and Darren Aronofsky's *Black Swan*.

If you've been around the business a while, you're used to working with film, you have a feel for how to expose it, you know how it will look and perform under most conditions, and you're probably familiar with almost every film camera in use today. Experienced camera crews are probably more familiar with film cameras than with digital. Film cameras and the lenses for them are readily available for rental, and neither design nor operation of them changes much from year to year. That means the crew can feel confident that any make of film camera will easily fall into a routine work pattern. The routine's important: The more you can rely on habit and practice, the less thinking you have to do about the equipment. Less thinking about the tools means more time to think about the unique problems that will inevitably crop up during the shoot.

So with all that going for it, why would anyone choose anything other than film? Well, there always money. Film stock is expensive; no matter how frugal everyone is, it's tough to have less than a 7:1 or 8:1 shooting ratio. For a roughly two-hour film, you'll be buying 70,000 to 100,000 feet of film, minimum. And every bit of exposed film has to be processed: more money. That gives you a negative, so now you need a print (the old way) or a transfer to some electronic display (usually a telecine so there can be dailies on tape, DVD, hard drive, or memory chip or card). This also costs money. And it takes time. If the company is shooting in a major city, with readily available services, dailies will likely be ready to view the morning after shooting. But on any location, you may have to wait a few days to see dailies. (Some folks call dailies "rushes," but in Hollywood I've never heard anyone call them anything but dailies, so that's what we're going to call them.)

The producer looks at the cost of film stock, processing, prints, and transfers. Then she ponders, wouldn't it be a lot cheaper to go digital? Buy some tape or a few cards? No processing, no transfer. Why not?

Well, other factors besides expense need to come into consideration in making the decision. One important question is, how is this film going to be exhibited? There's a big difference between seeing your movie on a 5-foot plasma screen at home and seeing it on a 50-foot screen at the giant multiplex. The same picture that looks great at home may be degraded under the conditions of professional theatrical projection. Whatever medium you use to shoot the movie, in a theater the image is going to be blown up hundreds of thousands of times. There has to be enough information recorded so that when it's spread out on the screen, the audience sees a highly detailed picture, not something with visible pixels. Film's grains are smaller than the pixels of any current digital process, so they give you a more continuous picture.

So if we're going for a theatrical release, the choice boils down to film (preferably 35 mm) or high-end digital. The choice of film cameras is Panaflex, Arriflex, and Aaton. A few older cameras, not made today, are still in use, like the Moviecam, but you'll mostly see Panaflexes or Arris.

The top-level digital cameras at the time of this writing are Panavision Genesis, Arri Alexa, Sony F35, Viper, and Red. And let's include the Canon D-5, a "still" camera with motion picture capability, used on such projects as Fox-TV's *House*. I say "at this time" because digital equipment—unlike film—changes all the time. That makes it much harder to keep up with every innovation. You and your camera crew may not be completely up to speed on every new make and model of digital camera that comes out. On top of that there are more differences in the operation of one make of digital camera versus another compared with film cameras that all operate pretty much the same.

The rental on high-end digital cameras is at least as much as for film cameras, so there's no saving there. The savings on media purchase and postproduction processing are too insignificant to matter on a big budget, but they might be a factor on more modestly budgeted projects. In the situation where the movie has a possibility of theatrical release but not the budget for film or high-end digital, there's the possibility of going with a lower-level but still professional digital camera. There are high-mid-level cameras like the Panasonic VariCam or the Sony F-900 (the first of the high-quality digital cameras, the camera Lucas used for the new *Star Wars*). These cameras and their associated workflows save a little compared to the high-end cameras. But they do not provide a RAW or full-dynamic-range picture, and they do not have the large amount of color-space information the expensive cameras do. They are more suited for television use, and in fact are used a great deal as high-definition cameras for television. Again, viewed on a home screen, the difference in quality between these midrange cameras and the high-end digital or film cameras is not too noticeable. But up on a theater screen the image provided by a lower-level camera does not compare with film or high-end digital.

Where the big savings come in is in using a "prosumer" camera. This class of cameras is intentionally on the border of professional and consumer use. Like consumer cameras they are small in size, have a small target area (often a $1/3$- or $1/2$-inch chip), necessitating the use of relatively wide lenses (more on this in Chapter 29), a short response curve to subject brightness, a restricted color palette, and an affordable price. Some of the best give great-looking images on a small screen, and a few films shot with them, such as *28 Days Later*, have had theatrical releases.

So why not use one of these lower-tier digital cameras? You'll save loads of money that you can spend on other things for the film. And while some of the audience might notice the less-than-pro picture quality, most of your audience will forgive that if your story, action, and characters are compelling. So you may be able to get away with it, but your film will lack the professional patina associated with theatrical films and HD TV.

Any time you're shooting high- or midrange digital, you'll want to hire a DIT (digital imaging technician), who's responsible for setting up the camera; making sure the picture is exposed well enough to be reproduced, not too overexposed so as to lose information, and in focus (something it takes a large, perfectly adjusted monitor to tell on); and maintaining consistency if you are shooting with multiple cameras. A DIT is a great help even on the lowest-budgeted production—maybe more so, since more things can slip past you.

The mid- and high-range cameras will usually be tethered by cables to the sound recordist (these cameras record excellent quality sound, and you have perfect sync with the picture). It's likely that you'll also have cables to the DIT and to the monitor used by the director to check on the frame (we usually call this video village because of the congregation of producer and writer types around these monitors). You may have a cable to some sort of recorder unless all the recording media are on board. All these cables get in the way on stage, and there has to be at least one person hired to wrangle the cables. On location, the cables will necessarily interfere with movement and are in danger of suffering damage. There are always developments in closed-circuit RF transmission (radio or TV wireless) that allow fewer cables. It's an ongoing story, but for now most cameras are used with physical cables.

Unless you record on tape (and very few cameras are made for tape these days), you will have some sort of recording medium (cards or hard drives). They are expensive; therefore, you'll have to use them over and over, and material recorded on them must be downloaded to another storage device. There should be two methods of storage (let's say hard drives) to insure against the possibility of damage to one of them. One of these must be sent to the editor for immediate editing. I know that we live in the digital age, and I know that digital copies are indistinguishable from the original, but after a number of computer crashes and the sudden unreadability of CD-Rs, I find it hard to trust digital media. The situation with these cameras is that you are downloading (copying) the original material to a secondary storage device. And then you are *erasing the original picture*! You are actually destroying the thing a large crew and group of actors have been working on at great expense. I feel very nervous, knowing that electronics are fragile.

I might be crazy, and I'm sure the loss of material is rare. But I have heard too many stories of lost files and "missing scenes" to be completely confident in digital storage. Where there is a greater likelihood of losing digital material than of losing film material, then the cost of possible reshooting must be factored into the (apparently low) cost of shooting digitally.

All electronic cameras have issues with internal heating. Feel your computer sometime after a lot of work; it's probably warm to the touch. In a real sense, digital cameras are computers attached to a sensor and a lens; they heat up, too. To keep from overheating, most have built-in fans. Of course, fans make noise; either they must be made silent (apparently not yet possible) or they must be turned off while shooting with sound in order to record a clean soundtrack. Operating the camera without running the fans for any length of time risks overheating. And overheating is a problem even with many cameras while the fans are running. Some of the DSLRs now being used to shoot movies because of their "hi-def video" capability overheat at the smallest provocation. While it is unlikely that the heating will damage the camera, the cameras must be allowed to cool, and this can cost precious production time.

The proliferation of choices available on the menus of digital cameras can prove, sometimes, to be more of a hindrance than a help. Some camerapeople enjoy tailoring the look of their picture to a specific job. But I advise you to retain as much information as the camera can give you so you can have the greatest range of options to make adjustments to the image in post. If you overmanipulate the image in the camera, you will be limiting your options later.

On digital cameras there are many settings that must be specified by the menu, and it is easy for many of these settings to be changed, consciously or inadvertently, without your realizing it. So unless you are continually turning on and off a display in the viewfinder, you may not know when a setting important to you has been changed. (You don't want to leave this display on all the time because it makes it difficult to see the frame you are shooting.) Film cameras have some settings that can be accidentally changed, too, but far fewer (usually only running speed, the inching knob, and shutter angle), and it is difficult to adjust them without a deliberate action.

Design of digital cameras has been improving rapidly. I worked with the Sony F900, the first professional digital camera, whose configuration was that of a news camera. It was very inconvenient to work with in a studio situation, and it was heavy and unbalanced. Most newer cameras are built more along the tried and tested lines of modern film cameras. However, smaller cameras, in particular, still have surfaces studded with buttons and switches in places that are almost impossible to avoid touching while operating. Again, the chance of error from inadvertently hitting one of these controls is always risky.

If your movie is to have any life to it, and especially if it looks as though it could make money after the original release, you'll have to think of storing it. This gets tricky. No one knows how long any current digital medium lasts. (None has been around long enough.) What we do know is that the specific method of storage changes often, rapidly, and decisively. You simply can't retrieve information from an old format. Remember the five-inch floppies? Tape formats change radically, too; it's hard to find a working two-inch or one-inch reel-to-reel videotape player anywhere, and that format was professional up to 30 years ago. Tape itself, although it keeps improving, does not last forever. Some archives find it necessary to fast rewind and fast forward their tapes to keep the oxide from flaking off the base.

And film? Black-and-white film on safety base has been proved to last at least 100 years. And you can project film shot 100 years ago on a modern projector—same sprocket hole, same format. The current standard for archival is color separations. (From the color original, three separate black-and-white masters are made, each through a separate precise filter: red, green, blue. At any time the three can be recombined into a color version.) This is the standard for high-end digital productions.

Well, I can hear you saying, "Couldn't I just make these separation negatives from my digital originals?" Yes, of course you can. You can do anything you want. This is America. But it will be expensive, and unless you have a surprise hit with an inexpensively digitally made film (*The Blair Witch Project*), you're not going to have the money for archival separations. Let's remember what Desi Arnaz taught us. When he produced *I Love Lucy*, everyone thought he was crazy to shoot on film. It's TV! It's gone after one show! Well, *I Love Lucy* is still showing on hi-def, wide-screen TV, and it's still making money, and you never heard of the other shows that were on 60 years ago.

As fair as I've tried to be, I am sure that by this time you are thinking I've been tough on digital and easy on film. The truth though is that at this time in the development of digital technology the savings of money on a professional feature film are not significant enough to recommend digital over film. Once you've canceled out cost, film just has a simplicity that electronics don't have. But in the area of documentaries and minibudget independent films, there is no doubt that digital is the way to go. Also, when you're first starting to shoot movies, you will feel more secure shooting electronically because you can immediately play back what you've just shot, making sure it's actually there. With film you have to wait until the film comes back from the lab to see what you've got. This can make novice filmmakers very nervous until they gain some experience with film. The bottom line is that you must learn to work with both film and digital cameras because, at least for now, film is not going away. It is still the professional standard on feature films and single-camera TV dramas. But don't worry. When we get to production, I will be telling you all about how to work with both film and digital equipment. Knowing both will allow you to feel confident about your work no matter what choice of medium is made.

Now that you've got your camera, you want to make sure it works. There are a few standard tests you should perform for every film camera, no matter how new it is or whom you got it from. By the way, your assistant can and should do these tests for you. It's up to you if you want to be present. If you have any doubts about the experience of your crew, it's a good idea to be there. Otherwise, leave it to them.

SHUTTER TEST

It's very rare, but it is possible for your shutter to be loose (not fastened tightly to the shaft it's attached to), causing fluctuations in exposure. The simplest way to check it is to shoot an 18% gray card (the standard for determining exposure in the middle of the scale). You don't need to shoot at any particular f-stop, just correctly exposed. Shoot about ten feet. When you look at the image projected or at telecine, there will have be an obvious pulsing (the card will get darker and lighter) if the shutter's off.

Chances are you'll never find this problem. In all my time in the business, I found this problem only once, and I've never heard of anyone else encountering this situation. In my case, the loose shutter was on an old Mitchell camera. We were going to use it for high speed shooting because of its rock-steady movement. It might have been the camera's age, or it might have been an anomaly. But if I had missed that one instance, a whole day's shooting would have been ruined, costing the show time and money. Just finding that one instance made the thousands of other times I did the test worthwhile.

REGISTRATION TEST

This is a little tougher, but the problem occurs much more often. There's always a chance that the pin holding the film in the gate will be worn or loose, so the film can move ever so slightly from frame to frame, either sideways or up and down. There will be a slight degradation of the picture, and multiple exposures will seem to weave with respect to each other. This is the characteristic we use to do the test.

First, make sure the camera is solidly locked down. It must be on a solid tripod and a solid head. Make it level, of course. If the tripod seems at all lightweight or tending to instability, weigh it down with sandbags or tie it down with a chain or a ratchet strap. Once you've framed the chart, lock the head down tight. It's better to close the eyepiece and not look through the eyepiece while shooting so there's no chance of unintentionally jostling the camera.

If you're using 16 mm or super-16, you don't need to mark the start frame, although you may choose to. Pull the lens, inch the shutter out of the way, and mark the film around the aperture with a felt-tipped pen. If you're using 35 mm, you *have* to mark the start frame. (You've got four sprocket holes, remember? You could easily reload the film one perf off, making the test pointless.) Mark the start frame just as with the 16. You may, in addition, use a hole punch to mark the frame. You would mark the frame, pull it out of the gate to punch, and then reload for the test. It makes it easy to find the start frame in the dark when you're rewinding after the first exposure. You don't need to be precise for your start frame, but it's nice, and it looks good.

Shoot 10 to 20 feet of a grid, like graph paper. You can find charts made especially for this test (you can probably get one from the lab you use). The lines should be about $\frac{1}{32}$-inch thick (so they expose clearly) and separated by about

¾ inch. It's easiest to find black lines on white card, but you can also use a black card with white lines. Expose normally, even though you're going to double expose the film.

Now the tricky part. Roll the film back to the beginning frame. This will be harder or easier, depending on your camera. It's easiest with cameras with a Mitchell-type magazine (like Panavision). These magazines have separate compartments for take up and supply, and there are no gears in the light trap. Arri 35s are not too hard; although you have to rewind through gears in the light trap, they move smoothly. The Aaton 16 and 35 and Arri 16 all have magazines that don't want you to rewind the film. You can do it, but it's a pain. Depending on the precise model of your magazine, it may be impossible. In that case, you've got no option but to cut the film, download it, rewind it carefully in a darkroom, and reload the magazine. This means you have to have a darkroom, and you should have hand rewinds (not used much since editing went to computers). Or you can simply rewind the film on to a core by hand. Come on, it's only 20 feet. Then carefully reattach the magazine to the camera. At this point it doesn't matter what frame you start on (unless you're working with 35 mm).

Now, looking through the viewfinder, unlock the head. Pan and tilt a very slight amount, just enough to offset the chart lines from the first exposure. A good amount is to offset the lines about ¼ inch both horizontally and vertically. You want both directions in case the wobble is only horizontal or only vertical. You only want ¼-inch separation so that the lines for the two takes will be in distinctly different places but close enough so that even the slightest movement will be obvious. When you get the footage back, I hope you don't see any movement. If you do, get a different camera body.

The shutter and registration tests apply only to film cameras. Digital cameras don't usually have mechanical shutters, and there's no question of registration because there's no moving film. If there is a mechanical shutter in your digital camera (check the manual or specs on line), do the test.

FRAME CHART

It's amazing to me that after all the care and experience we as DPs and operators put into precisely framing an image, movies are hardly ever seen exactly as the creators intended. Every theater has masking around the screen (that black curtain–like stuff) that can be adjusted to disguise errors in the projection setup, with the projected image either too large or too small for the screen. If the projector lens is too short for the throw, the projected image will be slightly larger than the actual screen. When this happens you can see the ghost image of the outside of the frame on the masking; and you know that part of the image is being cut off.

TV is even worse. Before digital broadcasting, there was no precise standard for TV sets. Most of them enlarged the picture slightly, overscanned. You got an image that seemed larger—and was—at the cost of losing information around the edges. This problem was so bad and so common that in shooting film for TV, viewfinders had three lines on the ground glass: the full frame (what was actually shot); "action" safe (a smaller area that you could be sure most TVs wouldn't cut off); and "title" safe (a still smaller area, designed for the convenience of commercials, within which you would frame the name of a product so that it could not possibly be cut off or obscured under any conditions).

And don't assume digital broadcasting and flat-screen TVs will eliminate the problem. Broadcasters still regularly overscan the picture—sending out less of it—to make sure no electronic artifacts like syncing signals appear in your living room.

So let's do the Frame Chart test. Again, set up your camera solidly mounted on a tripod. Set it about five feet from the wall, level on all three axes (to the horizon on x and y and no tilting on z). Mount a piece of stiff white card—foam-core is excellent—on the wall. One person looks through the viewfinder and directs a second person with a felt-tipped pen. The operator directs the pen person to make dots on the card matching each corner of the frame and the center as scribed on the ground glass. Then, with a straight edge, you connect the dots and make a cross at the center. It's a good idea to mark the name of your film and the aspect ratio you're shooting in. Figure 8.2 shows what you get.

You'll want to shoot at least 20 feet of this. If you're going to have film dailies (more power to you; they're a vanishing species), the editors will attach this as leader to every reel of dailies so the projectionist knows precisely how to frame the image. The editor can print the negative over and over to provide an adequate supply.

It's more likely you'll have electronic dailies, that your negative will be going to telecine, maybe without you. Having this chart as a guide for the colorist is vital. Telecine allows for the possibility of reframing shots by shifting the position of the frame and the size of the image. That's nice if you want to change what you've done, but if you want to see the image as you shot it, you need a way to be sure that the frame will be exactly as you intended. With the framing chart, the telecine operator can transfer it once and refer to it every time you have new dailies, ensuring that you'll see the image exactly as it was framed, without any art being chopped off and without seeing outside the frame you shot. Do this framing chart for HD as well as film. There's one more important test, and it's only for HD.

322-1179-04-1
ACAD, 4PERF
ANAMORPHIC (2.40)

ANAMORPHIC (2.40) = .839 X .700

FIGURE 8.1
Full frame lines on a ground glass.
Image courtesy of Panavision Inc.

FIGURE 8.2
Frame chart setup.

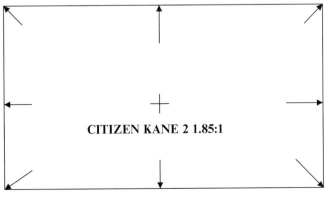

CITIZEN KANE 2 1.85:1

ISO TEST

You've got to know how effectively fast your camera is. The manufacturer will state an "equivalent" ISO number in the manual. That is, they'll tell you how its exposure compares to film. This is a good start, and if you don't know anything else, use it. But you want to know how the camera responds to your way of lighting and metering. (If you want to refresh your memory on metering, see Chapter 24.) Take your gray card, illuminate it evenly, set up the camera, and fill the frame with the gray card. Put the camera on auto exposure. Note what f-stop the camera indicates. Then take your meter, read the light falling on the card, and adjust the ISO setting on the meter until it gives you the same f-stop reading as you've got on the camera. This will be the ISO you will use to meter and to determine exposure. I know you just want to let the camera expose for itself, but that's not cinematography. Cinematography is setting a mood, exposing for that mood—not some abstract standard—and keeping a consistent exposure from shot to shot within a sequence. So you want to light and expose by your meter, not the camera's.

SECOND CAMERA

Often you will want to rent a second camera to have on hand. The main reason is to have a backup in case something goes wrong. When you're in town (whatever town it is that has a camera rental house), you can rely on your supplier to keep several camera bodies in house for emergencies. But on location, you're on your own. If you have a body go down, the time it will take to get a replacement means you might as well go home.

When you've lost the day, it can cost the production a lot of money. It may even cost you the location and the chance to shoot the scene. If you're really low-budget, the scene may never get shot. More often, you'll have to shoot the lost scene in a less-than-satisfactory location. No one's happy, but at least it's done.

It's also nice to have a second body for sudden inspirations. The director may decide to do a minor stunt or some action that can't be repeated. That's when it's great to be able to cover the action with two cameras. With film cameras and with high-end HD cameras, you'll only have to carry the body and the accessories (usually packaged with the body). You'll have lenses, magazines, and tripods on hand that should be enough to outfit a second camera.

If you're dealing with HD on a prosumer level, you probably aren't in a financial position to have two cameras. But even if it just means bringing out the old HandiCam, have something. There's nothing worse than being on a set with all the actors and a full crew and not being able to shoot because a camera broke down. You can work around all kinds of other equipment failures and glitches, but you can't do a thing without a properly functioning camera.

ACCESSORIES

Each camera has a standard complement of accessories. Either the manufacturer or the rental house will have fitted out a case with all the necessary items. It varies from camera to camera, but accessories include things like a sliding base plate, iris rods, matte box, follow focus devices, handles for hand-holding, and most other things you are likely to need. Most assistants have specific items and gadgets they've come to love working with; that's between them and the rental house. Also, assistants have their own personal gizmos that they've discovered or devised that they always bring along with them.

You don't have to worry about the accessories. If you're dealing with a reputable rental house, everything you need will be properly supplied, and the assistant will double check to make sure nothing has been left out.

CHAPTER 9
Selecting Lenses

Well, you've gotten a camera. Terrific! Now you need a lens, because it's the lens that takes the pictures. Let's talk about professional cameras first. Most of the prosumer cameras come with a lens permanently attached. There is not much to choose from there, but we'll look at a few options.

Let's make it simple. Every rental house has lenses, some that come in sets, that you can rent. If you look online, you will see lots of choices, especially Panavision, Zeiss, Cooke, and Leica. They make most of the lenses you'll be concerned with. It's fun to see all the stuff they have.

Don't be frightened by MTF numbers. You don't have to concern yourself with minimum focus, weight, or depth of field tables yet. For now, just enjoy the pretty pictures. We're going to make sense of this together. So remember, you've chosen a camera. You'll be getting it from a rental house that offers the best rates, the best service, or the friendliest attitude. Once you've made that choice, you're going to rent lenses from the same place. This should limit your choices to a manageable number.

If you're renting from Panavision, you've got the lenses they have. Besides their original lenses, they've got Zeiss and Primo (Leica glass) series. Panaflexes accept only lenses with Panavision mounts. And they've got anamorphic lenses. Anamorphics squeeze the picture so you can get a "Cinemascope" look, 2.4:1 frame ratio. If you're going anamorphic, Panavision has the best in the world. There are three series, each with its own distinctive look. But mostly you'll be shooting with flat lenses. ("Flat"—also called spherical—just distinguishes conventional lenses from anamorphic "squeeze" lenses.) Anamorphic movies cost more to shoot for many reasons. Mainly, the lenses tend to be slower, so you need more light and thus more electric power. To get the same vertical field of view, you need an anamorphic lens twice as long as a flat lens, and that makes pulling focus twice as hard. And the lenses are often heavier, so you have possible problems with Steadicam or handheld.

So let's say you're going flat (16 × 9 or 1.85:1). You want a range of lenses so you can shoot any frame you want, so you're not constricted inside small sets and so you can get the look you want. The look should really be the choice you make of a given lens for a specific shot. Wide lenses see a lot, show background, and have more depth of field than long lenses in the same situation. A longer lens is better as a portrait lens for close-ups and lets you shoot a small area from a distance and still fill the full frame. For 35 mm shooting, you want a selection like 14 mm, 17 mm, 20 mm, 24 mm, 29 mm, 35 mm, 40 mm, 50 mm, 75 mm, 100 mm, 125 mm, and 150 mm.

You may not need the 14 mm—it's very wide—or even the 17 mm, although I find the 17 can be a lifesaver on location. The 150 mm is a luxury, too, and the 40 mm is very close to the 35 mm and the 50 mm. The difference in the perspective look is greater among the short lenses; thus, a 17 mm and a 20 mm have a much greater difference in "look" than the 75 mm and the 100 mm. So let's say you've got this complement of lenses: 17 mm, 20 mm, 24 mm, 29 mm, 35 mm, 50 mm, 75 mm, 100 mm, and 125 mm. That should handle any normal eventuality.

"Wait a minute, Jack," you say, "I've always used a camera with one lens. It's a zoom, and it has all those focal lengths in it and more, and it works fine. So why am I renting a bunch of single-focal-length lenses?" You are doing that because you're in the big leagues now, and you want the best. But let me explain. For years, zooms were inevitably worse-quality lenses than primes were. Zooms have lots of elements (pieces of glass—11 and more). The more glass involved, the more chances to reflect light and to worsen the picture.

Zooms also have many more mechanisms in them. Just think about it. Of course, there's the mechanism that moves the glass around to make different focal lengths. Then there's the focus mechanism that keeps the focus the same at each different focal length you zoom to (remember, the position of the elements determines the focus, and you move the elements every time you zoom). And there's a mechanism that keeps the focal length the same when you're focusing (same deal). And there has to be something to keep the stop the same, no matter what the focal length. f/stop = focal length/opening. As the lens gets longer, the opening has to get bigger to keep the same stop. Pretty impressive trick, huh?

So many more design and structural elements have to go in a zoom that it's a wonder any zoom lenses actually work. But they do, and all this work makes them very expensive. Even a "cheap" zoom costs more than most prime lenses. But in the years before computer-assisted design, it was prohibitively expensive to design zooms of prime lens quality. So they didn't exist.

Even today, all things remaining equal, a zoom will tend not to be as sharp or as distortion-free as a prime. Many DPs in the past would not use zooms and primes in the same scene because the look of the lenses was so different that the cut between them was disturbing. But the professional zooms have gotten a lot better. Most zooms designed since 1980 will give excellent pictures that won't look out of place when cut together with shots taken with primes. Some of the newer zooms are so good that their pictures cut seamlessly with prime shots. But you still have to test them to be sure.

Now you are probably thinking, "If the new zooms are so good, why am I renting and carrying around all these primes?" Good question! But what about the maximum aperture of the lens? The fastest zooms are around f/2.8. (Angenieux has a zoom that opens to f/2.6, and some zooms for $^2/_3$-inch sensors—Panavision and Angenieux—open to f/1.6 to allow a shallower depth of field.) Many for 35 mm work are f/3 or f/4. What does all this mean? Well, if your lens only opens to an f/3, you will have to use fast film, no matter what you might want. Or you'll be boosting the gain and picking up electronic noise. You will need larger lighting instruments than usual just to get enough light for an exposure. I find most DPs want to shoot around f/2 to f/2.5 these days. With ISO 500 film and most digital cameras (usually ISO 320), that allows for using minimal light (saving on generator rental), and being able to capture the practical lights in a scene (say, store windows) in a natural way. It looks good and eliminates having to light the stores individually.

Okay, the truth is that every show carries a set of primes and at least one zoom lens. When I started, the standard was the primes we just discussed and two zooms: a 6 to 1 (20–120 mm, T/3) and a 10 to 1 (25–250 mm, T/4). The short zoom gave better picture quality, and in some cases it could be used indoors. The long zoom was for exteriors only, and the quality of the picture was barely acceptable.

Today, there are many more zooms available, including short zooms developed specifically for Steadicam®, so you may choose something other than our old traditional package. But it's a good idea to have a short and a long zoom so you cover the essential focal lengths when you have to use a zoom.

We're talking features here, so you're going to have very few occasions to use a zoom. Most DPs and directors still prefer primes for the picture quality and for the intangible quality you gain when you must accept the frame the lens gives you and you must move the camera, not the lens barrel, to change it.

This may be a good time to mention "target" size. If we're dealing with film, that's the size of the aperture; with digital it's the size of the chip. 35 mm has been the standard. However, even before digital became practical, many producers wanted to use super-35 mm. For super-35, the picture area is extended into the area normally reserved for the soundtrack. Usually, by the 1990s, super-35 meant shooting 3-perf (the camera pulled down the film at three perforations per frame instead of four). The useful area of the film was maximized, and 3-perf uses a shorter length of film for the same elapsed time. One thousand feet of film could last about 14 minutes instead of 10.

Since no projectors were made to handle film with 3-perf frames, the movie had to be optically printed to fit on 4-perf, and the picture had to be shrunk to allow for the soundtrack. And this meant extra money, pretty much eating up the savings of shooting 3-perf. These days, with digital intermediates the norm even for a film without effects, that's not a problem.

The camera department still had a concern. Given the design of lenses, that a specific lens was designed to cover a certain image circle and no more, the extra width of the super-35 frame meant that some lenses (usually the wider focal lengths) could not cover the whole frame. So the DP had to be careful to order lenses that cover the bigger frame.

If you're working with 16 mm (and I assume that would be super-16; no one uses the old square 16 mm anymore), your lens choice will be somewhat restricted. There's been less money in 16 mm production, and the lens manufacturers have made fewer lenses for 16. You will want to get the same approximate complement of lenses, but in shorter focal lengths: 12 mm, 16 mm, 25 mm, 35 mm, 50 mm, and 85 mm.

In 16 mm, a lens about half the focal length of a lens for 35 mm gives you the same picture area. You'll notice there's nothing comparable to a 17 mm; that's because an 8 mm or a 9.5 mm has been considered an "effect" lens. But you'll want one. And you'll want a zoom. I've never found a good 10 to 1, so I'd stick with the shorter zooms. In 16 mm, the longer zooms are often soft, and tend to breathe. (Breathing is the unwanted fluctuation of the size of the picture when you focus. Many zooms have this disadvantage, but most lenses don't show as pronounced an effect as the long zooms for 16 mm do.) And, of course, you have to make sure your lenses cover the super-16 mm frame area. Super-16 has become the norm only since about 1990; you can find a lot of fairly new lenses designed to cover only the frame area of regular 16. So check the coverage of your lenses carefully.

Now, what about digital? If you're working with the big stuff—Panavision Genesis, Arri Alexa, or Sony F-35—you'll be getting lenses comparable to the ones you would get for 35 mm film. These cameras mostly have a target (the chip) that's the size of a super-35 mm frame, so you'll have to make sure the lenses give coverage on the larger frame.

Most lens manufacturers have designed new lenses specifically for digital, and it's advisable to use them. Not only are they newer, and likely sharper, but they will handle the wavelengths that digital is sensitive to better than film lenses will.

And then there are the other professional digital cameras, the Sony 900, 950, and f-24, and Viper. They are cameras with $^2/_3$-inch imagers, and use different lenses from those with super-35 chips for the same reasons super-35 needs different lenses from regular 35 mm. Only in this case you're back to dealing with shorter lenses, as in super-16. And because the target is so small, and because the pixels are not significantly reduced, the lenses have to be much sharper to give a picture that will stand up to the greater magnification needed in exhibition.

Some professional digital cameras have their own proprietary lens mount, and you have to find a lens that fits. But these are mostly details. You can get most lenses in any mount. If you have enough money, you can get any lens with a new mount for the camera you choose.

The real questions are how sharp is the image formed by the lens, how fast is it, and how easy is it to use? You'll discover the answers to these questions as you use the lens. You'll get used to a set of lenses for your work, or you'll prefer one set for one kind of work and another for another kind of work. But when you're starting out or when you're interested in a group of lenses you haven't used before, tests give you vital information. Before you do anything, look at the barrel of the lens. Is it large enough to have a lot of room between the focus marks, and does it have a lot of focus marks? Your assistant will want to have enough marks so she doesn't have to guess at the focus.

I was assisting on a show once, using Zeiss lenses from the 1970s. They were nice, sharp lenses, and lightweight, but so small that the focus markings on the barrel of the 25 mm went 3 feet, 6 feet, 12 feet, 25 feet, ∞. You can deal with this at f/5.6, but we, of course, were at f/1.4, at night, on a crane. The action was to start on the star at a phone booth (if you don't know what a phone booth is, ask your father, or look for an old Superman comic) and to pull back and up to reveal the world. Well, I could set the opening focus—at 5 feet—and when I got to 12 feet, I was okay. But it was an act of magic to figure where on the lens 7 feet, 8 feet, 9 feet, and so on were. This was further complicated by the fact that it's notoriously hard to figure vertical distance, especially when you're on a crane moving up and away. I think I proved myself to the DP that night. When he saw the dailies, and when every bit of the move was sharp, I was in. But there's no reason to push your assistant that hard and risk a slight buzz in the focus.

And at night, it was almost impossible to see the tiny focus markings on the lens. These days almost every lens manufacturer has followed Panavision's lead and has large barrels with a lot of focus markings where it's critical, in the near-focus area. Most assistants have lens lights (also a rental item) so they can see the marks. I did, too, but I had to make my own or hold a flashlight in my teeth to see. Some lenses, notably from Cooke, have illuminated focus scales. (Where were you when I needed you?)

Any time you rent (or buy) lenses, you want to do tests. But when you're familiar with a line of lenses (say, Zeiss Master Primes), you're just checking to make sure nothing has gone wrong with the lenses. When they're new to you, you'll be a bit more rigorous.

Your assistant will run the first tests. She looks through the lens to make sure there's no obvious dirt, fungus, or clouding of the glass, and she closes and opens the iris (the f-stop ring) to make sure it's moving smoothly and accurately. Then she'll mount the lens on the camera, set up a focusing target, and check that the focus set through the lens hits the precise focusing mark on the lens as that indicated by a measuring tape. They'd better be the same. If they're not, she'll send the lens back and get another. Insist on it.

After these basics, it's time for your tests. Set up a color chart in an even light and shoot it once with each of the lenses. Ask for a one-light print or have the telecine colorist transfer every shot at the same setting. This will show you whether there's any obvious color cast to any of the lenses. With modern lenses, this is highly unlikely, but you may be working with older lenses. Then shoot some scenes, whether with actors or not. It's going to help you to shoot exteriors and interiors, to shoot at a range of f-stops from wide open to fully closed. You want to see that the lens doesn't vignette (transmit less light at the edges so it looks as though there's a shadow around the frame). You want to get a feel for the look of the lens: How sharp is it? How sharp does it feel? Is it hard and snappy like Zeiss lenses, or is it brilliant and forgiving like Primos?

These terms are not quantitative. I'm being deliberately subjective. You want to know if you like the lens and if its intangible qualities suit your film and your director's vision. You may find out in the course of shooting the tests that you like one lens or another for no reason you can state. Go with your gut. See if you can use that lens as often as possible.

At this early stage, it's great if you can shoot some tests with the actors. Just as all lenses have different personalities, they will treat the actors' faces differently. Usually the major modifications you make to the actors, close-ups are with makeup and lighting, but the lens may have a subtle effect as well. And shoot some close-ups with different focal lengths; usually I like to shoot close-ups with a 75 mm or longer (in 35 mm film terms) so I get a slight flattening of the features, which is usually flattering. The longer lenses put more air between the camera and the actor, so you're also getting a kind of cosmetic filter from shooting through the layers of air. It's subtle, but it's there. But you may find an actor's face loves a 50 mm or even a 35, a lens that's generally considered slightly distorting. You'll only know by testing. Test, test, test!

I've talked in film terms, but of course you'll be doing the same tests if you're shooting digital. And with digital, you'll almost certainly be dealing with diffusion filters. Filters have two basic uses: dealing with exposure and color, and affecting mood. The first kind you almost always carry. Back when I started, there was one color film: Eastman Color Negative 5247 (and 7247 in 16 mm), ASA 100, tungsten balanced. Shooting outdoors meant we needed a color correction filter (an 85) to cut out the excessive blue of daylight and usually a neutral density (ND) to lessen the amount of light and allow a good exposure. The NDs come in gradations of 30%, 60%, and 90%, commonly labeled .3, .6, and .9. Each drops the exposure by a stop. And you can get them combined with an 85 filter to simplify the process of using them: 85N3, 85N6, and 85N9.

These days, with film, there are several color films balanced for daylight. It's your choice, but it seems to me to make sense to use the daylight films outside and therefore to need one fewer filter in front of your lens. But you'll still want to carry NDs. The slowest film is ISO 50, and that will need an f/16 stop in bright sunlight.[1] You'll rarely want to shoot at f/16, since most lenses have a sweet spot at f/5.6 or f/8, so you'll need an ND.6 or ND.9 to cut down the light so you can open up the stop.

---

[1] A rule of thumb is that the exposure in bright sunlight at a shutter speed of 1/ISO in seconds (in this case, 1/50, the standard shutter speed for a movie camera) is f/16.

If you're shooting digital, it's a good idea to carry a set of neutrals as well. Every digital camera will have a built-in filter wheel with a couple of ND settings. But you can get more choices of specific exposure by using the NDs. And don't forget the infrared problem (see Chapter 24).

Always have a polarizing filter. You may not use it all the time—and it's only useful for exteriors—but it's great when you need it. Nothing else does what it can. The polarizing filter takes all the light coming from the sun and allows only those light rays parallel to each other to pass. The effect is to darken blue skies (sorry, gray and cloudy-white skies still look crappy) when the filter is pointed about 90 degrees to the direction of the sunlight. The polarizer can also eliminate or enhance reflections in glass, on water, and to some extent on reflective paint surfaces. The filter either comes in a rotating mount or can be placed in a rotating stage in the matte box (more later). Since it cuts down some light, the polarizer also acts as an ND; I allow it 1½ stops. You can determine how much you want to compensate for it by holding your meter steady, noting the f-stop, and then passing the polarizer over it and noting the f/stop you get this time. The difference between the readings is what your compensation will be.

You will also want to carry an optical flat. It is a piece of clear glass that you will sometimes use in front of the lens. It's optically clear ("optical"), and, like all professional filters, it has perfectly parallel sides ("flat") so it doesn't introduce any aberrations. The flat is put in front of the lens and any filters that may be there as protection when you're working with guns, explosions, bad weather, and mud or dirt. It's a lot less costly to replace a $60 piece of glass when the motorcycle you're following kicks a pebble right into the lens than to replace that $5,000 lens.

I've often used a flat to create my own diffusion filter. A thin coating of Vaseline can give a liquid, smeary look; a light coat of hairspray softens the light and the focus. By the way, maybe the most subtle way of making a hairspray filter is to spray into the air and then wave the optical flat through the spray.

That brings us to diffusion. (What a great segué, huh? I kill myself.) Diffusion is a catch-all term for a filter that obscures the image. Almost every filter that's not a color, an ND, or a polarizer is some kind of diffusion. I like to think of it as two general kinds. One, like a fog filter, a star filter, and many others, you will use primarily to affect the look of a whole scene. They're intended to give some emotional look—mysterious, romantic, you name it—to the entire scene you shoot. The others are intended for use on actors. There are dozens of kinds of diffusion, and every year new kinds are introduced. Again, the only way you'll know what you want, if you want any, is to test them.

I assisted a great DP, Robby Müller, for three years (*Dancer in the Dark, Ghost Dog, Breaking the Waves, Mystery Train, Barfly, Down By Law, Paris, Texas, Alice in the Cities, The American Friend*). Robby always insisted that he never wanted to use diffusion. He felt it was cheating and that he should make the effects with lighting. I learned a lot from Robby, including not to be foolishly consistent; we did use diffusion on a 50-ish actress when she was our star and producer. But you may feel like Robby that any diffusion ruins the beautiful photography you're doing. Nestor Almendros (*Sophie's Choice, The Last Metro, Days of Heaven, Claire's Knee, The Wild Child*), interviewed in *Visions of Light*, said the same thing. But using diffusion tends to go in and out of style. When I was a second assistant, every show used some kind of diffusion. As an operator, I saw hardly any. You must decide for yourself. Test!

Most camera rental houses and some filter manufacturers will gladly loan you filters to test for a few days or a week. Look online (Tiffen, Schneider, and Lee are leading filter manufacturers) to see what's available. Pick something. Until you've used a particular filter, you've got no basis for deciding, so pick anything you want. And, yes, test.

Shooting digital may present a different challenge. While some advocates of digital cinematography like the apparent hyper-sharpness digital usually provides, others find it annoyingly sharp edged, where film has a more "forgiving" look. You can use filters in front of or behind the lens. (Of course most digital cameras have menus that allow you to shape the picture to your liking, but that's another subject.)

Filters behind the lens have been used for years, primarily pieces of extremely fine netting. George Spiro Dibie, ASC, former president of International Cinematographers Local 600, was famous for his "Dibie net," a piece of fine French lingerie that he used on video cameras in the olden days of standard-def TV. As the most accomplished of the television DPs, Dibie (*Sister, Sister; Night Court; Barney Miller; Buffalo Bill*) gave all the credit to his beautiful pictures to the netting. I'm inclined to think his lighting had a lot to do with it.

But the point is that nets have been used behind the lens probably since the beginning of the movies. You can get a piece of netting (the finer the better; coarse nets tend to show their pattern, and dark nets, of course, reduce exposure). Cut it so that it's a little larger than the back of the lens. Use a small rubber band or some cement—nail polish is often the best—to attach it to the barrel of the lens. Please don't touch the glass. Make sure the net doesn't interfere with the lens mount and that it won't fall off into the mechanism. Many lenses have rings to attach the net with, and there are aftermarket devices that do the same.

You've got to be careful. I hate to repeat myself, but I want you to be sure the net or whatever you use to attach it doesn't interfere with anything in the camera and that whatever you've used to attach it is strong enough to hold up to use and yet easily removed. And if you get nail polish on the back element of the lens, you've just bought yourself a very expensive lens that won't take a good picture.

Like most judgments about filtration, the question of whether you soften digital is going to be a matter of your personal aesthetics. One thing you must be sure to do is to look at the results on a screen comparable to how the movie will be shown. Problems that don't show up on an editing monitor can be glaringly obvious on a big flat-screen TV and even more so on a theater screen. Test.

Part of your camera is the matte box. It is a vital part of working with the lens and with filters. You might not have much choice. The first thing is to get a matte box that will attach to your camera and fits it (you don't want it covering up the lens). With some cameras, you get what they have and that's it. The major manufacturers—especially Panavision and Arriflex, which have years of experience designing film cameras—will offer a choice of matte boxes designed for different purposes.

Following are the important concerns about your prep.

What size filters should I use?

The standard today is 4 × 5.650 inches, always called 4 ×5 inches. A 6 × 6-inch filter is often used, especially when, as with a graduated filter, it must be moved around the frame to get a precise effect. And many cameras used to use 4 × 4-inch filters. For smaller cameras, and since there's a lot of them around, you might be using the 4 × 4s. You'll probably have to use one size or another because that's what the matte box takes. I would recommend using 4 × 5s. They've been standard for 40 years, so there's lots of them around; you won't have a problem getting any filter you want in that size.

How many filters should I use?

When diffusion was a fad in the 1970s, I sometimes had four filters stacked in the matte box. Back then, you could only get two-stage matte boxes (holders for two filters). I had to remove the holders, tape three filters together, put them in the slot for the holders, and then tape the fourth to the front of the matte box. Besides looking amateurish and sloppy, this took time to set up and change filters and ran the risk of the last filter coming loose and crashing to the concrete. Now you can get three- or four-stage matte boxes, and I'm sure you could easily have custom sizes made.

But let's say you're stuck with old equipment. You've got a two-stage matte box and you want three filters. Well, do what I used to do. Matte boxes come with trays to hold the filters. The trays have some thickness; if you take them out of the matte box, you've got room for three filters sandwiched together. Clean them carefully, stack them on a clean surface, and carefully wrap tape around them. I recommend black camera tape (that's 1-inch cloth tape) because it won't rip easily. If that's too thick, use black photographic paper tape. Cut off any extra thickness of tape that laps over into the flat surface of the filter. It won't get in the picture, but you don't want it gumming up the matte box. Slide the filter pack carefully into the filter slot, making sure there's a bottom to it so the filters don't crash to the concrete. If there's not, you'll want to make a bottom for it. Tape a piece of showcard to it, and make sure it will hold. Then use another piece of black tape to cover the entry slot so that no light gets into the filter to flare the picture.

What kind of polarizer should I use?

A polarizing filter has to be rotated to work. You'll find two kinds: a "square" (or rectangular) stage with a regular filter tray that rotates on bearings and a round retaining ring at the rear of the matte box for a round filter. I like using the round filters. I can take the filter, mounted in its ring, away from the camera, rotate it to get the orientation I want, and hand it to the assistant to mount it just so (usually after having marked the top of the filter ring so it gets set precisely). With the square filters, I have to look through the lens with the filter mounted and rotate the matte box stage; there's no convenient way to set its orientation and then place it perfectly in the matte box.

What can I do about reflections?

Often in night scenes you see a car coming toward the camera and the headlights forming a ghost image and moving up and away across the frame. Most audiences ignore this as an unavoidable imperfection, but I hate it. With good lenses, the coating on the lens will prevent this ghosting so your only worry is the filter. We all used to pull the filters out of the trays and tilt them until the ghosting disappeared. Of course, this meant messing around again with taping the filters and figuring out a way to keep the filter in the matte box. Some years ago, William Fraker, ASC, designed a matte box with tilting filter stages so you could adjust the tilt of the filters and lock them precisely. You can get this kind of matte box for most major professional cameras, and it's worth having to eliminate the ugly ghosts.

Can I attach an eyebrow?

Most matte boxes have some sort of way of attaching a sunshade, universally called an eyebrow. You need this indoors as well as outside. It's your first line of defense against unwanted light hitting the filters (or the lens) and flaring the picture. Just make sure you can get an eyebrow and attach it.

Or you can do what I did when I needed shade, but there wasn't room for the metal eyebrow or there was danger an actor might run into it. I took showcard (showcard is incredibly useful, so have some of it around for a million reasons), cut out a shade, and taped it to the matte box. It still works.

Should I use donuts?

Yes, you took your fat pills before call time, but these donuts are a device to keep light from hitting the filters from the rear and causing flares or ghost images. (Yes, we hate flares like poison.) Something must fill the gap between the front of the lens and the back of the filters in the matte box. The oldest trick is to cut a donut shape out of ½-inch neoprene. The inner diameter fits the lens and the outer diameter is big enough to cover the rear opening of the matte box and small enough not to interfere with focus, zoom, and so on. Arri and some other manufacturers devised a rubber accordioning device that fits on the back of the matte box. The rear of the device is a plastic ring that fits snugly around the front of the lens. It's got a flexible rubber bellows to allow you to push the matte box as close as you want to the lens and to accommodate the breathing of any lens you use. I love this—neoprene donuts tend to gap and defeat their purpose—and I would suggest getting your assistant to adapt her matte box if it's not set up with the Arri donut.

If you're only going to use digital acquisition, you can skip this chapter. But you might want to have at least a passing acquaintance with some of the information here. Years ago, several companies made and marketed still and movie film stock: Kodak (United States), Fuji (Japan), Ansco/GAF (United States), Dupont (United States), Ilford (England), Agfa (Germany), Orwo (East Germany), Ferrania (Italy), and others all around the world. Some of these companies are out of business now, some are out of the film manufacturing business, and some are just out of the movie film manufacturing business.

Today only two manufacturers are left—Fuji and Kodak—and many of us are afraid that these companies may go the way of Polaroid: bankruptcy and dissolution. They're both well diversified, and I hope they survive to make motion picture film stock for many years to come. In the meantime, enjoy them while you can.

Up until the 2000s, it seemed to me that the choice between Kodak and Fuji was mostly a matter of price. Fuji was always less expensive, and many producers would insist on using it to save a little bit of money. When you consider the cost of film stock relative to the entire budget of a movie, it's minimal compared to expenses like studio rentals or actors' salaries. So choosing a film stock on the basis of price, when your whole movie depends on the quality of the stock, is short-sighted. Of course, the lower the budget overall, the more any little saving becomes crucial. On big-budget films it is not even a consideration.

Still, some directors and even DPs insisted on either Fuji or Kodak because they staunchly believed that one stock or the other had a special capability to affect the rendering of certain colors. Fuji was reputed to give especially good greens. I always felt that the amount of adjustment you could make in post—and this is photochemically, even before electronics revolutionized color adjustment—was so great that the small edge a film brand might give you in one color or another was negligible. But far be it for me to dispute a given DP's idiosyncratic choice. My eyes may just not be sensitive enough to distinguish the subtleties that these other camerapeople seem to see.

Now, in the twenty-first century, I would say your choice between Kodak and Fuji is strictly a personal one. Each company has a few stocks that are unique (like Fuji's Vivid series and Kodak's reversal and black-and-white stocks). Each film stock does have a distinct personality, but how you would define it is probably inexpressible in words. Shoot tests comparing different stocks and see whether you get any special feeling about one or another.

For all practical purposes, your decisions come down to fast or slow and daylight- or tungsten-balanced. It's really pretty simple:

1. If you're shooting indoors (day or night) or at night (exterior), use tungsten-balanced ISO 500 stock.

With this exception:

2. If you're shooting day interior and plan to light with HMIs or daylight Kinoflos, use daylight-balanced ISO 250 stock.
3. If you're shooting in bright daylight, get a daylight-balanced ISO 50 stock.
4. If you're shooting high-speed (high speed on the camera equals slow-motion footage) or in dim sunlight (late in the day), use daylight-balanced ISO 250 stock.

Really, that's all you need to know. But let's think about the reasons for these choices.

DAY EXTERIOR	50 D OR 250 D
DAY INTERIOR	500 T OR 250 D
NIGHT EXTERIOR	500 T
NIGHT INTERIOR	500 T

Most night work involves a lot of dark areas in your frame. You will be dealing with existent (practical) light sources: neon and street lights outside, household lamps inside. These sources can provide a significant amount of accent light if you are working with a fast film (high ISO). At your location, you will either be using household current —which will limit the size of the lights you can power—or you will be using a generator—and your producer will want you to get the cheapest one, which of course is also the generator that supplies the least power. No matter what, you will want the fastest film available.

I often hear inexperienced cinematographers talk about wanting more or less "grain." It's like a flashback to the 1960s. Back then, grain was a big issue when it came to the choice of film stock. That was because when shooting black-and-white, faster film (higher ISO) would always have significantly more grain than slower film (which was said to have a "finer" grain). Even in the 1980s, when fast color film became available, it was significantly grainier than slower color stocks. But modern film stocks are all so brilliantly formulated that there is essentially no difference in the size of the perceived grain between fast and slow films. In fact, I know some directors who say they want a lot of grain so their movie will look more "authentic." Authentic what? I don't know. Anyway, if you must have grain, it can be simulated digitally in post. I'm sure you've seen brand new movies that look grainy, scratched, and dirty all because someone wanted to suggest the olden days or old film. All that degraded look has been accomplished electronically; I assure you there's no chance that any of these imperfections are actually on the film as shot. I laugh. I cry. I think of the lengths we once went to to keep our film clean and grainless. You can only marvel at the power of fashion.

Back to reasons. Shooting day interiors with daylight-balanced films makes sense if you have a lot of daylight coming in through the windows and you don't want it to look blue; if you use tungsten film, it will. Combined with HMI lights balanced for daylight, you will get consistent color quality in the scene. Of course, you can choose to use tungsten film and accept the blueness of daylight as an expressive tool. And again, with contemporary emulsions, there is a greater tolerance of varied light sources so that even though there's a bluish tinge from the daylight, it will look "natural." (Digital, as I have mentioned, tends to be less forgiving.) HMIs tend to be large, expensive lights. But Kinoflos are small, cool, and use little power. They are a great choice for lighting indoors, and the daylight-balanced tubes will give you the same color effect as HMIs without the big generators and the heat. They are also much cooler and more energy efficient than tungsten lamps. So they make the choice of high-speed (ISO 250) daylight-balanced film practical, less expensive, and more comfortable (cooler sets).

Up through most of the 1980s, the only color negative stock in existence was a tungsten-balanced film. To get natural-looking color in daylight, you had to put an 85 filter on your lens to remove the excess blue. The advantage now of having daylight-balanced stock is that you do not need the 85 filter. Not having to put on an 85 means there's that much less dark glass in front of the lens for the operator to look through. A dark viewfinder can drive you crazy in bright light. I usually keep my viewing eye shut or wear an eye patch to keep my pupils open. And you're probably going to have to use some sort of filter to cut down the light (even a slow ISO of 50 needs an exposure of f/16 in bright daylight, deeper than you usually want to go).

High-speed daylight stock (ISO 250) is useful when you're shooting at high speed for slow motion. You will easily be able to maintain a decent stop at f/5.6 or f/8—one that gives you enough depth of field to hold focus—even though your exposure is ½, ¼, or less of the exposure at 24 fps. Running at 120 frames/second, a common slow-motion speed, means opening up 2½ stops from 24 fps. Since ISO 250 is two and ⅓ stops faster than ISO 50, you could have one camera running at 24 with ISO 50 and one running at 120 with ISO 250 and have essentially the same stop on each. The visual quality of the shots, insofar as they're affected by depth of field and the look of a particular stop, remains the same.

I mentioned black-and-white. Kodak makes the only black-and-white movie stock, so that's that. Of course, very few movies are released in black-and-white anymore. The few that have been recently are almost all shot on color negative and converted to black-and-white in the digital intermediate. Personally I prefer to shoot actual black-and-white negative. It hasn't been reformulated in 40 years, so it has all the characteristics, good and bad, of an older stock. I like the black-and-white grain structure. I like the fact that, unlike color stock, it does not have a black antihalation backing, so you get halos around car headlights, street lights, any other bright light sources. Antihalation backing prevents bright light from passing through the film, bouncing off the pressure plate, and reexposing the film in a halo around bright spots. It's an imperfection I love. Also, modern color stock has a much longer contrast range than black-and-white. Areas that would go very white or black in black-and-white stock will have detail when shot with color stock. Again, I prefer the imperfection in the old look. Since color film has three black-and-white emulsion layers with various dyes embedded in them, there's always going to be more detailed information in the color negative, even if it's drained of color. As a result, with any color stock trying to look like black-and-white, you have to increase contrast. Very few films shot this way are convincing. *Good Night and Good Luck*, shot by Robert Elswit, ASC, is one that is.

It's very unlikely that you'll ever shoot reversal film. That's film that produces a direct positive. It's a specialty item; it tends to have higher contrast than negative, and the stock and the processing are more expensive. I've only heard of its being used for music videos. Kodak has two: one that produces natural-looking color and one that gives more intense saturated color (somewhat like the look of Kodachrome).

Now, of course, you can choose super-16 or 35. (Regular 16 mm with a 1.33:1 format is effectively nonexistent.) The main basis for choosing super-16 over 35 is a matter of practicality. 16 mm is less expensive. 35 mm has more information and therefore better color, less contrast, less grain, and sharper focus, all of which contribute to better image quality. There are more cameras and lenses and more types of cameras and lenses available for 35 mm. 16 mm is smaller and lighter, and the support tools (lenses and accessories) are smaller and lighter. You will almost always choose 35 mm if you can; it's the traditional professional gauge, and it's more flexible. But super-16 can look great (e.g., Declan Quinn, ASC's *Leaving Las Vegas*, Matty Libatique, ASC's *Black Swan*), and the dollar savings and the ability to move faster are powerful arguments for some projects.

When you shoot electronically, the choice of medium (the term for whatever the picture is registered and stored on—the equivalent of film) is determined by the camera you've chosen. The manufacturer has decided on one medium—tape, memory cards, hard drives, DVDs—and that's it. Sometimes a camera can use either one of two forms of media, but mostly one of them is the manufacturer's preferred choice. The differences that distinguish film emulsions are in the cameras themselves: The imaging system may be a single chip or three chips; the chip size can be several sizes from $1/3$ inch to super-35 equivalent; and the chip may be a CCD (charge-coupled device) or a CMOS (complementary metal oxide semiconductor). Electronic cameras are basically computers with lenses on the front. Models are changing as fast as Moore's Law[1] predicts for computers. As I write, the newest digital movie camera is the Arriflex Alexa, but by the time this book is published, that will no longer be true. It's a wonderful and frustrating aspect of the developments in electronic movie equipment. Ultimately, the camera you decide to use will depend on the intended means of exhibition (big screen or small) and the cost and ease of use of a given camera.

Once you've decided on your film stock(s) or media, you can leave the ordering to your camera assistant and the production manager. With film or memory you need to be concerned that you always have enough on hand and that it's stored properly (for film, in a cool, dry, safe place). Care of the film or memory is also the responsibility of the assistant.

---

[1]The observation made in 1965 by Gordon Moore, cofounder of Intel, that the number of transistors per square inch on integrated circuits had doubled every year since the integrated circuit was invented. Moore predicted that this trend would continue for the foreseeable future.
In subsequent years, the pace slowed a bit, but data density has doubled approximately every 18 months, and this is the current definition of Moore's Law, which Moore himself has blessed. Most experts, including Moore himself, expect Moore's Law to hold for at least another two decades.
http://www.webopedia.com/TERM/M/Moores_Law.html

CHAPTER 11

Selecting a Tripod and Head

Now that you've selected your camera and your recording medium, you're going to need something to support the camera: a tripod, dolly, crane, or Steadicam. Don't think you can depend on hand holding. (For more of my diatribe against hand-holding, see Chapter 35.) Just as with filters and accessories, the camera rental house will have tripods, and sometimes they are part of a package. In that case you'll have little choice. But if you do have a choice, here are some things to consider: Is the tripod strong enough to support the camera? Cameras vary a lot in weight. It's important that you have a sturdy tripod. Otherwise your camera will wobble, and that only works if you're trying to convey the point of view of a character who is either seasick or drunk. Otherwise you want the camera to be steady as a rock. I like to get a tripod that might be a little too beefy for my camera, especially a light camera. I like the feel of a very solid platform under me. Part of the reason is that I tend to use my whole body when I'm operating a fluid head (I'll get to heads almost immediately, so hold on), and I want a platform that stands up to the weight of my body.

Another consideration: Does the tripod have a convenient configuration? In Chapter 34 I explain my dislike of spreaders, but some tripods have built-in spreaders, and they're great for one-man, run-and-gun shooting. You can pick up the tripod with one hand, set it down, and it's stable.

Also, no matter how beefy the tripod is, how much does it weigh? Is carrying it a burden? Who's responsible for carrying it? If you've got a full camera crew, your assistant is going to be carrying the camera and tripod, so maybe you don't care. But you do care that things move fast, and the easier equipment is to move, the faster the shooting goes.

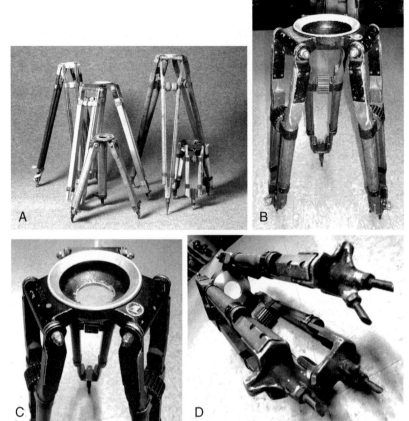

FIGURE 11.1
Wooden tripods.
Reproduced by permission of www.visualproducts.com.

FIGURE 11.2
Aluminum tripod with spreaders.
Reproduced by permission of O'Connor. www.ocon.com.

It used to be that when you got a tripod, you got something made of wood. That explains how tripods came to be called "sticks." In the 1970s, Ronford developed an aluminum tripod that became the standard of the industry and was copied by most tripod manufacturers. At some point, someone developed fiberglass tripods, making them lighter-weight, and finally came carbon fiber tripods, which are both lighter and stronger than anything else. Carbon fiber also has the advantage of not splintering like wood and not denting or bending like aluminum. You can probably see where I'm going: *Get carbon fiber tripods.* Of course, they cost more than any other kind, even to rent, but they pay for themselves in ease of use and time saved.

You probably noticed in Figure 11.1 that tripods with wooden legs come in different heights. Back when wooden tripods were used, you always carried three sizes and a hi-hat. The three sizes were regular, sawed-off, and baby. With those three, you could manage any height for the camera up to about seven or eight feet. The advent of Ronford legs reduced the standard complement of tripods to two: standard and baby. You'll always carry all the sizes, two or three depending on whether you've got wood or carbon, and you'll always carry a hi-hat

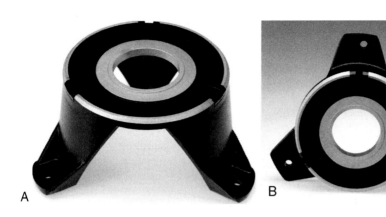

A   B

FIGURE 11.3
Mitchell top hi-hat and
lo-hat, not on plywood base.
*Reproduced by permission
of Film Tools®.*

(see Figure 11.3), mounted on a piece of plywood (watch out for the inevitable splinters), that allow you to get a low angle shot. You can also see a comparison of the sizes of bowl mounts (usually called ball mounts) in these figures.

I also fulminate about Mitchell tops and ball mounts in Chapter 34. But the point is you *will* have a choice. I would always go for the Mitchell top. It's the professional mount for heads, and it's universal for dollies and cranes, at least in the United States. But if you're using a lighter camera, and especially if you're doing documentary work, a ball top with a spreader makes leveling fast, since with a lightweight camera you can level with one hand.

Now that you've chosen your tripod, you will have to select the kind of head you want, the device that allows you to pan, tilt, level, and maneuver the camera. The main choice you'll have will be between a geared head and a fluid head. Friction heads are pretty much amateur stuff. The head, with its pivoting movement, is what allows the camera operator to manipulate the camera, to follow the action or change the framing smoothly and inconspicuously. If you're operating, make sure you're getting the kind of head you like, and make sure it's in good working order. You can tell just by panning and tilting. Does it work smoothly? Is there enough resistance, not too much, not too little, just so it feels effortless? Is the fluid head leaking? That's the silicone grease inside that damps the move and makes it smooth. (It needs to stay inside.) Does the head mount firmly without wobble in the keyway and without any tendency to loosen? Is there any slop, especially with a geared head, that you can't correct? "Slop" is any tendency of the head to wobble when you think you're holding it steady. (If you don't know how to adjust the head, have a technician do it and show you how.)

A geared head is an unlikely looking contraption. With its manually controlled wheels—cranking with the left hand to pan, with the right to tilt, but in directions perpendicular to each other—a geared head looks like it must have been inspired by the turret controls on the big military gun mounts we've all seen in WWII movies and docs. It's the most counterintuitive way of working you can possibly imagine. The direction you move your hands and the wheels does not

FIGURE 11.4
Hi-hat 150 mm bowl.
Reproduced by permission of O'Connor. www.ocon.com.

FIGURE 11.5
Panaflex Genesis on Panahead geared head.
Image courtesy of Panavision Inc.

FIGURE 11.6
Panaflex XL2 on Panahead.
Image courtesy of Panavision Inc.

FIGURE 11.7
O'Connor 2575D fluid head.
Reproduced by permission of O'Connor. www.ocon.com.

result in moving the camera in the direction you would expect. It's arbitrary, and you just have to get used to it. Everyone compares it to patting your head and rubbing your stomach at the same time. And they're right. Yet, in spite of that, a geared head is, in my opinion and that of most operators, the preferred head to use, the one that gives you the most control and ease of use. That's once you get the hang of it. You can find out how to do that in Chapter 35.

The fluid head, in contrast, is intuitive. The camera moves in exactly the same direction that you move the head. You just push it in the direction you want it to go. If you've done any panning or tilting before, you've used a fluid head or a friction head. You'll probably want to have a fluid head on hand even if you opt to use the wheels (the geared head). For tight spaces and for times an extremely fast move must be made, it's easier with the fluid head. Your choices here are mainly how heavy-duty you want the head (as with sticks, strong enough to allow you to work easily with the camera) and which manufacturer. Arri and Panavision both make regular and heavy-duty gear heads, and both are excellent. The choice between them is a matter of personal preference. You might also be able to find Mitchell gear heads or Worrall heads. Mitchell and Worrall are out of business, but the heads are still around. You can use the fluid head or the wheels with any support device—tripod, dolly, crane—as long as you have the correct mount for it.

My favorite head for some shots is a Mitchell Vitesse. It has the cradle (the part that holds the camera and tilts up and down) pivoting on a nodal point. Unlike other gear heads, the Vitesse can give you a full 90-degree vertical up or down from horizontal. Some fluid heads (like the O'Connor 2575D) give you a full 90-degree up and down, but most gear heads only give you about 30 degrees. Even with a tilt plate, they give you more tilt but not more range.

FIGURE 11.8
Mitchell Vitesse head.
Reproduced by permission of www.visualproducts.com.

One of the greatest challenges I ever encountered as a camera operator occurred when I was operating on a special slow-motion insert shot for the movie *Bird*. I had to keep an empty iodine bottle in the frame as it fell from Bird's hand after he tried to kill himself by drinking it. The bottle, which was actually only 1½ inches high, had to fill half the frame. Since we didn't have Forest Whittaker or a double to provide the hand that drops the bottle, the shot had to be done abstractly by dropping the bottle from outside and above the frame. I had to begin tilting as soon as I saw the bottle enter the frame, tilt with it for a reasonable length of time, and then let it exit the frame—at 128 frames per second. Let me tell you, that's very

FIGURE 11.9
Tilt plate on a gear head.
Image courtesy of Panavision Inc.

slow motion, and any mistake you make shows up on screen for a long time. And I made mistakes. Just trying to move the camera as fast as the bottle falls is very, very difficult. The bottle is a very small object; it may appear large in the frame, but it is so small that it almost exits the frame as soon as it enters. So the frame must move with it. There's an old gag: A guy says he'll give you a dollar if you can catch the dollar bill as he drops it. You position your thumb and forefinger on either side of the dollar bill, ready to pinch your fingers together and grasp the dollar as it drops. You never win. Your reflexes just can't respond as fast as gravity. It took a number of takes, but finally I got the shot.

What made it possible was being able to put the Vitesse in third gear (the fastest) and tilt it extremely fast, with an unmoving eyepiece. That is, the eyepiece pivots on its attachment to the camera, and it's connected to the head, like they are with all gear heads and movable eyepiece cameras, so it doesn't move relative to my eye. This makes operating fast and radical moves a lot easier.

And finally, as to the weight of the head, most manufacturers give specs that suggest the maximum and minimum weights their heads will carry. Again, I tend to like a head that's intended for a slightly heavier camera so I can set it at its maximum resistance and muscle it around. That's personal preference. I know operators who like the head so loose it swings freely. Whatever works for you is the only rule. Remember: Be comfortable with your tools, and you'll be able to do your best.

CHAPTER 12

What Everyone Else Is Doing to Prepare

You're kind of busy selecting cameras, lenses, and your support material—tripods, dollies, and so on. You're going to have a lot of help from your crew in ordering and checking out the equipment you want (making sure it works, making sure there's enough for the show, and loading and organizing it on the camera truck). You've spent some time, based on your analysis of the script, letting the key grip, the gaffer, and the first camera assistant know what sort of equipment you think you'll need. You've met with the production manager or the producer to sign your contract, and at that time you've gotten the crew list and the schedule. Right now, the schedule is still subject to change (and it will, all the time you're shooting; I'm talking about major changes here, like shooting in the Sierras instead of Malibu, and moving scenes up to the first week from the last). You may have had some input into the schedule, but not much; it's more a matter of when actors and locations are available and how they can be scheduled so their usage is consolidated. It's a lot about time and money. It needs to be.

From the script, you know what special items you might want. From the schedule, you know when you'll need those special items. You'll meet with the key grip, the gaffer, and the first camera assistant as far in advance of production as you can. Talk to the key about what kind of dolly you want and how much track. Track usually comes in eight-foot lengths, so guess at what might be the longest move and order one or two lengths extra. And always order some four-foot lengths to be able to fit into sets or locations where an extra eight feet is too long but you need some extra travel.

At some point there will have been some discussion—with the director at least, probably with the producer—about using Steadicam®. Someone will inevitably say, "Well, think of all time and money we'll save on dolly moves." No matter how ill-informed you know that statement to be, what you must say is "I love Steadicam®, but you've got to know it never saves time." And it doesn't. A Steadicam® shot takes time, thought, and a lot of effort to set up. In a way, it can substitute for a dolly, but the effort to have the operator suit up, set up the shot, be concerned with the rhythm of the shot, and work to eliminate physical obstacles often takes the kind of time that eliminates any saving you might get by not setting up track.

FIGURE 12.1
Garrett Brown, inventor of the
Steadicam®, with Stanley
Kubrick on the set of *The Shining*.
*Reproduced by permission of
Garrett Brown.*

FIGURE 12.2A
Steadicam®.
*Photos courtesy of The Tiffen
Company.*

FIGURE 12.2B
Operator with Steadicam®.
Photos courtesy of The Tiffen Company.

The Steadicam® was not designed to replace dolly moves. It was designed to substitute for and improve on handheld work. The idea was to allow operators to get into positions and places that no dolly or crane could manage. This can be done hand held, but at the price of shakiness and sloppiness in the shot. The Steadicam® eliminates the shake; with a good operator it eliminates even the float (the slow movement of the frame, like a buoy bobbing in the ocean, that's the mark of not-so-good Steadicam® operators).

A good operator will own her rig; you've got to customize it to make it work best for you, and she and her rig, and probably her assistant, will cost a good deal. I think the Steadicam® can be a great asset to a movie if it makes even one shot possible that you couldn't get otherwise. You may not be able to afford to hire an experienced operator. Here's where you settle for slightly less exquisite shots and find an operator who's still new to the rig and wants to build his reputation.

This brings up some advice I have if you're sort of young and in good health. Learn the Steadicam®. It's hard work, and starting out is expensive. But you vastly increase your value as an operator. You will get more jobs, and you are likely to get the more interesting jobs. The only real way to learn is to go to a class given by the Steadicam® Operators' Association (http://www.steadicam-ops.com/). The instructors are always experienced Steadicam® operators, often including Garrett Brown, the inventor of the Steadicam®.

If you decide on Steadicam®, you will either need to bring in the operator only for special shots or hire him for the entire show. What has become routine in the business for several years now is to hire the Steadicam® operator to be the A or B camera operator, have the Steadicam® rig on the camera truck for the whole show, and pay the operator his much higher Steadicam® rate only when the rig is brought out. When this happens, the producer is putting the screws on the operator. He'll say, "I love you, man, but I got to have you as an operator at

FIGURE 12.3
Western dolly.
Photos courtesy of Matthews Studio Equipment.

FIGURE 12.4
Doorway dolly.
Photos courtesy of Matthews Studio Equipment.

the [much lower] regular rate. But bring your rig on the show every day, and we'll pay you your (Steadicam®) rate when we use it." This saves the producer money, but it means the operator may lose high-paying one-day jobs. It also means the operator's expensive rig is just sitting there, acquiring debt, instead of working to amortize his bank loan (often over $100,000). In the contest between camera operator and producer, guess who wins?

You will always want a dolly whether you have the Steadicam® or not, and even if you think you're going to do the whole picture hand held. There will be decisions to make about what kind of dolly to get. Do you want a doorway dolly? A western dolly? Can you afford a crab dolly? If there's enough money in the budget, you want a crab dolly. It's the best camera platform there is. You (well, sure, the dolly grip) can move it around easily and position the camera precisely. You can adjust the height of the camera just as precisely. You can make linear moves on track or boards (a long piece of 1 × 12-inch pine is just as good as track and often more convenient) or move in any direction on what we call a dance floor, which is any smooth, flat surface. The grips will often make a dance floor out of ¾-inch plywood covered with masonite. It takes the bumps out of almost any surface.

Doorway dollies and western dollies are extremely useful; the doorway dolly is mostly used indoors, and the western dolly is for exteriors. Each is basically a piece of plywood with wheels and a steering mechanism at one end. With balloon tires, they can ride on a rough surface. A doorway dolly will also have track wheels to run on the same track the crab dolly uses. The doorway dolly was specifically made to fit through standard interior doorways. The smaller crab dollies (Fisher 11 and Chapman Super Pee-Wee) both fit through doorways as well. The western dolly is clearly a holdover from the days when Westerns were king in Hollywood. Its large wheelbase means it won't tip on back lot streets or sidewalks.

FIGURE 12.5
Fisher Model 11 dolly.
Photos courtesy of J.L. Fisher, Inc.

You can mount a tripod or hi-hat on either dolly. You want to fasten them securely, with chain or a ratchet strap (again, the grips do this). I've also often roped or screwed an apple box to the dolly platform, used it as a seat, and done hand held. You can get a hybrid look that way. You get some of the improvised feel of hand held along with the stable platform (so the operator doesn't have to walk) and a longer, often faster movement than the operator is capable of on foot. Both the doorway and the western are useful for hauling equipment when they're not being used to make a shot.

In most cases you can let the dolly grip and the operator decide on the dolly. They're not going to get something bad, and they probably have preferences either for convenience and habit or for what the dolly can do with what's needed for this movie. You may need items that might not be in a "standard package." There are several types of standard packages, mostly named as a two-ton, five-ton, or ten-ton package. That refers to the carrying capacity of the truck into which this package will fit. It's all the grips' decision, and you're better off staying out of it. And either the key or the best boy has a "best-boy kit," a large cabinet full of miscellaneous hardware, rigging devices, and homemade gizmos. You're going to talk about empty flag frames (to cover with specific diffusion or to use for special shadow devices), what size frames you need (12 × 12-foot, 20 × 20-foot, or maybe a special size to cover a large area), special rigging you will need (maybe you have a planned dolly shot that goes over a small ditch, so you'll need to bridge it), and extra amounts of normal supplies (speed rail is a convenient way to rig lights, cameras on vehicles, and so forth; maybe you have a big rigging job in mind, and the grips need to order extra speed rails and connectors).

FIGURE 12.6
Chapman Super
Pee-Wee IV.
*Photo provided courtesy
of Chapman/Leonard
Equipment, Inc.*

Over coffee and during your location scouts, you've talked over your electrical needs with the gaffer and the best boy electric. One thing all three of you will be sensitive to is dealing with a generator. You have to have enough power for your lights. While sometimes you can rely on house power, most of the time you don't want to take a chance. You rent a generator. For really small shows, you can get a putt-putt (a small industrial generator). But besides putting out only a limited amount of power, they're noisy. And as you may have heard, the producers are making all their pictures talkies these days. You want to help the sound department by shielding or reducing the generator noise.

Your best bet is a generator made for the movie business. They'll have a decent amount of power (a common size is 500 amps, big enough to power 50 1-KW lamps). And they're built to be quiet. The other thing they have is crystal control, a necessity if you use HMIs or Kinoflos that depend on line frequency to have correct color temperature and the correct amount of light output.

Most generators are diesel or gasoline internal combustion engines. Just like your car, the sound has to be muffled, and they have more or less effective insulation. Really, the sound shielding is good, but not quite good enough for movies. We are all convinced that sound mixers can hear grass growing. Usually the choice of a generator is up to the gaffer, but if you know you're going to have heavy power needs, you want to talk to your crew about getting a larger one or renting multiple generators. And while you're on location, you'll be looking for a place, preferably behind a solid wall, where you can put the generator so the noise is further baffled. But you have to be aware that for about every 100 feet of cable, the voltage drops by around 10 volts. And cable costs money to rent. So you'll be trying to keep the cable run from the generator as short as possible.

You also will be talking about the light package. Are you going to light with tungsten? (Conventional, usually used for interiors and stages, hot to run, takes more power per light output than other lamps.) Do you want to have a big HMI package? (More expensive but more efficient—more light for the same power, blue to match sunlight or to give a cold look to night.) Probably you want a Kinoflo package. (Very efficient in power use, perfect color balance for daylight, tungsten movie lights, or tungsten household lights, cool, lightweight, small, but generally not capable of large throws that you'll need on night exteriors.) And you may consider LEDs. (New technology, not as many styles of lighting fixture, very efficient, light, cool, often small, and easy to mount in awkward places.)

And these are the conventional lights. You may have an area of several city blocks to light. You'll probably opt for a Musco light or a variant. Musco lights were developed as "portable" lights for sporting events. I put portable in quotes because they mount on a large (eight wheels at least) truck. The Musco light is an array of HMI lights—for example, 25 5-KW lamps on a crane arm. They're all adjustable. I have seen the Musco give an f/2.8 (25 footcandles for ISO 500 film) at a distance of a quarter mile. So they're great for a basic ambient light, as well as a specific back, side, or front light.

You'll also convene with your crew and all the other departments at a production meeting shortly before the shoot, probably a week. At that event, the entire group (or at least all the keys and their main assistants) sit around a table while the AD reads the script, and the director comments on special needs for specific scenes. The AD checks with each department to make sure the necessary equipment has been ordered (say, we're shooting a car driving over and into a canyon; we want a crane to go with the car and then pull up for the leap and drop for the fall; grip, camera, and special effects have to be ready and able to coordinate). By the way, this meeting, just like working on the set or going to dailies, is not an occasion for offering any opinions. (This means you, too, Mr. or Ms. DP.) We expect you to be able to keep your crew under control, but don't let your intimate relationship with the director fool you. No one wants to hear anybody's opinions. Unless there's a disaster looming (and maybe even if there isn't), it's too late to make any major changes, and minor changes aren't worth talking about. And it's always too easy to hurt feelings or cast aspersions on someone else's work by a casual remark. Remember, everyone here is a professional, and any damage to someone's reputation can harm his or her livelihood. Your opinion could draw attention to someone's failing. Even if that person hasn't made any mistakes or done anything wrong, undue attention can—by the power of gossip and the power of the uncertainty everyone lives with—cause him or her to lose a job.

At various times during preproduction, with phone calls, during location scouts, after the production meeting, the DP has talked to the camera assistants about what to order. As with grip and electric, there's a standard package. If you've worked with your assistants before, they know what you like. If not, be sure to specify exactly what you want. You need to talk about how many primes and what focal lengths—likewise for zooms. What filters do you like, what ones must you have, what ones do you want to test?

Of course, there will be tests. If you're already a team, you can let the assistants do the shutter, steadiness, and framing tests by themselves. You may even let them shoot tests on the lenses for focus and color rendition. There will be other things to test. You may want to run an emulsion test. You may run filter tests; the filters may be an overall test (how does a shot of anything—a building, the landscape—look), or it may be a question of a cosmetic filter for an actor. With the actors, you want to test how the faces of the principals take light and by what kind of light and by what direction of light they are most flattered. In some cases you may want to work with wardrobe to be sure costumes look good. In the early days of Technicolor, some colors looked different to the film than they did to the eye. Wardrobe had to know how each color photographed in case fabrics or dyes had to be changed.

In the background of all this artistic fever, the transportation department has been prepping its vehicles. You may have a one-truck production; in that case, pile everything in the truck as neatly as possible and allow an extra half hour in the morning and the evening to unpack and repack. As soon as your budget gets realistic (say, over $1 million), you will be working with a separate truck for almost every department. Often grip and electric will share a truck. This shouldn't be a problem, but you must make sure the truck has a few basic features. You want at least one side opening and a rear overhead sliding door. It's better if you can have side doors on each side of the truck. That way each department can use one door, and can share the back. And the back must have a lift gate. Make sure there are portable steps to get to the lift. Not everyone is a kid, and it's safer to use steps rather than jumping up and down a couple of feet—especially when you're carrying equipment. Most teamsters will make sure the trucks are shelved—built-in, even if temporary—and that there are plenty of places for tie-downs. Of course, there has to be a connection for AC current, and it's a good idea to have a 12-volt (from the truck battery) wiring and lighting system, too.

Grip and electric trucks can vary from a tradesman's van for both grip and electric to 18-wheelers, one for each. The camera truck usually carries the sound department as well and often some of the AD's stuff. It all depends on the size of the show.

Your crews will take care of loading the trucks. At the end of prep—probably the last day or two for grip and electric and the end of the last day for camera—the drivers will get the trucks to the rental house. The best boys take care of loading, packing, labeling, and securing all of their equipment. The camera assistants do the same for theirs, although sometimes the camera rental house will load the camera truck after itemizing the equipment.

Everybody's making last-minute preparations. You're checking with the director and production manager to make sure you know about any changes or new problems. You want to be talking to your keys—gaffer, key grip, and camera assistant—to make sure they've got their equipment and crew under control. It's not a bad idea to visit them at the rental houses. This is also a good time to pick up some coffee and bagels, or donuts, or ice cream for the various technicians at the rental houses. They've been doing a lot of work for you, and their friendship can be a great help when it comes to dealing with equipment problems. And it shows your crew that you appreciate their hard work.

CHAPTER 13
The Night Before

There's not much more you can do. You've read the script a million times, you've talked about the movie with the director until you know it as well as he or she does, you've assembled the best crew you can find, and you've ordered all the equipment you can think of to shoot the picture. The call sheet has either been e-mailed to you or slipped under your hotel door.

Look it over. You should have no surprises. You know the schedule, and the call sheet should follow what's been scheduled. You'll find the name of the film, the date, the director's and producer's names, the scenes you're shooting, the actors, and which ones are called for the day. On the back is the crew list with their call times. Check yours and plan to be at least a half hour early. Take a look at the one in Figure 13.1.

Figure 13.1 shows the front and back of a typical call sheet. It should have all the information you need for the day and some notes about the upcoming days. It's the bible of the show. Nothing else—not the schedule, the budget, or even the script—is perfectly accurate and immutable, but the call sheet is. Check the call times; just make sure your time is earlier than set call (the time everyone's expected to be on the set to look at the first rehearsal) and that your keys' times are the same as yours or earlier so there's no chance you'll be waiting for them.

Because call times are often as early as 7 AM, you're going to have to be up at dawn to get to the set on time. So don't stay up late the night before. Have a relaxing dinner, don't drink too much, and settle in early. And if you can get a good night's sleep, more power to you. I'm always nervous the night before the first day. When I finally do get to sleep, I toss and turn. I have the standard "Oh, no, here I am on the set; I'm naked, and I can't remember how to do anything" dreams that wake me up three or four times during the night. Either I wake up an hour before the alarm or the alarm goes off, it seems, two minutes after I finally doze off. I used to work as an assistant to a very highly regarded DP who got incredibly sick before every show. Without fail, a few days before shooting started, he'd come down with a horrible case of the flu—sweats, fever,

FIGURE 13.1
Typical call sheet.

CREW CALL:	7:00 AM					*STARSHIP TROOPERS*
Shooting Call:		8:30 AM				Big Bug Pictures, Inc.

Director:	Paul Verhoeven	Sunrise/Sunset:	6:32AM - 7:07PM	DATE:	Tuesday, 9/10/96
Producers:	Jon Davison/Alan Marshall	Weather:	Morning Cloud Cover	SHOOTING DAY:	94 of 112
Writer:	Ed Neumeier		Afternoon Clear and Warm	Production Office:	
			Temperature: 65 - 95	Production FAX:	

All Departments: There Will Be A Daily Safety Meeting Before Work Begins

SET	SCENES	CAST	D or N	PAGES	LOCATION
To Begin:					Pyramid Arena
INT. EDUCATION CENTER - ATHLETIC FIELD & STANDS	15 - 25	1,2,3,9,53,	DAY 2	1 3/8	CSU - Long Beach
• The big game. Johnny triumphs over Zander and leaves with	(Parts)	(Stunts),			Merriam Way,
Carmen.)		(272 BG),			Near Atherton and Fanwood
		(300 Promo)			Thomas Guide Page 796 D-5
					(Miles R/T fr/ Sony: 56)
					Crew Parking:
					Pyramid Parking Structure
		TOTAL PAGES:		1 3/8	(See Attached Map)

	CAST	ROLE	CALL	MAKEUP	SET CALL	REMARKS
1	CASPER VAN DIEN	JOHNNY RICO	7:00 AM	7:00 AM	8:30 AM	
2	DENISE RICHARDS	CARMEN IBANEZ	6:30 AM	6:30 AM	8:30 AM	
3	DINA MEYER	DIZZY FLORES	6:30 AM	6:30 AM	8:30 AM	
4	JAKE BUSEY	ACE LEVY		(HOLD)		
6	MICHAEL IRONSIDE	JEAN RASCZAK		(HOLD)		
8	SETH GILLIAM	SUGAR WATKINS		(HOLD)		
9	PATRICK MULDOON	ZANDER BARCALOW	7:00 AM	7:00 AM	8:30 AM	
10	MATT LEVIN	KITTEN SMITH		(HOLD)		
18	CURNAL AULISIO	SERGEANT GILLESPIE		(HOLD)		
35	AMY SMART	CADET PILOT		(HOLD)		
51	ROB SULIT	STUDENT		(HOLD IF NOT FINISHED)		
XX	VIC ARMSTRONG	SUPERVISING STUNT COORD.		7:00 AM		
XX	DICKEY BEER	STUNT COORDINATOR		7:00 AM		
X1	JOEY BOX	UTILITY STUNT	7:30 AM	7:30 AM	8:30 AM	(DBL. "JOHNNY") TIGER
X1	TONY ANGELOTTI		7:30 AM	7:30 AM		(DBL. "JOHNNY") TIGER
X2	JAMIE KEYSER		7:00 AM	7:00 AM		(DBL. "CARMEN")
X3	DANA EVENSON		7:00 AM	7:00 AM		(DBL. "DIZZY") TIGER
X9	MIKE SMITH		7:30 AM	7:30 AM		(DBL. "ZANDER") GIANT
53	RON BOTCHAN		7:30 AM	7:30 AM		("OFFICIAL")
X	JILL BROWN		7:00 AM	7:00 AM		TIGER
X	PAUL ELIOPOLIS		7:30 AM	7:30 AM		TIGER
X	LEON DELANEY		7:30 AM	7:30 AM		TIGER FAN
X	TANNER GILL		7:30 AM	7:30 AM		TIGER FAN
X	MICHELLE BURKETT		7:00 AM	7:00 AM		TIGER CHEERLEADER
X	JIM PALMER		7:30 AM	7:30 AM		GIANT
X	MIKE PAPAJOHN		7:30 AM	7:30 AM		GIANT
X	KATHY MARSHALL		7:00 AM	7:00 AM		GIANT
X	EDDIE BRAUN		7:30 AM	7:30 AM		T.B.D.
X	JACK CARPENTER		7:30 AM	7:30 AM		TIGER FAN

STANDINS AND EXTRAS					SPECIAL INSTRUCTIONS	
No. Description		Call	Wardrobe	On Set	Properties:	Hero & Practice Jumpballs, Cheerleaders' Pom-Poms, Fall Pads,
3 Standins	(April, Lars, Jason)	7:00 AM	7:00 AM	7:15 AM		Players' Mouthpieces, Officials' Whistles, Fans' Pom-Poms
					Camera:	Steadicam, Beaumonte Camera.
272 Background, To Include:					Set Dressing:	Banner Regional Final - Uni High vs. Tesla Tech.
(Reporting to The Pyramid:)					Wardrobe:	Break Away Strap on Zander's Helmet, Team, Cheerleader,
12 Cheerleaders	(Tigers)	6:45 AM	6:45 AM	8:30 AM		Coach & Officials Uniforms, School Uniforms for 200 BG.
100 Spectators		6:45 AM	6:45 AM		SPFX:	Control of Scoreboard.
19 Jumpball Players		7:00 AM	7:00 AM		Production:	Add'l Production Assistants for Crowd Control, Promo. Audience
12 Cheerleaders	(Giants)	7:15 AM	7:15 AM			Load-Out at Parking, Etc.
5 Jumpball Officials		7:15 AM	7:15 AM		Locations:	Changing Areas for General Background, Locker Rooms for
4 Coaches & Ass't Coaches		7:15 AM	7:15 AM			Featured Extras.
100 Spectators		7:15 AM	7:15 AM		Transp'n:	Extras' Bus Shuttle from Parking Starting at 6:15AM,
20 Benched Jumpball Players		7:15 AM	7:15 AM			Quad Runner for Camera.
					Art Dept:	(Painter) Be Prepared to Touch-Up Floors at Wrap, If Required.
300 Promotional Spectators:					Stunts:	Boxes and Pads, Mini-Tramps.
(Reporting to Los Alamitos:)					Promo:	Los Alamitos Race Course
300 Jumpball Spectators		8:00 AM	N/A		Spectators →	N W Corner of Walker St. & Katella Ave. Intersection
					Parking	Enter off Walker St. approx. 200 yards N. of Katella Ave.

ALL DEPARTMENTS - PLEASE SEE ADDITIONAL INSTRUCTIONS ON BACK AND ANY ATTACHED SAFETY MEMOS

ADVANCE SCHEDULE

DATE	CAST	SET NAME (Synopsis)	D/N	PAGES	SCENES	LOCATION
Weds. 9/11	1,2,3,9,53,	Continue & Complete:				The Pyramid Arena
(Day 95)	(272 BG),	Int. Ed. Center - Athletic Field & Stands	Day 2	1 3/8	15 through 25	CSU Long Beach
	(300 Promo BG)	• (The big game. Johnny triumphs over Zander and			(Parts)	
		leaves with Carmen.)				
Thurs. 9/12	2,35,36	Int. Fleet Trainer - Lunar Orbit		2/8	61	Sony Studios
(Day 96)		• (Carmen weaves in and out of fleet traffic. She				Stage 29
		points out the Rodger Young.)				(Small Gimbal)
		To Begin:				
	2,9	Int. Rodger Young - Life Pod Bay	Day 22	2 6/8	158,158B,	(Large Gimbal)
		• (Carmen and Zander enter, jump into lifepod,			158BA,158BB	
		blast out of burning lifepod bay...)			(Parts)	
Fri. 9/13	2,9	Continue and Complete:				
(Day 97)		Int. Rodger Young - Life Pod Bay	Day 22	2 6/8	158,158B,	
		• (Carmen and Zander enter, jump into lifepod,			158BA,158BB	
		blast out of burning lifepod bay...)			(Parts)	
Mon. 9/16	2,9	Int. Planet P - Bug City Cavern - Lifepod	Day 22	2 2/8	163A,163B	Sony Studios
(Day 98)		• (Zander hits his head. Smoke fills the cockpit.)				Stage 30
		Int. Planet P - Bug City Cavern	Day 22	3 6/8	164,166pt.	
		• (They blow the hatch, roll out. the pod starts burning.)				

** NO FORCED CALLS WITHOUT PRIOR U.P.M. APPROVAL - ALL CALLS SUBJECT TO CHANGE BY THE A.D. **

Unit Production Manager:	Robert Latham Brown	Assistant Director:	Gregg Goldstone

A

FIGURE 13.1—
CONT'D

STARSHIP TROOPERS			Date:	Tuesday, 9/10/96
Big Bug Pictures, Inc.			Shooting Day:	94 of 112

NO.	PRODUCTION (2000)	CALL	NAME		NO.	ADDITIONAL CREW	CALL	NAME
1	Production Manager	O/C	Robert L. Brown					
1	1st Assistant Director	7:00 AM	Gregg Goldstone					
1	2nd Assistant Director		Kenneth Silverstein		NO.	SET LIGHTING (3200)	CALL	NAME
1	2nd 2nd Ass't Director	6:15 AM	Peter Hirsch		1	Chief Lighting Technician	7:00 AM	Jim Grce
1	Add'l 2nd Ass't Director	T.B.D.			1	A.C.L.T.		David Christensen
1	Assistant Director Trainee		Joth Riggs		1	Lamp Operator		Lou Ramos
1	Assistant Director Trainee		Staci Lamkin		1	Lamp Operator		David Slodki
1	Production Assistant		Michael DeVaney		1	Lamp Operator		Greg Kittleson
1	Production Assistant		David Smith		1	Lamp Operator		John Owens
1	Production Assistant		Susan Blanchard		1	Lamp Operator	↓	Ron Kline
1	Production Assistant		Jennifer Biskup*					
1	Production Assistant	6:30 AM	John Hayes**					
1	Production Assistant	7:00 AM	Bob Hume					
					NO.	CAMERA (3300)	CALL	NAME
	** Report to Los Alamitos to Re-Direct Extras To Pyramid.				1	Director of Photography	7:00 AM	Jost Vacano
	* Report to Los Alamitos to Load-Out Promo. Spectators.				1	Camera Operator		Billy O'Drobinak
					1	Camera/Steadicam Oper.		Mark Emery Moore
1	Script Supervisor	7:00 AM	Haley McLane		1	1st Ass't Camera	6:42 AM	Gregory Irwin
NO.	PROD'N OFFICE (2000)	CALL	NAME		1	1st Ass't Camera	7:00 AM	Todd Schlopy
1	Production Coordinator	O/C	Daren Hicks		1	2nd Ass't Camera	6:42 AM	Joy Stone
1	Ass't Prod'n Coordinator	(Per Hicks)	Janet Campolito		1	2nd Ass't Camera	7:00 AM	Tom Vandermillen
1	Ass't Prod'n Coordinator		Lisa Hackler		1	Camera Loader	6:42 AM	Jerry Patton
1	Production Assistant		Wayne Lamkay		1	Production Assistant	7:00 AM	James Ferrera
1	Production Assistant		Robin Berk					
1	Production Assistant	↓	Kurt Valles		1	Stills Photographer	8:00 AM	Stephen Vaughan
NO.	ART DEPT. (2200)	CALL	NAME		NO.	SOUND (3400)	CALL	NAME
1	Production Designer	O/C	Allan Cameron		1	Sound Mixer	7:00 AM	Joseph Geisinger
1	Art Director		Steve Wolff		1	Boom Operator		Raul Bruce
1	Art Director		Bruce Hill		1	Utility Sound Technician	↓	Jack Wolpa
1	Assistant Art Director		Bob Fechtman					
NO.	SET OPERATIONS (2500)	CALL	NAME		1	Video Assist Operator	7:00 AM	Aaron Katz
1	Key Grip	7:00 AM	Gary Dagg		1	Video Assist Operator	7:00 AM	Dan Dobson
1	Best Boy Grip		Joe Kelly		NO.	TRANSPORTATION (3500)	CALL	NAME
1	Dolly Grip		Tom Miller		1	Transportation Coordinator	O/C	Jim Chesney
1	Company Grip		Steve Iriguchi		1	Transportation Captain	(Per Chesney)	Ken Moore
1	Company Grip		Leo Behar		1	Transportation Captain		John Armstrong
1	Company Grip		Paul Rychlec		1	Transportation Captain (2nd U)		Joe Feeney
1	Company Grip		Peter McAdams		X	Drivers		
2	Add'l Grips	↓	(Per Kelly)			(All Transportation Equipment & Personnel Per Chesney)		
1	Standby Painter	7:00 AM	Richard Girod		4	Single Room Cast Trailers	Rdy@6:00 AM	(Cast: 1,2,3,9)
					1	Two Room Cast Trailer		(Prod'n, Cast: 53)
1	Crafts Service Employee	6:00 AM	Eric Winn		1	Two Room Cast Trailer		(Prod'n, Cast: XX)
6	Add'l Crafts Service	7:00 AM	(Per Winn)		1	Honeywagon		(Stunts)
NO.	SPECIAL EFFECTS (2600)	CALL	NAME		1	Director's Trailer		
1	SPFX Consultant	O/C	John Richardson		1	Extras Bathroom Unit	↓	
1	SPFX 1st Unit Coordinator	7:00 AM	John McLeod					
1	SPFX Technician		Nick Karas		6	Promo. Spectators Busses	Rdy@7:30 AM	At Los Alamitos Parking
X	Add'l SPFX Technicians		(Per Richardson)					
X	SPFX Technicians @ Shop	(Per Dept.)	(Per Richardson)		NO.	LOCATIONS (3600)	CALL	NAME
NO.	SET DRESSING (2700)	CALL	NAME		1	Locations Manager	O/C	Bill Bowling
1	Set Decorator	O/C	Robert Gould		1	Locations Manager		Patrick Mignano
1	Leadman	(Per Gould)	Scott Bobbitt		1	Ass't Locations Manager	↓	James Lin
1	On Set Dresser	7:00 AM	Mara Massey					
NO.	PROPERTY (2800)	CALL	NAME		X	Security Guards	(Per Loc'ns)	
1	Prop Master	7:00 AM	Bill Petrotta		X	Fire Safety Officer	↓	
1	Assistant Prop Master		Jennifer Dawson					
1	Properties Person	↓	Mike Gannon		1	Set Medic	6:00 AM	Brian "Doc" Maynard
					NO.	CATERING	COUNT	NAME
1	Weapons Coordinator	O/C	Rock Galotti		X	Crew Breakfasts	Rdy @ 6:00 AM	Michelson's Catering
NO.	WARDROBE (2900/3000)	CALL	NAME		X	Extms Breakfast Buffet		
1	Costume Supervisor	O/C	Nick Scarano		20	Drivers Lunches	Rdy @ 12:30 PM	
1	Key Costumer	(Per Scarano)	Anthony Scarano		155	Crew Lunches	Rdy @ 1:00 PM	
1	Key Costumer		Carolyn Dessert		245	Extras Lunches		
1	Specialty Costumer		Laura Baker		300	Promo. Spectators Lunches	↓	
X	Set Costumers (Extras)	6:30 AM	(Per Scarano)		720	Total Meals		
1	Set Costumer (Principals)	6:42 AM	Brian Callahan		X	Additional Seating for 1st & 2nd Units Combined, As Required		
1	Set Costumer (Principals)	6:12 AM	Lisa Buchignani					
NO.	MAKEUP & HAIR (3100)	CALL	NAME		NO.	VISUAL FX (4400)	CALL	NAME
1	Key Makeup Artist	6:12 AM	John Blake		1	VFX Producer	O/C	Laura Buff
1	Makeup Artist	6:12 AM	Bill Myer					
4	Makeup Artists (Extras)	6:30 AM	(Per Blake)					
1	Key Hairstylist	6:12 AM	Jan Alexander					
1	Hairstylist	6:12 AM	Mary Hart					
1	Hairstylist (Extras)	6:30 AM	Caroline Elias					
5	Hairstylists (Extras)		(Per Alexander)					
NO.	YAGHER FX M/U (3100)	CALL	NAME					

ADDITIONAL INSTRUCTIONS & INFORMATION

Safety Hotline:		Daylight:	12:35 Hours	Closest Hospital:	Beach Community Hospital
Security (Emergency)		Dawn:	6:07 AM		
Safety Office		Sunrise:	6:32 AM 83° Azm.		
Hospital:		Transit:	12:50 PM 61° Alt.		
		Sunset:	7:07 PM 276 Azm.		
		Dusk:	7:32 PM		

B   Production Manager: Robert Latham Brown   Assistant Director: Gregg Goldstone

CREW CALL:	7:00 AM	*STARSHIP TROOPERS*

Shooting Call:	8:30 AM

Big Bug Pictures, Inc.

Director:	Paul Verhoeven	Sunrise/Sunset:	6:32AM - 7:07PM	DATE:	Tuesday, 9/10/96
Producers:	Jon Davison/Alan Marshall	Weather:	Morning Cloud Cover	SHOOTING DAY:	94 of 112
Writer:	Ed Neumeier		Afternoon Clear and Warm	Production Office:	
			Temperature: 65 - 95	Production FAX:	

All Departments: There Will Be A Daily Safety Meeting Before Work Begins

SET	SCENES	CAST	D or N	PAGES	LOCATION
To Begin:					Pyramid Arena
INT. EDUCATION CENTER - ATHLETIC FIELD & STANDS	15 - 25	1,2,3,9,53,	DAY 2	1 3/8	CSU - Long Beach
• The big game. Johnny triumphs over Zander and leaves with	(Parts)	(Stunts),			Memam Way,
Carmen.)		(272 BG),			Near Atherton and Fanwood
		(300 Promo)			Thomas Guide Page 796 D-5
					(Miles R/T tr/ Sorry: 56)
					Crew Parking:
					Pyramid Parking Structure
		TOTAL PAGES:		1 3/8	(See Attached Map)

	CAST	ROLE	CALL	MAKEUP	SET CALL	REMARKS
1	CASPER VAN DIEN	JOHNNY RICO	7:00 AM	7:00 AM	8:30 AM	
2	DENISE RICHARDS	CARMEN IBANEZ	6:30 AM	6:30 AM	8:30 AM	
3	DINA MEYER	DIZZY FLORES	6:30 AM	6:30 AM	8:30 AM	
4	JAKE BUSEY	ACE LEVY		(HOLD)		

FIGURE 13.1—CONT'D

delirium. Then, as soon as he got on the set, all that would instantly disappear and he'd be fine. And you'll be fine, too. All the preparation you've done during the preproduction phase should give you confidence that you have all the tools and resources at hand that will allow you to exercise maximum creativity when you're actually shooting. Lack of preparation will mean you'll waste time, money, and mental energy on the set solving practical problems instead of being free to concentrate on making great art (or at least good entertainment). It's all up to you.

PART 2
Realities: Production

CHAPTER 14

On Time and Ready to Shoot

Finally, after all the weeks of preparation, we are actually going to show up on the set and shoot something. Every set follows a common routine. There are, of course, individual variations on exactly how things are run. But the key thing to keep in mind is that the way you and your crew—and everyone else working on the set—conduct themselves will have just as much impact on the quality of your cinematography as all that planning you did during preproduction. The guiding principle should be that the more artistic and creative freedom you want for the work, the greater the corresponding level of discipline and order you need. If some of this seems militaristic, it is. Well, let's say it requires military discipline. But it is also absolutely necessary. There is zero tolerance for chaos on a film set. So let's consider some of the unwritten laws of set behavior.

GET THERE EARLY

This is the First Commandment. You are *never* late. Traffic? Allow for it. Don't know how to get there? Get a GPS, go to MapQuest, or Google the location. Figure out how long it will take to get there—and double it! You don't have a car? Make arrangements to carpool, or use public transportation. And allow 15 to 30 minutes for the inevitable "unforeseen" problems. The Academy Award–winning actress Nina Foch, who taught me at the AFI, gave me this mantra: "Early is on time; on time is late; late is unforgivable." Cos Cosentino, a great AD, impressed me with his observation that "no one has ever been criticized for being early."

EAT ON YOUR OWN TIME

Let's hope your producers have some snacks or breakfast on the set. This is usually called Craft Service, from the name of the union (Crafts Services) that used to shovel up the horse leavings in the silent movie days and is now responsible for snacks. Most shows will at least have coffee. Allow plenty of time to chow down. Even if you just want coffee, give yourself extra time. On one show a novice assistant was still drinking coffee when he was supposed to be getting the camera prepped. When asked with mocking solicitousness, "Oh, don't you have enough time to drink your coffee?" he naively explained, "It's not the time, it's the temperature." Suffice it to say that he soon found himself with plenty of time to wait for his coffee to cool. Bottom line: If you don't have time to get yourself some breakfast, that's too bad. I'm sorry if that sounds harsh, but that's the reality. It's your responsibility to take care of your needs before it's time to be working.

CALL TIME IS NOT WHEN YOU SHOW UP

You will get your call time from looking at the call sheet given to you the night before. The call sheet is the final word; follow it like it's your bible, unless you get a phone call from the AD changing your call time. Let's get something straight about call: Call is not when *you* arrive at work. Call time is the time you're supposed to have your tool belt on (maybe metaphorically) and be ready to work. You'll notice two call times on the call sheet—one next to your name and one at the top of the first page that says "set call" or "shoot call." Shoot call is the time that the entire cast and crew is expected to be on the set ready to rehearse and shoot. Your personal call will be earlier. It's like the following schedule. (Notice that the camera assistant has a different call than most of the rest of the crew. More about that in a moment.)

Stupid o'clock:	ADs and teamsters are already there
6:00–6:30	Camera assistants arrive
6:30–7:00	DP and rest of crew arrive
6:42 (6.7 military)	Camera assistants' call time
7:00	Crew call time
7:30	Shoot call time

Every department has some sort of tools; even makeup has to check the powder, creams, sponges, and powder puffs. Camera has a lot of tools. The assistant has to build the camera—make sure it's working; warm it up if it's a film camera; mount the lens; attach the accessories; load the film, tape, or cards—and get the camera out to the set to the spot where you'll be shooting.

So because the camera assistant needs extra time to prep the camera, he or she is always given an 18-minute early call (earlier than most of the crew) to build and service the camera. You might be wondering, why 18 minutes? And why should the assistant get an earlier call? Well, it goes back to the early days of the union and to when every camera department had a time clock, and you had to punch in—early, that is, before your call time.

The 18-minute early call is a union rule, and even nonunion shows have adopted something like it. The notion of giving the assistant a slightly early call comes from the days when the assistant would pick up the camera at the camera department at the studio. The camera would have been serviced by the machinist, a regular employee of the camera department; the magazines would have been loaded and the batteries charged by loaders in the loading room; and all the equipment would have been loaded onto some kind of cart (we used to call them lungs, because they reminded us of iron lungs; look it up). The assistant dragged the cart (or, if he got lucky, had a little tractor drag it) to the stage. He had to be on the stage by call, so he got a few minutes extra to drag the lung all the way from the camera department to the stage. Sometimes it was 20 feet to the stage, sometimes a quarter of a mile. That few minutes' official early call could put the assistant into meal penalty (everyone else breaks for lunch after six hours; the assistant at six hours and 18 minutes, so he's 18 minutes into penalty) and that meant a few extra bucks a week back when it mattered. It's 18 minutes and not 15 or 20 because at some point the union got a deal that fractions of an hour worked would be in military time, which is divided into tenths of an hour, or six minutes per tenth. Therefore, the assistant got a three-tenths early call, or 18 minutes. And it's still the rule. Some things never change.

As opposed to the camera assistant, the camera operator has very little to prepare, and the standard joke on the set is you'll know when the operator has arrived by the sound of his Porsche's brakes screeching into a parking space just as the AD yells, "Rolling," for the first shot. By the time the slate's in frame, the operator is sliding onto the dolly seat, turning on the camera, and asking the assistant, "What's the shot?" That's an exaggeration, of course, but not by much.

QUIET ON THE SET

Movie sets are noisy places. There's always a lot of work to be done, and much of it necessarily involves noisy equipment and people giving verbal directions. So the less you talk unnecessarily, the better. If you want to chat with friends, take it away from the work area. If you must remain in the work area, curb your need to chatter.

And don't think you can get away with spending much time off the set. If you're on the grip, electric, camera, or sound crew, you must be on set all the time. Others who must stay are the script supervisor, the first AD, and usually one PA (so the AD has someone to go running for people and things).

KNOW YOUR PLACE

Basically, you could say that although the producer and director are the ultimate bosses of the film, the first assistant director and the director of photography work in tandem to run the set. And while you're on the set, you must pay attention to your supervisors. This involves keeping them in sight at all times—no matter how physically difficult that may be—and tuning your ears to recognize their voices. And respond instantly.

When you're given a direction, feed it back:

> **First Assistant:** Judy, get me the two-inch lens.
> **Second Assistant:** 50 mm coming in.
> **First Assistant to DP:** 50 mm on, boss.

When you complete a task, it's not always necessary to inform the DP, but it's often a good idea, especially if you (gaffer and electrical crew) are carrying out the DP's orders to change the arrangement or setting of lighting instruments. It is not always obvious to a DP that a requested change has been completed. There are a lot of instruments, they're probably up high, and it takes a few minutes to make an adjustment, so it's not on the gaffer's or the DP's mind. By having the lighting crew report the completion of a requested change, the DP will know the adjustment has been made and he or she can now check to make sure the change works.

FIGURE 14.1
Sample chart of the chain of command on a movie set.

It's tough to chart the chain of command on a movie set, but this diagram will give you some idea of what it looks like.

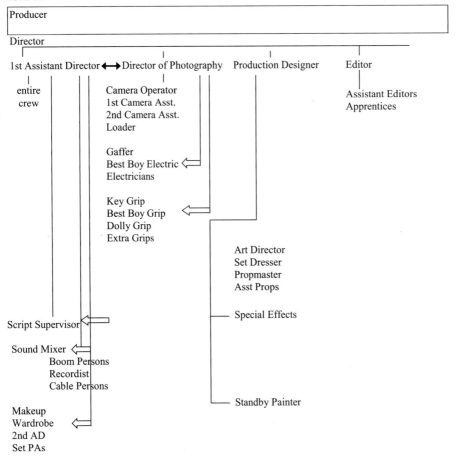

"DUMMY UP"

I once worked with a veteran assistant whose main advice to me was "Punch in, be on time, and dummy up." As oppressive and undemocratic as that sounds, he did have a point. Your freedom to express yourself on the set is determined by your place in the hierarchy. As a DP you'll be fairly free to express yourself, though always with deference to the producer and director and possibly the star(s). The operator defers to the DP and everyone the DP defers to. The second assistant defers to the first AC, who in turn defers to the operator and DP, and so on. The chart gives you a good idea of who defers to whom. The grips, electricians, and even the prop people defer to the DP and to the heads of their own department.

Anyone above you in the hierarchy can give you orders at any time, but you will usually only get them from your immediate superior. And if you have questions or suggestions, voice them only to your immediate superior. That means, as a second assistant, talk to the first assistant, not the operator. Oh sure, you're buddies with the operator, but your job is to keep the first happy and do what the first expects you to do. He or she is more experienced than you are and theoretically understands the situation on the set better than you do. The first is likely to be more politically savvy and can judge whether it's worth taking what you have to say up the ladder, often saving your butt by keeping you from committing some unpardonable set taboo. Work hard, and one day you'll be at the top of the ladder.

In the meantime, for those at the bottom of the ladder, the set is not the place for suggestions, bright ideas, or arguments. If the show is at all well run, all issues involving opinions will have been worked out in prep. If you didn't get the chance to put in your two cents' worth then, probably no one wants to hear from you. And if the production is poorly organized, and things are being conferenced on the set, then everything is going to hell anyhow, and you don't want to be part of it.

This is important: *The set is no place for thinking.* Of course, you have to be thinking and alert to do your job, but if you didn't get everything taken care of as part of your prep, you will be perpetually behind the eight ball. Occasionally some improvisation will be called for, but if you can help it, make it the rare exception. Production time is too scarce and too expensive to waste on work that should have been done earlier.

BEHAVE YOURSELF

Back in the 1920s, someone said, "Motion pictures are made by ladies and gentlemen." We all know that there's no literal truth to this, but the concept can be helpful to you. Think about it. You're thrown together with 20 to 100 people you don't know, many of whom you wouldn't choose to socialize with, and now you have to spend 12 hours of every day with them, working hard on this one-of-a-kind project, with people giving you orders and you giving other people orders, and never enough time and never enough money, and sometimes people not in the best mood because they had an argument with their husband or their wife or their teenage kids, or their car isn't working right. Do you think this is fertile ground for angry outbursts and fistfights? Don't laugh, it happens.

Anyway, you don't want to be part of any improper emotion, or even be a witness to it. So use some social lubrication. Say "please" some of the time, and say "thank you" a lot. Maybe instead of "Get me the friggin' hammer," you could say, "Could you please get me a hammer?" And go easy with the cursing. Yes, everyone has become immune to the words, but hearing them all day can make an unpleasant buzz in your ears. If you are someone's assistant, and he or she is working hard and nonstop, and you have a minute free, make sure you know how that person likes his or her coffee, and go get a cup. Or water, or soda, whatever you know he or she likes. It's just friendly, not subservient. Don't ask the person—no one needs to be bothered that way—just get it. Even if the person doesn't want it (although 90% of the time it is welcome), he or she will think better of you, and be a little happier on the set.

Of course, you could just apply all the lessons Mother taught you:

- Don't talk with your mouth full.
- Always say please and thank you.
- Take a shower every day.
- Dress nicely.
- Be polite.
- Always be on time.
- Do unto others as you would have them do unto you.
- Don't cross the street without first looking both ways.

Do these things, and it will keep the set happy and productive.

CHAPTER 15
First Day/First Shot

Now that we're all on our good behavior, let's start looking at the work that goes into making a shot. As DP you've arrived on the set early. You've gotten coffee. You've found the catering truck and the honey wagon (where you go after visiting catering). You've said hello to your crew and to some folks in the other departments. You check in with the AD and make sure he knows you're there. If any horror has developed overnight, he'll be the one to tell you.

You'll wander over to camera; if you have an idea for the first shot, you'll suggest a lens to the assistant. Usually the assistant will have put up whatever your "standard" lens is. (Every show has a lens you use most often to shoot the masters.) It's probably a 25 mm, but it might be a 32 mm or a 35 mm. If it's a TV show, he'll put up a zoom, usually a 5 to 1 (20 mm–100 mm). By the time the camera is cleaned, oiled, and assembled, the dolly grip will have rolled the dolly, ready to mount the camera, over to the camera truck or next to the camera room on stage. The second assistant will have put on the head, and the first will have put the camera on it and plugged it into the battery, and the dolly with the camera on it will be wheeled to the set. If you're out in the desert or on some other rough terrain, the first assistant might put the camera on sticks and carry it on his shoulder—sticks, head, and all—to the spot where you'll be shooting. After the first day, it is likely that the DP and the director will have discussed the first shot for the following day at the end of the previous day's shooting. That way the DP is able to tell the assistant exactly where the camera needs to be placed first thing the next morning.

So the camera is now on the set. The AD (assistant director) yells, "We're in!" for the crew to get working and "Quietly!" to ensure that the director and DP can hear each other talk. By and large the AD runs the set—at least in terms of logistics. The idea is to relieve the director of practical concerns so he or she is able to focus attention on the creative aspects of the work. At this point the AD is everyone's boss. The precise order of the next few events may vary (the director may want to clear the set—that is, have the crew move away—to do some private rehearsals with actors). The AD will let all involved know where they're supposed to be—and where they're not.

Now, as DP, you'll be working with the director to determine the first setup. If you've planned well, you should have a very good idea of what you intend to do. As the director blocks the scene with the actors, the DP and the director will move about, sometimes using a director's finder, looking at the rehearsal and deciding on the best camera position for the master. The actors continue to rehearse, accommodating to the set. If allowed, the crew watches, anticipating their role in executing the shot. The director and DP might also discuss the other shots that are on the shot list and may set tentative positions for those shots. It is also possible that the director will suddenly decide to completely disregard the shot list, coming up with entirely new ideas now that you're on the actual set. The reality is probably somewhere in between.

Meanwhile, the camera crew will be hovering nearby, picking up on what the first setup will be. The key grip and gaffer will stand by for hints about lighting. Once the blocking is set, the second camera assistant will "put down marks." Marks are pieces of tape put on the floor in a "T" shape at the actors' feet to assist them in finding the places they are supposed to stop and stand during the scene. The standard mark is a T, the crosspiece between the actors' toes with the upright pointing back toward the actors.

And there are other situations. I have worked with directors who would walk on the set in the morning, tell the second to lay marks, and proceed to run the scene by themselves, setting places for every actor before the actors ever appeared. The first time I saw this, I was shocked. I have always considered the actors' blocking to be a vital creative tool for both the director and the actors. To see actors being arbitrarily assigned places to walk and stop seemed an artistic crime. And yet it worked perfectly well. This was not a heavily artistic show with actors who took themselves too seriously. It was a programmer, and the actors were able to accommodate to preset blocking as the crew is usually able to accommodate to the actors' choices.

The marks serve as a memory aid to the actors, the stand-ins, and the first assistant, who does the focusing. Stand-ins are surrogates for the actors who perform during the technical preparations and rehearsals. They are able to duplicate all the movements and much of the dialogue of the principal actors. (And good stand-ins, who look like the actors and remember all the nuances of the actors' moves, are a treasure.) This way while the stars are off in makeup, wardrobe, hair, and rehearsal, there are flesh-and-blood models for the DP to light and to practice camera moves with. Often the principal actors will have been called to the set just as they've arrived and will not have had time to get made up or costumed. So they are off doing that while the lighting is getting set up, or they may also use that time to run lines, rehearse, or discuss the scene with the director. As soon as the actors leave, the AD will ask the DP how long lighting will take.

Uh oh. How long *will* it take? How do you know? Well—you guess. After you've lit a certain kind of set several times, and after you've worked a few shows with the same crew, you can give pretty good estimates. The first time is one more example of the sheer terror that filmmaking, like battle, provides you with. If you've actually never lit a set, you're probably with a lot of people who are also first-timers, so do your best, and after a day or two you'll be able to give a useful time estimate. Usually a DP will have worked as a crew member before he has a chance to shoot; that's a good time to watch other DPs and see how long they take to light a scene. Figure you're going to be slower, and add 30% or so more time. The AD will be looking at his watch all the time. A good AD will let the DP know when half the estimated time has elapsed; he may then ask for a new estimate. And a good AD will be letting the DP know when he's got ten minutes, or five (by the DP's own estimate), or when the director is about to say, "Shoot, no matter what it looks like."

The DP lights the set, working together with the gaffer and the key grip. Of course, this involves the entire electrical and grip department. Lighting is always the part of making a movie that takes a lot of time and gets everyone not directly involved feeling impatient. Everyone working on the show, especially the director, is frustrated by how much time it takes to light. The few times I've directed, I was no different from any other director—my first thought after rehearsing the actors was "Why is the lighting taking so long?"

No matter how well you've planned, there just never seems to be enough time for lighting. Learning how to be effective in a limited amount of time will put you in great demand as a DP. Chapters 21 through 24 discuss lighting in more detail.

Meanwhile, every other department is preparing for the shot. Every department has something to do. Hair, makeup, and wardrobe are busy making the actors look pretty and, seriously, making sure their looks will match from shot to shot. Props is making sure that the set is dressed properly and will match the other scenes shot on the same set. Sound is finding hidden places for microphones and booms and making sure their placement does not cause the lights to throw weird shadows onto the actors or the sets. And, of course, the camera operator is looking through the viewfinder, making sure no lights or C-stands will be in the shot. The first camera assistant is measuring the distances from the camera to the actors (probably to the stand-ins at this point) for focus. The grip crew is building track to allow for dolly moves and doing dry-run rehearsals using the stand-ins to duplicate where the actors will be at various points in the scene. All these tasks will be illuminated in chapters to come.

A word about stand-ins: A good stand-in is a precious resource, far more than the "warm body" the title "stand-in" implies. They're usually professional extras who have come to specialize in this job. Some have formed a special relationship with a particular actor, and that actor will always request that that particular stand-in be hired. I have worked with stand-ins who could tell you on exactly what line or cue the actors they are standing in for will move, how fast they will move, how they will stand (or lean or slump), what kind of idiosyncrasies they have (like always being a foot off their marks), and when you'll need to look out for those idiosyncrasies. Some of the best stand-ins I've ever worked with were on the film version of *Noises Off* (the hit Broadway play). The producers had the actually smart idea of hiring a Burbank theater company that had just completed a run of the show. These actors could play out any scene, while the "first team" was off getting ready to shoot. Of course, they knew all the dialogue and all the complicated running around. (*Noises Off* is one of those door-slamming farces.) Imagine the difficulty of lighting and rehearsing the scene for camera moves if the stand-ins weren't able to reproduce exactly what the principal actors would do when they came on the set to shoot the scene. Without stand-ins the actors would have to be on the set for these preparations, and that would take away from their rehearsal time, delay makeup, hair, and wardrobe, and cause them to use up valuable energy that is better used in their on-screen performance.

Also working with the stand-ins, the DP is determining the precise location of the camera. Although the director almost always specifies a rough placement for the camera, most directors are not sensitive to the details the DP has to consider—nor should they be. So the DP (and/or the operator) looks at the intended shot to see if the actors will block one another (we call it stacking), if a set piece is obtrusive or will appear to be growing out of the actor's head, what height the camera needs to be to see the action but not see beyond the edges of the set, what exact lens should be used, and on and on.

When all this work is completed, the DP informs the AD that the camera is ready to shoot. Well, to be honest about it, the AD has been right on hand all the time, breathing down the DP's neck and hustling the crew along. So, as often as not, the AD is telling the DP when the work is done: It's done when the AD says it's time to shoot.

Now we're approaching the moment of magic. Let's hope you're happy with the lighting (or you've just had to say "Good enough"). The AD calls the actors to the set for shooting. Of course, a good AD will have been checking on the actors to make sure they will be finished with their preparations and will be ready to come to the set the moment lighting and camera rehearsals are completed. The AD has also been keeping the director up to date on the progress of the work, while the director is running lines with the actors or planning his next shot (or talking to his stockbroker).

Finally, everything is ready and the actors are brought to the set. The director will have the actors do one or two rehearsals, ostensibly just for them. But while the actors are rehearsing, every department is refining its work and making sure there are no unforeseen traps lurking. Maybe one actor blocks another; maybe an actor speaks too quietly. Each problem must be dealt with. The crew is supposed to know what to do to make the shot work and to do it quickly and quietly. I think of shooting as involving at least four performers besides the actors: the camera operator, camera assistant, dolly grip, and boom operator. I might also include the sound mixer. Each of them must move in complete sync with the actor. Whatever the actor does, whatever unexpected changes, these crew members accommodate with second-to-second adjustments. Often you'll see the boom operator have to go to an unplanned position in order to catch an actor's line and in the process do a little dance to avoid standing where a light might throw a boom shadow into the frame. It's a beautiful thing to see these professionals perform the exquisite ballet that allows the shot to be made and without calling any special attention to themselves.

I have worked with dolly grips who see when one actor is blocking another and move the dolly imperceptibly an inch or two to one side or the other to keep the actor clear and save the shot. They do this without looking through the viewfinder or seeing a video feed. Through lots of experience they've come to be able to recognize problems just by observing the position of the actors relative to the camera angle.

Of course, the camera assistant has to do the impossible: focus without being able to see the image. Everyone is shocked when they first find out that the person focusing doesn't look through the viewfinder. There is only one viewfinder, and the operator is looking through it to compose the shot and execute the moves. Although the assistant has laid marks and carefully measured their distances from the camera, instantaneous adjustments of the distance setting must be made every time an actor fails to hit the mark (which is a pretty frequent occurrence). And the assistant must also mentally calculate depth of field to ensure that the key elements in the shot will stay in focus. And if that isn't enough, the assistant is simultaneously floating a zoom, keeping its moves invisible while changing focal lengths.

Meanwhile, the camera operator is adjusting the frame to avoid cutting off an actor who has missed his mark, or is leaning in a way that throws off the composition of the shot, or suddenly jumps up out of his seat, or performs any number of unplanned moves in the middle of a take. All these adjustments are made on the fly and completely imperceptibly. The operator, and the rest of the crew, is expected to be able to accommodate these unplanned occurrences. It's part of the job. The actors have to be free to express themselves and can't be expected to limit themselves for the sake of the crew.

When the director feels the actors are ready, the AD calls, "Picture up." Of course, the entire crew has to be ready, too, but it's the director's prerogative to say, "We're going to shoot *now*." A director may ask if anyone needs another rehearsal, but believe me, you don't want to be the one to say you need one. "Ready to go" is the only answer you want to give. Some directors may actually be concerned that the crew has had adequate rehearsal, but beware, others just want to look as though they've considered the crew's needs—or, more sinisterly, want to be able to divert blame from themselves when something goes horribly wrong by pointing out that they offered the chance for further rehearsal. This may sound a little paranoid, but believe me, these things really do happen. If you know and trust the director, you may want to ask for another rehearsal. It always saves money and time in the long run. But too often the director has to be concerned with giving the appearance of working fast to a producer who might be applying pressure because of lack of money. So be discreet. If you're positive everything is going to be ruined without another rehearsal, see if you can get one. If you can't, just do your best and pray that if you screw up the take, one of the actors blows a line on the same take, and you get another chance to make the shot. If no one else screws up, you'll be stuck having to ask for another take. You don't want to have to do that. So just be perfect.

So it's time to make the first shot of the first day. The AD may call out, "Who's not ready?" (which is better than "Is everyone ready?," to which no one ever answers). Don't be not ready. The response of makeup and hair might be to suddenly rush toward the actors to make last-minute touchups. To anyone not in the business, and to a lot of us who are, this seems ridiculous. Didn't these folks just spend two hours making our actors beautiful? Why do they have to run in and do something else now? Sometimes I wonder if doing that is just a way for those departments to make sure they get noticed. They're dependent on the goodwill of the actors, and want to show them how attentive they are. But then I remember that makeup and hair are responsible for making the actors look good and for maintaining continuity (they have to make sure that the actors always look the same, from take to take within a scene and from scene to scene within the movie). It is unforgivable for an actress go from perfectly coiffed to windblown to coiffed in three shots, all interiors and all in a time span of seconds, which actually happened in a film I shot.

Finally, the AD calls, "Roll 'em." (It's always the AD's responsibility and privilege to initiate the actual photography.) The sound mixer turns on the recorder and calls "speed" when it locks in to sync. Sound always rolls first, a throwback from the 1950s and before when the sound department actually turned on the camera, through a synchronizing arrangement that relied on large electrically synced motors. These days it may save film to wait for sound to roll first, especially if the director runs in for a last-minute note. Saving film is not an issue with digital cameras, but no one, especially the editor, wants a lot of unusable picture to look at before the scene actually begins.

"Speed" is the signal for the camera operator to turn on the camera. Sometimes the assistant will turn on the camera. Personally I don't like that; I think only the operator, who is the one person who can see what is actually being filmed, should turn the camera on or off. Anyway, the camera is now running.

Now the second camera assistant holds the slate up in front of the camera, calls "Mark," and bangs the sticks. On a really, really, really low-budget film, the second might voice an audible slate (calling, "Scene 3, take 2") just before hitting the sticks. (I know we've all seen that in movies that show a film being shot, but it's not what really happens.) If done this way, the operator will turn on the camera right after the audible slate but before the sticks are banged. (The idea is to save money on film stock or at least not to turn on the camera until everything is definitely ready. That way no film is wasted waiting for someone. Realistically, you save so little film this way that it's pointless, even if your movie is so low-budget that film cost is a serious matter. But it looks good to some producers.) Normal procedure is to have the sound mixer, using a mixing panel with an announce microphone on it, do the verbal slate. The assistant will only call "Mark" and hit the sticks.

The director calls "Action"—and only the director. The actors act; the first camera assistant focuses and zooms; the operator frames the picture, pans, and tilts; the dolly grip maneuvers the dolly; the boom operator swings the boom; and the mixer records the sound—all in perfect synchronization.

When they're finished, the director calls, "Cut." Once again, *only* the director does that. Sometimes, if they're sure of the situation, the camera operator might call "Cut" (say, the prop person inadvertently walks into the frame), or the sound mixer might (if jets flying overhead are completely drowning out the dialogue). But you want to be very, very careful about doing that. The director may only intend to use parts of a take, so the part the prop person is in may not be a problem. The director may love the acting in the important parts of the shot and not want to cut off the performance due to a technical concern. Conversely, the director may love the visual performance of an actor and be willing to fix it in postproduction by replacing it with good sound from another take or with ADR (automated dialogue replacement). So the sound mixer would not have wanted to stop the shooting. It is best to just leave it to the director.

The AD repeats "Cut" in a loud voice. Unfortunately, there has been a tendency of late for the many second ADs, listening on their radios (what civilians call walkie-talkies), all to repeat, "That's a cut" in the loudest, most annoying voices possible. Someday they will reap their just rewards, and it won't be pretty.

Now, everyone prepares for the next take. Even if you think you know without a shadow of a doubt in your heart of hearts and with complete certainty that there won't be another take, be ready for another take. You don't want to be the one who holds up shooting because you're unprepared when the decision is unexpectedly made to do another take.

If the director is satisfied with a take, the director calls, "Cut! Print!" (This is so exciting. One shot down, a million to go.) Right after completing a print take (unusable takes are not printed), the first camera assistant checks the film gate in the camera. If there's a hair in the gate, the shot will have to be redone. Don't let this happen. Everyone will hate you.

Another relatively recent development, but one I find exceedingly annoying, is the tendency for the AD to yell, "Check the gate!" when there's a print take. Checking the gate is the first assistant's job; he opens the camera, takes the film out of the gate, removes the gate, and inspects it for "hairs"—small buildups of scraped-off emulsion that will look like hair when projected. It has always been the procedure to check the gate for each print take. The assistant routinely does this quickly, quietly, and unobtrusively. For most pros, it was always a matter of seconds. I find it very insulting to have the AD act as if the camera department has to be told to do it. Making the AD call for checking the gate is unnecessary. Besides the insult to the assistant's tender ego, it provides unwanted noise and disruption on what should be a quiet, competent set.

Of course, with digital equipment there is no gate, so this issue becomes irrelevant. Sometimes the assistant will check the last take to make sure there were no electronic glitches. He'll rewind the tape and play it or simply click over to the card, go to the last clip, and play it.

Now, if all has gone well and the director doesn't want any more takes for this shot, the AD hollers, "That's a print! New deal" (or something to that effect). In any event, it means we're going on to whatever is the next shot the director wants to do. It might be coverage of the scene you've just shot. It might be a pickup within the scene (in those two cases, it's not really a new deal). Or it's moving on to another scene, or perhaps another set. Sometimes the AD will say, "FDR!," which is universally known to mean "New Deal." Or "We're on the wrong set," clearly meaning we're moving to the next set on the call sheet. Or maybe just, "Moving on." One way or another, everyone will know what is going to be happening next.

So we've now completed the first shot of the day. Now take everything you've just done to create one shot, and repeat it over and over again a thousand times for every additional shot in the film. Pretty easy, huh? Of course, this chapter only describes the process of shooting in the most simplistic terms. In the following chapters we'll explore in more detail how each step of the process is accomplished; how the DP lights and composes the shots; how each member of the camera, grip, and electrical crew performs his or her individual job; and how they all function together as a team. Let's get started.

CHAPTER 16
Shooting Masters

So now you have a generalized idea of the procedure on the set for making a shot. But the big question now is, how do you actually design and choreograph shots, and how is your plan executed? Let's do a "Groundhog Day" and relive that first shot of the first day of shooting.

It's pretty likely that you've decided to shoot the "master" first. Remember that in simplest terms this is the shot that pretty much covers the entire action of a scene. Don't worry—we'll talk about exceptions very soon. The master is invariably the first shot made; no one starts off shooting a scene with a close-up or an insert. There are many reasons for this, but a primary one is that you want to know how the whole set will be used and what all the action of the scene will be so you can match the movement and lighting when you move in for closer shots. Reverse the process and you'll have a big mess on your hands with no reference point for how to shoot.

So here you are on the set with the director watching the actors rehearse. You've spent days or even weeks planning shots for the movie with the director. That's nice, but have you really pinned down exactly what this master shot will be? Maybe not.

Let's say you'd planned to set up the camera left-of-center on the set and envisioned a relatively wide shot that would show the complete set and all of the actors in the scene. No problem, except now that you're actually there, you realize that the 25 mm lens you wanted to use isn't going to work. Or any other lens, for that matter; the blocking now makes the actors look as though they're crowded into the right-hand side of the frame. And besides, one of the minor characters is blocking the star. Meanwhile, the entire crew is standing there waiting for you to give the go ahead so they can get to work on the shot. Whatever you do, don't panic. As you walked around during the rehearsals, you will have considered any number of camera positions and gotten an impression of how to get the most effective shots now that you are seeing the actual blocking of the scene. If your brain hasn't been bubbling with ideas by now, you might want to consider another profession. Ultimately, of course, the director makes the final decision, but if he has any regard for why he hired you in the first place, you will have a great deal to say about what to do.

What is the master, and what do we expect from it? Often the master is defined as a wide shot of the whole set, lasting through the full length of the scene. ("High, wide, and stupid," as one of my associates often says.) Or it is more narrowly thought of as a shot that covers a portion of a scene, maybe not the whole length, but definitely in wide shot. Another way to look at it is that the master is the shot that defines what must be matched in the other shots, the "coverage" of the scene—matching for screen direction, for actors' positions, for use of props, lighting, on and on. That's why it's referred to as the "master."

Always keep in mind what you're trying to do with the master. *Master* is a flexible term; it can mean something different to different directors. If your director is Orson Welles (*Magnificent Ambersons, The Stranger, Lady From Shanghai, Touch of Evil,* and, of course, *Citizen Kane*), the master might be the only shot for an entire scene. Try to watch the scene in *Citizen Kane* where Mrs. Kane sends little Charley Kane off to school with Mr. Thatcher. First we see Charley playing in the snow outside his mother's boarding house and hear her calling to him from inside. Welles cuts to Mrs. Kane inside, and the rest of the interior scene is shot in one long, uninterrupted, unedited take with the camera following the actors as they move about the room discussing what will happen to young Kane. This is a master that is continuously recomposing, starting from a wide shot of the interior of the boarding house, then morphing into close-ups, two-shots, and small group shots. But it's all one continuous shot, and it's the master by default. Welles uses this approach over and over in most of his films. The opening shot of *Touch of Evil* is still considered one of the great *tours de force* of filmmaking history.

Director Jim Jarmusch in his early films—watch *Stranger Than Paradise* if you haven't yet—has a different take on shooting a scene covered with only an uninterrupted master shot. In *Stranger* each scene is done in one shot, and the shot is a master; it's fairly wide, and it shows the entire set and all the action of the scene. But the camera doesn't move. Yet it works for the comedic irony that is Jim's trademark. Because Jim didn't have much money for film stock, he made a virtue of necessity and let each scene play "in one."

Most directors you work with will not be cinematic geniuses, so you will more likely be shooting a more conventional master and a fair amount of standard "coverage." (By "standard coverage" I mean a master, small master, two-shots, over-the-shoulders, and singles for every part of the scene. It can take a lot of time and a lot of footage.) When there's a strong director with a unique vision, standard coverage is less likely. When a producer is in charge (like a Thalberg at MGM in the 1930s or most TV shows now), coverage is more likely. In the first case, you'll find yourself advising a little more coverage, and in the second case a little less. If full coverage is asked for, you'll want to suggest ways to do it that will take less time. Conversely, if you're asked to shoot the scene entirely in a single setup, you'll be advising some coverage. The director will decide whether he wants the one, perfect shot (like the Wellesian master just described) or extensive coverage so he has all kinds of options when it comes to editing the film. When you have the perfect shot, most directors will not want to break it up with closer shots. ("Break up that shot and you're putting your foot through a Rembrandt.") I have to tell you, even after all my years on the set, I find it awfully hard to tell whether the scene we've just shot will play in one, and most directors will admit that they can't either. Swept up in the theatrical excitement of a great live performance, many directors will think they need no coverage. Later in the editing room they see the shot on the screen, without the excitement of the set, and the scene falls flat. So you can see why you might want to nudge the director a little to get at least some coverage, a couple of close-ups, or some overs. The editor may well find that the perfect shot is perfect, but that it's good only at the beginning of one take and at the end of a second. To use a part of each take, you must have a shot that allows you to bridge from one to the other. Your coverage!

Now there may be some directors you don't want to do that with. On his first day working on a Woody Allen film (Woody's well known for long takes without coverage), a very famous, Academy Award–winning cinematographer suggested to Woody that he shoot some coverage on a scene. "No, I don't think so," said Woody. Fine. The next day, the famous cinematographer suggested the same thing. "No, I don't think so," said Woody again. The next day, there was a new DP. Know your director.

When the director wants to cover every action with numerous shots, you're going to end up with long days, a bored crew, and tired actors. If you can, try to get close-ups before the actors have lost the freshness they first brought to the scene and before they look tired. Most experienced directors realize that not every part of every shot will be needed or used. If there are flubs in a two-shot, they may never be seen because the close-up gets used for those lines. Help the director be aware of these things. You'll cut down on the time spent shooting, and you'll lessen the mass of footage the editors have to deal with. You'll make friends and save money.

Blocking the actors for the master is very important; you want to be sure you're not painting yourself into a corner by allowing blocking of action that will be confusing when the audience sees it on the screen. For example, two people, a man and a woman, are in a room, talking. So far, so good; the man looks left, and the woman looks right. The man walks to the window; he crosses the room, so now he's on the left, and his looks are to the right, and the woman's are to the left. But no one's talking when he crosses, and so we get no coverage of the looks after his move. Later the editor decides to cut to the woman's look to the man. But all we have is her looking right from the talk and from the master; we *can't* go to a close-up of her because the look will be wrong, so we're "forcing the master," making an editing decision that wouldn't be what you would choose. If, however, the master had been from a different angle—set up so the man is always on the woman's right—the editor could have used either shot. Or if we had dollied across the set (going right to left, countering the man's move and thus keeping him on the same side of the line as the woman), the editor could have used either the master or the close-up. Of course, we could just have covered the woman in close-up through the entire scene. Often the director will be resistant to coverage, thinking that the producer will insist on using the coverage in the final cut. And the director doesn't want that. You're there to let the director know that there may be a problem, and you're there to offer a solution, and you're just being a friend. You're not his enemy (taking sides), and you're not trying to take over the picture. And you don't have a stake in what he does except to help him make a good movie. So you're acting as a friend, not a boss, not a parent, not a rival, and not a jerk.

Notice I mentioned solving a problem by using a dolly. A crab dolly is one of the indispensable components of any camera package (yes, the grips take care of it). You may find yourself on a show that can't afford a crab dolly. You may need to shoot mostly from a tripod. That's not bad. The movie business started with static shots, and plenty of great movies were made with little or no camera movement. I've never worked a show that didn't have a dolly, but if you're stuck, then for goodness sake, at least get an inexpensive doorway dolly.

The simplest master would be a static wide shot. Sometimes it works out that way. More often, the dolly is used to adjust the frame as the actors move. We may need to move to uncover an actor as he is blocked by another actor, or we may have to move to keep the composition balanced.

What is more interesting is the designed master. A planned master has a lot in common with Welles's lengthy shots that do the majority of a scene in one take. With this approach, you will not see the whole set or action in a wide shot, or only for part of the time. In our previous example, with the man and the woman, let's say the woman leaves the room and another man walks in and stands at the window with the first man. In that case, we might start on a two-shot of the man and woman, widen and counter as he goes to the window, and push in a little as she walks out, picking up the second man and pushing in further with him to end up in a two-shot at the window with the two men. We've gotten the whole scene in one take, and we've seen a lot of the set; we've seen the set in relation to the characters, so we'll recognize where they are when we see them later only in a closer shot. We have a master that the director could use in one, or she could decide to break it up by coverage: close-ups, two-shots, and so on.

Sometimes the coverage will include a "small master," with the majority of the scene shot fairly close in on the main characters. The director may want minimal coverage, but he doesn't want to see the whole room every time he returns to the master. The audience is oriented to the scene in an initial wide shot, and then, say, after cutting to a close-up, the small master can be used for the rest of the scene or parts of the scene.

You will often find that you need to get a reverse master. In this case, you've got action that happens all over a set or covers 360 degrees, but it's only possible to shoot one side of the set at a time because of the necessity of setting up lighting on the other side. After you've shot the master on the left side of the set, and after you've done coverage there, you'll shoot a master on the right side of the set. You want to make sure you get all the coverage you need on one side before turning around because shooting this way means two entirely separate lighting setups, and believe me you don't want to light the same thing twice. It's a pain for you, and the producer won't like the time and money it takes. Make sure you double check with the director to be absolutely sure you're done with shooting any action on one side before you break up the lighting and start to set up on the other side. Give the director a chance to dream up any extra coverage he needs, and get assurance from the AD that there will be no going back to the other side again. That way when the director has a bright idea about going back to the first lighting setup, the AD can tell him no, and you don't have to be the bad guy. Being the bad guy is the AD's job (regardless of the AD's gender; take my word for it: there are plenty of tough female ADs).

If you're really unlucky, you may run into a director who thinks it's necessary for the actors to be letter perfect for every moment of the master. It's boring and expensive to shoot a master over and over—I've seen 10 or 15 takes—and usually unnecessary. A standard master will rarely be used for more than a few seconds at the beginning, maybe a few seconds somewhere in the middle, and a few seconds at the end of the scene. As I've said, the master establishes geography and screen direction and gives the actors a chance to play out the whole scene. Unless you're shooting a carefully designed Wellesian master or a one-shot-does-it-all Jarmusch take, the master just doesn't need to be perfect. If it does need to run in one, the AD should insist on a lot of rehearsals. And if it seems impossible to do a clean take, maybe it will be necessary to rethink the scene and do it in coverage.

I have seen some directors, using digital cameras, act as though they can shoot a master as many times as they want. The tape or the card is practically free, and you can record 20 or 40 minutes without stopping. And some of them say, "Hey, let's shoot the rehearsal. We could get lucky." Watch out for this. First of all, the crew needs rehearsals as much as the actors. Everyone needs time to find the best way to make a shot and the chance to see the rough points and stumbling blocks. Often after one rehearsal, every department makes small adjustments, and shooting goes smoother because of those changes.

The other problem with falling in love with "Don't cut—keep rolling—back to one and do it again" is that it takes time that you know no one has. Young, inexperienced directors, especially, have a hard time telling when they've gotten the take they want. They keep shooting, hoping lightning will strike. As they take this time, you'll find that you have less time to light and to block, and your work suffers. And believe me, when the producer or the executives want to blame someone for being slow, they always point fingers at the DP. Guess who gets fired?

We've looked at a master shot with a static camera and one shot with a moving camera. I should make it clear that with the camera on a dolly, you can do a tracking shot—you lay track and move in a straight line—or you can move the dolly on a "dance floor," which allows you to change direction anytime you want during the shot. For this the dolly needs to be on an extremely flat, perfectly smooth, absolutely level surface with no bumps. A dance floor might be the stage floor or a smooth floor on location. More often, the grips will build one for the shot; they'll lay down ¾-inch-thick plywood (standard 4- × 8-foot sheets) wherever the dolly has to move. The DP and/or the operator will have worked out all the separate positions and moves with the dolly grip—in essence separate shots—for the scene. The dolly grip marks where the dance floor needs to be constructed. Then the rest of the grip crew comes and lays down the plywood. To make the surface even smoother, they lay smooth-surfaced ¼-inch Masonite over the plywood, slightly offsetting the seams of the plywood and the Masonite, then taping the joins with 2-inch-wide paper tape. Now with a dance floor in place, it is possible to dolly fluidly in any direction and to make invisible adjustments as the actors change position.

Building a dance floor or laying track might sound like a lot of work, and you might be thinking, "Hey, wouldn't a Steadicam® be a great alternative to dollying, laying track, and/or building dance floors?" If you remember, we talked a little about the Steadicam® back in the preproduction section of this book (see Chapter 12). There's no question it's a magnificent tool, but, as I've said before, it's not a substitute for a dolly. Believing that a dolly shot and a Steadicam® shot are interchangeable really does a disservice to both; the movement of each has a distinct feel, a unique purpose, and a specific reason for being used. A dolly shot is solid, and it is either a straight line (on a track), or it's filled with pauses where the camera does not move (dance floor). A Steadicam® shot is more free-form, rarely in a straight line, and almost always moving. And Steadicam® gives the impression of floating, although a good operator will not let the camera weave as though it's on a pendulum.

And don't think planning, rehearsing, and carrying out a good Steadicam® shot is any easier than making a good dolly shot. Consider what goes into making a good Steadicam® shot. If you trust your Steadicam® operator, and you'd better, you'll let the operator design the execution of the shot. The director and the DP have an idea of what they want. Based on that, the Steadicam® operator can determine how to get the shot and what help will be needed from the other members of the crew. The operator must be able to physically negotiate a path through the available space, with workable "stopping" points (not so much stopping as places where the shot changes direction or pauses briefly), no hindrance from props or set decoration that could interfere with the physical movement of the rig, and absence of bogeys from lighting. (Bogeys are any problems—flares, ugly shadows, a piece of the light in the frame.) The DP will be responsible for making sure the lighting works for the entire course of the moving shot. A good operator is specific about what he will see in his shot, but since he's often following or leading an actor, the shot may not be precisely as rehearsed. Since a unique quality of a Steadicam® shot is that it is free-flowing, make sure none of the lighting instruments are placed where they might creep into the operator's shot or anywhere they might end up in his path of movement. For a Steadicam® it is usually best to light from above so you can keep the instruments off the floor, out of the way, and out of the frame.

Contrary to popular opinion, a Steadicam® does not necessarily save time. Some producers and directors will want to use it as a time saver. Know that designing the shot, making sure all the obstacles are out of the way, rehearsals, suiting up, and finally making the shot all take time. It could be faster than making a comparable dolly shot, or it could be slower, or there could be no difference at all. In any case, beware of budgeting less time for doing Steadicam® shots because someone wants to think it's going to save so much time.

Remember that some of the appeal of the Steadicam® is that it can make possible those "Wow! How did they do that?" shots. The first feature film ever to use a Steadicam®, *Bound for Glory* (1976), had an exterior crane shot that, as the camera dropped to ground level, continued on through a door and into the interior of a building. No crane or crane arm could have fit through a doorway and then turned and moved around once inside; it was and still is a great shot that makes the most of the Steadicam's® special capabilities. Steadicam® artist Larry McConkey's marathon shot through the basement of the Latin Casino in *Goodfellas* is certainly one of the most impressive Steadicam® shots ever done. Ray Liotta and Lorraine Bracco enter a back door from the parking lot; they descend some stairs, while we and she are wondering what's going on. We see the kitchen personnel, people racing back and forth, people squeezing past, and finally we ascend and erupt out onto the floor of the Latin Casino, where a table is brought for them stageside. It's a great metaphor for Liotta's rush of Bracco and for the rhythm of continuous, thrusting movement of the film. To make this work, Scorsese and McConkey had to constantly block the actors and the atmosphere, moving and talking, to keep the shot interesting. Remember these examples, and make it a point to work and plan with the director in prep and the operator on set to achieve those shots that will dazzle the audience.

The advent of the Steadicam® also made possible the shot you often see with actors briskly walking or rushing down corridors while earnestly engaged in conversation, the camera just in front or right on their tail. This kind of shot became a distinctive style for two shows in particular: *ER*, when dashing through obstacles in the emergency room, and *West Wing*, when rushing around the White House. It has since become a staple of TV drama. They became signatures of these shows because of the speed (*West Wing*) and the athleticism (*ER*) in their shows. This kind of Steadicam® shot borders on a "substitute for a dolly" that I suggested you should never use. But a dolly probably could not have done most of these shots as they look on the screen. I mention this to you as two brilliant examples of making lemonade out of lemons once the Steadicam® became available. Long dialogue sequences are a mainstay of TV, and they are antithetical to the concept of motion pictures; they're radio. So the creative talent on these shows took one possible boring shot—two people talking—and combined it with another boring shot—two people walking from one place to another—and turned the combination into an engrossing trademark shot.

CHAPTER 17
Close-Ups and Coverage

125

Okay, we've thought out our master shot and talked a little about coverage. Let's suppose for the moment that we've done the master and now we're on to our other shots. Let's start out with faces. All actors will tell you that it's vital to see their eyes. Yes, the eyes are the windows of the soul, blah, blah, blah—but they have a point. (Let's remember that a large proportion of directors have been or are actors, so we'll face this demand throughout our careers.) The camera might not be able to see souls, but it can read minds; if an actor is fully in his part and understands the inner life of his character, the camera will magically pick this up. To do this magic you want to see the actor's face, and especially the eyes, arguably the most expressive part of the face. Now some actors will argue that the set of their mouth or the tilt of their head or the way they hold their shoulders is just as important. But no one ever complains that they can't see an actor's mouth, and you'll get holy hell if you can't see the actor's eyes.

The closer we get to an actor, the greater part of the frame that is taken up by the eyes. And it's better to see both eyes. So avoid profiles or the backs of heads. Sure, you can get a lot of mileage out of profiles, but that's a deviation from the norm; like all deviations and rule-breaking, it's a tool to be used sparingly so it retains a special impact. (Profiles can, for example, indicate a distancing between characters, a moment of introspection, or a deliberate hiding from another character in the scene.)

The rule is "two eyes." Whenever you're shooting a full close-up, always show both of the actor's eyes. A common use of this technique, showing both eyes, is in complementary cutting among actors having a conversation. Always make sure the actor's eyeline—the direction in which he's looking at the other actor in the conversation—is almost right into the lens—but not quite. You will convey the full impact of the actor's personality by showing as much of his face as possible. This is practically a law with close-ups; in wide shots it's more acceptable to shoot the actor in profile or looking off to one side.

When you move into a close-up from your master, you'll need to change the placement of the camera so that the actor is looking closer to a line drawn straight through the camera lens. This change of angle is necessary for editing. Cutting from a master and a close-up that have both been shot from the same camera position will result in a jarring jump as the editor cuts back and forth between the wide shot and the close shot. By changing the camera position or angle on the subject for each shot, you will smooth the transition between the shots.

In shooting close-ups you'll be concerned with "headroom" (the amount of space in the top of the frame above the actor's head) and "nose room" (the amount of space in the frame between the actor's nose and the side of the frame). Nothing looks worse than a lot of empty space above the actor's head or to have his nose up against the edge of the frame. Since the actor is looking off camera a little, the operator must lead the actor—even if only a little—by allowing some space on the side of the frame in the direction of the actor's look.

Let's talk about headroom. It's the operator's responsibility to keep headroom—the room over the character's head—consistent from shot to shot. The proportion of the headroom to the rest of your frame differs from close-up to midshot to wide shot. It looks really stupid if you cut from a close-up of actor 1, whose head is ½ inch below the top frame line, to actor 2, whose head is 2 inches below the top frame line. The inconsistency is ugly and upsets the audience.

How does the operator know exactly how much headroom to leave? That a good question. Many DPs have decided views on how much headroom there should be; others leave it to the operator to decide. In any case, the operator needs to have a clear idea of how much headroom each DP he works for likes, even if he needs to do it by mind reading. One DP might tell the operator to allow "this much" (space), holding a hand at a specific distance directly over his own head. And he'll insist that that's the only right way to do it. And the next DP the operator works for will want it twice as big, and the operator just has to adjust. When the operator has a DP who wants to be the one to determine the headroom, the operator must do exactly what the DP wants. It's difficult when what the DP wants is different from what you would normally do. You will have to pay extra attention to maintaining the desired headroom in every shot until it becomes routine, almost reflexive to you. When I do my own operating, I find that for close-ups I like to have a space over the head equivalent to one or two fingers. I imagine two fingers on edge set on top of the actor's head, the top finger touching the top frame line. When I go to a midshot, I'll double that. And for wide shots or masters, it usually becomes a matter of balancing out the overall composition of the frame.

In dealing with close-ups of two actors looking at each other, it must be framed so that one actor is looking to the right and the other is looking to the left. Thus it appears that they are looking toward one another. Remember we'll know the orientation of these shots from how the actors were positioned in the master. Otherwise they will look as though they're looking not at each other but off to some object out of the frame. Here's where we come up against the 180-degree

FIGURE 17.1
Examples of headroom.
*Reproduced with
permission of GVSU
Summer Film Project.*

rule, or what is referred to as "crossing the line." We'll be dealing with this in detail very soon, but for now it's enough to stress that once an actor is moving or looking in the one direction, he must be kept looking and moving in the same direction. No greater source of disagreement and wasted time occurs on sets than discussions about crossing the line. Woody Allen even makes fun of it in his film *Hollywood Ending,* on top of the joke that the director in the film is hiding the fact that he's gone blind and the DP he's hired doesn't speak English.

FIGURE 17.2
Actors looking in opposite directions. *Reproduced with permission of GVSU Summer Film Project.*

FIGURE 17.3
Actors looking in the same direction. *Reproduced with permission of GVSU Summer Film Project.*

In order for the director, the DP, and the camera operator to be able to easily communicate regarding the kind of shot they want to make, there's an established nomenclature that all film professionals use to define and describe all the standard shots. Most of the shots you're likely to make fall into the following categories. There are at least four standard close-up shots:

FIGURE 17.4
A choker.
Reproduced with permission of GVSU Summer Film Project.

1. *Choker:* An extreme close-up where the top and bottom framelines cut across the forehead and the chin. This shot isn't used too frequently, but it's great for extreme emphasis. Look at Sergio Leone's cinemascope compositions of Clint Eastwood's eyes in his early spaghetti westerns (*A Fistful of Dollars, For a Few Dollars More, The Good, the Bad, and the Ugly*). Overuse it and it becomes obtrusive. Save it for special occasions.

2. *Collar points:* Looser but still pretty tight. The bottom of the frame cuts across right about the level of the actor's collarbone, and there's little or no head room at the top of the frame. This is a frequently used shot in TV but less so on theatrical features. With this shot the actor's head is very large in the frame; on your home TV screen it's reasonable, but on a 60-foot screen at the multiplex, it's overwhelming.

3. *Second button:* The location of the bottom of the frame is self-explanatory; there's usually a little headroom. This is probably the most frequently used close-up in feature films.

4. *Two tees:* Use your imagination to figure out what this means. The frame cuts at the elbows. If you run an imaginary line across the body from one elbow to the other, you'll find it crosses the body just under the breast. Hence, two tees, also known as a Montana shot (because it shows a pair of beauts). It may be time to retire that name. No doubt the term harkens back to the old, old days of movies, when the camera crew was entirely men. As an assistant, I worked with a DP

FIGURE 17.5
Collar points.
Reproduced with permission of GVSU Summer Film Project.

who insisted that two tees was the only surviving term from a full tee system that covered shots from head to foot. (E-mail me, and I'll tell you the other points.)

Next we have the waist shot, knees, and a full shot. All self-explanatory, but I should mention the cowboy shot, also the cowboy close-up. This shot cuts just below the hands when they're hanging at the side. It's also known as "guns," since the shot is designed

FIGURE 17.6
Second button.
*Reproduced with
permission of GVSU
Summer Film Project.*

to show the western star's guns, or to show him on a horse with an indication of the horse. Despite its origin, it's still a useful shot in any genre. And by the way, never frame a shot so that you cut a person at the ankles. It's ugly and awkward, and professionals will make fun of you.

We've gone through shots that show increasing amounts of the body and end up with a frame whose height is just a little more than one full figure tall. Often the director or DP will want to know what the boundaries of a shot will be. If the shot is wider than the shots we've been talking about, one of the best ways for the operator to describe it is to call it "one figure," "two figures," or "three figures" (as though they're standing on one another's heads). That defines the height of the frame. That gives the director or DP a clear idea of the coverage of the shot. Any bigger, and there are other ways to describe the shot. All the names for shots are fairly standard, and it's important to use them when communicating. With video assist, often there's no need to ask what the operator has framed; the director can see it on the screen. But when asking for a shot, or talking to other operators in a multiple camera situations, or for talking over the radio (action sometimes requires widely spread-out camera positions), the terms are still useful. And if you know them, you'll look cool to the crew and mysterious to outsiders. Remember, it's important to look cool, and we want to keep what we do a mystery.

Other important compositions are the over-the-shoulder (showing a bit of the back of one actor in a close shot of another) and master. Although not strictly a shot, I need to mention matching action. We always shoot with an editor's mind. It's up to the actors and the script supervisor to make sure that different angles of the same action have the same movement taking place at the same moment each time the scene plays. It's up to the cinematographer to shoot setups that overlap action and that can be cut together. For example, if

FIGURE 17.7
Two tees.
*Reproduced with
permission of GVSU
Summer Film Project.*

you cover a scene in only a choker and a full shot, you'll find the cut is awkward. It's way too much of a jump in space. You won't have a problem if you shoot something in an intermediate range that will ease these transitions.

By now the standard shots are a syntax understood by all moviegoers. In fact, you could say that they are a "language" the audience is fluent in. When audiences first saw a wide shot,

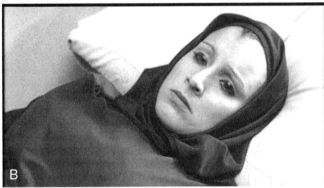

FIGURE 17.8
Waist shot.
Reproduced with permission of GVSU Summer Film Project.

FIGURE 17.9
Knees.
Reproduced with permission of GVSU Summer Film Project.

FIGURE 17.10
Full shot.
*Reproduced with
permission of GVSU
Summer Film Project.*

A

B

FIGURE 17.11
Cowboy close-up, "guns."
*Reproduced with
permission of GVSU
Summer Film Project.*

they knew they were watching a presentation as seen through a window or a stage proscenium. And they had little trouble accepting close-ups as a way of seeing important details of a scene. Some early movie producers objected to the use of close-ups for the silly reason that as long as they were paying for whole actors, they wanted to see the whole actor and not just parts of actors.

But it soon became apparent, even to these producers, that the intensity of a drama or the amusement of a comedy could be greatly enhanced by using a variety of shots intercut. The audience wanted to be able to zero in on the most important person(s) or action in the scene. Audiences knew that they were seeing only a portion of what might be going on in a scene, but they were able to accept that the story was being told from a specific point of view. In contrast, moviegoers were less receptive when they first encountered Jean Luc Godard's extensive and deliberate use of jump cutting in his film *Breathless* (1959). You might say that jump cutting left filmgoers in the lurch until *A Hard Day's Night* and MTV came along and made the use of jump cuts commonplace.

By now the standard shots—close-ups, medium, and wide shots—are so familiar that they've become compositional elements without inflection. That is, they carry a weight of meaning, but their meaning is pretty straightforward, and that meaning is the same to everyone. In fact, in using standard shots, the director and cinematographer are modestly expressing their choice to be transparent storytellers, just telling the story without any unusual point of view. Maintaining balance in the composition of your frame, using the rule of thirds, and favoring the look or movement of a character (leaving nose room, weighting the frame so there is more space in the direction the actor is looking or moving) are also so standard that they don't convey an unusual or idiosyncratic point of view. Their commonness is a source of strength; they imply normality. Then when you break from the norm, from observing these "rules," it's possible to elicit a dramatic reaction from the viewer, provoking an immediate sense of discomfort or unease, or at least the notion that something is out of the ordinary.

FIGURE 17.12
Over-the-shoulder.
Reproduced with permission of GVSU Summer Film Project.

Breaking the rules this way is like adding spice to a recipe. Used judiciously, it is a pleasant shock to the audience. Moderate amounts of rule-breaking delight the audience, and makes them pay attention. But shooting everything unconventionally can result in sensory overload, just as shooting everything conventionally leads to dullness, sameness, and boredom.

A movie or TV screen is a two-dimensional display that is able to create an illusion of three dimensions (and more and more so every day). Compositionally the cinematographer enhances or diminishes this illusion by the degree to which modeling with light, composing in depth, and short or long lens lengths are used. A feeling of great depth is achieved by staging (as in *Citizen Kane*'s famous boardinghouse scene), by the choice of wide lenses (Welles, again: the use of wide lenses to see a vast background with an artificially close foreground), or by simple devices such as putting stage pieces in the foreground (Hitchcock's glass of milk in *Suspicion*) or by having the main characters play in the background while some secondary action is going on in the foreground (almost anything by Altman). Some of the power in emphasizing depth results from the audience's sense that they are in the picture. Some of it comes from the optical fact that a wide lens, with the same composition as a long lens (frame lines identical), will show more of the background—that is, more of the area the characters are living in. A brilliant example is in *The Usual Suspects*. Verbal's story—the lies he tells—is shot with long lenses, so that the audience's field of view is compressed and limited. The objective story—what really happened —is shot more with wider lenses. The audience is allowed to see more. This device is not completely consistent in the film, but it is used enough so that there is a pervasive sense that something is being obscured when Verbal is talking. In consonance with the script, the cinematography helps to keep us in suspense right up until the end of the movie. Even if there's no compelling dramatic reason for it, the use of foreground objects (even just a corner of a table in a restaurant scene, for example) will almost always make your composition more interesting.

FIGURE 17.13
Foreground.
Reproduced with
permission of GVSU
Summer Film Project.

FIGURE 17.14
Frame within a frame.
Reproduced with
permission of GVSU
Summer Film Project.

Using foreground objects heightens the audience's perception that the characters on the screen inhabit the real world and do not live in isolation on a movie set where all obstructions are cleared away. Depth and reality are enhanced by the sense that we have to look past or through objects in the front of the actors.

The use of an iris to isolate a small portion of the screen is rarely used these days except self-consciously. But a variant still employed in many films is when an architectural element (such as a doorway) or a natural element (such as an overhanging tree) is used to create a frame around the action. One of the most memorable shots of this kind occurs at the end of *The Searchers*, where director John Ford frames Ethan, played by John Wayne, with the camera shooting from the dark interior of a cabin, through the cabin's doorway, out to a harshly bright, barren sunlit exterior. The view of Ethan standing outside all alone, silhouetted in the frame of the doorway and the cabin's dark interior, expresses more about Ethan's isolation than any words ever could. This is the power of cinematic imagery. Use it well.

So now it's time for you to try making these shots yourself. Following are instructions for an exercise I call "standard shots." Follow the instructions, do the exercise, then look at the page titled "What You Should Have Learned from the Standard Shots Exercise." Remember: The best way to learn something is to make mistakes, so do the best you can and then evaluate where you might have gone wrong.

17A • SECOND EXERCISE: THE STANDARD SHOTS

Okay, we've just been talking about the "standard" shots. Let's take some time now to work on them. I figure you own or have access to some kind of camcorder or digital video camera, and I'm assuming that it has a zoom lens, as everything made today does. For this exercise, I'm happy for you to use any camera available. Film cameras are not as readily available, and at this stage there is no advantage to working with film, since we're not concerning ourselves with visual quality or lighting at this time. Go ahead and use whatever you have access to. If you're not sure how to use the camera, consult my Camera Tutorial in the "Cheat Sheets and Checklists" section.

17A • SECOND EXERCISE: THE STANDARD SHOTS—CONT'D

Grab some friends or family to help you shoot and to be your actors. Or if no one wants to help, use a doll or a Wilson volleyball. Don't worry too much about lighting right now. Just make sure you have sufficient light to get a good, clear image. You can shoot indoors or outdoors or both. The main thing is to concentrate on executing each of the shots as described following. Have fun, play around, but for each type of shot, be precise in your framing.

➔ **SHOOT AT LEAST 10 SECONDS PER SHOT** so the image will be on the screen long enough to be able to make some judgments about it.

CLOSE-UPS: Shoot all the different types of close-ups described in this chapter, framing your actor exactly as described: choker, collar tips, second button, and so on. Do this using a wide lens setting, then a midlength setting, and finally a long lens setting. One thing you'll quickly discover is that each time you change your focal length, you have to change the placement of your camera—the distance of your camera from your subject—so that you'll be producing exactly the same framing on the actor with different focal length lenses. You don't have to be specific about the exact focal lengths of the lenses you use as long as they fall into the approximate ranges of wide, medium, and long. Every electronic camera has a different size target area and a different range of zoom. Many won't have any focal length markings on the barrel of the lens; you will just see a bar in the viewfinder indicating approximately how long the lens is from W to L (or possibly T, for telephoto).

1. SINGLE/ WIDE LENS: This is the smaller number on the lens barrel or in the viewfinder. Remember, precise lens length doesn't matter; just shoot so the bottom of the frame is where it's supposed to be.
2. SINGLE/ MEDIUM LENS: This is a number in between the wide and the long lens settings on the lens barrel or in the viewfinder.
3. SINGLE/ LONG LENS: This is a large number on the lens barrel or in the viewfinder.

OVER-THE-SHOULDERS (**OTS**): Each shot framed *exactly the same* with the actors *in the same relation to each other* using different-length lenses (and, of course, moving the tripod to a new position to shoot over the shoulder of each actor and changing the distance from the camera to the actors when the lens length changes).

4. OTS/ WIDE LENS
5. OTS/ MEDIUM LENS
6. OTS/ LONG LENS

TWO-SHOTS: Each shot framed *exactly the same* with actors *in the same position* using different lenses (and, of course, moving the tripod).

7. TWO SHOT/WIDE LENS
8. TWO SHOT/MEDIUM LENS
9. TWO SHOT/LONG LENS

WIDE SHOTS: Frame each shot *exactly the same* with the actors *in exactly the same positions* using different-length lenses (and, of course, moving the tripod). This may

(Continued)

17A • SECOND EXERCISE: THE STANDARD SHOTS—CONT'D

seem weird, but you can make a wide shot using a wide lens—as almost everyone always does—or you can make it on a long lens, like Kurosawa. You have to place your camera very far away from the actors to get the same field of view with a long lens that you get with a wide one. When you view the results, you'll see the different effect you get using the different lenses.

10. WIDE SHOT/WIDE LENS
11. WIDE SHOT/LONG LENS

PAN on a close/medium-close shot.

12. Follow your actor (in waist shot) walking across a background.
13. Pan across the *same* background *at the same speed* without an actor in the frame (this is called an unmotivated pan). You'll see why in a minute.

ZOOM

14. Zoom in on an unmoving actor.
15. Zoom (in or out) and pan *simultaneously* as your actor walks across the frame (try to start and end the zoom and the pan at the same time).
16. Zoom *out* while holding the framing in close-up of your actor as the actor walks directly forward toward the camera.

See if you can plan the order in which you'll do these shots so the exercise gets done in the fastest, most efficient way. Think about how to minimize the number of times you'll have to change your camera position. (Who wants to lug around a camera any more than necessary?) There's a smart way to do this and a stupid way. However you do it, you'll learn a lot. After you finish shooting, screen what you've shot and read "What You Should Have Learned from the Standard Shots Exercise." Then we'll get back to the set. Following is a checklist you can use to make sure you've got all the shots.

	WIDE LENS	MEDIUM LENS	LONG LENS	ACTOR	NO ACTOR	ACTOR WALKS ACROSS FRAME	ACTOR WALKS INTO FRAME
CLOSE-UP							
OVER-THE-SHOULDERS							
TWO-SHOT							
WIDE SHOT							
PAN							
ZOOM							

17B • WHAT YOU SHOULD HAVE LEARNED FROM THE STANDARD SHOTS EXERCISE

Now let's look at what you shot and see what you have learned from the exercise.

CLOSE-UPS: You should now be familiar with how to frame close-ups from super-tight to somewhat loose. You'll observe that a choker is a shot that really calls attention to itself, while 2Ts is very neutral and without any special dramatic impact. You'll observe that you have to adjust your headroom depending on how tight your shot is. You'll notice that the perspective changes with different length lenses. The wide-angle lens will have given you more three-dimensionality and slight distortion. In practical terms, noses will look more pronounced and other features will be more prominent due to the greater sense of depth (although the ears may seem to recede). The longer lens will have given you a flatter, less distorted look. Using a longer lens on close-ups usually gives more flattering results; noses don't stick out as much as they do with a wide lens, and most everyone looks better with the long lens. You also know now that you have to move the camera further from your subject if you use a long lens. A danger of using a zoom lens is that you'll just plant your camera close in to the scene and then stick with that placement, allowing it to arbitrarily determine the focal length. This is what people do who are taking snapshots. A professional cinematographer selects a lens for the effect it will give and then positions the camera based on that choice. Using long lenses is a powerful creative tool, so take advantage of it. Working in close quarters on a small set may limit what you can do, but there will *always* be practical limitations to what you can do.

OVER-THE-SHOULDERS: What you learned regarding close-ups also applies to OTSs. In addition, since an OTS has two people in relation to each other, not just an isolated single figure, your choice of lens will have a significant effect on the sense of the dramatic tension in a scene and on the sense of relationship between the characters. A short lens will exaggerate the perceived distance between two actors facing each other and will make the foreground figure appear relatively large. This can be artistically useful if you're portraying one character as more dominant than the other. Conversely, a longer lens will compact the space between the actors, giving you a more intimate sense of the relationship between two people. It tends to diminish the difference between their sizes; it also lets you include only a sliver of the character whose back is to camera. You can see that for a love scene you might want to shoot with a long lens, keeping the characters equal in size and close together. To do that you will have to place your camera far away from the actors. That may seem a weird thing to do when you are shooting an "intimate" scene, but don't confuse the sense of closeness you are trying to create on the screen with being physically close to action when you're on the set.

In composing your OTS you will have discovered that there are choices to be made regarding the left/right and/or up/down offset of the actors. You may have chosen your camera angle simply to produce a generally visually pleasing and balanced composition, or you may have based your decision on the desire to convey a specific dramatic effect. The composition of an OTS shot can emphasize the closeness or coldness of the characters' relationship. It can also convey the relative importance of one character compared to the other. The person lower in the frame is almost always

(Continued)

17B • WHAT YOU SHOULD HAVE LEARNED FROM THE STANDARD SHOTS EXERCISE—CONT'D

perceived as being inferior, so you might be shooting that person from above. Dominant characters will be higher in the frame and likely to be shot from below. Of course, when your camera is high for an OTS, the foreground person is lowest in the frame, and the person facing us is looked at from above (and vice versa). It's an odd apparent reversal of the high camera/low camera→inferior/superior effect. You will have to decide in your case whether, for example, a high camera tends to diminish the foreground figure or the character facing the camera. It doesn't just always follow the "rule." How much you show of the actor who is facing away from the camera will have an impact on the scene. By including only a sliver of the shoulder of the foreground actor, you diminish the audience's consciousness of that character. On the other hand, if there's a lot of shoulder included, that character will loom large in the audience's awareness. And watch out for the horror of the white shirt. If the guy you're shooting over wears, say, a white T-shirt, that T-shirt will be the brightest thing in the frame and will draw undue attention from the audience. It's not a movie about a T-shirt. So you want to consider wardrobe carefully; maybe no one in the cast should be in a white shirt. If you must deal with one, try to take light off the shirt by flagging it (use any solid that will block the light). Or frame the shot so there's only a sliver of the bright white shoulder showing.

TWO-SHOTS: The first thing we want to ask ourselves here is "What is the accepted definition of a two shot?" It is *not* just any shot that has two people in it. In doing this exercise some people have produced shots where you see two tiny distant figures surrounded by a vast landscape like the Grand Canyon, or you see two heads close together filling the frame. Neither of these fits the common definition of a two-shot. A two-shot is a medium-wide shot of two people with the bottom of the frame between the actors' knees and waist (and a balancing amount of headroom). It's tighter than a full-figure shot and looser than a close-up. It's a fairly neutral shot; not much is implied in the way of relationship between the characters. It's often just an efficient way to shoot dialogue. But as you have seen, how you compose your shot can always influence an audience's reaction to what's happening on the screen.

The main effect of using different focal length lenses will in this case not be on the characters themselves but on their place in the world. A wide lens will show a great deal of background; it suggests that the characters are involved in a big world. A long lens tends to isolate the characters from the rest of the world; it shows less background, and the shallow depth of field throws the background out of focus, further suggesting the alienation of the characters. But notice how with a long lens the distant background is brought close to the characters.

WIDE SHOTS: Once again, you can see the effect of the choice of lens length. Shooting your wide shot with a short lens will give you more depth and will show more of the background, left-to-right, than a long lens will. How much of an area you want to or can afford to show (you'll be limited by the size of sets or by having to avoid unwanted elements in the frame) and how far or near to the action you can set up your camera will often dictate what length lens you'll have to use. But if you do have a choice, again remember even a wide shot can be impacted by the lens length. With a long lens you can get a Chinese/Japanese feel with a flattened perspective or use a short lens to get a deep perspective European Renaissance painterly look.

17B • WHAT YOU SHOULD HAVE LEARNED FROM THE STANDARD SHOTS EXERCISE—CONT'D

PANS may be the most misused camera technique, with the possible exception of hand-holding (but that's another subject). Somehow, bad filmmakers have convinced the world that the way to show where we are is to pan across a landscape or a room from left to right (or R to L). This is just plain wrong. Not only is this kind of panning shot incredibly ugly, it is also boring and tends to strobe. Strobing occurs as an apparent jittering of objects when they are close to the camera and the pan is fast; it stems from too great a lateral displacement from frame to frame of the object shot; our eyes can't integrate the successive frames into continuous motion; hence we see strobing.

Panning this way is an attempt to duplicate the point of view of a person looking around his or her environment. It doesn't work because our eye/brain system does not see the world by looking around in a pan. In reality, as we turn our heads or bodies to look around, our eyes light briefly on one "shot" after another as we take notice of individual objects of interest. We are conscious of, but barely notice, the areas between the interesting things. Nevertheless, our brains have no trouble piecing together these discrete images into a cohesive impression of a place.

The pan you did where you had a subject to follow shows that if you have a person or object in the frame that stays in approximately the same position on the screen, you can eliminate strobing. It's actually still there but only in the background, and since the audience is not looking at the background, they don't notice it. They do notice Cameron Diaz, who might be the star of your movie and is definitely an object of interest. Panning with something that's moving is fine, but don't pan over air. There are lots of more interesting and more effective ways of showing the audience where they are. Think about it.

Finally, **ZOOMS.** Maybe I was wrong about pans. Zooms may be the most misused film technique. So let's make sure they're useful, informative, beautiful tools and not poor substitutes for dolly moves. In your exercise you shot a straight on zoom in/zoom out on a stationary subject. This kind of zoom is ugly and obtrusive. It throws the audience out of the story by pointing out the flatness and two-dimensionality of the screen and by drawing attention to the artificiality of photography. The other zoom you did should have shown you that it's possible to disguise or hide a zoom (the camera crew calls it burying the zoom) when it's combined with actors moving (here, a pan; even better with a dolly move). The third zoom you did should have shown you how you can fake a tracking shot that, if the rhythm is right, can substitute for actually moving the camera—when you don't have a dolly or don't have room to move. Any professional camera will have a motorized zoom and zoom control. The professional controls can be adjusted for speed and can be varied during the zoom; they can also be started and stopped smoothly—"feathered," we say. Your prosumer digital camera will have a zoom control, but none of them is well made. When you figure that a professional zoom control usually costs more than the whole camera you're using, it's no surprise. I'd say the best thing to do is never to zoom until you get good equipment. Now, I have faith in the human spirit, and I know that if you're motivated enough, you'll figure out how to get a beautiful, invisible zoom out of the worst equipment. If you want to, bravo. Every skill you pick up will pay off somewhere down the line. But don't let trying to master an amateur zoom control take up all the time you need for shooting.

(Continued)

17B • WHAT YOU SHOULD HAVE LEARNED FROM THE STANDARD SHOTS EXERCISE—CONT'D

I'm going to assume that you've had some help with this exercise, and everyone will want to look at the results. Well, sure. It's their first dailies, and they're excited. Bring everyone in front of the TV, break out the beers, and savor your accomplishments.

Let me take this opportunity to explain screening room etiquette. First of all, you never know who's in the screening room with you. It might be someone who could hire or fire you, so behave. Look good. If someone in the room has worked on the film you're screening (and someone always has unless you're alone, and even then), don't make any comment on that person's work. No matter what, you're drawing attention to it, and you don't know if that helps or hurts. You are a nice guy or gal and you don't want to hurt anyone, or you're not so nice and you just don't want to make an enemy who'll get even.

Usually there's a lot of money at stake, and everyone's nervous (remember William Goldman: "Nobody knows anything"). They might be looking for a scapegoat or a whipping boy. Don't volunteer.

So like so much else in life, your best bet is to behave as your mother wanted you to: Be quiet and polite, sit quietly without fidgeting, and say nothing if you can't say something positive (and it's always better to say nothing). If you have to give an opinion, you can always rely on "I've never seen anything like it" or "You've done it again!"

Having completed the Standard Shots exercise, you will have gotten a taste of what it's like to be a camera operator. I determined what the shots would be, and you made the shots I told you to make. On the set, the director and/or DP will determine what the shots will be, and the operator needs to execute all the shots exactly as he or she has been instructed. Aside from possessing the manual and technical skills needed to execute shots effectively, a good camera operator must be able to discern exactly the framing and movement the director and DP have pictured in their minds. You can see why there is terminology to describe shots: to facilitate communication. But it takes more than that. To be a success as an operator, you must have excellent communication skills. And being psychic doesn't hurt either.

Now, not every director knows shot terminology, and some are not good at expressing what they want pictorially. (So why were they hired to direct? Maybe it's because they know how to hire people who know what they're doing. Like you, right?) In any case, the DP will be there to translate the director's wishes into meaningful directions. Presumably, you're very tuned in to how the DP works and what the DP wants (that's why he hired you). If you're not familiar with the director or DP from working on shows with them before this one you're on, you'll have to figure out what they want from the feedback you get as you go along. And you'll have to pick up on that fast because no one wants to spend a lot of time tweaking shots. Once again, mind reading is a useful skill to have, and you also have to develop rhinoceros skin to deal with critiques of your framing. Try not to yell the way one operator did when he was frustrated by an inarticulate director: "Damn it, Ted, I'm not one of your [expletive deleted] brain cells!" This will not promote a productive work environment. Whatever the case, listen to the director, and try to understand what he or she wants.

In some cases the DP will do the operating, sometimes to save money on low-budget projects (it's one less salary to pay) or to eliminate having to explain what is wanted to another person (it's easier for some DPs to just do it themselves). On bigger-budget projects and network TV, having an operator is the rule. In fact it's a union rule. Even if the DP wants to operate on a union show, you must hire an operator (called a "stand-by") who will have to be paid even if that person never touches the camera.

It sounds like featherbedding, but it's not. The first reason for this rule is that without it, too many producers will pressure the DP into operating just to save a buck. It's common that a DP will want an operator. Being a DP and being an operator are two different jobs. During lighting and setup, the operator is supposed to be working out and rehearsing the shot with the assistant and the dolly grip. Meanwhile the DP is working with the grip and electric crews to light the set. If he has to do both, the DP is likely to shortchange one of the jobs, probably operating. During shooting, the operator is fully occupied making the shot, keeping the frame balanced and the movement smooth, keeping the actors well in frame, and remembering everything that's not perfect so he can tell the director about the shot. The DP is standing nearby. These days he's probably watched a rehearsal on the monitor, so he's made sure the operator is getting the shot he wants. He's spending his time during shooting watching the lighting on the set, sensitive to the smallest shadow in the wrong place, or an actress not looking her best, or any imbalance in the light. It's possible to be aware of the lighting while operating; I've done it, and some DPs are great at it—but again, there's only so much concentration available. If you're looking at the lighting, you're neglecting the framing and vice versa. That's why we want operators, and we don't want the job classification to disappear.

The reason for the standby rule is to discourage the producer from forcing the DP to operate by saying, "You want the job or not?" Show business can be brutal. (A regretful note: Recently the union signed an agreement that allows the producer not to hire an operator if the DP "wants" to operate. I'm happy that some low-budget films can now be made with union crews, but you know this agreement is going to be abused by producers who care only about money.)

As an operator, if you're not the DP, you will have to please both the director and the DP. Let's hope the DP will be in complete sync with the director and their opinions won't differ much. If there is a difference, the operator will have the dilemma of who has the last say on what the operator should do. The director mostly has the final word. I just hope you don't get caught in a squeeze play between them. Sometimes you can't win.

Every show is different, and you will know pretty quickly whether the director likes to give you the shot or the DP does. In most cases, you have an idea of what kind of shot they're going to want (master, two-shot, single), so you should direct the dolly grip or the assistant to put the camera in an approximate position. That gives your boss something to approve or, if there's a very different shot, to change. Just by listening to the director and DP—carefully, from the first minute—you will see how much they want to determine the shot and how much they're happy to leave up to you. I've had directors who would let me set the shot and never even look through the viewfinder. Then I've had directors who love to sit on the dolly and move it around and then say, "Something like that," so I get to refine it. And I've even had one or two directors who say, 'Give me a 35 (mm) right here, four feet off the floor, on the star." Well, when they know lenses, it's heaven, but don't expect that from most directors.

Where to begin? The first thing to do is "clear your space." (I got that bit of advice from an experienced operator.) That means make sure you know what you're doing, make sure nothing is in your way (physically or psychologically), know that you're ready to shoot, and don't be rushed. Never let anyone on the set rush you. It's a sure way to make stupid mistakes. Be as fast as you can, and know when to ask for time and when to give in.

Part of your preparation is making sure the head is adjusted just right for you and for the shot. If you're on the wheels, put it in the gear with which you're most comfortable. If you've got a fluid head, adjust the tension so that it's tight enough for some control and loose enough to change the speed of your move during the shot. Make sure you can stand or sit comfortably, and stay balanced. Most shots involve some athletic move by the operator; you don't want to fall down or slide off the dolly because you haven't found a comfortable place to be. And when you can, when you're working on a dolly, get a lazy Susan seat. It's made so you can twist around while you're operating (the regular seats are stationary). The lazy Susan seat lets you operate with your butt, which has many more muscles than the rest of you (and maybe more brains). It's best to find the end position of the shot, make yourself stable and comfortable there, and then twist your body around to get the beginning of the shot. You can always start unbalanced because you're going to move and you don't have to hold that position long. Besides, you're fresh when the shot starts. By the end, you may be exhausted from your move, and yet you have to hold that shot and that position until the director says, "Cut!"

Even though the assistant is responsible for keeping the camera level, you must be aware of the level at all times and be sensitive to it. There will be moments when, although the camera is perfectly level according to the bubble, the picture will seem off. This might happen because you have dominant lines in the frame that are themselves not square to the horizon (a grove of trees growing slightly off vertical, say), or a part of the set might not be plumb, or the angle of the shot and the way the lens forms an image may make the picture skewed in reference to the frame lines. Remember that you're dealing with an artificial situation: The frame lines are powerful, and the audience will feel them as the correct reference for level. So if you have any of these situations, level the camera to the frame. And rehearse: Make sure that you haven't set up the frame so it gets worse at some point during the shot.

When you're looking through the viewfinder, look at what's really going on in the frame, not what's in your mind. Novices often make the "snapshot mistake." You've seen this: Pop takes a picture of Mom to prove they were at the Lincoln Memorial. He places her on the steps, and then he steps back. It's a big building, so Dad makes sure he gets the whole thing in. He thinks what a great picture this will be, but when he replays the shot or gets a print made, he's shocked to see a picture of a giant building with a little smudge that might be Mom in front of it. He can't figure out what happened, because when he took the picture, he could see Mom clearly. That's because he was thinking about *her*, and that's where his attention was. He saw Mom as much as he saw the building, and he thought the camera would too.

So make sure that what you're taking a picture of is in the frame and is the right size. Then look at the edges of the frame. What's there that shouldn't be? Are you off the set? Is the foot of a C-stand coming in? Make sure the entire frame is clear. Look for electrical cables that will lie in wait for you in corners and under furniture. Be sure that all the props in the shot belong there (you can check on this with the prop master or the script supervisor). Have the second assistant pick up any marks that might show up in the shot. Rehearse the shot, especially if it involves any moves (pan, tilt, dolly). You want to be sure you can make the shot—that the head is in the right gear or is stiff or loose enough for you to perform the mechanical requirements of the shot easily. And, again, you're looking to see if any of these moves takes you off the set.

You must look at the frame lines all the time. Be concerned with the overall balance of the composition, and don't shoot anything that shouldn't be there. Film camera viewfinders all show a little bit more around the edge of the frame than will actually be recorded on the film. Because of this, the operator can see when some unwanted object is about to creep into the frame (uh oh, there's that light stand) and can modify the shot before it's ruined. You can't do this with most electronic viewfinders (digital), and I hate that. But if that's what you're working with, be extra aware of what your safety margins will be. That means you have be much more aware of the boundaries of the set and the possible pitfalls on it for you, and you have to be able to sense problems coming even though you can't see them in your viewfinder.

DPs will usually give you a lens size and a position. Your job then is to refine it. Make sure no poles are growing out of the actor's head, make sure you're not off the set, and make sure you're matching other shots in the scene. You may have to change the camera position slightly, but be discreet. You will always match angle, distance, and focal length in complementary shots (like close-ups in a conversation) so the editor can cut smoothly. You may want to check with the script supervisor to make sure a close-up you are going to shoot six hours after the matching shot does actually match. A good camera assistant will usually keep records—lens focal length, distance of the person from the camera—and an excellent camera assistant will have his records and will make sure the script supervisor has them, too. But be ready to do it yourself just from memory.

Also, in regard to the lens, the camera assistant and the grips should be taking care of lens flares. The operator should tell them about any flares he or she sees so they can be eliminated. Lens flares are easy to see and kill. Stick your head in front of the lens looking toward the set, and you'll immediately be aware of any lights in your eyes. They have to be flagged off the lens. Have a grip put up a flag between the light and the camera. (Flags are light control devices handled by the grips. An opaque fabric is stretched over a wire frame, giving you something that will block the light. They can be any size from 2 × 12 inches to 4 × 8 feet. All of them have stems that are part of the frame so they can be mounted in a clamp. The clamp is usually a gobo head on a C-stand. (More on C-stands in Chapter 22.) If the flag gets in the frame, direct the grip how to move it until it can't be seen; you may have to put it closer to or farther away from the camera to have it work. You see the light become covered, and the grip can see the shadow of the flag fall on the lens or the matte box, and that way you know when the flare is gone. Using the principle "the angle of incidence equals the angle of reflection," you can look into the lens from the side of the camera opposite of where the light is that's causing the flare, and tell the grip where to place the flag. Now

FIGURE 18.1
Camera, light, and viewer finding which light is flaring.

you're thinking: the angle of what? Okay, your geometry might be a bit rusty; just think about how you'd calculate the angle you'd use when trying to sink a ball shooting pool. Never played pool? Find a geometry book.

Be aware that some viewfinders display artifacts that won't appear in the filmed or recorded image. Often flares appear that are only in the viewfinder. I have also found that double images, caused by points of light (headlights, candles), often show in the viewfinder and on the monitor but not on the film/chip. At first the director will be very concerned when he sees these flares on the video feed monitor. Explain that they will not be seen on the film or recorded image. As soon as the director screens the dailies and sees that there are no flares, he will trust that you know what you're talking about. Just make sure you're right and there are no flares.

Because of varying formats, one of the joys of operating is dealing with the multiple scribing lines you see in your viewfinder. (Well, maybe not *that* much of a joy.) Anyway, back when the proportion of TV screens was 1.33:1, looking through your viewfinder to shoot a feature in 1.85:1, you'd see at least three different lines: full frame, 1.85, and TV.

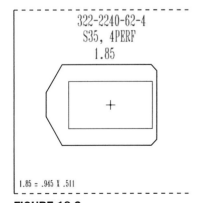

FIGURE 18.2
1.85 scribing lines on ground glass.
Image courtesy of Panavision.

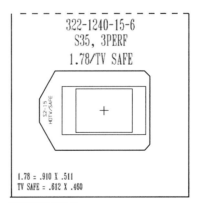

FIGURE 18.3
1.78 + TV action safe.
Image courtesy of Panavision.

FIGURE 18.4
Balanced composition.
Reproduced with permission of GVSU Summer Film Project.

Now you've got ground glasses that will have full-frame 3-perf plus TV plus 1.85 plus 1.75 (for HD). Be prepared to be told, "Keep it all safe," and then when you say, "I can't get the actors in without going off the set in 1.85," to be told, "Don't worry about it." Remember, "better safe than sorry," so play it safe and keep everything bad out of all the frames if you possibly can. Or get the script supervisor to make a note that the director okayed it. The script supervisor's notes are official, and having a note in there might save your job.

Pretty soon you'll learn to split your attention among all the different things you're supposed to keep an eye on: 80% paying attention to the format you're supposed to be shooting and 20% making sure no lights or stands get in the other format, and that all the important action is in both formats. It can be frustrating, and I'm hoping there will be less of it now with the advent of HDTV.

Some of the fun of operating is composing on the fly as a scene plays out. Even when you just frame-up a supposedly static shot, there's a good chance it will be necessary to make undetectable adjustments to the frame as the actors move about or just lean a little one way or another. The trick to adjusting is to be ready to make it at the drop of a hat and to move when the actor makes a slight move—a slight glance is enough—to distract the audience's attention. It's up to you to keep a well-composed frame at all times, even as you are making sure to include everything that needs to be seen. Strive for what is regarded as a balanced frame. That doesn't mean keeping the subject centered—that's hideous—and it doesn't mean that everything in the frame is symmetrical. To me balanced is an indefinable quality. To paraphrase what a Supreme Court justice said regarding pornography, you just know it when you see it. I admit that might not be very helpful, but there's an assumption that if you were drawn to cinematography you will likely have some innate sense of composition. Analysts of fine arts, photography, and cinema have written plenty about composition. I refer you to those sources if you would like to read more about it. (See the bibliography.) Figure 18.4 shows an example of what I would consider a balanced shot. Figure 18.5 shows an unbalanced shot.

FIGURE 18.5
Unbalanced composition.
Reproduced with permission of GVSU Summer Film Project.

I use the unbalanced shot to convey some uneasiness to the audience or to suggest a character who is off-kilter in some way. When you have a dolly shot, you will be expected to lay it out. You'll work with the dolly or key grip, of course, and with the DP and the director. But mostly you're expected to determine the start and end of the shot and the placement of the track. First, you need to be sure to get the shot you've been assigned. Make sure you can see the actor(s), and make sure you're positioning yourself to keep them in frame. You don't want to be too close or you'll have to use a very wide-angle lens. Likewise, not too far away, or you'll be fighting a long lens (the small angle it takes in will advertise every small mistake you make and every bump in the track). If the move is fast, make sure the dolly grip can push. You've got the choice of push or pull, and most grips will want to push because they can see where they're going. You have to be comfortable on the dolly. If you have to hang off the front with no place for your feet, you'll be unstable and likely to blow the shot or fall off the dolly. And you don't want to have to shoot over the back of the dolly—where the handles and the arm control are. Unless you're on level ground, think about the precise path of the track: Will it require bridge-building to make a flat surface? Try to minimize the amount of cribbing (the wedges, apple boxes, and pieces of wood used to raise and level the track) and ingenuity the grips have to use.

FIGURE 18.6
Diving board on a Fisher dolly.
Photos courtesy of J. L. Fisher, Inc.

Once the track is built and the dolly's lifted or rolled onto it, the assistant will ask (the dolly grip) to put the camera on the dolly. The dolly grip will do some runs to make sure there are no bad bumps. Then you need to mount the dolly (ask the dolly grip first) to see if you find any bumps. It's best to do this while looking through the lens you're going to shoot with. If you just ride the dolly, I guarantee you'll find bumps; your butt is a lot more sensitive than your eyes. So make sure you don't see the frame wobbling; that's all that matters. You may need help supporting yourself. There are all kinds of platforms and extensions made, and usually the grips will know what's best for you. Eventually you'll get used to them and know when to ask for a pork chop or a diving board.

Actors are fun. I love actors, and they're the reason for our jobs. Sometimes we have to talk to them. There are a few who are old-time pros, the ones who always hit their marks and understand when you need a look or a move cheated. But you're also in the position of teaching. Sometimes you will want the actor to cheat his look. What you need is to see both eyes (usually a rule), but you can't move the camera (maybe the background's wrong, maybe it would take too long). So you give them an eyeline that looks good in the frame even though it makes no sense to the actor.

FIGURE 18.7
Two pork chops (front boards) on a Fisher peewee dolly.
Photos courtesy of J. L. Fisher, Inc.

And you must be vigilant that the actors' eyelines match when you're shooting complementary close-ups. It must seem as though they're looking at each other, and you must find a place for each actor to look that convinces the audience that they're looking at each other and that, again, maintains "two eyes." All too often, an actor will say, "But I was looking over here," and position his head so you can't see both eyes. Here's your politics and psychology again. Usually you can say, "It's okay; the camera makes it look like you're looking over there," and the actor will accept it. If the actor is still unsure, it's worth the time to put the actor at the viewfinder and to show him—or, better, have the stand-in show him—how the shot looks. Sometimes you just have to say, "Trust me, it works," and move ahead with the day's work.

The physicality of actors often defines them, but you have to be aware of their habits and idiosyncrasies. Many actors have a tendency to lean, and this can either take them out of the frame or unbalance the frame for you. You can often compensate by invisible moves (do it when the actor moves, or when the other actor is talking, or when anything else distracts the audience), but if there are two actors in the frame, you may be faced with cutting one of them in half to keep the other in frame. That's when you want to encourage one of them to lean on his opposite foot. Most actors can manage this without distracting them-selves, and it saves your shot. I try never to ask actors to do something that's so much trouble it might hurt their acting. It's not good for the movie, and it's a good way to get the director mad at you.

Sometimes you need help from the actor when he's simply walking from one point to another. Often enough, the actor's path will take your frame offstage or into part of the set you don't want to see. Or the actor may block himself or another actor from the camera. Once again, if I can move the camera, I will. But sometimes it's necessary to have the actor modify his move. In these cases, you might ask for a banana: put a curve into the walk. It's up to you to design it so it's not an obvious curve but just so it uncovers or hides whatever is your problem.

A constant dilemma is bringing an actor out of a seated position. Sometimes you have to hold others in the shot, or sometimes you would go off the set (usu-ally this is a case of seeing over the set). So you ask for a Groucho. In tribute to Groucho Marx and his bent-at-the knees walk, you're asking the actor to stand up at an angle or a crouch—rather than straightening out his body vertically on his rise—so that his head stays in the frame and your frame stays on the set. What you're doing during the stand-up is raising the camera or moving it so that the frame is recomposed and you can hold his height without going off. Again, you want to help the actor and yourself: Make sure it's not obvious that the actor is crouching a little. It should look like a normal, slightly slow move, and your repositioning the camera and reframing will hide the artificiality.

Whether or not you need help from them, dealing with actors is never straight-forward. Or it may be, but you have to know the actor pretty well. Often directors will declare that no one is to talk to the actor except them. The idea is to keep the actor from being confused as to whose directions to follow, but it can get silly when you just want the actor to make a quarter turn. Make sure the director is comfortable with you talking to the cast. Then remember that actors may be high-strung, sensitive, artistic, whatever adjective you want. They're involved in a different kind of job from you. It's no more or less artistic, but it all comes from inside. There's technique, but they don't have the advantage of a machine to play with. So they may seem scattered or standoffish when they're just concentrating. Be considerate; don't interrupt their personal preparations. Try to talk to them as you would to your mother. She doesn't know anything technical either, so you'd have to choose your words carefully and work extra hard to make yourself understood. Choose your moment, be polite, be clear, and don't act as though they're members of an exotic species.

You're going to need to do handheld work. It should be partly intuitive, but it works differently for different cameras. With traditional, professional, film-style cameras, the biggest issue is weight. It's an advantage to have some heft to the camera; it gives you a way of maintaining stability. But if it's heavy enough to stay solidly on your shoulder, it's heavy enough to tire you out. I think one of the worst giveaways of bad hand-holding is the fatigue tilt. As the day goes on, your shoulder gets tired, and the camera tilts more and more to the right. Of course, the picture tilts to the left. It's never pretty, and it can be very annoying when it becomes common in a movie.

The first solution is not to let yourself get too tired. If you're doing eight or ten takes, ask for a break at some point. You won't need a long time—just enough to get rid of some of the lactic acid in your muscles. Two or three minutes should do it. Next, use a brace. Many different types are available. I like the one I bought years ago. It's sort of a combination of a weightlifter's belt and a Sam Brown belt (like grade school hall monitors wore). The part that goes on my shoulder has a pouch fitted to it with different thicknesses of rubber wedges. The wedge shape puts the camera on the level by eliminating my shoulder slope. I can use one or more, depending on how much cushioning I need and how high I want the camera to be. Of course, you want it as low on your shoulder as possible so you're not fighting a high center of gravity. It's important that the camera be balanced back-to-front so that where it rests on your shoulder it's neutral, neither tipping forward nor backward. Any Panaflex or Arri will be like that. Some HD and digital movie cameras will be configured that way, some not. Know for sure what you'll be working with and if you have to, build your own shoulder mount.

Several manufacturers today make mounts for various digital cameras, especially for HDSLRs, which have to be adapted for movie-style work. Find something in your price range. Most mounts will be a kind of triangle brace, with the base of the triangle holding the camera and running back to your shoulder, the hypotenuse running from the camera to your belt, and the third side imaginary. Most of these don't have a provision for balancing the weight; you have to have the whole camera in front of you, so all the weight is pulling you forward and hurting your back. Figure some way to balance the weight so it's centered; all the weight will go straight down your body to your feet. You'll be able to shoot more easily, and you'll need fewer pain pills. The best thing to do is to extend the base of the triangle, the rods or plate the camera is mounted on, back over your shoulder and put a weight on it equal to the weight of the camera. And pad your shoulder; it's going to be a long day.

As with all work, clear your space. Make sure the viewfinder is locked off, or it will droop in the middle of a shot—and in a comfortable position. Make sure the handles are just where you want them. I try to orient them so I can pull my elbows into my body, giving myself additional bracing. You may use the handles that come from the camera's manufacturer or aftermarket handles, or you may do as many of us do and grab the matte box (make sure it's tied down tightly and that it's sturdy) or the iris rods. Look out for cables that might trip you up. If you must have trailing cables, have a trusted assistant wrangling them. Your first assistant will be at your side to focus and, more importantly to you, to take the camera off your shoulder when you're not actually shooting. I got trained as an assistant to expect the operator to let go and walk away, and the camera had better not fall. I urge you to do the same. After you've shot a take, you need to talk to the director or the actors, and you must relieve yourself of the weight of the camera and the stress—both physical and mental—you've been under trying to make the shot.

And when making the shot, design it. Figure out a way you can be steady when it's necessary not to move. Make sure you've got solid footing and a way to make a bipod of yourself, with your legs in a stable position. If you can, figure out how to have something to lean against (it could be one of the crew) when you make the pauses during the shot. The moves will look best if they're fast. Slow moves will show any shakiness or unsteadiness. The faster you can move, the cleaner it will be. Avoid those slow, long pans, which are mostly ugly anyway. And be prepared to kill people. There's no room for politeness. If you're moving through crowds, you're what matters, not their health. I do not set out to bang into extras and hurt them, but if they get in my way, I'm happy to mow them down. The shot is what's important. And I've never sent anyone to the hospital. The determination to make the shot, no matter what, and to do the fast moves is part of the most important aesthetic of handheld: Be specific. It's altogether too easy to squirt the lens around randomly as if it were a hose. Every moment of your handheld shot should be as precise and as well-composed as any tripod-mounted shot.

All this has involved working with relatively heavy professional cameras. When you're dealing with prosumer or amateur digital cameras, you've got a machine that's so light it might float off if you're not careful. It's these cameras that provoke my tirades against hand-holding. As I've said, it's all too easy to use these cameras without a tripod. The result is almost always sloppy, but it doesn't have to be.

You can choose to take advantage of the light weight of the cameras. They're so small that you can make almost any move without being restricted by gravity or momentum. There are inexpensive, lightweight jibs on the market. With some imagination and minimal skill at fabrication, you could make a jib of your own. Or you could devise another method of mounting the camera. Imagine if Garrett Brown hadn't had to work with 35 mm cameras when he invented Steadicam. What devices might he have come up with? I think very little has been done to take advantage of the intrinsic qualities of these small cameras. Working with them need not be only an imitation of working with large, heavy cameras.

But if you're going to use them the way we've been using big cameras, you can't just grab them and run. Most of them have viewfinders (or LCDs) in inconvenient places. You have to hold the camera out in front of you to see, and there's almost no way to take advantage of the stability of your shoulder and body. So buy or make some sort of rig for shoulder mounting the camera.

Although it seems silly, you might want to take this nice, light camera and put some weight on it. The heft and therefore the momentum of a heavy camera contribute to the solidity of the shots you get from them.

FIGURE 18.8
Shoulder support allowing repositioning of the camera.
Reproduced by permission of HabbyCam, LLC, www.habbycam.com. Inventor: Richard Haberkern.

We've previously talked about how making a shot depends not only on the performance of the actors but also on the performance of the camera operator, the dolly grip, and the camera assistant. The movements and focus have to be as perfect as the actor's performance, if not more so. You'll sometimes see some lousy acting in films, but you won't see jerky out-of-focus shots. The minimum standard for the operator's and assistant's performance is "perfect."

After you've completed a shot and the director asks you, "How was it?," you have only two possible answers: "Good" or "I need another." Even though the director and DP will have been watching the take on a monitor (unless there's no video assist), most of them will still ask you whether the shot is good. They are concentrating on the things that most concern them, so they need your professional judgment as to the usability of the shot. As I said, you're expected to be perfect; the director doesn't want to have to lose a great acting performance because the operator or assistant screwed up. The director will be extremely unhappy if the shot isn't usable because of operator or assistant error.

And be judicious about calling for retakes. This means that in the fraction of a second after you turn off the camera and the director says, "How was it?," you've got to review the shot in your mind and decide whether anything unforgivable happened. It's nerve-wracking, and you have to rely on your instincts about the shot more than any concrete assessment. Sometimes you'll tell yourself that a shot is "good enough." This is a very important judgment to be able to make. I know what you're thinking: How come you were just saying the operator had to be perfect and now you're talking about "good enough?" I admit you've got me there. It may sound as though I'm telling you to settle for second or third best, but the reality is that 100% perfection may not be an achievable goal. You are going to have to develop instincts for how much error is acceptable. Knowing what's "good enough" enables you to do professional work and do it in a reasonable amount of time. As an assistant, you have to know "good enough" in terms of focus, and you've got your depth-of-field charts or calculators to help you. As a DP you will always be deciding that the lighting is okay, even though it could be better, and that you just can't waste any more time on it because the AD needs to be able to go ahead and shoot the scene. As an operator you must state with confidence whether a shot is good or not, and you must make that assessment instantly. Nothing will destroy the trust of the director and DP in an operator faster than hesitancy about whether a shot is good. You must be fast, and you must be right.

Whatever happens, don't contradict the director if he wants another take, claiming there was a problem with the operating or focus. Even though you may think your work was perfect, you never know why the director is saying that it wasn't. I remember an occasion when I had perfectly completed a really tricky shot, only to have the director announce in front of the whole crew, "Oh, Jack missed the shot. Let's do it again." Now, one of the rules of the set is you never call out anyone in front of the whole crew. It's a professional insult, and it's just not done unless you want a punch in the nose. So I was stunned when the director did this. I knew this director. I'd worked with him off and on for ten years, and we always got along, and I thought we respected each other's work. Seething at this injustice, I jumped out of my seat on the dolly, and got in the director's face. "Hey, Bob, what's up? You know I didn't...." Then suddenly seeing a certain look on Bob's face, I finished, "... mean to mess it up. I'll fix it." And I quickly returned to the camera. What I saw in his look was that the star had screwed up badly. But the star was the star, and the star was the producer, and the star was in a bad mood, and the star would be insulted if Bob said the performance was bad, and that's why he needed another take. The only way to get another take was to blame it on a technical problem—someone else's fault. And since we were friends, Bob figured he could get me to take one for the team.

When I was promoted from first assistant to operator, a friend who'd made the move a year earlier told me, "This is an even bigger change of job than you think, because you're going from technician to politician." At the time, I wasn't sure what he meant. It was an odd thought, but it turned out to be true. The professional operator has to have the facility to make other people (the director and DP) comfortable with allowing someone else to take charge of the important function of composing the shots and being the one who is looking through the viewfinder when a shot is made. You have to be able to interpret the director's verbalized thoughts of images in his mind into equivalent visual images on the screen, and you have to be able to direct and coordinate your efforts with the other crew members who are working with you to accomplish the work.

I'm not sure that there are any exercises you can do to be a good politician. You'll pick that up from the advice and feedback of the more experienced people you work with. What exercises can do is help you hone the manual and mechanical operating skills that are essential. So go ahead and do the next exercise.

18A • THIRD EXERCISE: OPERATING SKILLS

The following exercises are intended to help you hone your skills as an operator; on low-budget films the DP will also double as operator, so you'll want to develop good operating skills. For this exercise it doesn't matter what camera you use, but you do want to be working with a decent tripod and head. O'Connor heads are the original fluid heads, and the old O'Connor 100 is a beautiful head. The new ones are great, too. Look for your head's weight-bearing capacity; that's an indication of how much resistance you'll have when operating. Get one that fits the weight of your camera. Other excellent heads are Cartoni and Sachtler. Sachtler heads tend to be used a lot, although I find their click-stop controls for resistance don't give me the flexibility the other heads do. Your mileage may vary. The geared heads are Panahead and Arrihead, although you might be able to find old Worrall and Mitchell heads. (Consult Chapter 35 for directions on mounting the head, or ask the rental technician.)

If you can get hold of a gear head and a fluid head, I suggest you perform these exercises with both so you can compare the operation and results of one compared to the other. You don't have to record your practice shots, but if you're using reusable media, it might be a good idea to do so. Seeing what you've done on the screen may look different from what you envisioned as you were shooting. And relax: It takes a lot of practice to get good at this. So repeat each movement over and over until you're satisfied with your performance. No, it won't happen in one day; you'll get bored before you get good. And the first few times with the gear head can be very frustrating. However, you'll find you're drawn back to it the next day. Keep at it. One day you'll mysteriously do everything perfectly, and you won't notice any effort. Hooray!

1. Stand Up and Sit Down

It doesn't take much to describe this exercise. Set up your camera on a tripod at about a height of four to five feet. Use a medium lens so you can frame a tight waist shot. Have someone sit in a chair about 8 feet away. Begin shooting that person sitting in the chair. Then follow the person as she stands up, walks to another chair about 15 feet from the first (and again at least 8 feet from the camera) and sits down. You can have your subject go back and forth between the two chairs as you try to keep your camera movements smooth and your frame well balanced.

Doing pretty well? Now try this exercise with a longer lens (tighter shot) and with a longer lens at a greater distance. Then try it with a wide lens at different distances. There are infinite variations of this exercise. You can have the camera higher or lower, you can have a taller or shorter person, the actor can walk fast or slow—try as many different ways as you can.

2. Follow a Subject Entering an Empty Frame

Set up your camera on a tripod with a medium-long lens, with your subject about 10 feet away so he will be cut at the waist or elbows. Start shooting on an empty frame. Have the subject walk into the frame from one side or the other, and then continue to walk as you frame up on him and follow his movement.

The trick here is to establish your frame as soon as the actor enters it. Timing is crucial. Be careful not to overly anticipate the subject's entrance, but likewise don't

(Continued)

18A • THIRD EXERCISE: OPERATING SKILL—CONT'D

let him get halfway across the frame before you pick up on him. As a rule, you'll want to give the actor some nose room so there's space in the frame ahead of the actor's direction of movement. What you want to do is tense your muscles and prepare yourself mentally to begin the pan as soon as you see your subject enter. This physical and mental preparation will allow you to overcome the slight time lag you would otherwise have. The lag would mean the subject is at least to the middle of the frame before you move; with your mental prep, you'll catch him before that, and he'll never get beyond the middle of the frame. You'll want to maintain consistent framing for the duration of the shot as you follow the actor's movement.

Once again, the difficulty of executing the shot will be affected by the lens you're on and the size of the subject in the frame. So also perform this exercise with a wide lens and a long lens and with the actor at varying distances from the camera. If you're a whiz at this, fine. Use a tighter lens. Keep making it harder—can you do this shot when you're framed as a choker?

3. Follow a Subject Ascending/Descending Stairs

Start off with your actor at the bottom or top of a flight of stairs. Place your camera about 10 feet from the bottom of a flight of stairs, and, using a midlength lens, frame your subject in a waist shot. Follow the actor as he ascends and then descends the stairs.

You can set up your camera in varying positions relative to the stairs: facing the stairs head-on, at 90 degrees (sideways) to the stairs, or at any angle in between. You'll want to try all of these setups. Each presents a different challenge. As your operating improves, try a longer lens and/or move the camera closer to the stairs.

The trick here is to keep the subject in the frame and to keep the frame steady. Don't try to adjust for the up-and-down bounce of the subject. Your job is to keep the camera moving so the lens describes a smooth diagonal. The subject's head will rise and drop slightly in the frame; this won't be annoying unless you let them leave the frame.

4. Follow Patterns Drawn on a Wall

Put a big sheet of paper on the wall and draw zigzag lines or diagonals or circular lines on it. (Panavision has ready-made practice charts, a classic one with diagonal lines and cloverleaf curves, that you can use if you're lucky enough to be near one of their offices.) Try to follow the lines. Then try doing it quickly and smoothly. Use different-length lenses at different distances from the wall.

5. Shoot an Unpredictable Erratically Moving Subject

Find a subject like children playing, pets romping around, an amateur sporting event, any active subject. With your camera on a tripod, practice following the movement. Use wide, medium, and long lenses at varying distances. A friend of mine borrowed a geared head and an old viewfinder, set it up in her livingroom, and followed her kittens. Kittens are fast and totally random; if you can follow them, you're good.

18B • WHAT YOU SHOULD HAVE LEARNED FROM THE OPERATING EXERCISES

When it comes to operating, we all have a particular bugaboo, and you will have now discovered yours. The chair thing, though, is a bear for everyone. If you can work out a way to get good at it, you'll have the skills to perform almost any tough move, and you'll make a good operator of yourself for what is probably one of the most common moves camera operators have to make.

Having done this exercise, you should now have renewed respect for all the operators who have made this move look invisible on the screen, and you will appreciate how much practice it took to master it. Next to bad focus, bad operating is almost as annoying and equally unforgivable, and yet they are both taken for granted when done well. That is why, in spite of all the jokes that are made on the set about how easy the operator has it, there's an unspoken regard for the hard work that goes into becoming a really good operator.

When dealing with actors rising from and sitting down in chairs and walking from one chair to another (situation #1), you're faced with transitioning from a tilt to a pan and back again, while keeping the actor in the frame, with good headroom, leading the actor as he walks, and neither getting ahead nor behind (losing the actor from the frame or having him bump up against it). It's like the old patting your head while rubbing your tummy challenge.

You will have noticed immediately that you tend to let the actor rise before you tilt so his head goes past the top of the frame, giving him a "haircut." Then you'll find yourself lagging behind as the actor moves toward the other chair. You'll be fooled by the fact that, depending on his changing angle toward you, the actor seems to go faster or slower in different parts of his move. And you'll have difficulty keeping the nose room consistent. When the actor gets to the other chair and starts to sit down, you may (in a reverse of the start) let him drop into the bottom of the frame as he sits. And finally, you'll be plagued throughout by the need to keep consistent lead room and headroom.

In addition, everyone gets up and sits down and moves differently. Young actresses, maybe because they weigh so little and have so much energy, seem to rocket out of their chairs. Older people may first bend forward before they actually rise to generate momentum to get them up off their chair. Some people move immediately, and others pause—for how long? Who knows? You will be dealing with every one of these moves in your career, so have a bunch of different subjects for your practice sessions. The only true way to overcome these problems is practice. As you will on the set, have rehearsals. Whenever you see the actor sit or rise, see how he moves. This means during "actor only" rehearsals, when there's just concentration on lines and characterization. Even if the rest of the crew is ordered off the stage, you can sit quietly in a corner and observe the actors. Every one of them will have a "tell"—the little unconscious move that poker players look for in their opponents. At least you can memorize the cue at which the actor rises and how soon after the cue the actor moves; it could be a line, or it could be another actor's movement.

In situation #2 you are trying to anticipate an actor's move (as you did in the chair exercise) but now you do not have a subject in your starting frame. Whenever

(Continued)

18B • WHAT YOU SHOULD HAVE LEARNED FROM THE OPERATING EXERCISES—CONT'D

something—an actor, a car, a basketball—enters your frame, you have be able to lock onto that object instantly from a static position and then follow it smoothly, while maintaining a consistently well-composed frame. The art of operating is to make these moves so smooth that nobody notices them and the audience is never distracted from the actors by unsettling movement or composition.

It is most likely that you'll lag behind your subject. Either this will remain consistent during the shot and it will look like the subject is pushing the frame with his nose, or you will play catch-up. Catch-up is continuously trying to adjust. The tendency is to do too much, putting the actor at the edge of the frame where he entered, then slowing so he gets ahead of you, and so on. You can see this in sports coverage of race cars going around ovals. The operator wants to keep a consistent speed, but even though the car is at a constant speed, his apparent speed varies because the track curves.

The solution here, besides practice (sound familiar?), is to imagine—just mentally—that you're making the moves (with the head) that you would make to follow the subject and to try to feel the acceleration and deceleration that's due to the curving of the movement. Sometimes you have to get above the scene physically to see the exact path of the subject. So if you need to, find something to climb on (a ladder, a chair) and get a bird's-eye view of the scene. You'll find that this need occurs to the focus puller as well. You can work on it together.

In situations #1 and #2 your moves were essentially vertical and horizontal (tilting and panning), but in situation #3 you will have had to combine them to produce a diagonal move. This is generally not hard with a fluid head. It is one of the killers for a novice on the wheels. If you don't blend the moves of your right and left hands, you get a jerky look we call "Etch-a Sketch."

The cure for "Etch-a Sketch" is, yes, practice. And make a point of being conscious of how your work looks. Try to critique it in your head. If you're on a show that records video assist, always look at it. Figure out what you could do better, and identify precisely the point in your move that you screwed up.

Practicing by following lines on a wall (situation #4) is another good way to sharpen your skills without having to ask another person to spend hours being a subject while you practice. You'll want to spend more time than he or she wants to give you, so practicing this way allows you to spend all the time you want and need without annoying your friend. After you've practiced, get your subject back in and try #1 and #2 again. See if you've improved.

When I was first learning to use the wheels, the classic advice was to tape a flashlight (these days it's a laser pointer) to the head (you don't even need a camera) and try to write your name on a wall. I didn't get this at the time; I thought unless you're using a can of spray paint, you can't see the result. And the thing is, we don't draw with the head; we follow a moving subject. Of course, this would work all right if you had your name (or any words or shapes) written on the wall and you manipulated

18B • WHAT YOU SHOULD HAVE LEARNED FROM THE OPERATING EXERCISES

the head so that the light shone on the writing on the wall as you followed along the outline of the words.

With situation #5 you will have been required to perform your framing and moves quickly and spontaneously without rehearsal or foreknowledge of what the animals or people will do. You will be cursing the wheels and itching to take the camera off the tripod and handhold. Resist the impulse and force yourself to work with that head. It's the only way you'll become a really good operator.

CHAPTER 19
Still More Composition, or Follow the Money

A DP and an operator have dozens of instantaneous decisions to make to keep the composition of a shot working throughout a take. Even in a shot where the camera doesn't move and things appear as simple as possible, an actor can move, and the subtle alignment of the shot will change. It may be a simple two-shot (any shot in which only two actors appear) in which the characters move closer together; the operator must make invisible pans to keep the shot balanced. It may be a large master (a shot that shows the entire action or setting of a scene); characters move forward and back and to the sides, and the operator wants to maintain a balanced frame, so it's time to work with his dolly grip not to lose actors or, worse, cut them off with the frame line.

For every shot, you've asked yourself the question "What do I want the audience to see?" You're telling stories; you want the action and intent of the story to be clear. You also want to persuade the audience to feel a certain emotion or see things from a particular point of view, in keeping with the director's intent. All of this requires making numerous decisions that impact the effectiveness of the shot.

First, there are decisions to make even before the camera is set. Thinking of the character and the actor (we always think of the actor; the rule is stay on number one, the person at the top of the call sheet, the lead), we need to know how to present him or her. The angle on the actor is usually the most important consideration. In masters (or master shots), the aim is to see the whole action; that's important to get a feel for the story and the setting. To show character, we may use increasingly closer shots that feature the actor. So how do we shoot the actor?

Usually star power takes precedence: Get a full frontal view, keep both eyes in the frame (and when lighting, make sure the eyes are well lighted, with a twinkle in them). But there are times when the physical blocking of the scene or the psychological demands of the story prevent getting a full face.

For example, the actor may be looking out a window. We need to see the actor to know who she is, but we have to see what is outside the window. So we're probably going to go with a profile or a one-quarter shot (a shot framed from the rear and to one side of the actor, showing slightly less than a profile), and everything will be fine. Maybe the director will have the actor turn away from the window in contemplation, into a full-face close-up.

A canny actor will always find a way to face the camera in a scene—even exiting a door. Look at *Touch of Evil*; after Quinlan (played by director Orson Welles) has killed Grandi, Welles leaves the room. But as his bulk fills the frame, Welles reaches for the door across his body with his right hand. This causes him to turn into profile, but as he closes the door, he turns back to look at the results of his mayhem, full face to the camera, and the neon light effect comes on just then to light him. It's a brilliant piece of choreography and serves the story well.

You will have to choose how you'll show the actor. First, you need to think about what best serves the story. Do you really want to see the actor face on, or would it be better to keep the character somewhat hidden (three-quarter shot [analogous to a one-quarter shot, but showing more than a profile] or profile)? Is he subordinate to what else is in the frame (one-quarter shot, back of head)? Usually these choices are made almost by reflex, and in fact, the director more often than not decides the angle he wants on the scene. But as long as we're becoming tomorrow's cinematographers, let me encourage you to think about the proper shot for the movie. Often enough, the director says, "Give me a close-up," and leaves the operator to his own devices. If you're ready, if you've read the script and thought about it, if you've been paying attention to the character and to the director's sense of the work, then you can make a decision that looks good and gives the director something extra, something he or she hasn't asked for. These moments endear the DP and operator to the director. Besides making a good movie, working this way can get you your next job.

The cinematographer and the operator (the person actually looking through the camera, setting and adjusting the frame; today often called the cameraperson) must always think about editing. If you break up a two-shot of a conversation into three-quarter shots, both actors should be in three-quarters for smooth cutting. When moving into close-ups, it is standard to vary the angle and usually to move in so that more of the actor's face shows—a 50/50 two-shot (usually a shot with the actors in profile; always a shot in which the actors show the same amount of face), three-quarters, or full singles (another word for close-up, calling attention to one actor). Of course, the actors must be looking slightly off camera, one to the right and one to the left, to create the sense that they are conversing with each other. This is following our famous 180-degree rule. Sometimes it may mean cheating, which is adjusting things in the frame so they make sense on the screen. It's a much-used term signifying in this case we, the filmmakers, are setting the shot in a way that doesn't precisely correspond to the master. We cheat a lot in making a movie. The trick is to make the audience believe they are seeing everything in temporal and spatial continuity. Of course, almost nothing "really" is. So as I say, it may mean cheating the actor's look—either at an angle or a direction not used in an earlier take—so that it works for the camera. The actor may have to look in a direction that seems counterintuitive to her. Take a little time; explain it's a technical thing; tell her it has to do with the stage line; make sure the actor knows that she will look better with the cheat; and never try to explain the principle. You'll drive yourself crazy and be there all day. If the actor needs more convincing, explain that this is her close-up. An actor once told me, "A master shot buys me a Chevy, but a close-up buys me a Cadillac."

Sometimes, however, you want to break the rules, with one actor in profile while the other is full face. Let's say you've got two characters making a deal and one of them plans to double-cross the other. The victim benefits from a full face shot; a profile of the betrayer lets the audience know subliminally that he's not to be trusted: we can't see all of him, so he's hiding something.

Every time a cinematographer sets up a shot, he must decide where to set the camera and at what height to shoot from. These days the standard camera height seems to be about 4½ or 5 feet off the ground—what I call the cow's-eye height. This height tends to keep the actor in perspective, emphasizing neither the top nor the bottom of his body. It's sort of boring, but it's perceived as neutral. The audience gets no particular emotional nudge from it.

It's likely that this practice results from the idea that the camera reflects the audience's point of view; this height more or less duplicates our visual experience when standing. I realize that most of us are taller than 4½ feet, but it seems to work. The point is that it's neutral and that it's important to know why and when you deviate from the norm. There are always practical reasons (you want to see over everyone's head, so you put the camera high). The unusual choice of camera height is most interesting when it's used for its emotional connotations. It's a truism that high views (looking down at a subject) give an audience a sense of power and expansiveness. Low views (looking up at the subject) give a feeling of wonder or of the point-of-view (POV) of an inferior. A shot from below of a person emphasizes his dominance, stature, authority; a shot from above diminishes him or her.

These ideas may seem clichéd because stating them baldly in words makes them seem superficial or shallow. Always remember that you are dealing with visuals and emotions, not words and meanings. Very often talking about a camera technique will sound simple or simple-minded, but the effect visually on the screen will be extremely expressive. It's a difference in the "language." I wish there were a word for the syntax of pictures other than "language," but I'm stuck with it. (Please e-mail me if you have any suggestions.)

Then there's always the element of movement. Actors move; they have to be followed and focused. So the camera must move. You may have tried moving the camera by hand or in a shopping cart, or a car, or a skateboard. Good for you for trying; probably you got yourself a jittery mess. Movement is tricky for everyone, although experience helps.

FIGURE 19.1
Matthews doorway dolly.
Photos courtesy of Matthews Studio Equipment.

Movements convey feelings of their own. Sadly, there are few rules to guide us. A horizontal movement can be calming or boring or white knuckle exciting. So let's think of what you're facing now and what you will have to face as you advance. Everyone has trouble executing pans and tilts, and at first it's an irresistible temptation to zoom in and out excessively.

And what happens when you use a dolly? Usually you hurt yourself. With any luck, you can find a doorway dolly, the simplest professional moving camera platform (a sheet of plywood 28¼ by 51 inches with interchangeable balloon and track wheels, usually with a rudimentary steering mechanism). Pros use them all the time, but crab dollies are preferred. I've found most schools and small rental or production houses have made the investment in a doorway dolly. Doorway dollies are fairly inexpensive, they can be used on track or on the flat, they're slightly steerable, and they're hard to break. You can even build a reasonable facsimile yourself. Look at the pictures on Matthews's website,[1] or check out magazine articles, particularly in *Student Filmmakers*. A lot of camerapeople build their own equipment, and they get by surprisingly well with it. What you're going to want to do is design and execute interesting moves.

It's not too hard to put a tripod on the doorway dolly and push it around. But to make a good shot, the camera movement has to have a purpose, and it has to be well designed. Well-designed means that the movement is neither too long nor too short, and you are able to make the shot without contorting yourself.

Sometimes the purpose of a shot is just to follow or lead a character as he moves. Certainly this is what most of you will want to do most of the time. Almost as common is moving toward, or less commonly away from, a character to emphasize an emotional point. With overuse this can easily become absurd, creating a sense of exaggerated cheap melodrama. But used sparingly, it can be effective. These are motivated moves; action or emotion causes them. And there are unmotivated moves. Fellini's films are loaded with these. *8½* could be a primer for the unmotivated or unlikely move. Often Fellini will dolly without apparent reason, but soon a character enters from behind camera, and we follow her, so it's semimotivated. Sometimes the dolly will move one way (say, pushing forward into the scene) and the characters will move in a contrary direction—perpendicular to the dolly's track or randomly in and out of the frame. Fellini will use this also as a character's POV shot, into which the character often enters—and sometimes exits, the shot continuing further even without the main character. There's a thrill and a dreamlike quality that Fellini gets from these moves. They're hard to pull off, but if you can do it, they add great excitement and energy to a shot.

[1]http://www.msegrip.com/mse.php?show=product&cat=422&products_ID=26251

Designing a dolly shot begins simply: Where do you want to start? Where do you want to end? Really, all you need to do is determine those two points, lay track (or not), and roll. You may want to consider a few aspects: If you can, be on a flat surface. Dollies just don't work on bumps or inclines. If it's the least bit uneven, you'll have to lay track. (A dolly track can be as simple as two flat boards, or professional aluminum or stainless steel tubing designed to fit special hard rubber tires.) Although you may have a dolly, it's less likely that you'll have track. But— good news—renting track is usually relatively inexpensive.

So you've got the beginning and end of the shot set. Good! Think about it a little bit more. Is the camera facing mostly in one direction, or would the operator have to climb over and around the dolly and make a 270-degree shot? I've done a lot of that. Usually it's poorly laid-out shots that turn you into a pretzel. You can probably get an effective shot without this kind of move. If you've got a shot that picks up your hero walking, leads him, lets him pass, and follows him, you've got a 180-degree shot. It's hard to do, and you have to ask yourself, "Is it worth it?" My philosophy is that the drama should be on the screen, not behind the camera. Some shots will always be tough, but you should avoid unnecessary difficulty if you can. Think about where the lens is pointed; this will determine whether the dolly grip pushes or pulls the dolly. (You don't want the grip in the picture.) Another consideration for crab dollies is the operator's comfort. Yes, we're all prima donnas, but comfort means you'll be able to make the shot more efficiently. It's important that the operator has a place for his or her feet and is able to see through the viewfinder easily.

Laying track is a skill, and I recommend that you find a professional grip and have him or her show you and your crew how it's done. If that's not possible, remember the idea is to have the track all at one level, from side to side and along its length. Before you've got it leveled, make sure it runs in an absolutely straight line from one end to the other. Keeping the track level is vital, and so is keeping it in a straight line. Otherwise, you've got a crooked, wobbly roller coaster.

To avoid the roughness, you should level the track by putting wedges under the joints in the track and adjusting them until a long (at least 3-foot) level shows the bubble centered. You can rent the wedges from equipment houses, or if you're handy, you can make them by cutting 1-foot lengths of 2 × 4 inches diagonally. It's best to use two wedges, with the pointed ends overlapping and facing each other so you've got as flat a surface as possible to adjust the level. You'll probably have to use some kind of cribbing (any sturdy lumber, usually 1-foot lengths of 2 × 4s and one foot squares of ½-inch or ¾-inch plywood) in some places to compensate for lower ground levels. Remember, the track has to be as high as the highest point of the ground, so it's likely that you'll need cribbing. Apple boxes are most often used to support the track to the uniform height. Anything sturdy and nonslipping will work. Sometimes grips put a 1 × 1-foot piece of ¾-inch plywood under the joints on top of the wedges. This gives more support area, and it's a nice, safe technique. The wedges have to be oriented in line with the track so the ends don't stick out. Otherwise there's a danger they'll be kicked and displaced.

FIGURE 19.2
Grip wedges (for leveling).
Photos courtesy of Matthews Studio Equipment.

FIGURE 19.3
Dolly track leveled with wedges and cribbing (for height).
Photos courtesy of Matthews Studio Equipment.

Disaster alert: Here's what can happen if you disregard this advice. Back when I was an operator on the TV show *Mad About You*, I had a lot of chances to do dolly shots on our back lot New York street of Paul and Jamie walking along the sidewalk, talking about life, and running into friends and oddballs. One day we had a shot running the whole length of the street. Since our back lot was an old driveway behind another stage, the contour of the land was sloped and uneven. No concession for movies. It was about an 80-foot tracking shot, the full length of the street, requiring 10 lengths of 8-foot track. At the start, the track was on the ground, but because of the slope, the track had to be cribbed up a full 2 feet at the end. The grips probably used every apple box in the department, and they certainly took painstaking effort to achieve this with perfection. Now one rule of track is that no one walks on the track or steps over the track. No one—*ever*. If the dolly grip absolutely has to when pulling the dolly, or if the actors have to while the camera's rolling, that's okay. Everyone else must go to the end and walk around the track. (The exercise won't kill you.) The grips, especially the dolly grip, all keep an eye on the track, and they warn everyone away from the track, but it doesn't always work. The cruel truth is that there are always producers on the set. And on TV, most producers are writers, so they think rules don't apply to them. On this particular day, someone (and I'm guessing it was a producer) walked on the track, tripped on a wedge, and kicked it out of place. This is bad enough, but it's only the second worst sin. What's the worst sin? He pushed the wedge back where he thought it belonged and did not alert anyone to what had happened. Civilians don't have a clue how to set up a track, and they should stay away. If they must mess around, they should have the decency to tell a grip when they've screwed up. There's nothing worse.

So we're doing the shot. Paul and Helen walk quickly, so the dolly is moving at quite a clip. I have my eye to the viewfinder, and it's a nice shot. Suddenly the viewfinder rips itself away from me—the nice shot is gone, and I'm looking at the world—and my ride is as rough as a mile of bad road. Our dolly's speedy skateboard wheels, in their special sled, had hit the wedge that the culprit had "replaced." The dolly popped off the sled; hit the track, knocking it over; and everything—dolly, camera, and operator (me)—went airborne. The resulting imbalance on the camera separated it from the tripod head and hurled it toward the pavement. Half a million dollars' worth of camera and lens, not to mention the film, headed to destruction.

Acting on pure adrenaline-induced instinct, I grabbed the camera and kept it from hitting the ground. Here's a hot tip: Never hurt yourself to save the camera. They can always make more. But assistants are trained to marry their cameras, and I was trained as an assistant. Anyway, the camera was saved with only minor repairs. No one was ever caught. But this is why you're careful with your wedges, and this is why dolly grips scream at the idiots walking anywhere near the track.

By the way, this was a Fisher Model 9 dolly, 700 pounds of aluminum and steel, $80,000 if they sold them (like a lot of specialized equipment, they're only rented). It's called a crab dolly. Crab dollies are the fancy hydraulic ones, dollies that can move forward and back, side to side, and often in a circle around its center. It's a lot more dangerous than your doorway dolly but much more versatile, since you've got a built-in rise and drop and the ability to move in multiple directions.

Back to the present. You've got your shots laid out and the track built and leveled. Now comes the interesting part: the time for real teamwork. The dolly grip and operator are dependent on each other. In fact, the dolly grip is as much a member of the camera department as of the grip department. The operator has to be able to design the shot, to communicate it to the dolly grip, and to work with him or her to make the shot happen. This is a prime example of the way crew members must engage in the cooperation that is a byword of filmmaking.

Whenever a scene is shot with actors, there are at least five performers involved in making the shot: the actor(s), of course; the boom operator (the person holding the boom—it looks like a broomstick or a fat fishing rod—on the end of which is the microphone); and the camera crew: operator, assistant, and dolly grip. It pays to think of the work done by these crew members as a performance, not just as technology. A successful shot requires an intuitive interactive relationship among these five.

Working with a dolly requires balletic skills. The operator has to find a position from which he or she can make the shot without straining muscles and without falling off the dolly. The camera assistant has to be nimble, avoiding the track and making sure the dolly doesn't hit her or roll over her feet. She must maintain a position from which she can operate the focus knob and zoom control while keeping an eye on the action. The dolly grip has to start and stop smoothly, feathering the moves, has to match the walking pace of the actors, must be alert for changes, and must be aware of the boundaries of the frame.

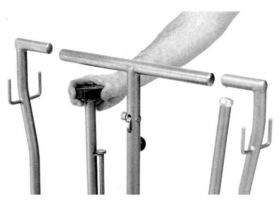

FIGURE 19.4
Arm rise and fall control.
Photos courtesy of J. L. Fisher, Inc.

Feeling the frame takes experience. You get that experience by paying attention to how wide the shot is (ask the assistant what millimeter size the lens is), by realizing that each lens has its own effect on the actors' moves, by being aware there's a chance that an actor will stack—block—another, and by getting to know how much compensating movement by the dolly the operator can deal with. It's fairly complex, and demands a sophisticated understanding of the dynamics of the scene.

Should you find yourself pushing a dolly, here's a few hints: Make sure you know—without looking—how to operate the rise and drop of the hydraulic arm that supports the camera and operator. Which way do you turn or push the knob? Find the friction point (the point at which the control engages, when the arm starts moving, usually ⅛ of a full turn)—most dollies aren't perfect, so the arm is unlikely to move as soon as you start turning the knob—and mark it with tape or a grease pencil. Then when you have a rise or drop coming up, you can set the knob to just before it starts to move, and you'll start your move precisely on cue. Spend some time rehearsing when you're not shooting or rehearsing with actors. And remember to ask the electricians to drop a stinger (an extension cord to civilians) close to the dolly so you can pump up the hydraulics. (Most dollies have an electric motor to pump up the pressure that controls the arm move.) Figure out how you want to mark the dolly so you can hit a precise position every time. Mark it any way you want, but *be consistent*. If you use different systems of marking your start and stop positions, you're going to forget what the mark means, and you'll have another chance to embarrass yourself. The best way I've seen is to mark a rear wheel with tape or chalk at the wheel's hub. The hub is always going to be within a fraction of an inch of the correct position, and the rear wheel is the least likely to go out of alignment. (With the weight of the camera, the operator, and sometimes the assistant, the dolly tends to move on a diagonal, not on a line parallel to its chassis.) Pay attention to what the operator wants; he's the dolly grip's boss, no matter how stupid or demanding he seems. Be sensitive to what the actors are doing and saying. If your move is cued by a line of dialogue, memorize the line before it so you're alert and ready to move when the cue comes. And when a cue is coming up, tense yourself; you are preparing your muscles and your mind so there's no lag time between the cue and your move.

Now let's say you're working as a camera assistant. The left side of the camera (right and left are from the operator's perspective behind the camera, so that means on the operator's left) is called the smart side because all the markings and controls you need are built on that side. Try to work on the smart side. If you can't (say, without falling into a ditch), prepare yourself by marking the lens on the dumb side so that you can read focus marks wherever you are. (Some lenses come marked on both sides; some can be mounted in any configuration so you can read the focus marks from anywhere; be sure you know what you've got.)

Remember that the dolly is 400 to 800 pounds of steel and aluminum, and at least 100 pounds of operator. Once it's moving, it doesn't stop on a dime, so don't get in the way. Toes don't grow back. If you have a critical focus (a shot in which you must be precisely at the correct focus mark, one that gives you no help with depth of field), you may want to set marks by the side of the track so you have a reference for where the dolly is at any point in time. *Don't do this routinely*. Many dolly grips feel that the assistant's marks mock the grip's ability to hit his marks accurately. So talk to the dolly grip, explain that it's *you* who has the problems, not him, and ask if it's okay for you to lay reference marks. You're going to need diplomacy and an appreciation of selective truth all during your career. This is a good time to practice. And remember that the closer you get to the subject, the more critical the focus becomes due to decreased depth of field. So don't freak out about your focus at every point; know what's critical on the lens you're using, and concentrate on that area.

You'll have to zoom and focus and walk at the same time; I know—it's impossible. But you have to do it. So on your downtime practice with the zoom. Find a speed that usually works for you, realizing that you can set the zoom control to move faster or slower from your set speed by pressing the knob or trigger on the zoom control either harder or gentler. Get used to how long it takes to zoom a certain number of millimeters so you can hit your marks closely without looking at the lens. This shouldn't take you more than a year or so to perfect, so start right now. And remember: A good assistant never sits on the dolly unless it's impossible to walk. It's a courtesy to the grip (why should he or she have to push your fat ass?), it leaves more room for the operator, and staying on your feet keeps you more alert so you focus better. See Chapter 30 on focusing for more information on these functions.

When you finally get a chance to operate, you'll think you've died and gone to heaven. You don't perform heavy physical work, and you get to sit! Then you discover that you're responsible for setting the shot. You've got to be able to set the start and stop of the dolly move so the director gets the shot he wants, so it's physically possible for the dolly grip to make the move, and so you can be comfortable while operating. (No one cares whether you're comfortable. But remember, a more-or-less comfortable operator will be able to make shots more smoothly and with better composition.)

Work with the dolly grip to set the beginning and end points of the shot. Together, you can implement the shots the director needs, without setting up an impossible layout for the track. Before you lay track, or before you rehearse with the actors, rehearse with the dolly grip and assistant (and stand-ins, if you have them). Pay attention to how hard it is for you to get into position all during the shot (if it is). You can manage some discomfort at the beginning, and a little less during the shot, but be in a stable, comfortable position at the end, where you're likely to have to hold on the shot after the move. You will need to decide the orientation of the dolly. Is it better if the grip is pushing, or can you make the shot better if he or she is pulling? Should you have the dolly at a 90-degree angle to its orientation (so it moves in a line parallel to the actors, moving right to left or left to right, rather than forward or back)? You may be better off standing rather than sitting. I have found that if I use the seat, I prefer a "lazy Susan" style seat rather than the usual fixed seat so I can use my butt to move the seat and still keep myself on it. Be considerate of the assistant and the dolly grip, but remember that above all you must get the shot and execute it well. See Chapter 18.

It may be intimidating, so remember how beautiful and exciting a good tracking move can be. Keep working at it. Your best bet is to assemble a consistent dolly crew (remember: camera operator, camera assistant, and dolly grip) that work together often. You'll become familiar with each person's methods and idiosyncrasies, and you'll be able to function as a single unit, a perfectly coordinated team.

CHAPTER 20

The Horror of the 180-Degree Line

Would you like to drive yourself crazy? I told you how to do it before: Try explaining the 180-degree rule to an actor. Or just argue about screen direction with the script supervisor. Everybody will be yelling within two minutes, you can make a lot of new enemies, and more than half the people in the "discussion" will think you're nuts. And if you're right about where the actor should move, 95% of your coworkers will think you're out of your mind.

For a matter so basic, so integral to conveying information to the audience, the 180-degree rule, or the stage line, or screen direction is a boogeyman to a lot of people in the business. Most simply do not understand it. Most of those who have some idea of what it's about—and they're the ones in on the argument— only vaguely have a sense of what it is, and have no systematic way of thinking about it or applying it.

I'm good at this. I really understand what's going on. And I'm never wrong. (See what I mean about going crazy?) I will take you through this in an organized way with a few principles you can hang on to and use whenever the question of screen direction comes up.

What are we going to call this? I just mentioned most of the common expressions used to refer to the problem. I'm mostly going to call it the line (short for stage line). What is it? It's the issue of making sure the audience is oriented in space, that they know who is talking to whom, who is chasing or following whom, and who is looking at what.

The situation exists because of the essence of pictorial representation: We're taking something we all know to be three-dimensional, and we are trying to represent it in two dimensions. If we were actually working in three dimensions, and we could move the audience around, we wouldn't have any problem. We'd just all walk around to the side to see where the people are. If you try that, you'll find yourself looking at a line; the screen is a very thin thing.

Proscenium theatre

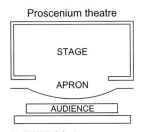

FIGURE 20.1
Proscenium theater.

A lot of film derives from theater; as soon as someone decided to shoot actors instead of just the reality outside the front door, theater sneaked in, and it's not going to leave. So we have artificiality, and we have words and concepts from the theater. So although you don't do theater, you will have to learn a few theatrical terms and concepts. We've already seen the first: *stage line*.

Imagine a theater. The actors are on the stage. The audience is in front, physically separate. Maybe the stage is raised; maybe there's a curtain that rises to signal the beginning of the act and falls to indicate the end. There is, in any case, something that separates the audience from the area where the action takes place. (No, I'm not talking about *avant-garde* theater, and it has nothing to do with us right now.) The separation is the stage line. All the action, and the actors, stay behind it. Actors move left and right, upstage (away from the audience) or downstage (toward the audience), but they stay on the stage.

No, we don't have a stage when we do movies. But the camera sees one way, and the action takes place in front of the camera. Look at Figures 20.1 and 20.2. You can see similarities. In both cases, the diagrams are drawn as though we are looking from above; temporarily, we are gods. There are more similarities. The theater is labeled clearly: You see the stage, you see the audience, you see the proscenium that separates them. It's not as clear in Figure 20.2, a lighting diagram of a movie set.

Let's remove the lights so they don't distract us, and let's put in what passes for the proscenium. Now we're calling it the stage line (Figure 20.3). We have a very simple illustration of what happens. The stage line is an imaginary line set up by the master, the first shot in a sequence. It separates the camera from the subject.

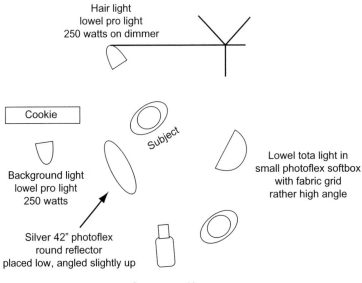

FIGURE 20.2
Standard camera setup.

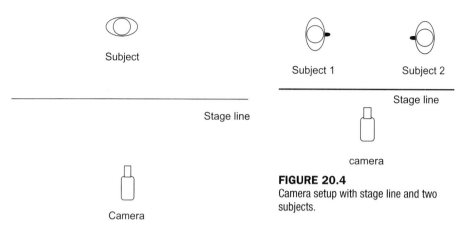

FIGURE 20.3
Camera setup with stage line.

FIGURE 20.4
Camera setup with stage line and two subjects.

Figure 20.4 shows a practical situation. Here we have a camera looking at two people talking to each other. We know where they are, and we know where they are in relation to each other. We can see that subject 1 is looking at subject 2 and vice versa because of the clever noses. All is fine when we have them both in the shot. They can move around; they can change places. But what happens when we want to shoot close-ups?

FIGURE 20.5
Close-up on subject 1.

We move closer (or put on a longer lens), and we change camera position. We change position to vary the angle a little to make a pleasing cut and to get a better look at each actor's face. Our next shot is set up like Figure 20.5. The shot we make looks like Figure 20.6.

We want to get a shot of the person subject 1 is talking to, so we get what is shown in Figure 20.7. As we have talked about, we get a shot with the actors looking about the same size (it's a 2Ts shot), with them on opposite sides of the frame and with them looking in opposite directions with room in the direction they're looking. Figure 20.8 shows how we get that second shot.

FIGURE 20.6
Close-up on subject 1.
From the film *A Moment of Grace*.
Reproduced with permission of GVSU Summer Film Project.

We've moved around to shoot subject 2. We've made sure the frame is the same size, and we've got 2 looking at 1. This is pretty straightforward. But what if we have another person there, someone next to 2, and we want a close-up of him? The setup will be as shown in Figure 20.9. And all we have to do is move the camera around to get what's shown in Figure 20.10.

So we move the camera around to get a shot of #3. We've got three singles,

FIGURE 20.7
Close-up on subject 2.
From the film *A Moment of Grace.*
Reproduced with permission of GVSU Summer Film Project.

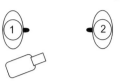

FIGURE 20.8
Close-up on subject 2.

like in Figures 20.11, 20.12, and 20.13. But when we get to editing, what happens? We put them together, and suddenly #3 is not looking at #1 when he talks to him or to #2; the looks are the wrong way.

What happened was back when we set up the master (Figure 20.14). The line is between the camera and the actors. We can move the line around as long as the actors and the camera stay on their own respective sides (Figure 20.15). It's when we think we're being smart and getting a good shot by moving the camera and not the actors that we get into trouble (Figure 20.16).

As you can imagine, when we're dealing with a large number of actors, especially when they walk around and the action takes place on every side of the camera, that's when we have the biggest trouble. Let's call them the biggest challenges.

Why is this happening to you? You're a nice person, and all you want to do is tell an interesting story. And

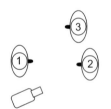

FIGURE 20.9
Close-up on subject 2.

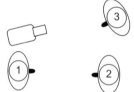

FIGURE 20.10
Close-up on subject 3.

FIGURE 20.11
Close-up on subject 1 (drawing).

FIGURE 20.12
Close-up on subject 2 (drawing).

yet the gods of the movies seem intent on frustrating you. Sadly, this is an inevitable consequence of our living in a three-dimensional world and shooting movies in a three-dimensional world but having to show movies in a two-dimensional world. Working in three dimensions gives you immensely more information than working in two dimensions. All I have here is a two-dimensional instrument, the printed page, so it will be tricky to give you the difference between working in two and three. Although I assume you know something about both.

FIGURE 20.13
Close-up on subject 3 (drawing).

When you, like a camera, are an observer in three dimensions, the information provided by your binocular vision allows you with the slightest movement to determine the relationship of objects to one another in space. But we know that when we take a picture, it's from one point of view. A photograph partakes of a tool of Renaissance painting—perspective—which itself came from the invention and use of the *camera obscura* (ancestor of our HandiCams). In some of the tracts on perspective, painters pointed out that they worked by projecting the real world (3D) onto the world of paper or canvas (2D). When that occurs, the picture may mislead the viewer by hiding objects behind others. It also determines the two-dimensional relationships between them.

It makes no sense to say about the real world that a person is looking right or left to see another. It only makes sense to specify direction from the point of view of a viewer. If the viewer is not the actor, then the viewer (we're talking about the camera here) is determining the direction the actor must look every time. Look at the two-person setup in Figure 20.17. We see #1 looking right and #2 is looking left. If we go to a close-up of #1 looking right, we assume that #1 is looking at #2. If we go to a close-up of #1 looking left, we assume he's looking at something else. Fine. No confusion. But if we try to show a conversation, this means that #1 must look right in the close-up and #2 must look left in his close-up. If we show #2 looking right while engaged in dialogue with #1, we are confused. We *know* #2 is talking to #1, but we also *know* that he's not looking at her.

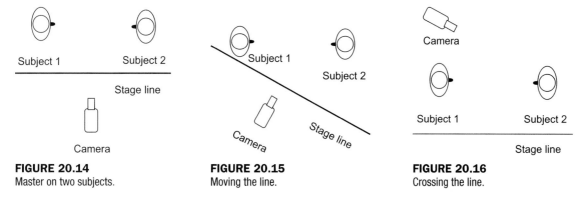

FIGURE 20.14
Master on two subjects.

FIGURE 20.15
Moving the line.

FIGURE 20.16
Crossing the line.

FIGURE 20.17
Two-person setup (from side).

Reducing the problem to a two-person dialogue is simplifying more than you need to, but I think it tells you something important:

First rule: Once an actor is established looking at something in a given direction, he must *always* look at that object in that direction.

This should be easy for you to remember and to apply. And you can see why, in our example with three people, we ran into trouble. What happened is that the people are in the same relationship to each other—that fooled us—but we have let #3 look in a direction different from the direction he looked in the master.

Unless you let yourself get spooked by the idea of "stage line" and "180-degree line" and "continuity" and "matching"—all those words that we use but are just our jargon—you should not have trouble with screen direction. It's mostly a matter of common sense. And the easiest way to know what to do is to remember which way the actor looked.

At this point, I want to make sure you know the difference between the *actor* and the *character*. I've been cavalierly using the terms interchangeably. The character is the fictional person in the story. His consistency is what concerns you. But the actor lives in three dimensions. So he may not understand what happens when we put him into two dimensions. And sometimes actors will argue with you about their look or what they perceive as the wrong camera position. Once again, *do not get into an argument.* Just tell them it's a technical question and that everything will work out okay when it's cut.

What you're doing is keeping the character looking and moving in the correct way, in the direction that seems consistent to the audience. The audience has, in effect, lost information (the positions in 3D space). You have to help them by providing clues (consistent directions) they can't perceive otherwise. You have to do consciously what gets done automatically or intuitively in the real world.

Remember how we discussed leaving "nose room" or "look room" in a close-up so the character's nose doesn't seem to bang up against the screen? That's part of what gives us information about where the character is looking, whom he is seeing, and what direction he's going to go in.

The other rule of not crossing the line is:

When you want a character to change screen direction, he must do so *within* a shot.

Okay, I know what you are thinking: This is crazy, Jack! You just said they have to move the same way. Yes, and that's true; if you have a character running from right to left, then in successive shots he must continue to run right to left. But if, during a shot, he turns and starts running left to right, in successive shots after that he can run left to right. You have shown the audience, in two dimensions and within the time constraints of a shot, that he is going in a different direction. And they're satisfied.

There will be occasions when you must have your character talking to different people in the scene at different times. It's important to know how the movie is going to be edited. Of course, no one knows until it's too late. You must think of the order of the scene and then think of where the master—or whatever shot has established the line—was shot and where your character was relative to the others in the scene. Rarely it may seem that you need to shoot it "both ways"— that is, shoot your character looking both left and right to the same person. Try to avoid it, but you may need to do it in order to save the editor.

I know that a lot of this, like much of a serious discussion about how to shoot something, can sound very simple verbally. Believe me, when it comes down to determining correct screen direction on the set, it is neither simple nor trivial. The arguments can be heated. Unless you have a firm grasp of principles, you will become confused, frustrated, and angry. With a firm grasp of principles, you will be able to stay calm in the midst of a storm. Others may get angry with you, but eventually they will see you're right. You get nothing out of that except a better movie.

CHAPTER 21

The Good, the Bad, and the Ugly (But Not Necessarily in That Order)

When it comes to cinematography, nothing is as shrouded in mystery to most everyone on the set, outside of the DP and the lighting crew, as lighting. And lighting is probably the most challenging aspect of learning cinematography. Part of the problem is just knowing where to begin. You're the DP, and you've got a set to light. How do you do that?

Now there are some DPs who get by just by being very good politicians, which mostly involves hiring a really great gaffer who does the lighting for them. When it comes time to light, they say to the gaffer, "Key from the back right and give me a 4 to 1 fill." Then off they go to drink coffee and flirt with the makeup girl (or guy). I swear, I'm not kidding. Let me suggest that a better approach is to actually know what you're doing.

With fledgling cinematographers who are new to lighting, the most common mistake you'll see is overuse and/or misuse of frontlight. You can tell frontlight because it comes from the front. (Surprising, huh?) More precisely, it is light that comes from the camera's position or behind the camera that throws light all over everything in front of it. Just about everyone starts out lighting this way. You're looking at a scene from behind the camera, so the tendency is to put your lights back there too where they won't be in the way or get into the picture. I mean, what else can you do? Put your lights *on* the set?

I made the mistake of frontlighting—over and over. Working with film, before the advent of digital media, you didn't get to see the results of your work until the next day at dailies. It meant you had to think a lot, meter carefully, and be able to visualize the image without being able to see it on a monitor. This is great training, but it can make you paranoid and overly cautious. You think, "Geez, I'd better use a lot of light so I'll be sure you can see an image on the film." So you use too much light.

Many beginners confuse the job of lighting with the job of illumination. The words look as though they mean the same thing, but they don't. Illumination just puts light in, making things visible. Illuminating something—a room, a scene, a desk—means only that you can see it. I have a lot of respect for illumination, since my dad was actually an illuminating engineer. He designed lighting for businesses and factories so working people had plenty of light to see their work and wouldn't damage their eyes.

Now it's easy to think that's the job when you're shooting a movie. Back in the old, old days, at the end of the nineteenth century, film stock was very slow and needed a huge amount of light just to get an exposure. Cleverly, Edison built a shooting stage on a circular railroad track so that the stage could be rolled around and repositioned as the day went on, taking advantage of the brightest light as the sun changed position in the sky. Lumiére and most other early filmmakers shot their movies outside, in daylight, only. After ten years or so of this, some movies were shot inside. The indoor sets had either giant windows or Cooper-Hewitt lights—Mercury Vapor lights that were essentially large and very bright fluorescent tubes putting out a lot of blue and UV light. This was indeed illumination only. You can look at early films, and you will see no modeling, no use of shadow, no directionality to the light. It was enough for them just to get a picture, and the audience was satisfied.

Now I assume that you want your lighting to do something more than just light up the actors and the set. Of course, you want to create striking images, but, even more, you want to produce expressive lighting that adds to the impact of the movie. So how do you do that? Well, first of all, stop worrying about whether or not you'll get a picture. Today, any film stock and any digital camera you use will easily register an image no matter what. With some cameras and stock you could shoot in a coal cellar at midnight and still get a picture of the black cat walking around down there.

If you're working digitally, you have a monitor that shows you that you're getting an acceptable exposure. You're relieved of the simple worry "Will I see a picture or will it be blank?" Of course, you can't trust it. In order to trust the picture you must have a monitor that's calibrated precisely; that usually means getting a video engineer to set it up. Then you have to make sure it doesn't lose its adjustment in transport and that no one fiddles with it on the set. (Fat chance.) You should have a DIT—digital imaging technician—on the set to make sure your cameras are calibrated and give identical pictures. Now we're talking about professional movies, and no one will have a simple pullout LCD screen on those anyway.

The worst thing about frontlighting, besides being a reaction to an unreasonable fear, is—in plain English—it's *ugly*! There are a few exceptions—mostly situations in which the natural light comes from behind the camera and you like the look (I've used patterns of windows throwing light on the subject), times when the fill is as bright as the key (a rare occurrence), and beauty light on your actor. But in most cases frontlighting flattens the image, destroying the illusion of three-dimensionality. Frontlight works against modeling, making your subject seem flat, literally two-dimensional. It is promiscuous; it lights everything equally, so there's no difference between the star of the movie and the furniture. Frontlighting will throw the shadows of your subjects behind them. If they're close to a wall, you'll have ugly and distracting shadows on the wall. If you have several people in the scene, some behind others, the people in front will throw ugly, obscuring shadows on the ones in back. As soon as you try to record sound, the boom mike throws a shadow all over the actors, the set, and the background. If your light stand is kind of low, the light will be behind the camera, and it'll throw an incriminating camera shadow all over the scene. So you can see that one concern you will always have with lighting is the creation of unwanted and ugly shadows. Always be watching out for these and take note that they don't occur only with frontlight. (You will also be concerned with the creation of beautiful shadows, but more about that later.) Frontlight ignores the reality that in real life interiors are lit by a variety of multiple lighting sources that differ in the same locale depending on time of day.

Using frontlight on night exteriors presents additional problems. If everything in your scene is evenly illuminated, your lighting will be essentially the same as if it were lit by sunlight. If it's properly exposed, it will look like day. If it's not, it will just look dim, not like night.

I once worked with a DP who lit a graveyard scene with 12K HMIs, all from behind the camera, all frontlighting the cemetery. The gaffer, the electricians, even the grips and makeup people were perplexed. There was grumbling all over the set, and it came down to "Doesn't this guy know anything? Hasn't he ever heard of backlight?" Well, I guess he hadn't. The shot went into the picture, and it looked like hell. (I don't think that DP ever got another job.)

So we get it: no frontlight! So what do you do? Well, if you're not going to light from the front, how about lighting from the back (yes, we call that backlighting, as shown in Figure 21.1) or the side (no, we call that cross lighting)? It's good to have a default strategy for lighting. Not every scene has a strongly dramatic drive to it. If there is no compelling reason to put lights in a specific place—though there usually is, and you want to search for it—begin with back cross lighting.

To back cross light, you begin by placing your lights above and about 45 degrees behind your subject. You can vary this basic setup depending on your specific situation. For example, on practical locations you'll have to find places to attach and hide lights. One good way to do that is to mount your lights on special vertical poles wedged between the floor and the ceiling. (Matthews makes a telescoping pole called a Matthpole, shown in Figure 21.2.)

Any way to mount lights that takes up less space than conventional light stands is a great help on cramped locations, as most locations are. A wall spreader (a piece of lumber between two metal braces with a screw adjustment like a turnbuckle) puts the lights high and off the floor (Figure 21.3). If you

LIGHT

SUBJECT

CAMERA

FIGURE 21.1
Backlight.

FIGURE 21.2
Matthpole.
Photos courtesy of Matthews Studio Equipment.

A   B

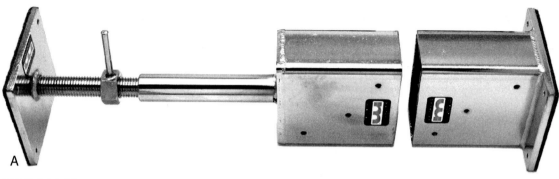

FIGURE 21.3A
Wall spreader
courtesy of Matthews Studio Equipment.

FIGURE 21.3B
Best boy electric Christopher Porter hanging from a well-mounted wall spreader
courtesy of Jack Anderson.

FIGURE 21.4
Truss.
*Photo courtesy of Global
Truss America.*

have the room, use a truss system like the ones for rock concerts and theaters (Figure 21.4).

I learned back cross lighting from George Spiro Dibie, ASC, former president of the national cinematographers' local and one of my mentors. Dibie revolutionized the look of multiple-camera shows (sitcoms) with *Barney Miller*. He brought to television the lessons he had learned gaffing with James Wong Howe, ASC (*Funny Lady, Hud*, over 100 others), and other top DPs. Instead of building a "wall of fire," 5Ks and 10Ks ringing the set from the front and side, Dibie used lighting from the back and at an angle to put modeling light on the actors. One character's backlight became another character's key light. The set had a dimensionality about it that differentiated it from all other sitcoms. It became possible to do moody lighting by varying the amount of front fill (soft, secondary lighting, not the primary, bright frontlighting of the past). And he taught his style to anyone who asked, sparking the revolution in multiple cameras and building the generation of cinematographers working today.

Let me say it again: Do not use frontlight. You'll constantly be tempted to, but try to be strong. Find a way to light your characters from some other direction, preferably in a way that avoids ugly shadows and simultaneously gives modeling to faces and bodies. Look for a window, a door, a light fixture on the wall. There's always something that "justifies" your placement of a light. Or invent a light. Many times I've had to say (to myself), "Okay, there's a high window on the back wall, and a bright street lamp is outside, and it's lighting my character." Of course, we don't ever see a window; I use it as a mental trick. It helps me to remember the quality, direction, and amount of the light. It's a justification (granted, only in my imagination) for putting a light in a particular place. More importantly, it lets me keep consistency in the look by remembering my invented light source.

Frontlighting often goes hand-in-hand with another sin: over lighting. Thank goodness for the evolution of faster and faster film and the development of highly sensitive chips. With them, the perceived need to use a lot of light to get a decent exposure has disappeared. But the tendency to over light has not. There are DPs who fuss and fuss with their lighting, using a ridiculous number of lighting instruments to pick out this and that little area of the set, insisting it's necessary to do this to get a really "beautiful" image. This is called "painting," and that's not a compliment. If there's time to bring out specific areas with subtle additions of light, that may not be bad. But all the attention paid to lighting little bits of a shot works against your goal: place, time, emotion. You can become involved in a kind of navel-gazing, totally occupied with the beauty of your handcrafted frame to the detriment of the whole work.

"Painting" is most common in the shooting of commercials, where there is more time to light. Although on movie/TV sets we all complain about too little time to do the work, it's often a blessing to be constrained by a schedule. Just as the sonnet form imposes limits on a poem and yet produces perhaps the greatest poetry, the limit of time keeps us focused on the primary expressive elements (place, time, emotion) and away from the merely decorative.

Another kind of over lighting is less interesting than painting. Sometimes a DP will flood a scene with light so that everything in the scene is brightly illuminated even where there should be shadows. It's fast and easy. It's a way of not having any shadows so the DP doesn't have to worry about creating bad shadows. But shadows help to convey mystery, enhance three-dimensionality, and obscure areas of less interest in the frame. You always want to keep the audience following the primary action, and you can achieve this by allowing the rest of your frame to fall into shadow.

One of the most common instances of over lighting occurs when shooting night exteriors. Often you'll see a shot of a street at night that's been illuminated by a

LIGHT

SUBJECT

CAMERA

FIGURE 21.5
Diagram: Light at a kick angle.

FIGURE 21.6
Frame still: Light at a kick angle. From the film *A Moment of Grace.* Reproduced with permission of GVSU Summer Film Project.

giant light (at one end of the street) throwing a wash of light on a facing wall or pointed into the camera, giving a flare and usually lighting up moisture in the air. If you're going for a "mystical" effect, this flaring might work, but forget conveying any sense of naturalism. The reality of night time for most of us is that there are a very few bright areas and a lot of dim and dark areas. To convince the audience you're really showing them night, you need to make the lighting very spotty. There must be an area or two of bright light (as from a store window) and possibly pools of light from streetlights. But streetlights do not cover a large area. Light from them, from stores and signs, and from traffic falls off very rapidly. Unless you are in a highly developed urban area with store after store, no gaps between them, every store lit, every store with a lit sign, you will not have an evenly lit exterior.

Also, how you want your exterior to look depends on the time of night you want to show. Nine o'clock Friday night in an area of restaurants, shops, and theaters is going to have a lot of lights and activity. Four in the morning in the same area will have almost nothing lit except streetlights and the occasional car headlight. There's far more black and unrelieved shadow at 4:00 AM.

Now that I've warned you against over lighting, let's talk about under lighting. This may be a problem for you if you are working on low-budget projects with not enough money to rent lamps and a generator or if the schedule is so tight you don't have time to light. If you have to light a relatively large area with too few lighting instruments, think about how you can make each lamp pay off. You will probably have one or two actors in the scene, and you want to see them. If you can, let them play at least part of the scene in silhouette. You can light a background and have the actor play in front; you get a sense of the geography and you can see the actor's presence. The silhouette also gives you more of the feel of night by hiding some of the actor from the audience.

You can make use of smaller lights by not lighting everything up to key. Again, darkness and dimness are part of what makes night night. Let a small lamp cover a larger area. Back it off—move it further from the subject or dim it with scrims and nets—and it will never make the background bright, but it will show the background and will be consistent with a night feel. But do not make the mistake of underexposing the entire shot. It is a good idea to have something—even if it's a glint of chrome on a car or a bit of rim light on your actor—that is fully exposed ("up to key"). The audience reads that as a reference; its brightness, even though only a tiny part of the screen, gives them something to hang their eyes on. They see that bright spot as a realistic bit of light, and they read the darker areas as darker than the bright spot, consequently darker than normal, thus like night.

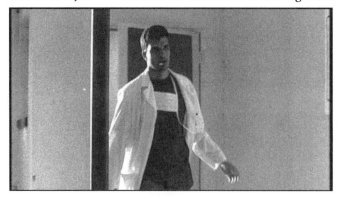

Remember that backlighting and rimlighting (light hitting your subject that gives only a sliver of light on one side) allow you to light a scene with small instruments that use less electrical power. That is because the kick angle of a light (the light hitting a subject and bouncing off it, like billiard balls off a cushion) appears brighter than the same lamp frontlit.

If you have very small lights and not many of them, you can light a large area by hitting specific key areas, letting the light fall off between them. You'll create a mysterious and nightlike feeling with a sense of space. You can also put a number of small lights behind a large piece of diffusion (material that softens and spreads the light, like tracing paper, made by the same companies that make gels for lights). By making sure the lights hit the diffusion evenly, you will have one large backlight.

The same approach works when you're fighting time. I think of all these tactics as sketching in the shot rather than lighting it. I think you will find that they are often more effective than if you had used a lot of lights or taken a lot of time.

Remember that you can also get light onto your actors' faces by using a bounce card. Rather than directing light onto the actor, you direct your light onto the reflective surface of a lightweight board, and then bounce the light reflected from the board onto your subject. You can devise a bounce board from many things; I often use foamcore (from most art stores), showcard (from film supply houses), or bead board (Styrofoam sheets—insulation from home improvement stores: cheap and available). Use anything you can find that works. Usually you want to have the bounce be bright enough to read emotions and expressions. But at night, you can sacrifice that to a moody look. If you don't have enough lights but you want to see some of the character's face, you can angle a bounce card so it picks up one of your backlights and throws that reflection into the character's face. It may be three or four stops down from key—almost invisible—but it will give you a glint in the eye, and it will give you an exposure just slightly better than total darkness.

You might be thinking, "All this is fine, but I'm working with three photofloods and some old music stands." Maybe you are, but I like to remind myself of something Roger Deakins (*True Grit, The Company Men, A Serious Man, No Country for Old Men, Jarhead, The Big Lebowski, Fargo*) said at a Cinematographers' Guild (Union) Lighting Workshop I attended. He talked about the early years as a DP he spent working on documentaries. Referring to the times when all he had were a couple of harsh bright lights, he told how he managed to discover soft directional light. He could use these ugly bright lights by bouncing them into a white reflective surface or by letting them shine through something translucent. And what was the bounce and the diffusion he used? More often than not, it was a bedsheet borrowed from one of their subjects or from a neighbor. Deakins has become one of the world's most acclaimed cinematographers, but he still works with homely, do-it-yourself rigs. Just recently he talked about this in *American Cinematographer* while discussing his work on *Revolutionary Road*. In this film, two characters are arguing in a room where Deakins wanted a ceiling fixture with a hard edge. The ceiling fixture wasn't visible, so he used an 18-inch ring of 60-watt bulbs surrounded by silver foil instead. Your imagination is always more important than your equipment. Use it.

The time has now come to talk about *three-point lighting*, which is a lighting setup that uses three lighting sources: key, fill, and backlight or kicker. You may have read about three-point lighting in some filmmaking texts or have heard about it in a film class. All I can say is, I worked for 25 years on Hollywood camera crews, DPing for 16 of them, and I never heard the term *three-point lighting* used on the set. I never heard the words, never heard a reference to it, and never encountered any DP who lit that way. And yet many books on movie lighting and some teachers refer to it. The bottom line is, just as there's no crying in baseball, there is no three-point lighting in movies. Erase it from your mind.

The problem with "three-point lighting" is that it is divorced from place, time, or emotion. It's useful for shooting still portraits and documentary interviews (talking heads). Those situations are not drama; you're just trying to create a pleasing look. In making movies—and some TV—you're interested in the expressive qualities of lighting. How do you achieve a compelling sense of place, time, and emotional attitude? As I have said (and will keep saying), it all comes from the script. The motivation for your lighting should always proceed from the story.

Relying on three-point lighting will inevitably create an artificial look to your work. Three-point lighting is arbitrary and unmotivated. Besides being a one-size-fits-all solution, three-point uses frontlight with all the disadvantages I've previously mentioned.

You might be thinking that using back cross lighting as a default strategy is just as arbitrary. The difference is that back cross lighting is an approach to a lighting plan, not a prescribed arrangement of lights. It's a strategy that prevents you from frontlighting without a good reason to. Sometimes you'll be lighting to duplicate natural light, and other times you'll be lighting to convey emotional truth, irrespective of natural light. No single setup can serve all your needs.

So this is all well and good, but right now you're feeling stuck with lighting your small movie with what you've got: three guys and four lamps. Don't despair. There's no reason you can't use some version of all the techniques I've talked about or that you can't avoid the pitfalls I've warned you against. Use shadows for effect and eliminate shadows that are ugly. Remember source lighting; shoot the same room with different "imagined" sources of light. Get to work and screw up. You will; it's not hard. (The desire to frontlight will be irresistible.) And pay attention to how your work looks, on the set and on the screen. Many, many ways of lighting are good, even more are bad, and way too many are ugly. Don't make anything ugly.

CHAPTER 22
Learning the Hardware

You will want to know something about handling equipment. Of course, you're a DP, and DPs don't have to put up lights or set flags; that's why you have a crew. But there are some good reasons for knowing this equipment and being able to use it.

First of all, if you know how the equipment works, and now and then show that you can use it, you will gain the respect of your crew. They will always be happy to know that you're not afraid to get your hands dirty—you don't think you're "above" them or too good to do the kind of work they do. Just being able to set a flag indicates that you know at least as much as they do and therefore you have a kind of moral right to be in command. It's one thing to get hired to be the boss; it's another to earn your crew's respect so you don't have to order anyone around. You will be able to run the set just by asking politely for specific jobs to be done.

Another reason to know the equipment is that you will be able to tell at a glance whether the crew you have is capable of doing the job. Sometimes you've got a new guy (this always happens, but it will happen more when you, too, are beginning) and you'll want to help him out or get another one of the crew to show him how to do the job. Sometimes you will have gotten stuck with someone who knows nothing and can't do the job, and really should be fired. You hope your gaffer and key grip will notice and tell you, but they don't know who hired that person. What if she's the director's cousin? If they badmouth her, they might get fired. So you need to be able to suggest getting rid of her and hiring someone who is qualified.

The more you know how to handle equipment, the better able you are to suggest a specific solution to a problem on the set. Most of the time you won't have to; your crew will know what to do. But occasionally you will want a job done a specific way. If you know how to work the equipment, you can tell your crew what solution you want, and they'll respect it.

And don't be afraid when you're just starting to take on jobs as a grip or an electrician. Not only are you making money (we hope), but you're getting experience on a set, you're meeting people, and you might learn something. Many of the best DPs have put in time on the grip and electrical crew. It broadens their knowledge and adds to their appreciation of the job.

The list of specialized grip and electric equipment is almost endless. We're not going to think about that. We'll concern ourselves with the most basic tools and procedures. First of all, safety matters more than anything. The cinematographers union has a motto: "No shot is worth a life." We all know this, and we've had to bring it up several times as some of our members, for whatever reason, have been killed on the job. Don't get hurt, and don't let others get hurt. In some ways, this is heavy industry. And there's always equipment being used in precarious ways, equipment that can cause serious harm if something goes wrong. Don't forget that because of the artistic nature of the business, every shot and setup is being done for the first time. To an extent, routine will keep everyone safe, but the novelty of each setup forces you to think carefully all the time.

So wear gloves. Any grip or electrician handles dirty, sharp, heavy, and sometimes electrified equipment. Fingers don't grow back, and sturdy work gloves are your first line of defense. You don't have to buy the $60/pair kind; you can get perfectly serviceable gloves at the 99¢ store.

And don't wear open-toed shoes (sandals, flip-flops, etc.). Toes also don't grow back. Most people on the set wear athletic shoes, and most of the time that's fine. If you're lifting or hauling heavy things, you might want to wear work boots.

You want to have and carry a couple of tools. Everyone needs a knife, and many crew members always carry Leatherman-type multitools. Everyone needs a flashlight. It's often good to have a screwdriver, and you can buy a good 4-in-1 inexpensively anywhere in the country.

The basic tool for lighting is the lamp. You should be familiar with the basic look and parts of a Fresnel spotlight, the workhorse fixture of the business. Figure 22.1 shows a Mole-Richardson 2K.

FIGURE 22.1
Mole-Richardson 2K.
Photo courtesy of Mole-Richardson Co.

Lamps go on stands. Remember a few things. Always put a sandbag on a stand. Once you've placed the lamp, bag it so it won't fall over. If it's big, use a couple of bags.

Righty-tighty, lefty-loosey. Say that a few times—out loud and with an audience. You'll feel foolish, but you'll remember. There will come a time when you're trying to loosen a nut on a stand. It won't budge, and you'll be thinking, "Maybe this is a reverse thread. Maybe I'm just going the wrong way. Maybe...." Stop! If you want to loosen it, turn left (counterclockwise). If you turn it right, you'll be tightening it. The exceptions are few and far between.

When you've got your light up and mounted, you'll probably want to control the light with a flag or a net. It's a good idea to train your grips

FIGURE 22.2
C-stand with a gobo arm.
Photos courtesy of Matthews Studio Equipment.

FIGURE 22.3
Standard Edison plug.
Reproduced by permission of FilmTools®.

automatically to bring a C-stand, a flag, and a sandbag to place by every lamp. It'll probably be needed. Figure 22.2 shows a C-stand with a gobo arm. So one more time: righty-tighty, lefty-loosey, and sandbags.

I want you to know something about basic electricity. You should be able to wire a standard Edison plug, and it's good to know how to repair the wiring on a lamp. I suggest you practice wiring a plug with scrap wire and an old plug. But *do not* use anything you've wired unless you get taught and you have your work checked out by an electrician. Electricity is too dangerous to mess with. Figure 22.3 shows a standard Edison plug.

If you can, find an electrician to show you how to handle and wrap a stinger (what civilians call an extension cord). This may be the fastest way for you to set yourself apart from the rest of the new kids. Once you know how to wrap it correctly and you do it, you save yourself and everyone working with you a lot of time and trouble.

CHAPTER 23
Why We Light

Okay, we get it: less lighting, no frontlight, maybe back cross light. How else can you deal with a scene? Well, you can try turning off all the lights in the room—movie lights and work lights—and then turn on one light and see what it does. Move it around until you like the look. It will suggest something to you. It may suggest that you need a lot more light. Or it may say, "Hey, this single source looks interesting. How can I get it to show what needs to be seen?" It's rare to be able to get away with only one lamp, but add your lights one by one—don't set up a bunch all at once—so you can see the effect of each light. You will probably need fewer lights than you first thought.

Another approach, particularly on location, is to look at the natural light in a place. (If the natural light is banks of fluorescents, or if you're on stage, this may not tell you anything except to start from scratch. But remember the film *All the President's Men*. The *Washington Post* newsroom is a classic of imitating one look—fluorescents—with tungsten lamps, a totally different animal.)

What does the normal, existing light in a scene do? Take a naturalistic approach. What does the light do naturally? What does it want to make your set look like? And then, being perfectly realistic, how can you fake it? The existing light should give you clues as to the mood of the place, which may be the reason the director chose it. It certainly gives you clues to light so the scene won't look "lit." I know that seems perverse, but you will find that it's easier to convince the audience of the truth of your story if there are no obvious clues that it's "lit."

What are some obvious clues? These can be hard shadows, brightly lit corners, shadows on the wall, or rimlight everywhere. Showing a light source in a scene and having your light coming from a different direction isn't a good thing. Most of these factors can be useful in some situations, but they're specialties. Looking at the light as it is will help you to avoid these clues and keep them from being problems. Working with fewer lamps will help you as well. The fewer you work with, the more control you will have. You will be able to see right away where unwanted light or shadows are coming from. It's easier to correct with fewer lights. And stand back and take a look at the scene as the lights are going up. You

FIGURE 23.1
Viewing glasses (aka viewing filter) color #2.
Photos courtesy of The Tiffen Company.

may see something you like before you've had all the lights up that you thought you wanted.

When you look at the scene, you'll want to judge how it looks on your recording medium. I have used various contrast filters like those Tiffen and other manufacturers make as contrast viewing glasses for cinematographers (Figure 23.1). The idea is that the viewing glass darkens the scene and takes away some color, so you can judge more easily where it's overlit or where the shadows are too dense. It's a good tool, but I find I prefer to view the scene in two dimensions. That's one reason many DPs light through the viewfinder. You see the image with one eye— monocularly, 2D—on a ground glass that itself is a flat surface. I have also used Polaroids; they are no longer available, but you can get a Fuji film if you like this tool.

I would shoot 3200-speed black-and-white film. It abstracted the picture for me by being in black-and-white, by its flatness, and by a very high contrast. I could look at the scene without the distraction of the work on the set going on, and I could judge whether I needed more or less light anywhere. Cameras and film for these Polaroids (the kind Stanley Kubrick and John Alcott used) are harder to come by today (Figure 23.2).

Another excellent form of previsualization of your scene is a digital still camera. In fact, most advanced digital cameras allow you to set ISO and shutter speed (1/50 second) to correspond to the film you're using. You can shoot a still and look at it immediately on the LCD display of your camera. Or you can download it to a laptop and see a large image of your scene. Many DPs will return to this image later and manipulate it in Photoshop or a similar program to come close to the precise color, contrast, and density they want in the final film. It's then easy to e-mail the manipulated shot to the timer or colorist. He's got a precise reference to use to make your dailies look exactly the way you want.

FIGURE 23.2
Polaroid 110A Camera for lighting.
Reproduced by permission of Michael Joachim.

While we're talking about dailies, let me remind you always to use a reference for the timer. I use a gray card. Most labs have a gray card or a color chart that they will be happy to give you. After the scene is lit, put the gray card in the key light, expose it as you plan to expose the scene, and shoot about ten seconds. The timer can use the card as a reference to set up his printer lights or the settings on the telecine. You may want to light the card separately when it's difficult to put it in the key. In that case, use your "white" light: your neutral light, the color temperature that will give you a shot without coloration on the gray card. It's best to light it to key, but as long as it's properly exposed, the exact f-stop doesn't matter.

One way to help the timer is to have an assistant hold the card so we see skin in the frame, and the timer has a skintone reference. Check with your timer/colorist before you start the project. Some prefer a gray card, and some prefer a color chart. Yours may have a specific chart she likes to use. If so, get one and use it. You're buying insurance that your dailies will look good.

When you're lighting, you've got control of the characteristics of light: quality, quantity, angle and direction, and color. Let's talk about the quality first. You can have hard or soft light, direct or indirect. Each choice makes a statement, evokes emotion. Hard light tends to look artificial. Look at any film noir—*Out of the Past* is a great one. It's easy to see that most of the film is shot with hard light, light that's not diffused or bounced, and that this allows great specificity in placement of the light. But it also has an extreme directionality; it looks "sourcey"—in other words, you can tell that it's been lit and see where the light is coming from. A lot of recent films, especially those going for a realistic story, will use soft light. *American Beauty* is a good example. In almost every scene, you are not aware of the presence of lamps; there's light, but it is soft, so it doesn't advertise its presence. These two films provide a great example of direct versus indirect lighting. In *Out of the Past*, people are lit, and there is obviously a lamp set to illuminate a character on a specific mark in the set (Figures 23.3 and 23.4).

FIGURE 23.3
Levels of lighting (film noir lighting). Jane Greer and Robert Mitchum in *Out Of the Past*, shot by Nicholas Musuraca, ASC.

FIGURE 23.4
Illusion of natural light. Annette Bening, Kevin Spacey, and Thora Birtch in *American Beauty*, shot by Conrad Hall, ASC.

Often soft light is used as a shorthand for nondirectional light, but this isn't necessarily so. Indirect light will almost always be soft light, since it's not really possible to have indirect hard light. But soft light can be directional. A great example is Kinoflos. With these fluorescent lamps, the light is soft (at least to a degree) and can be aimed to specific places, thus being directional. It is also a standard technique to put diffusion in front of a hard light (Figures 23.5 and 23.6). It thus stays directional, but it is softened.

FIGURE 23.5
Kinoflo fixture.
Photo courtesy of Kino Flo Lighting Systems.

FIGURE 23.6
Kinoflo lighting subject.
Photo courtesy of Kino Flo Lighting Systems.

FIGURE 23.7
Frieder Hochheim, the inventor of Kinoflo.
Photos courtesy of Kino Flo Lighting Systems.

When light is bounced, it can be slightly directional, but almost all bounced light is indirect. That is, it comes from a given direction, but because the light waves scatter, the directionality of the light is not perceived as much as it is with hard light.

Bouncing is a great tool. You can bounce using any light source. An advantage is that lamps that would be terrible as direct lighting—too harsh, not enough control—will be fine as bounce lights. For control there is nothing as good as Fresnel lights (the standard movie spotlight, invented by Mole-Richardson in the 1920s).

You will be considering the direction of light. Where is it coming from, and at what angle? We are used to seeing things lit from above—we evolved with the sun, after all—and the majority of your lighting will be placed at least slightly elevated. It's best always to consider a justifiable source of light. Is there a window? Would there be a light fixture at some point? Audiences tend to react unconsciously to a justification for a light source. If there's nothing on the set or in the picture, you can make up your source. Just pretend that there's a window, a lamp, a fire, and so forth just off screen. Light from there, and your scene will look good. If you do something to identify the "source," such as putting a cutout of a window frame made from cardboard in front of the lamp, you may convince the audience of the actual existence of a fictional source.

All light has a color—that is, a characteristic wavelength. Mostly we're concerned with color balance, keeping the source light compatible with the film stock we're using. Or if we're doing electronic work, keeping a consistent white balance. But colors have a place in creative cinematography.

The most common use of color is blue to simulate daylight when contrasting it with warm tungsten light or moonlight and orange to simulate the sun (when contrasting it with cool daylight) or tungsten light. They work as accent colors contrasting with the "white" light of a scene. If you're shooting a day interior, tungsten balanced (3200° K), letting in some daylight will make the areas hit by the daylight look blue. Likewise, if you're shooting a day exterior lit by the sun (5600° K), having a powerful tungsten light inside suggests the warmth of electric light. Often we will use tungsten for night interior, and to have some accent light on the exterior, we will use a light with some blue gel on it. The interior is 3200° K, normal "white" with tungsten balanced film, and the exterior is blue, giving us a bluish exterior at around 4000° K.

You will also be concerned with the amount of light, and that is usually a question of exposure, covered in the next chapter.

CHAPTER 24
Exposure

It seems to me that how we expose film is one of the great nightmare beasts to aspiring cinematographers. Exposing video and HD seems easier; in fact, it looks as though you can just glance at your monitor or LCD display on the camera. True, you can get a somewhat acceptable picture that way, but you don't know how to expose, and you don't know what you're doing when you light.

It always pays to know what you're doing and why you're doing it. You know that you're not lighting for illumination; you're putting music on the film. You're setting time, mood, style, and emotions. You have to think about how the shot is going to look, and you need to understand exposure to do that. You will quickly find that hit-and-miss-lighting, relying on a monitor to balance and adjust the lights, will take longer than lighting conventionally. And producers and directors will look unkindly on your taking a lot of time. And don't forget that occasionally you will have to "light air." You're just not always going to have the luxury of a cast and a set before you start.

Look at the extremes of lighting styles. With film, the good old conventional way, you as the DP light knowing what you want your key to measure and then you balance by eye. With video (the progenitor of digital), there is no DP. The lighting director sets up lights, metering to make sure they're within the contrast range of the system, and the engineer sets brightness (puts on the stop). In both systems, the guy in charge uses a meter. In film it's most often an exposure meter; with electronic it's usually a foot-candle meter. The big secret is that these two meters do the same thing: They read the light falling on the scene to be shot. A foot-candle meter reads foot-candles (lux in the metric system). It's a measure of light falling on a surface, and that's all you need to know, unless you want to work with foot-candles, in which case you need to know how many foot-candles are necessary for a given exposure. For example, Figure 24.1 shows Kodak's table for exposing 5219 (7219). Figure 24.2 is General Electric's idea of a foot-candle.

Lens Aperture	f/1.4	f/2	f/2.8	f/4	f/5.6	f/8	f/11	f/16
Footcandles Required	5	10	20	40	80	160	320	640

FIGURE 24.1
Foot-candle/stop table.

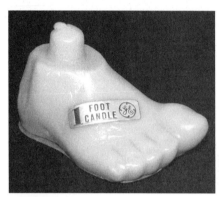

FIGURE 24.2
General Electric's "foot-candle" advertising novelty.
Reproduced by permission of Schenectady Museum and Suits-Bueche Planetarium.

There will be some difference in your lighting between film and digital. The major questions are contrast and range. Relative to film, all digital cameras except the highest end will not handle extremely bright and extremely dark areas of your shot as well as film will. That means that you must make sure that the brightest area is only, say, four stops hotter than your key (where you set your meter) and the darkest area is only three to four stops under key, if you want to hold detail. You will know the range of film after having done the "Emulsion Test" exercise (Chapter 24a). You can and should perform the same test with your digital camera, and it will tell you whether you can hold detail in an area of the shot four stops over key or if maybe you can get away with only three stops over. You will also have done the "Contrast" exercise (Chapter 24c) to see how your particular film or chip shows contrast, how much or how little detail it holds, and what looks flat and what looks too contrasty.

With that knowledge you have an idea of how to light for whatever medium you use. Then you need to remember that digital, as an electronic medium, cannot handle anything that is "too bright." What is too bright? Once you have reached 100% of your digital camera's exposure, anything brighter will "clip." That means there is no picture at all. It is not like extreme underexposure where no picture at all means a black, featureless area. Clipping looks like a hole in the picture. It is white, but not the white of a bright subject. It is the white of too much information for the chip to handle, and so it, again, looks like a hole. You can get away with minor clipping, as in bright specular reflections (from a car's surface, say), but any moderately large area looks like hell. You must set your exposure so that "nothing"—that is, nothing except small spots—is over 100%. Thank goodness we have the zebras to tell us when we reach 100%. (Zebras are indicators that can be set to show in an electronic viewfinder. Cameras allow one or two settings. The zebra—diagonal lines—shows up when the exposure in a given place in the frame exceeds the percentage you've set. Many people use 70% for skin tones and 100% for too bright. I prefer 50%—for faces—and 100% to warn me when I've clipped.)

In some cases—such as the sky—we have large bright areas in our picture. The only way to avoid clipping is to stop down (toward larger numbers, smaller apertures) far enough to bring the sky under 100%. The downside is that you may be underexposing other areas of your frame. You have to add light to them or selectively filter out the sky. A very useful tool is the polarizing filter. It cuts

FIGURE 24.3
Zebras in viewfinder.
Reproduced by permission of www.EyeFish.tv.

out about 70% of the light overall, and limits the light reaching the sensor or film to parallel waves. The effect is to darken the sky without darkening the rest of the picture. But its use is limited to sunny days, and it's less effective if it's not at 90 degrees to the sun. There are graduated filters that theoretically let you dim the sky without affecting the rest of the picture, but they have a line where the filtering stops, and unless you're in a desert, something always goes above that line, and it's visible in your frame, and any illusion of reality flees.

So for electronic imaging you really have to add light. Unless you have large lamps (12 K HMIs and bigger), you won't have any artificial light that can compete with the sun. You can use reflectors and bounce cards. Reflectors are best to redirect sunlight and then to be bounced off a white card. If you can get a bounce card in sunlight, that will work. But bounce cards are usually only good for tight shots. For wider work, I will use a 20 × 20 frame with Griffolyn—a kind of silver or gold reflector—on it to bring up the unlit area by one-half to one stop.

Okay, you're on the set, and you need to know how to deal with the light. What color is it, how much of it is there, and what's the range between the bright and dark parts? If you're on a stage set, it's about 95% likely that you'll be using tungsten lights. You'll use tungsten-balanced film, and any other color of light (whether from a light source with a different color temperature or from gels on lamps) will be an accent.

FIGURE 24.4
Griffolyn on frame. Photo courtesy of Matthews Studio Equipment.

While I'm on tungsten, here's an interesting fact. Tungsten light is conventionally described as 3200° K, but I always use a color meter. I like to check the lamps on my sets. I have rarely found a tungsten lamp that is up to 3200° K. The best I've seen was at Mole Richardson. Larry Parker (the head of Mole, a passionate and reliable source of lighting information, and a helluva nice guy) brought out a new light: brand-new housing, new and clean mirror, new and clean lens, new bulb. It measured 3150° K. Now that's not much of a difference; even the most sensitive

recording material would consider that close enough to 3200° K. But that was a brand-new lamp. Most lamps are old, dirty, and not in prime condition. Even the most enthusiastic best boys don't clean their lamps every day, and that's what's needed. And although quartz-halogen lamps don't darken and change temperature as they get old, if they're dirty they're going to lose temperature. The usual standard for studio tungsten lights is 2900° K. I've found this by measuring them, but here's another way to know. Kinoflo makes fluorescent tubes that are perfectly balanced to color temperature. They have 5600° K (daylight), 3200° K (tungsten), and 2900° K (warm tungsten). If you use the 3200° K tubes with most tungsten fixtures, the Kinos will look blue. I've done it for effect, and you can see it with your eyes. Kinoflo saw this early on, and brought out their 2900° K bulbs, which match tungsten lights perfectly. Then there are household bulbs. Tungsten, yes, but usually around 2700° K, sometimes lower.

This talk about color temperature, while fun, is also to introduce the idea of using a color temperature meter. With the digital revolution, the use of color temperature meters has diminished somewhat. They're available on eBay now for a fraction of their original cost. The idea is that since digital cameras can white balance to almost any wavelength of light and give you a good picture, no one needs color temperature meters anymore. I think there's some worth to this argument for still photographers. But I think that cinematographers still have good reasons to own and to use color temperature meters.

Relatively few cinematographers use or have used color temperature meters. In my experience working with other DPs, it has seemed to me that they simply took the nominal color temperature of the main light source (3200° K or 5600° K), used the appropriate film or conversion filter, and didn't worry about it. This approach has worked fine. At least since the major shift to color in the late 1960s, labs have been able to modify small problems in color to make the photography look natural. Today, with the preponderance of even film-originated projects getting an electronic finish, the vast capabilities of electronic finishing can correct or adjust any color variation in the original.

I will still argue for the use of a color temperature meter in order to know what you're doing. Here's the situation: Almost all film stocks and most digital cameras have a tolerance for mixed light—light of different color temperatures in the same shot—that would have seemed like a fantasy 15 years ago. Given this, there is less need to gel (with color correction filtration) lamps or to filter cameras. But again what we're aiming for is not just a decent picture. We're trying to make something meaningful, and to do that, we have to know what we're doing.

One way I was alerted to the lower than 3200° K temperature of movie lights was by looking at my printing lights. I like to have the lights around 30 to 33. (You can refresh your memory about printing lights in Chapter 37.) I was on one film consistently getting lights for interiors lit with tungsten like 31-30-24. That's 31 Red, 30 Green, 24 Blue. That meant the blue-registering layer of the emulsion was thinner than the red and green layers. In turn that meant that it was being less exposed. Why? I cudgeled my brain, and all I could come up with was that the lamps were deficient in blue. I checked the lamps, and as I've said, they were mostly around 2900° K. On my next picture, I had an enthusiastic gaffer who loved working with the color meter. He took the meter, and had his crew correct every lamp we had to either 3200° K or 5600° K (depending on what light we took as white). In some ways that film has my favorite photography because it has all its light sources color-balanced.

What I believe happens with too little blue is, strangely, more a problem with focus than with color. Or I should say sharpness. The blue layer appears to me to be the layer with the sharpest image. I have come to this conclusion through playing with color film. I have shot it through color separation filters, R, G, B, one at a time. Color separation filters are designed to let through all the wavelengths of light that expose a given layer in color film and only those wavelengths. So what I did, in effect, was separate the color film into three different monochrome films. Red is by far the softest layer. You may be able to notice some of this effect yourself in commercial movies. There will often be largely red light used for party scenes or some kinds of action. Look closely, and odds are that the scene will be softer than the rest of the picture. I won't guarantee it, because there are many ways to give your scene a red look, but I have seen it. The green layer is the next in clarity, and the blue has the best image on it. I could speculate on why this is, but that's not what I'm writing about, and that's not what you're interested in. You want to know how to do good cinematography. I'm saying that making sure your lamps are all color correct is a good way to start.

You already know that you will find every sort of lamp made by GE on any given location:

Sun	5600°	White or blue
Tungsten	3200° (2900°)	White or yellow
Cool white fluorescent	4800° or so	Bluish with a green spike
Warm white fluorescent	4000° or so	Slightly bluish with a green spike
Sodium vapor	~2600°	Very yellow-brown plus green
Mercury vapor	~5000°	Very blue-purple plus green plus ultraviolet

You want your shot to look good. Maybe you can just let all the lights go; it has been done, most successfully in *The American Friend*, shot by Robby Müller, but there's a good chance that you're going to have two predominant colors fighting it out, and that's not a pretty picture. (Pun intended.)

To balance the different sources—at least to get close—you can gel the lamps, filter the camera, or both. Gels are what we call the plastic filters (originally gelatin) that are made to go on lamps. Originally for the theater, now they come in both theatrical colors and color-temperature correct versions. There are CTB—color temperature blue—to cool off lights (to a higher color temperature—I'm sorry about the terminology) and CTO—color temperature orange—to warm them up (to a lower color temperature). There are gradations in each of them—$\frac{1}{8}$, $\frac{1}{4}$, $\frac{1}{2}$, and full—so you can create any degree of color shift you want. I will tell you right now that CTB does not convert tungsten to daylight. You need at least 1¼ CTB to do that. And to know how much to use, you need a color meter.

As I have said, plenty of DPs have shot films over the years without using a color meter. But you'll have more control if you use one. Let's say you've got a day interior. There are practical tungsten lights all over the location, and you want to use them. There's only a little sunlight coming through the windows. So you figure it's easier to gel the windows than to gel all the lamps. That's a good thought. Besides having to modify fewer sources, gelling lamps blue cuts the amount of light from them in half. You can't afford that unless you have a lot of big lights and a generator to power them. So you put CTO on the windows. Now here you have a chance of doing some creative work. Instead of trying to bring the sunlight to the same color temperature as the tungsten, if you leave it slightly blue, you give a cool and distant look to the exterior, separating it from the interior, and simulating the way our eyes register daylight when we're in a tungsten-lit area. So you use ¼ or ½ CTO, you bring the exterior light closer to the interior so your media don't have to deal with a giant discrepancy, and you've actually lowered the (very bright) intensity of the exterior light a little, so it's easier to balance the light levels.

You use the color meter to determine the colors of the tungsten lamps and the daylight, and you put up the gel accordingly, checking to see that it gives you the difference you want. You can get a rough indication by eye, but the film or chip will always be more sensitive to the difference in color than your eye is.

You also want to use the color temperature meter when you're confronted with any gas-discharge lamp: fluorescent, mercury vapor, or sodium vapor. Besides being an odd color, each has a discontinuous spectrum (the sun and tungsten lamps have continuous spectra). So what colors exist are in spikes, not a continuous flow. You can use the color temperature meter to find out the Kelvin degrees of the light source and use the two buttons—for blue/orange and green/magenta—to determine a light's distance from a standard. You can use charts to adjust the color temperature (available from gel manufacturers), or you can use different gels and combinations placed over the sensor of the meter to get the result you want.

FIGURE 24.5
Continuous and discontinuous spectra.

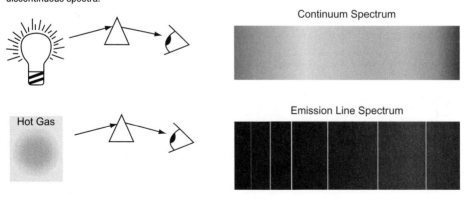

Continuum Spectrum

Hot Gas

Emission Line Spectrum

Remember I said you could use filters on the lens? Well, if you shoot tungsten film outdoors, you always use an 85 filter to remove the excess blue in sunlight. You can use an FLB (for tungsten film) or FLD (for daylight film) on the camera to remove the green from fluorescents. There's no standard, either in filters or gels, for working with mercury vapor or sodium vapor lights, although Rosco makes a nice gel, Urban Vapor, that simulates the look of sodium vapor lights when it's put on a tungsten or HMI source.

Using a color meter instead of just using the standard gels as a one-size-fits-all solution lets you know precisely the differences you are establishing between your light sources. It gives you a basis for lighting the set as you have previsualized it. Since your eyes will accommodate to any different color of a light source and see it as "white," the meter helps you to stay honest, to remember what color you are using as dominant on the set. And using the meter allows you to shoot the gray card, the reference to the timer or colorist, with light of a precise wavelength. You know what that is, you know its relationship to the colors of light on the set, and you have a clearer idea of how you want the shot to look.

The predominant color of the shot, like so many other things, you can "fix in post." It's true, and it's been possible for years, even photochemically and even with the old, less sensitive emulsions. We've all done it, either premeditating it or making the best of a bad situation, when we don't have the material to correct the color in the camera. You may not have had a chance to scout a location—it had to be added at the last minute—and it's nothing but fluorescents. You have no minus green gel (the standard to take out the green spike), you're hundreds of miles from the nearest source, and you have to shoot. So you shoot, you—your assistant—make notes on the camera report, and you trust the timer/colorist to make the dailies look good. It seems easy. Why not do it all the time?

Because it's not a good idea. First, you have to have that scene color corrected at every stage of postproduction; that takes time and money. It's not that much, but the producer will notice, and he'll blame you, and you'll have a hard time getting the next job. Second, if you want to adjust the color in the scene, you have limited yourself by already having added a lot of magenta (same as eliminating green) and not leaving room to do more in the green/magenta area—without spending too much time and money.

If you're Roger Deakins, these caveats about time and money don't have to apply to you. You're working on big-budget movies, and you have a terrific track record. But for you and me, the workers in the mine, no one cuts us any slack. It's better to think ahead, to solve problems in advance, and not have to be putting out fires all through postproduction. Besides, "We'll fix it in post!" is a well-known joke on any set just because everyone knows how much it's going to cost.

Now, say you're using a digital camera. There are a few things you will need to deal with that do the same things as your adjustments to film. You won't have to concern yourself with different film stocks. Any media you use will record the picture as you define it. Of course, you will want to white balance to the dominant light in the scene. If it's mixed daylight and tungsten, decide what look you want. (Do you want daylight to be "white"? Then the tungsten will look orange. Is tungsten "normal"—white? Then the daylight will look blue.) You may want something in between so the daylight is bluish but not too blue and the tungsten is warm but not too orange. So remember: When you white balance, you're telling the camera what "white" light is. No light source is really white, of course; it is really the neutral color or light for you.

Now, if you call sunlight (5600° K) "white," then anything lit by tungsten (3200° K) will look sort of orange. What if you want the sunlight to be cool but not white or real blue? You can white balance either by getting both sources to illuminate the same white card, or—better—you can use a colored card. A blue card will make light warmer, and an orange card will make the picture cooler. It's a matter of complementary colors. You'll remember that when you work with film, you have to think positive/negative, and you realize a *bright* light—to get a bright area in the picture—gives you a *dark* space on the negative. It's the same thing with electronic. You have to think of complementary colors, and you remember that shooting a card of one color will give an overall look to your picture of the complementary color. The camera will try to read your card as white. If it's blue, the computer in the camera will remove some blue from the record of the scene. Removing blue is equivalent to adding yellow or orange. *Voilà!* You've got a warmer picture. Vortex Media (http://www.vortexmedia.com/), a great resource for electronic imaging, makes a nice set of white balance aids called warm cards. A full set includes several shades of blue; it also has some green cards you can use to remove the green from a location lit all by fluorescents.

Then there's exposure. With electronic cameras, you face a situation similar to film cameras in that daylight exteriors are a lot brighter than artificially lighted interiors. (I bet you guessed that already.) With film, we use a slower speed film, or we use neutral density filters in front of the lens. The neutral density filters (NDs) cut down the amount of light reaching the film, so we can use a lower f-stop so we are not faced with light so bright it will overexpose the film.

When you're working electronically, you usually have NDs built into the camera. They're controlled on the sides of most cameras by a dial, and they're calibrated differently from the way conventional filters are. NDs are made in gradations of .1, from .1 up to as high (and dark) as the manufacturer wants. Most commonly we use three NDs: ND.3, ND.6, and ND.9.

And the way we talk about NDs is weird: We call them "enn dee three," and so on. Do not say the decimal point. And then you'll be working hard on a show, and some joker is going to say, "Give me a 30 neutral." Huh? Okay, sometimes the NDs are written as ND.30, ND.60, and ND.90 instead of ND.3, ND.6, and ND.9. So some DPs will call out the 30, 60, or 90. You know it can get boring on the set, and having different names for things is one way to liven it up.

Each three-tenths of a gradation equals one stop, so you have an easy conversion of your exposure. You can either open one stop from your meter reading or you can set your meter to an ISO half of normal (ISO/2 = one stop). In video and digital cinema cameras, the NDs are usually stated as reciprocals of the filter factor. Thus, 1/2 ND (camera terms) equals a Filter Factor of 2, which equals ND.3, which in turn equals 1 stop.

It's complicated either way, but I think the electronic system of notations is worse. (Yes, no one asked me.) They're made for autoexposure anyway, so most users don't care what they're called. Since you're setting your own exposure manually—you're an artist, right?—just make yourself a cheat sheet to make your life easier. A friend of mine, a cameraman named Matt Irwin, worked it out. Here it is:

1/2 ND = FF of 2 = ND.3	1 stop
1/4 ND = FF of 4 = ND.6	2 stops
1/8 ND = FF of 8 = ND.9	3 stops
1/16 ND = FF of 16 = ND.12	4 stops
1/64 ND = FF of 64 = ND.18	6 stops

Now, you *can* use NDs in front of the lens, but you may run into another situation. Most sensors are extremely sensitive to infrared light (IR). Ordinarily, there's no problem; infrared is a relatively small component of the light. But when you cut down visible light with NDs, you're not cutting down on infrared. The infrared becomes proportionately greater, and it will mess up your picture. Some cameras have filters or circuitry built in to compensate for this problem, but with many, you'll need to add an infrared-cutting filter. Tiffen, for example, makes a combination ND and infrared-cutting filter (http://www.tiffen.com/pr_infrared_filters.html).

Working with gels on lights and playing with color temperature are the same as working in film. It's just that you have decided what the camera is balanced for (white balancing), not the folks at Kodak or Fuji.

Okay, you know what color temperature your lamps are. You know what you consider "white" light (the neutral standard from which you work when you do effects with color). You're ready to start lighting. And I bet you have your exposure meter all ready. Is it hanging around your neck? Every meter I've ever bought comes with some kind of cord or chain to hang around the neck. I've seen some guys deal with this, but very few. I find that when it's around my neck, the cord is too short to put the meter where I want it. Or it's too long, and it swings around, getting in my way and probably hitting something and breaking. So the first thing I do is get rid of the cord. The second thing I do is get a case I can wear on my belt. A few meter makers—Spectra is the only one I can think of—give you a hard leather case with the purchase of a meter. All the others give you at best a thin vinyl case that protects against nothing. You're going to have your meter on your hip; it's the most convenient way to carry it, and makes it easy to get to. And you have to protect the meter. It's fairly expensive, and besides it's no good to you if it's not reading accurately. I always have a hard leather carrying case with a belt loop on it. Sometimes you can buy these; they're a custom item and not always available. I have made my own, which isn't hard if you have the time and some clamps. Ever since I had my spot meter pop out of the small joke of a case the manufacturer provided, I have used a case with a positive latch that will protect me from bumps and weather. I once wore two meters through 12 hours of rain in the High Sierras. The cases were a little worse for wear, but the meters were in good shape.

Whether you buy a new meter or get one used, you want to be sure it's reading accurately. If you can trust the manufacturer to make a good meter, I think you should be able to trust it to have it correctly calibrated when you get it. But don't. Even if it's new, and certainly if it's used, have it checked and adjusted if necessary. The one place I know, the place that Hollywood cameramen have been using for years, is Quality Light-Metric, 7095 Hollywood Blvd, Suite 550, Los Angeles, CA 90028-8903; 323-467-2265; Fax: 323-874-0421. Send it in, and it will be back in a week. I've worked with meters that had gone off accurate calibration. Thank goodness my gaffer always carries a meter. We check them at the beginning of the show to see that they read the same (within $1/3$ of a stop). And we talk about the stop all the time. Any discrepancy is a red flag, and we check the meters. I always carry at least one extra meter (just in case); that's usually a good reference. If two of the three meters say the same thing, we figure that's correct, and I'm sending in my inaccurate meter the same day.

Let me tell you a little about buying meters. There are two general classes of meters: incident and reflected. You will be using an incident meter. A reflected meter has no use on a movie set except for a specialized kind: the spot meter. I own a reflected meter, but over the years I have acquired a lot of meters I don't use very much. A reflected light meter reads light reflected from an object and tells you what stop to use to render that subject middle gray (also 18% gray, the middle of the scale from black to white as measured for a given ISO).[1] Using a reflected meter and measuring a white card and using the f-stop it gives you, you will get a picture in which the white card is gray. Using a reflected meter and measuring a black card and using the f-stop it gives you, you will get a picture in which the black card is gray. You can begin to see that you'll have trouble from shot to shot. If one shot is mostly bright, the reflected meter will give you a stop that darkens the brightness to gray. If one shot is mostly dark, the reflected meter will give you a stop that brightens the darkness to gray. Everything goes to the gray, but a given subject—say, an actor—will be a different color or shade, depending on his surroundings.

This kind of work will get us fired fast. What do we do? We get an incident meter. An incident meter reads the light falling on a subject; it then computes (or lets you compute) the stop that will render an 18% gray card as 18% gray. For whatever light level in the scene, an 18% gray card will always look the same. This implies that any subject, given similar lighting conditions, will look the same. And this guarantees that from shot to shot your actors will look the same. Of course, they will be highlighted or shadowed, depending on your lighting. But if they are lit the same, they will reproduce the same tone, irrespective of their surroundings.

---

[1]Check out http://en.wikipedia.org/wiki/Exposure_meter for more information on how meters work.

What kind of meter should you get? You should get an incident, but now there are two classes of incident and several manufacturers. The classic meter is an analog meter, designed in the 1930s and 1940s. Since the 1980s there have been digital meters. DPs who have been in the business for a long time still tend to use analog meters. Most younger ones use digital. I leave it up to you. Each has its advantages and failings. The analog meters all have a mechanism that is similar to a mechanical watch. There are springs and other delicate elements to the mechanism; if you drop the meter, it's almost always broken or at least out of calibration. Some analog meters are direct reading (they show you the f-stop without your having to work the disks on the meters that are mechanical computers), but most are not. But analog meters are often more compact, and they do not need batteries. This last fact is the reason I always have a backup analog meter. Digital meters must have batteries, and they tend to be physically larger. But they can be used in any light situation (analog meters require inserting a slide to cut down light for exterior use). They are direct reading: Once you set parameters—ISO, shutter speed—the reading you get is the f-stop you use. However, the settings disappear each time the battery is removed. I take out my batteries at every wrap. I don't know when I'll use the meter next, and I don't want the battery compartment to get corroded from an old, leaky battery. And they all have buttons that are easy to hit accidentally, buttons that change your settings and can screw up your exposure. So always check the settings on the digital meter before using it.

FIGURE 24.6
Digital meter showing buttons.

The companies still manufacturing analog incident meters are Spectra and Sekonic. Both are descendants of the original Norwood meter from the 1940s; the Sekonic is an older design. Either works fine. When I started in the business, you were not a professional unless you had and used a Spectra. I worked with one man who used a Sekonic, but he had 30 years of experience, and no one was going to mock him. There are other analog meters around, but most of them do not have a setting for 1/50 second shutter speed, the standard at 24 fps. The standard still camera shutter speed is 1/60 second; it's only ⅓ of a stop difference, but why annoy yourself with either the discrepancy or the need to adjust for it every time you work?

The manufacturers of digital meters for cinematography are Spectra, Sekonic, Kenko, and Gossen. There may be others, but I have not come across any. For some reason I have never seen anyone use a Gossen meter. They have a good reputation but no presence in Hollywood. Kenko took over the Konica/Minolta line of meters a few years ago. The Minolta digital meter was the first one to be used in Hollywood, and many cinematographers who adopted it in the 1980s and 1990s still use them. I imagine the Kenko is similar, but again, they're not in common use here. In fact, the old Minolta meter may be the most common digital meter now used; you can usually find them on eBay. The Spectra, coming as it does from a long line of meters made for cinematographers, is particularly easy to use. It has good ergonomics and doesn't have a lot of unnecessary options. The relatively new Sekonic L-758 Cine is a combination incident and spot meter. The combination is very attractive, since you have to carry only one meter. It works well, and Sekonic has been making great reliable meters for at least 50 years. Sekonic makes several similar models for still photography, and

FIGURE 24.7
Sekonic L-398A Studio Deluxe III.
Reproduced by permission of Sekonic©.

FIGURE 24.8
Spectra professional light meter (P-251 Classic). *Reproduced by permission of Spectra Cine, Inc.*

you want to be sure to get the Cine model. Again, it's a matter of shutter speed. I don't think you can go wrong with any of these meters.

Now you're on the set, you've got your calibrated meter, and you're going to light. I see a lot of novices, and I see them holding their meters with a death grip, brandishing them like a totem, and measuring everything in sight—with a frightened, querulous look on their faces.

Back off on the metering. What you want to do is decide what's your key. The key is the main light and probably what lights the most important thing on the set, what you want the audience to pay attention to. Set that light. Meter it. Is it reasonable? Reasonable means does this stop seem like a good one for this scene? And what's a "good" stop? That's what the DP—you—likes. Laszlo Kovacs once said he liked to light interiors to an f/4 so he could use a long zoom inside if he felt the need. Many TV shows when I was an assistant lit to f/3 (¼ stop deeper than f/2.8) because we used zooms that were f/3 at maximum aperture. I like to shoot at around f/2.5 (⅓ stop under f/2.8) because it gives me some depth of field and yet it usually allows me to use practical lights and keep them looking natural. I once worked for a DP who liked to shoot at f/1.4 or whatever widest open was on the lens. We assistants called that WFO.

You will find a stop that seems congenial to you. It will no doubt be different for different shows. If you have a musical comedy, you'll light it brighter to a higher stop to carry all the movement in focus. If it's a mystery, you'll light to a wider stop to allow a shallow depth of field to provide some uncertainty.

And now, light to f/2.8. It's a good stop; all the lenses except some zooms will open that wide, and you can use relatively less light (and therefore power and heat) than a higher stop requires.

Set your light. Have the lamp operator flood it and spot it so you can get an idea of its coverage. Set the center of the light on the subject. You'll find the center by spotting and putting the hot spot on the subject or by using a gaffer's glass,[2] looking through it at the light, and telling the operator where to aim it. Then measure the light. You have the choice of pointing the hemisphere on the meter toward the light or toward the camera. All the books say point it toward the camera. This way you get the light falling on what you will see, and you will have an accurate and consistent exposure. I have found that this is true for black-and-white photography, which was the dominant style when these meters were invented. But working in color, I find that pointing the hemisphere toward the camera tends to give me a slight overexposure. I prefer to know what I am getting from the light; that way I can decide to make where it falls middle gray, or not, as the case may be.

From this point on, put away your meter. Yes, it's a fabulous tool, and it may be your worry beads, but once you have the key adjusted, everything else relates to it.

---

[2]A gaffer's glass is a very dense filter. When you look through it, you can see the center of the light without hurting your eyes. Several companies make very nice and very expensive glasses. Or you can use a dense welder's glass, which is fairly cheap at your local hardware store.

It is likely to be the brightest area in the shot, but not necessarily. Put in your other lights and fill and adjust them by eye. You will have done an exercise to show you contrast ratios (Chapter 24c). You won't want to trust your eye at first, so measure the intensity of these other lights where they fall on the scene. Do one at a time, and calculate the ratio it gives you. You will know what ratio you want; make sure you're getting it. Then try to commit to memory how it looks. This is a process of training your eye so you will eventually be able to light entirely by eye and be accurate.

An exposure meter is essentially a very simple tool. You hold the meter in the light. You read what the meter says either with a needle on a scale or from an LED screen. You put that f-stop setting on your lens. You shoot. It can really be that simple. Both film and professional chips are made so well today that if you are anywhere in the ballpark with your exposure, you will get an image—maybe even a pleasing image. So if you're new and the idea of exposure terrifies you, loosen up. You may screw up, but you probably won't ruin the movie. And you'll learn.

Mistakes can be, and have been, made. The easiest is to let your meter go out of calibration. It doesn't happen easily; I've had meters that haven't needed adjustment for years at a time, but if they go off, you might not notice. So check your meter against other meters and have it checked regularly at the factory or at Quality Light Metric.

It's easy to get the settings wrong. With an analog meter, you must read the needle on the dial, take that number and put a pointer against it, and finally go to a third indicator to find the stop. It's easy to read wrong or to set the wrong number against a pointer. It's also easy to accidentally move the ISO setting while you're doing all this calculating. With the direct reading Spectra, you won't have that problem. A slide calibrated for a specific ISO goes in a slot behind the hemisphere. As long as you have the correct slide in, you read the f-stop without any intermediate steps. This may be one of the best features of an analog meter.

Digital meters all have buttons that must be used to set ISO, shutter speed, and sometimes other parameters. These buttons are intentionally easy to reach, but they can be hit or pushed accidentally very easily. They'll reset your meter; if you don't check at every reading, you run the risk of following a mistaken reading.

Of course, there are other, simpler ways of screwing up. You could have the wrong ISO on your meter because the wrong film was loaded. You think, "But who could be so stupid?" Don't be mean. I have a friend who as an assistant once loaded several magazines with a slow film instead of a fast emulsion because the labels on the film cans were identical. You probably won't experience that circumstance, but it's easy to misread any label. You and your assistants need to establish routines— like putting big homemade labels on cans—to make it impossible to make that mistake. Another friend, who working for the first time with a DP, automatically switched from fast to slow film when the company went outdoors after shooting an interior. Much to his chagrin, the DP wanted to keep using the fast film. It was his good luck to find out after only a couple of shots; he was doing the conventional procedure—fast inside, slow outside in day—but he was assuming the DP was working that way. By now you know not to assume—ever. Always talk to each other. Tell your assistant what stock you want to use, and make sure he checks with you whenever he's going to go to a different emulsion.

Using filters opens up a Pandora's box. Many filters need to be compensated for on the stop. If you don't know that a filter is in or the assistant forgets that he's put in a filter, your exposure will be off. This too is a matter of metering. Usually what I do is to figure the compensation for all the filters in terms of stops to be opened; then I convert that to a changed ISO, which I enter on my meter. It's simple: Every time you cut an ISO in half, you are indicating a situation that is one full stop less sensitive. Here is an example: In an identical lighting situation, ISO 500, stop f/4; ISO 250, stop f/2.8. Now it would be possible to have ISO 500 film that you want to use outside, where it's much too fast for the normal range of f-stops (1.4 to 22) at $\frac{1}{50}$ second. And the ISO 500 films are balanced for tungsten, and of course we're now in daylight. I first put on an 85 filter to remove the excess blue from the sunlight; it holds back $\frac{2}{3}$ stop, so the ISO goes to 320. Then I know I want the film speed around 40.[3] To reduce the effective speed of the film, I have to keep some of the light from reaching it. We use neutral density filters. Neutral density filters are gray—they have no color effect at all—and are calibrated in tenths. Three-tenths equals one stop. An ND3 (one stop) puts me at ISO 160, ND6 at ISO 80, and ND9 at ISO 40. *Voilà!*

What if your assistant doesn't put on the filter and you've compensated for it? You will have a badly overexposed shot. What if she puts on the wrong filter—say, an N9 when you wanted an N6? Then of course you're underexposed. To try to eliminate this problem, it is industry standard for the assistant to put a label on the camera left side of the matte box to indicate what filter is working. When I was an assistant, I had a bunch of 1-foot-square pieces of plastic that I carefully labeled for every filter with press-on letters, and I put Velcro on the back of them and on the matte box. Now there are even companies that make these labels, neatly engraved and in different colors. It's possible that the assistant will still forget something, but if you follow this routine, you will always be looking at the matte box to check on the filters, and you'll often ask the assistant what the filters are as a reminder to double check. Again, screwups are possible. I know one assistant who put a gelatin filter behind the lens, forgot about it, and put the same filter, glass this time, in front of the lens. The film lost two stops and was severely underexposed. Nothing is foolproof.

As I said, you'll always get a picture no matter how you meter. But we've spent this whole book trying to get a more precise understanding of ways to do things so we can have full control over the photographic process. Let's apply that to metering, since the stop you put on the lens is kind of important.

Everyone meters differently. You can read in *American Cinematographer* magazine about different camerapeople discussing film speeds (ISOs). One will say he thinks the film is faster than the ISO 500 the manufacturer gives it; he calls it 1000 ISO. Another will say the same film really is an ISO 320. (And the same

---

[3]How do I know? A rule of thumb says that the correct exposure in bright sunlight is f/16 at 1/iso sec. The shutter speed on the camera is 1/50 sec, so I know I could shoot at f/14 ($\frac{1}{3}$ open from f/16) if my ISO is around 40.

situation occurs in rating electronic cameras. Many manufacturers will indicate an ISO equivalent rating for the camera. It's an equivalent because there's no international standard for rating the speed of digital cameras. But DPs test them; just as with film they'll often say a camera is faster or slower than the maker says.) So are all of them nuts?

Maybe, but not necessarily. The speed rating for a film is arrived at by careful laboratory testing according to standards set up by the Society of Motion Picture and Television Engineers (SMPTE). It's not a matter of opinion. A certain amount of light exposing the film for a fixed amount of time yields x density; therefore, the film is rated at ISO XYZ. But everyone works differently. You will have shot an emulsion test (Chapter 24a). Part of the reason to do this is to learn how the system of film + you + laboratory + timer works and how the film looks best. If you shoot that test with an ISO 500 film and find that the results are best at one stop overexposed, then you will effectively be calling it an ISO 250 film. It may be due to your personal taste, but it is more likely a result of the way you meter. Depending on how I hold my meter, I can easily get results up to one stop off plus or minus. What's important is not that you conform to the manufacturer's rating but that you are consistent in the way you hold your meter and in the way you judge what readings it gives. As long as you are having a consistently exposed film that has a good density (the lab can read the density and let you know), you're in good shape.

I previously mentioned contrast ratios, and I said I would talk about the use of spot meters. A spot meter is a reflected light meter with a telephoto lens and a narrow band of acceptance so it can read the exposure of an arc as small as 1 degree. Since it's a reflected meter, it will tell you what stop to use to get a rendering of your subject at 18% gray. So you don't use it to set exposure, but you can use it to see the relative brightness of different areas on the set. And since it's a little telescope, you can read these areas without going to them; you can stand right next to the camera.

I use my own understanding of Ansel Adams's Zone System with the spot meter. I'm not going to try to explain it here. It's valuable to know, and you should read his book, *The Negative*, to get an understanding of the Zone System. For our purposes, the system divides possible exposures into ten zones, each one stop apart. Zone V is 18% gray, Zone VI is "skin tone" (Caucasian skin), Zone 0 is black, and Zone X is white. His system is based on sensitometry, the science of measuring the sensitivity of photographic materials. I recommend that you learn something about sensitometry, but not here. Read Kodak's *Basic Photographic Sensitometry Workbook* (http://motion.kodak.com/US/en/motion/Education/Publications/index.htm). Adams uses the zones to determine where he will put the exposure of his still photographs. I use the idea of the system to tell me the ratio of light to dark in a scene. I know that the incident reading of the key has given me a stop that will reproduce an 18% gray card as 18% gray. And I know that the spot meter will tell me how to make anything else 18% gray. I take the readings from the spot meter, and I can tell how much brighter or darker than key an area is.

Say my key is f/2.8. If I put an 18% gray card in the key and read it with the spot meter, I will get a reading of f/2.8. If I read a bright area of the set and get a reading of f/8, I know that is three stops brighter than key. If I read a shadow area and get f/.7, I know it's four stops under key. I can do two things with this information. I can adjust the contrast of the scene up or down, and I can make sure the lighting has kept the frame within the possibility of keeping a good image on the medium. Anything can happen now, but you've prepared yourself pretty well. Now it's time to get out there and shoot. Good luck.

24A • LIGHTING EXERCISE #1 • EMULSION TEST

When you're shooting an actual movie, this is part of your prep. I do it every time I start a project, and so should you. Even if you're shooting digital, you need to know how your picture is going to look. The idea of the test is to see how the film or chip you're using responds to light. It also tells you how it relates to your lighting and metering. As I've said, some cinematographers like to rerate the ISO of their stock to accommodate their ways of lighting and metering or the way the lab and timer/colorist treats the picture.

I freely admit that my test is adapted from the one described by Steven Burum, ASC, in *Reflections*, a book I highly recommend. If you look at the article, you will see that I have changed all the lighting instruments. Burum had access to plenty of large lights; I didn't, and I don't expect that you will. You can use any lamps you want, but you must have the setup bright enough to allow for over- and underexposure.

Set up two pieces of card or fabric, one very black and the other very white, as the background. Have two subjects, one in front of each color. Seat them enough in front of the background so they don't throw shadows on the background. Place an 18% gray card in front of the subjects. Light the setup evenly to an f/4 or f/5.6.

Here are some things to remember:

1. It's good to have the two subjects as different in skin tone and hair color as possible so you can see how the film will show these extremes together and see the difference in the effect of backlight on different hair color.
2. You can use anything for the black and white backgrounds. I use highly absorbent black velvet and white felt. The velvet shows detail only at the greatest overexposure, and I'm interested in extremes. The felt is fairly nonreflective so I don't have distracting specular reflections. I have found that it's also a good idea to have pieces of black and white showcard in the background. They are similar to what you will encounter in smooth surfaces.
3. Make sure the gray card is close enough to the camera to be read easily and far enough away to be in exactly the same light as your two actors.
4. If you can include slates in the frame, good; but I find I don't have the space.
5. The frontlight doesn't have to be soft light, but I find it's easier to get an even coverage if I use a large source(s) through diffusion.
6. Run enough footage so you have time during dailies to examine the picture for all the information you can get from it.
7. The precise over- and underexposures are up to you. My first test is three stops over and three stops under.

To get a finer sense of how the film works, I would take the exposure I like best, establish that as normal, and shoot a test in ⅓ stops, one stop over and under.

24A • LIGHTING EXERCISE #1 • EMULSION TEST—CONT'D

What You Should Learn from this Exercise

Here are some major points:

1. Notice how the film looks in the one-light print. The over- and underexposures in these tell you how your picture will look when parts of it are over- and underexposed. You can take for granted that any film handles overexposure better than underexposure. But how much detail is there in the overexposed take? Is there detail in the bright areas? Likewise, the test will tell you how much detail you will retain when you have areas of underexposure.

   Remember, you will always have areas of under- and overexposure in a given frame; not everything can be up to key, and you wouldn't want it to be. You can begin to learn how much latitude you have in the film and how much is pleasing to you. If something looks like a horrible mistake, maybe it will work as an effect in a certain kind of movie.

2. Look at the timed print. You can see how well the film can be printed, how it can be "saved" from bad exposure. One or two stops over and one stop under can be made to look almost as good as a print from a correctly exposed negative. But you will notice that there is slightly less detail in the highlights of the overexposed take. Likewise, you start losing detail in the shadows of the underexposed take. In the two- and three-stop variations, you see what loses detail quickly and what holds at least some information.

3. A telltale problem can be the look of blacks in your picture. They need to be "thick" so they seem solid, but not so dark that they lose all detail. (Assuming you don't want a featureless black area, which you may.) Blacks that are too thin we generally call "milky" or sometimes "smoky." This happens because of the negative/positive printing process. When the entire shot is underexposed, the negative is thin. Light goes through it easily to the print material. As a result, to make it look "correct," very little light is used to print the film. But that means so little light is exposing the print stock that in the clear negative areas, which are the blacks, there's not enough light to expose the print stock fully. Hence, thin, milky blacks. Of course, this thinness is true for the whole frame, but it's most noticeable in the blacks.

A few points are very different for digital shooting. The first thing you notice is the danger of clipping and how quickly that happens in bright areas. The next point is that digital cameras tend to dig into the shadow area and show detail that film hides. You can see that things you might get away with in film—like running cable in dark corners—may well show up when you shoot digitally.

Since there is no ISO standard for the speed of a digital camera, the manufacturer gives an equivalent speed. Before you do any tests, you have to make sure this is correct. Set up the camera pointing at a gray card. Put on the autoexposure function, and let the camera set its stop. Then use your exposure meter to read the card. Adjust your ISO settings on the meter until it gives you the same stop as the camera did. The ISO you land on is the basic equivalent ISO for the camera. You'll start with that and go three exposures up and down.

(Continued)

24B • LIGHTING EXERCISE #2 • DIRECTION OF LIGHT

This is the first of a series to show you how to make use of the qualities of light. Use a camera, tripod, and 1 light source (I like to use a 650W Fresnel). Shoot the following. To evaluate directionality of KEY LIGHT, shoot a medium close shot:

1. Front
2. Back
3. Side Left
4. Side Right
5. 3/4 Front Left
6. 3/4 Front Right
7. 3/4 Rear Left
8. 3/4 Rear Right

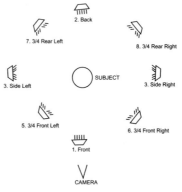

FIGURE 24.9
Light placements.

Then add one bounce light (Try a 1K Fresnel with beadboard or Fomekore). To evaluate the effect of FILL LIGHT:

a. Repeat (from the previous six shots) 1, 3, 5, and 7, and add fill light (use two light sources).

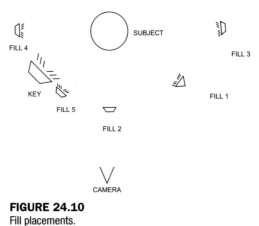

FIGURE 24.10
Fill placements.

24B • LIGHTING EXERCISE #2 • DIRECTION OF LIGHT—CONT'D

b. Vary the amount of the fill light to create different ratios:

1. 2:1
2. 4:1
3. 8:1

When setting your fill, use this rule: Each stop up or down equals a doubling or halving of light. So a 2:1 ratio means one stop difference between the key and the fill. Set your lens stop to the key. For example, if the key reads f/4 and you want a 2:1 ratio, set the fill so it measures f/2.8. I find that you will get a better look with a bounce fill; use a white card and bounce the fill light off it. And an easy way to do this set of exercises is to set the 2:1 ratio first, and from then on leave the key and the fill in the same places. You can then adjust the fill by putting a double scrim in the lamp or a double net in front of the lamp. Each double should reduce the light by ½ (check it to be sure). So, in our example, with one double on the lamp, the fill would read f/2, and the ratio would be 4:1. (It's 4:1 because f/2 is two stops down from f/4, and each stop down is ½ the light. ½ × ½ = ¼.)

What You Should Learn from this Exercise

The first thing you will notice is that it's confusing to meter the light when it's coming from different directions, especially from the back. Try it with the meter pointing from the subject to the camera, and try it with the meter pointing to the light. You will get very different readings and very different effects.

You will notice next that you don't know what the ratios are. For simplicity, let's call it the ratio of key to fill. For 2:1, the key is twice as bright as the fill. As noted in the preceding directions, since each stop is equal to doubling the light, there should be one stop separation between the key and the fill, such as key = f/4, fill = f/2.8, and there will be two stops difference for 4:1 and three stops difference for 8:1. It may surprise you to see how flat 2:1 is and how 8:1 is dramatic but not overwhelming.

And you don't know where to put the fill. Here's a chance for more improvisation. Most cinematographers will place the fill either directly from the camera—that is, frontally—or at a position 180 degrees from the key. Try those positions. Do you like the way they look? Would you be happier with the fill at a 45-degree angle to the camera? Some people will put the fill on the same side as the key. I think this is pointless, but maybe you will like it. There cannot be a right or wrong for this technique. What's right is what you like and what you think best fits the film you're shooting.

You will learn to light by eye, and the way you learn is to train your eye consciously. Setting ratios by meter and memorizing the way they look will give you the ability to set ratios by eye. You'll notice that the result on film or on digital is more pronounced than it is to your perception by eye. This, of course, is a consequence of the fact that all recording media are less sensitive than the eye and consequently look more contrasty.

24C • LIGHTING EXERCISE #3 • QUALITY OF LIGHT

Using the same setup as in exercise #2, shoot the following:

1. One high-contrast shot, one low-contrast (two shots; same subject, same framing)
2. One silhouette, one semisilhouette (two shots; same subject, same framing)

(Continued)

24C • LIGHTING EXERCISE #3 • QUALITY OF LIGHT—CONT'D

3. Hard and soft light setups, each with a 4:1 key to fill ratio. (One shot all hard light and one shot all soft light [two shots; same subject, same framing])

As in the first exercise, the pairs of still shots, you'll have to use your own judgment as to what is contrasty.

Silhouette is less subject to personal judgment. A real silhouette is a black cutout against a white background. You can vary this somewhat, but there should be no detail in the subject. The idea of the semisilhouette is to play with small amounts of detail showing in the face. This is, for example, a standard technique in film noir or to show a character with something to hide.

Hard light is direct light without diffusion. Soft light can be light through diffusion, bounced light, or a naturally soft source, like Kinoflos, directed at the subject, diffused, or bounced.

What You Should Learn from this Exercise

The effect on the audience is marked. The softer the light, the more it is usually perceived as natural. Hard light looks theatrical and dramatic. Contrast provides interest and three-dimensionality to the subject; high contrast tends toward the dramatic, and low contrast toward natural and peaceful.

What's important is that you find out what kind of light, what kind of diffusion, and what contrast you can make with different setups. You will find styles you like best and will want to use. You will also figure out how to create effects that will be useful in different dramatic situations.

24D • LIGHTING EXERCISE #4 • LIGHTING THE FACE, THE GREAT LANDSCAPE

You will light and shoot a glamour portrait setup, testing the best light for the subject. Remember what you have been doing for the last three exercises, and think about the ways you can shape the light:

1. *How do different directions and amounts of light work?* You have at your command back, side (½ light), ¾ front, ¼ rear, frontal. What direction of key works best for the subject?
2. *How does light vary in quality?* Vary the amount of the fill and think about the contrast: Should the shot be high or low contrast? Should the fill smooth out shadows or just bring out the features?

   Work with diffusion and bounce: Which works best for the subject? What do you prefer to work with? How hard or soft should the overall look be to bring out the best in the subject? Here are some characteristics of light to keep in mind for every setup:

   Placement/direction (angle)
   Distance from subject
   Size/intensity
   Hardness/softness
   Color
Remember: Place one light at a time!

CHAPTER 25

Exercise: Shooting Your Project on Film

Now it's time to shoot a project with a film camera on film stock. This will be the final exercise in the book and will call into play everything you've learned. I won't be telling you what to shoot. I told you long ago that I'm not going to tell you what subjects or stories to do, just how to do them. Here's the chance to fly on your own. I suggest you make a movie you will be proud of and think other people would like to see, but that's up to you. You might just be interested in personal expression, and that's okay, too. But remember: This is going to cost a bit of money, so it will be to your advantage to end up with something you can at least show to people to get a job. Do your best work possible, and in line with that, don't get in over your head by getting too ambitious for this first film project. It's always better to do a small project well than a big project poorly.

The first thing you're going to need is an idea or script for this exercise. But you're a cinematographer. No one expects you to have ideas for scripts. Find a writer or director who has a script and offer to shoot their film. If necessary, entice them by offering to get all the crew and equipment and pay for the stock. That should be a very attractive offer. Or for the sake of this exercise, you could come up with a little idea of your own. Try to think of something that will allow you to use lots of the cinematic techniques we've been talking about in these pages. Remember, the less dialogue the better. They're called motion pictures because they move and because they tell the story in pictures. And dialogue is hard to do well. As a showcase for your cinematography no one is going to be overly impressed looking at nothing but dialogue scenes.

Once you've got the project set you'll be going through all the steps we talked about in the preproduction section of this book. Even a small project requires preplanning. The first requirement you'll encounter is getting access to a 16 mm film camera. If you're in film school, that probably won't be a problem. If not, you will have to borrow or rent a camera. So you have to know something about 16 mm and super-16 mm cameras. By far the most popular 16 mm and super-16 mm cameras are the Arri 16SRs. If you can get your hands on one, that's great. My school has several Aatons; our equipment manager got them because they're quieter than Arris. But both Arris and Aatons are expensive, whether they are new or old models. The great Arri S and M models were workhorses of non-sync filming in the 1970s. They're still great cameras, and you can buy used ones for a pittance. If you're not recording dialogue, they'll be fine. If you are, you'll need a quiet camera and you'll need a sound recordist; they almost always come with their own equipment. If you're in school, you'll get your sound equipment from the school.

There are probably a lot of Éclair NPRs around; these are great cameras, but they have a tendency to get dirt in the gate. If you don't mind windup, spring-driven cameras, the Bolex 16s are good nonsync cameras. And, of course, there's the Bell and Howell Filmo, which was designed as a combat camera during World War II. It's so rugged it can be used as a weapon. Unless they've been converted, all the Bolexes and Filmos, all the older Arris (S and M), all the Eclairs, and many of the 16SRs and the older Aatons (LTR, XTR) will be regular 16 format, 1.33:1. That's not a serious problem, but it's good to be aware of it. My recommendation is to shoot with them, but imagine a wide-screen frame (1.85:1—movie standard or 1.75:1—HD) while you're filming. If you can remove the ground glass and you have the nerve to try, you can use a very fine pencil to scribe the frame lines. Any of these cameras can be fine for your purposes. As long as you've got a camera that works and is good enough to have been used by professionals, you'll be in good shape.

Then there's the matter of lenses. It's important to have good lenses. If there's anything to splurge on, make it lenses; they make the picture. Most of these cameras come with lenses made for them. Again, they're basically all good enough for your purposes. I want to encourage you to use prime lenses. Zooms are attractive to people, especially those on tight budgets, because it looks like you're getting dozens of focal lengths for the price of two or three primes. But zooms tend to lead to sloppy work. It's all too easy to put in a "tracking shot" that's just zooming. It's aesthetically repellent. And using primes will force you to think about the choice of lens focal length and the precise placement of the camera.

Beware the Canon Scoopic camera, which has a built-in zoom and too much automation to give you control over the picture. You'll have to learn the basic handling of these cameras—loading, lens mounting, tripod mounting, and a few controls (on/off is important). You can get manuals for all of the cameras from the manufacturer, or you can go online to a number of places[1] to buy old manuals or reproductions. An indispensable tool is David Elkins's *Camera Assistant's Manual*. It is, bar none, the best book ever written on the job of the camera assistant. It has threading diagrams and basic instructions for all makes of cameras in common use. Another great source is the *ASC Manual*, although it is both very technical and whoppingly expensive. Finally, you could look

---

[1]Do a search or start with these:

http://www.butkus.org/chinon/on-line_manuals.htm

http://cameras.about.com/od/usermanuals/Digital_Camera_User_Manuals.htm

into Verne and Sylvia Carlson's *Professional Cameraman's Handbook*, also full of diagrams and pictures and descriptions of cameras. Obviously, if you are at school or know someone with film experience, you could seek their help. Or if you can't do anything else, find a camera rental house and ask them to run you through the basics of the camera. A lot of great people work at rental houses, and I have always found them to be knowledgeable and generous with their help. Refer back to Chapters 8, 9, 11, and 18 for help with using this new equipment.

Next, you are going to need film stock. As I've said before (Chapter 10), it's not too complicated these days because you'll choose either indoor or outdoor, depending on the needs of your project. If you're really going to do this right and learn the most, you'll want to do some lighting. Access to lighting equipment again depends on your resources—film school equipment, rental, make your own. You'll also need a light meter and need to know how to use it so you can determine and set your f-stop. You can begin to see that for this exercise or project you'll be putting into play pretty much all of what you've learned so far from this book. If you don't feel prepared, go back and reread.

Remember that it takes a lot of people to make a film. Don't worry about getting a 100-man Hollywood crew, but don't try to do it completely on your own either. I'd say a minimal crew is six people plus the director: one camera assistant for you, three grip/electricians, an AD, and a PA (or runner—someone you can cut loose from the set to do errands or handle emergencies). Up until now you've probably gotten by shooting by yourself and with a few friends. Now you want to graduate to a new level of professionalism.

So how are you going to get yourself a crew? Lots of people want to make movies. You can check Craig's List—for example, http://losangeles.craigslist.org/tfr/, which is the Los Angeles Craig's List and go to Jobs and then to tv/film/video/radio jobs. Here is an example of a listing:

Cinematographer (Southern California)
Date: 2010-07-30, 9:09AM PDT
Reply to: xxxxxxxxxxxxxxxxxxxxxxxxxxx [Errors when replying to ads?]
We are looking for a cinematographer to work on an ultra-low-budget movie.
Day rates INCLUDING EQUIPMENT are $200.00 a day.
Filming from August 2nd to Sept 2nd with 10 days off in between in Palm Desert, CA.
PLEASE ONLY E-MAIL IF YOUR DAY RATES ($200) INCLUDE EQUIPMENT.
We also provide meals; accommodations (3 people sharing room); gasoline allowance to commute to Palm Desert. We also provide one grip person to help as gaffer and boom operator.
Please provide the package of lights, HD camera, and cinematographer for $200.00. Prove that you own it, please. DP promised he had equipment, but it didn't belong to him, now, a day before production, we found out that his DP friend got a gig and needed his equipment back.

P.S.: Please only apply understanding that we cannot afford more than $200.00 a day.
P.S.: Please specify (tell the truth) the equipment you have. Don't think that you'll be able to convince me to rent because our budget is very low.
P.S.: E-mail us your reel.
Thank You.

Of course this person wants you to have your own equipment. Be careful of that kind of deal. Sometimes it's their way of getting equipment on the cheap, and they don't care about your work. But it may be legitimate; they could be maxing out their credit cards to make an art film, and they need you as a collaborator and a sort of financier. In any case, don't go out buying equipment until you have a feel for what you like to work with and what equipment producers are looking for. There's no point to getting an old 16 mm camera if everybody wants to shoot super-16. There's no point to buying an HD camera that's too expensive for you. You've got to figure out how you can amortize the cost either by actually renting it or by getting jobs partly because you own equipment. And that means getting lots of jobs. Balance your acquisition of equipment so that the equipment either makes money for you or helps you to get jobs. Don't get saddled with so much expensive equipment that you have to work jobs that may be morally or artistically repugnant to you just to pay off the cost of the equipment.

If there's a film school or film enthusiasts' organization where you live, check with them for possible crew members. If not, look for people who do jobs or have skills similar to film jobs: makeup artists and hairdressers, obviously; carpenters and construction workers for grips; electricians to light; antique store and thrift store owners for props and costumes; community theaters for actors, directors, lighting designers, costume designers, set designers, stagehands, stage managers (great ADs); accountants or bankers for producers; sports team coaches for ADs and production managers; and amateur photographers for the camera crew.

For this venture make sure you've got a script you like and a director you respect and get along with. You never know how good a movie is going to be, so just start with a congenial group. You're going to make great cinematography anyway, right?

Do a very short movie. I recommend five minutes or less. First of all, you're shooting film; the stock costs money, and so does processing and transferring it to digital so it can be edited. Also, a very short movie can be shot without pain, difficulty, or long hours over a single weekend. Everybody has fun, no one gets overtired, and no one has time to make enemies. In Los Angeles I took part in a friendly competition called the 48-Hour Film Project, where groups of people get together and shoot, edit, and screen their films all in a 48-hour period. It's a lot of fun, and you'd be surprised at how good some of these movies turn out. Check it out.

- http://www.48hourfilm.com/
- http://www.nytimes.com/2010/06/09/movies/09time.html
- http://www.sa48hr.com/

These organizations hold competitions all over the United States, and you could meet people you'll keep as colleagues for years.

So shoot it, cut it, record some local musicians for the soundtrack, and show it. Find a place that can accommodate 50 or 100 people; everyone who worked on it will want to bring his or her family and friends. Make the show a big deal, and start looking right away for your next project. You're king of the world! (Okay, so it took James Cameron another 12 years to make another film, but that doesn't mean you have to.)

Now that the film is done, let's talk about what you will have learned from shooting it.

25A • WHAT YOU SHOULD HAVE LEARNED FROM THE SHOOTING ON FILM EXERCISE

You're going to show your work to a lot of people. Let's review screening room etiquette. (You've got no control over everyone else, but you can be polite and maybe get your main crew to be like you and set an example.) First of all, you never know who's in the screening room with you. It might be someone who could hire or fire you, so behave yourself. Look good. If someone in the room has worked on the film you're screening (and someone always has unless you're alone. Even then), don't make any comment on that person's work. No matter what, you're drawing attention to it, and you don't know if that helps or hurts. You are a nice guy or gal and you don't want to hurt anyone; or else you're not so nice and you just don't want to make an enemy who'll get even. Remember, just do as your mother told you to do.

Now, what are you going to see? Either you will love everything or you will hate everything. Almost everyone seems to fall into one of those two categories, at least at first. They're both wrong. Nothing is so cut-and-dried as great/horrible. Try to be nuanced in your reactions. Things will look different the next time you watch dailies, things will look different in the editing room, things will look different when the film is done. You can, however, look for a few points that are unambiguous.

Exposure/Lighting
- How's the exposure? Does it seem to be mostly correct or at least close enough so the density can be adjusted in post?
- How do the actors look? Are they attractive, or at least appropriate to their characters? Do you see a nice modeling to their faces?
- How is the contrast ratio? Is it too contrasty? Or is it verging on flat?
- Do you see distracting shadows? Worse, do you see a boom or a camera shadow?

Operating
- Is the operating smooth? Is head room consistent? Do you lead the actors in the direction they're talking, looking, moving?
- Is the size of your lead consistent looking?
- Do you fall behind in the lead and have to catch up, or never catch up?

(Continued)

25A • WHAT YOU SHOULD HAVE LEARNED FROM THE SHOOTING ON FILM EXERCISE—CONT'D

- Do the pans and tilts work without being jerky?
- What do you think of the composition of the shots?
- Are they well composed and stay composed as the actors move?
- Are they beautiful, or at least pleasant?
- Did you accidentally show something that is not part of the scene, like a lamp or stand?
- Did you shoot off the set?

Assisting

- Are the shots in focus? If you have zooms, the best you can hope for is that they're undetectable. If you can see them, do they start and stop smoothly?
- Is the speed of the zoom appropriate to the rhythm of the shot?

Dolly

- How are the dolly moves?
- Do they start and stop in sync with the movement in the frame?
- Are they fast enough? Too fast? Smooth? Bumpy?

Art

- Do the shots give you a sense of the emotion of the scene?
- Does it seem as though you have enough coverage of the scene?

You will be asking yourself all these questions and maybe more, depending on the particular circumstances of your shoot. (For example, did the polarizer hide all the reflections in the car windows? Did your car mount work without coming loose? There will be a million things that can go wrong, and you will be hypersensitive to every one of them.)

Remember your dailies etiquette: Be polite, say very little, give only compliments, and give them only when you're asked. There's plenty of time later to do a postmortem and to drag everyone over the coals. You'll do this privately, with the director and with individual members of your crew.

You can relax for a while after shooting and after dailies. During the film, you'll have new footage every day, but after the first day you should be less apprehensive about dailies. You will have fixed the obvious problems. Be careful not to change your methods of shooting too much in reacting to the dailies. It's important to stay consistent through the film. You've made your plans, you've practiced the craft, and you should be pretty good. You're not perfect, and you'll always find room for improvement. But if there's something big bothering you, think it through. Is the film consistently over- or underexposed? Don't change your lighting or metering. Call the lab right away. Find out how dense the negative is. It's possible that the timer or colorist is trying to "save" you by making the dailies look a certain way he thinks will please the producer.

Of course, you need to check with the lab if there are scratches or dirt on the film. The negative has to be inspected. You may have to go to the lab and look at it yourself. Even if you're not sure what you're looking for—you want to check negative density, but you don't know how—ask. For the most part, lab workers know their stuff, and they're happy to teach you and set you straight. After all, their reputation, as well as yours, is riding on the look of your film.

25A • WHAT YOU SHOULD HAVE LEARNED FROM THE SHOOTING ON FILM EXERCISE—CONT'D

A particular problem I have seen in the last few years is a disappointing telecine transfer. Plenty of things can go wrong. You can forestall some problems by shooting a frame chart so the film is transferred as you framed it. And shoot a gray card for every scene; either the colorist will time the scene as you want, or you'll see by looking at the gray card that it's too light or too dark, or you'll see that you need to adjust your method of exposing the gray card. But the most common problems I have seen are excess video noise, which can sometimes look like film grain.

I can guarantee you that with any modern emulsion, properly exposed, you won't have visible grain. If it's there, either you metered and exposed incorrectly or the lab screwed up. You probably have a pretty good idea of the accuracy of your exposure. To be sure, again, go to the lab that processed the film. Ask them to read it on a densitometer. The readings they get will be an absolute indication of the adequacy of your exposure. Then talk to the telecine operator.

I have had mostly excellent relationships with colorists and with the companies doing telecine. But I know a lot of people, mostly starting out and mostly poor, who have tried to cut corners on telecine. In every case, their work has suffered. Sometimes the telecine company will not admit a problem and will not offer some correction. They're stuck with an unsatisfactory film. Don't let it happen. No matter how low budget the film is, there's got to be money for good technical work. If the producer insists that there's no money in the budget or she wants to go to a lab you know is cut-rate, you've got decisions to make.

If you feel the producer's attitude is typical of the way the film is going to go, and you can afford to, turn it down. You don't want to work hard and put your heart into something you'll be ashamed of. But the likelihood is that you won't have your choice of jobs. So you might as well take it and get some experience. Do the best you can and try to make sure your part of the film is done well. If it's a disaster, ask them to take your name off the film. Honestly, if it's that bad, it's unlikely that anyone will see it. But you never know.

However, if you decide to do this film because it has many attractive qualities, you have to shoulder the responsibility to get the best work you can from the lab and the telecine house. Go to them well in advance. Meet the owner, and get to know the staff who are likely to be handling your film. Most places will assign a timer or colorist. If you can meet several of them, find someone you like who seems sympathetic to your way of working. Specifically request him or her; after all, it's in the lab's interest to keep you happy. You never know: you might be the next Vilmos Zsigmond. Have coffee with your contact, buy him lunch, spend some time becoming more than a number or name to him. Find out what kind of instructions he likes to get. Does he like gray cards or color charts? Would he like to have e-mailed instructions for the dailies, or does he like to talk over the phone? Does he like getting stills you've manipulated in Photoshop as a starting point for the look? The more you do, the more likely you'll be happy with the dailies and with the film as a whole.

After the film is edited, you will have a final chance to tweak the look when you time the finished picture, whether photochemically or electronically, and probably with the director.

PART 3
Realities: Postproduction

CHAPTER 26

Postproduction: Timing and Transferring

Hey, the shoot's over! Hooray! I'll bet you thought this day would never come. You've managed to get a good night's sleep for two days in a row now. You're feeling human again. Of course, now you're getting nervous about your *next* job.

It's always this way. Even Oscar winner Jack Lemmon used to say he worried he'd never get another job. When you feel that way, it means you're really in show business. Luckily for you, you'll be called up in a couple of weeks or months by the director, who wants you to time the picture. Whether you've shot on film or digitally, timing is essential. Like cleaning up, it doesn't happen after the job; it's part of the job.

After the film is edited and the picture locked, you will work with the timer at the lab or the colorist at telecine to "time" the film. *Timing*, a term left over from earlier days, means adjusting the picture so the color and density are correct for every shot and consistent within the scene. (In the United Kingdom and some parts of the United States, it's called *grading*.) A great change can result from a small adjustment to the brightness of a lamp or the relative intensities of color. You'll go through the film shot-by-shot, often with the director present, to ensure the finished film looks exactly as you and she intended.

Timing is as important as preparatory discussions with the director when you decide on a look for the film. I have seen scenes shot in the summer be manipulated in timing to look convincingly like a wintry landscape. That sort of extreme manipulation is unusual. But even small adjustments affect the audience's emotional response to the film. Every artistic or practical decision made has an impact on realizing the director's vision. You can change a shot from one that is bright and simply gives the audience information to one that is dark and creates a sense of mystery.

Keep in mind the entire emotional and narrative thrust of the film. The director has the final say, but you are the person who knows what the original intentions of the cinematography were. You're the only one who knows exactly how the lighting was done to fulfill those intentions, and you can make or prevent changes that will alter the impact of the film.

Your first experience doing timing will be intimidating. You know what you want the film to look like, but how do you describe it in words? How do you talk to the timer (for brevity, I'll say "timer," and you'll think "timer or colorist" from now on)? It can be tricky, no doubt about it, and you can get flummoxed when you hear the terms of art—*midrange, crush blacks,* and so on—that are completely foreign to you.

Don't worry. To begin with, you're the customer. They want to make you happy. And your timer is an experienced technician; he knows what he's doing, and he's done it a lot. (I will have to tell you that you may get an inexperienced timer, and you may be screwed. It's often luck of the draw, but if you have a tight budget and the producer made a deal with the lab to get a good price, it's likely that you'll be assigned the least experienced timer. Why should they give you the best when they've got work to do for a big company?)

Let's assume you get a timer who's as new as you are. You know how to deal with this: Don't try to impress her with what you know, and try to establish a good rapport with her. Of course, that should be your approach with the oldest, most experienced timer in Hollywood. If you try to act as though you know what's going on or try to play the great artist, most people will see through you and will resent you. But you're a nice person, and you wouldn't try that act (would you?).

Most people will be happy to talk you through the process, and they love to show you how their profession works. Use that, and ask questions. Use a technique that I've always followed and have been very happy with: Let the timer do a first pass on his own. Most timers will want to. They know how to make the gross corrections, and can give you a look that's consistent at least within a scene. If your dailies are close to what you want (and if they're not, it means a miscommunication with the lab; look at Chapter 37), the timer will turn out a product close to your original intentions.

Then you and he will watch it together. You can talk about changes you'd like made—using common terms like *brighter, darker, more blue, more orange*—and you'll get another trial print to go through together again. The number of trial prints you get will depend on your producer's deal with the lab, but any lab will give you at least two prints before wanting more money.

If you're finishing electronically, you'll be in the timing suite with the colorist. Everything I just said about personal relationships holds true. One difference in an electronic lab is that the colorist can make changes as you sit there, and you can see them immediately. It's a lot faster, and can be more efficient. You and the colorist can go through several stages of adjusting the look of the picture, stages that would have taken days with a traditional photochemical approach.

It helps to have a vocabulary in common. When working photochemically, your talk will be fairly simple: lighter or darker, and more or less color, which is RGB (red, green, and blue, and their complements, cyan, magenta, and yellow). Your only other real control is whether to print on conventional film stock or a higher-contrast stock that gives thicker blacks. Both Kodak and Fuji make different printing stocks, and there's a difference between them you may prefer.

Electronics gives the colorist a very powerful tool, but it comes with more jargon, both from engineering and the complexity of the process. Instead of density (lighter or darker), you have control over three areas of the image: the blacks, the gamma (midrange), and the whites. Blacks and whites make sense to anyone. You will need to use the term *gamma*, but don't confuse yourself with thinking about the gamma that defines the contrast of negative film. Just think of it as the middle exposures of the shot. You can raise (lift) the blacks, showing more detail but risking making your blacks milky. You can lower (crush) the blacks, making them denser and darker but losing detail. You can raise or lower the whites, but you must be careful about raising—brightening—the whites so much that you clip them (as in original digital photography, this is losing all detail and making it irretrievable). Midrange—gamma—is less intuitive. Most skintones will fall in the midrange. So you can lift or lower the midrange primarily to make the faces brighter or darker. It might be done as a correction to your exposure, or it might be a particular look you want.

Besides the speed of correction, your advantage in electronic timing is being able to try out different looks, see them immediately, and keep or discard them. The colorist will urge you to start with a standard scene that you two can correct to your satisfaction. He can then use that as a template for any similar scenes and as a general idea for the whole film. He'll know if you want faces to pop with brightness like fashion photography or to be dense and detailed like a documentary. All telecine bays have a frame store; the colorist will put one frame from each corrected shot in the store as a reference. If your eyes start getting tired, and you feel confused as to whether you're keeping the look consistent, you and he can refer to the frame store. Budget is, of course, a big consideration in telecine. Time in the telecine bay is very expensive; a lot of equipment has to be amortized, and the company has to make a profit.

In a conventional lab what you take away is a print, 16 mm or 35 mm, depending on your original. It's called an answer print; you've approved all the changes to it, and the settings are saved so that every print of your film from now on will look the same as your answer print.

When you telecine the film, you will ideally be going in with an EDL (edit decision list) the editor has prepared. The lab uses this to find the parts of your original and put them together. All of this is in the realm of electronic data. When you are happy with the look of your film, you have many choices of the final media. You can pretty much narrow it down to tape or hard drive. There are several kinds of tape you can use, and of course there are choices of hard drives. The choice of tape is up to your producer and the postproduction supervisor. What you come out with is essentially a negative of the cut film, and it's used to make all the copies whether film or digital. Your interest is in keeping the best picture. You'll get it with the media that can retain the most information. It's up to you to push hard for the highest quality; at this point money is likely to be tight, but it's false economy to settle for anything but the best-looking film.

CHAPTER 27

Postproduction: Putting Together a Reel

You're out there now. You've practiced your craft, you've met people involved in the business, and you've shot some film. You're going to be looking for your next job. How do you find it? Well, don't ask me! The only advice I have is that you should stay in touch with everyone you know in the business. Jobs come from connections—let's call it networking—and you never know who might turn you on to a job. Besides camera crew, directors, and producers, I've been recommended by grips, gaffers, assistant directors, prop masters, art directors, and script supervisors. I've also tried cold calls, but I can't recommend them; the return isn't enough to justify the time.

However you make the connection for that big feature, you're going to meet people who say, "What can you do?" And you're going to show them. You're going to put together a demo reel. Don't worry if you feel you don't have enough material. The truth is that the shorter the reel, the better. Its maximum length is five minutes. Even though a director wants to know how good you are, no one wants to watch a demo reel. This is marketing, and you have to sell your reel as much as you have to sell yourself.

And every reel is a work in progress, no matter how many times you've revised it. It's likely that you will always be shooting something that looks special or is exceptionally stunning. Every time you shoot a movie, think about what you might want to use from it for your reel. There's no guarantee that any technique will work best, but I've found a few rules it helps to follow.

First of all, go through all your work. I guess this brings up a point: Make sure you get high-quality copies of everything you shoot. It should be part of your deal, especially if you're working for little money or for free. High quality means the best copy you can get, easily duplicable, with the most information on it. For example, don't settle for a DVD; most DVDs will incorporate a lot of compression from the original. Try to get copies of the master of the film or at least duplicate copies of the dailies of the scene you like most.

Once you have the material, label it and store it carefully. Short of vaulting it in an old salt mine in Kansas, keep it dry, reasonably cool (60° F to 65° F, if you can), and out of direct sunlight. (Sunlight won't hurt, but it will heat up your material.) These conditions apply to almost anything—film, tape, solid state memory, and hard drives.

Go through your films. It's best if you've been able to get or make a viewing copy of the film. You can watch that over and over without damaging the original. And you're going to watch it over and over. Make notes of scenes and shots you think are particularly good. Do they show off lighting, operating, composition, beauty, well-known actors? All of these are good reasons to pick them out. Think about transitions. If you have, say, a couple of good right-to-left moves from different movies that would cut together and make a nice, kinetic, seamless transition, that's impressive.

Definitely note all the work you consider the best looking. Then go through your notes and begin making a continuity. (My editor friends call it a "paper cut"; I just like to say that for the pun.) Anyway, write out what you think would make a good sequence for the reel. Think about these rules:

- Start with the best. A lot of the time that's all anyone will watch: the first 30 seconds.
- Finish with your second best. If they get that far, you want to leave them dazzled.
- Arrange the rest so it makes a natural progression.
- Think of thematic sequences: action, scenic, and so on.
- Don't put in dialogue. Half the time the producers watch reels with the sound off anyway.
- Cut fast; there's less story to engage the audience than in the whole movie, but don't confuse them.

Group all the shots from one film together. There's some difference of opinion here, and it's this: Do you put all the pretty shots together, then all the action, then all the night shots, and so on, like a picture book, or do you put little movies on one after the other? I think everyone tends to look at a succession of shots as a sequence, and makes up a story whether a story exists or not. Take advantage of that. You've got stories there; use them, and your viewers are likely to get involved, feel the time is passing quickly, and have a more favorable opinion of you and your work.

Now it's time to put it together. I am assuming you have an editing program at home. If you don't, it'll be easy to find someone who does. You don't need an editor, but it's a good idea, especially when you get down to a fine cut. Start by assembling the material in the order you've decided. See if you like it or if you want to rearrange it. When you have the order the way it works for you, do a second cut for rhythm. After you have that, it's time to get opinions. Remember, this isn't a work of art; it's a demonstration of the art you can make. Any smart person is a good test audience, but it's probably better to show it to people in the business. And don't show it to everyone at this stage. Reserve some people, especially if you have some higher-up contacts in the business, so you can get fresh viewpoints for later versions.

You will want to put a soundtrack on in case your prospective employers do watch the reel with the sound on. This can be tricky. As I said, don't include dialogue—no words at all if you can make sense of the pictures without them. And you should be able to. You're a cameraperson, right? Use music you love. I have watched a lot of reels. I caution you against using popular music. First off, most of it has lyrics; your audience will listen to the lyrics, and it will distract them from your pictures. Next, be careful of using anything that might appeal strongly to one group; it's just as likely to offend another group (think rap and hip-hop). You may love it. I hate it, and I'm typical of my age group. Don't put yourself behind the eight-ball.

Here's a cautionary story. Years ago, I went to college in a town near where Rod Serling, creator of *The Twilight Zone*, had a summer vacation house. Rod was a wonderful man who wanted to give back some of the riches he had gotten from the business. So he offered to come by one day, look at our student movies, and offer some constructive criticism. It was great; not only did he give all of us ideas about how to improve our work, he managed to say something positive and encouraging about the worst, most incomprehensible, out-of-focus junk anyone has ever seen. But he was stumped by one film. There was someone singing on the soundtrack. You could see Rod didn't like it, and he was trying to find a diplomatic way to encourage the filmmaker to change it. He offered the advice, "Since you're not doing this for commercial purposes, why not use something from a record rather than having your roommate singing off-key?" We all sat there, stunned. No one made a peep. Finally, one of us had the courage to speak up and said, "Uh, Rod … that's not his roommate. That's Bob Dylan singing." "That's Bob Dylan?" Rod exclaimed, shocked. "Well, he's lucky to be making a living."

And your music, no matter how good you're convinced it is, will turn off your audience if you're not careful. I've tried jazz and classical. They can be good, but they also tend to overpower the images, and the musical phrases are often too long for a short sequence. I've had my best luck with soundtrack music, and I recommend it. The composer wrote it for movies, and it goes well with all kinds of pictures. But don't worry; they'll probably turn off the sound anyway.

You've got the scenes you want, they're cut pretty well, the order works, and you've got music for the track. Now you need titles. All you really need is your name, followed by "Director of Photography." Some DPs will put phone numbers, e-mail addresses, website URLs, and more. I think that's all counterproductive. If you'd like a second opinion: If you're going to put your reel on your website, you will want to include contact information in the titles. You want to make sure they know whose work it is: your name. And make sure they remember you're a DP. They'll have the DVD cover (again—not if they're looking at it online). You're submitting this as a DVD because that's today's standard. But remember: Retain all your material in the best form possible. I've gone through ¾-inch U-Matic tape, ½-inch VHS tape, and DVD as demo reel formats, and I've only been doing it for 25 years. Formats will change for you, too. You want to design a cover for the DVD—and a label for the disc—that's beautiful, striking, identifiable with you, and professional looking. Presentation is vital, and the better your physical reel looks, the more professional everyone will think you are.

And on the DVD and the case you will put your name, phone number, e-mail address, and website if you have one. Make them clear and legible, and put them on both the disc and the cover. Agents and producers get a lot of reels, and they're not as careful as they could be, and you don't want them to lose track of you.

I can't say much about websites. I'm sure you know more than I do. But whatever you do, make it visually striking; you want to impress viewers even before they see your photography. And look around for places you can deposit or showcase your reel. There's a fair number of websites that exist just to show reels. Your research will give you an idea of the competition out there, too.

And, although you've probably decided by now, there is the question of length. Remember this: They don't want to see your reel. A DP friend of mine says that most reels become expensive coasters for the producers' coffee cups. How much time will they give you? How much time would you give anyone? How long do you think they can stand to watch anything? The commonly accepted rule of thumb is five minutes, not a second more. When you start, you'll be lucky to have a minute and a half of good material. Don't pad it. Wow them, and leave them hungry for more.

PART 4
Technicalities

CHAPTER 28

Cameras: Black Boxes

Movie cameras—and I mean film and digital and any other methods of image acquisition yet to be developed—are magic devices that produce the illusion of continuous movement by putting together a succession of still pictures, with slight variations from frame to frame, viewed so quickly as to fool the audience into thinking they're seeing real motion. Generally, the phenomenon is called *persistence of vision*. It's not a perfectly accurate term, and you can find the best explanation I've seen in Bruce Kawin's book *How Movies Work*.[1] So we have a box that can record millions of still pictures that, when shown in succession and alignment, create the illusion of motion. How does it do that?

MOTION PICTURE CAMERA

Any camera is basically a box closed off to light with a hole in the end to let a small amount of light through. A box with a tiny hole in it is a pinhole camera. It can make a perfectly good image, though in slightly soft focus. To improve the focus, we put a lens in the hole. A lens bends light rays. If we get the right lens, we can make it converge the light rays passing through so they are sharply focused at one point.

So far we've got a fairly unsophisticated piece of equipment. A box with a lens like this was used by painters, beginning in the Renaissance, to throw an image on paper. The image could be traced, and we have art. The box was called a *camera obscura* (dark room) or, in a slightly different arrangement, a *camera lucida* (bright room).

You can see a giant camera obscura today at the beach in Santa Monica. It's a dark room where you enter, close the door, and turn to see a beautiful picture of the beach—upside down. So that could be a problem. Fortunately, when we take a still picture, we can turn it right side up to look at it. A movie is projected through a lens that turns the upside-down picture upside down, hence right side up.

---

[1]Kawin, Bruce, *How Movies Work*, Macmillan, 1987.

But we want to preserve this picture so we can look at it later. We put a light-sensitive substance (film, CCD) on the side with the image. Given a lot of engineering, we can take this light-sensitive material, make the image permanent, and use it in many ways later. This is our photograph. Put a lot of still photographs through a projector and we have a movie.

GATE • SHUTTER • MOVEMENT

It's easier to understand film first and then, by analogy, digital. Film came first, and that makes the camera a nineteenth-century technology. Most of us are at least somewhat conversant with mechanical devices, so we can understand the concepts. Electronics came after—so it did develop as an analog to film—and it certainly is harder for me to understand, so I figure it will be for you, too.

We've got tough, flexible film (thank you, Eastman Kodak; more on this later). The standard for professional movies is 35 mm with four perforations per frame. When we use film in our later movies, it'll be 16 mm, one perforation per frame. The film comes in long rolls, usually 1,000 feet for 35 mm and 400 feet for 16 mm. The perforations are designed as holes for a hook in the camera's mechanism to grab the film and pull it through the camera. The film has to rest for a moment (less than $1/24$ second, since we have 24 frames per second) in the gate, through which light from the lens enters and exposes the film. Then the film has to move and stop—24 times a second. That's fast—90 feet per minute. Uh oh, now we're in trouble. Did you ever try to start and stop quickly—over and over again—fast? Twenty-four times a second of anything is a fast pace for human beings and most machines. As tough as the film has been made, it would be easy for it to break under the stress of fast speeds and sharp stops. It's even easier because the film is being continuously fed and taken up on the reels in the magazine. The unexposed film is held in the light-tight compartment of the magazine, fed through the camera mechanism as it is exposed, and then taken back up into the magazine, where it awaits processing.

FIGURE 28.1
Panaflex movement.
Image courtesy of Panavision Inc.

Think about this. The mechanism of the magazine is operating continuously, but the mechanism of the camera is working intermittently. The result is the film bunches up in front of the gate. Pull it down quickly, and the film hasn't come out of the magazine enough, and it breaks, or at least it's strained and scratched at the top of the gate. How can you remedy this problem? The answer is, with the loop.

Some very smart people as far back as the 1890s came up with the idea of placing a loop between the continuously moving drive sprocket and both the top and bottom of the gate. Figure 28.1 shows the Panaflex movement. You can see how a loop forms in various threading diagrams in Chapter 34.

Meanwhile, there's a pin moving on a cam in, down, and out, grabbing a sprocket hole, bringing the film down and preparing for the next frame to sit in the gate and to be exposed. It's really quite beautiful. It's like a sewing machine inside a box.

Of course, the light from the lens has to hit the film while it's held steady by two more pins—registration pins—and it can't hit the film while it's moving to the next frame (or else it will blur). So we have a shutter that opens and closes in synchronization with the film and the pull-down claw; the shutter is a disk with part of it removed. Usually the shutter is split in half, so for half the time of the rotation of the shutter, the film is being exposed. This gives us a nice, easy way to figure exposure: The shutter is open half the time, and the film moves 24 times a second, so it's in the gate for $1/24$ of a second. (It's exposed for $1/2$ its time in the gate, then it moves and is not exposed for the other $1/2$ the time.) One-half of $1/24$ is $1/48$, so the exposure time is $1/48$ second; we round it off to $1/50$ second for convenience.

VIEWING SYSTEM

These days, almost every camera has a reflex viewing system. The light that comes through the lens goes to the film half the time; the other half of the time, it goes to the viewfinder. How does it do that, you ask? Well, with great difficulty. The front of the shutter is a front-surface mirror (or sometimes there's a separate mirror shutter; same thing, more engineering). The light hits the mirror, is reflected at an angle through a system of prisms and lenses, arrives upright and fairly bright at the objective end of the eyepiece, and goes right into the operator's eye. Lots of work goes into making sure the viewfinder picture is bright and upright and it's in focus—*exactly* the same focus the film is getting. Briefly, the ground glass (on which the viewfinder image is formed) is just on the viewfinder side of the shutter and placed at exactly the same distance optically from the lens as the film is. Therefore, the light traveling to the viewfinder travels the same distance as the light that travels to the lens. So if the picture in the viewfinder is sharp, so is the picture on the film. The lens, the piece that lets light enter, is in front of the movement, attached to the outside of the camera. We'll talk more about the lens later.

FRONT: MATTE BOX, IRIS RODS, FOLLOW FOCUS

The front of any professional movie camera has a geared knob attached to the lens so the assistant can focus, a matte box to shade the lens from unwanted light and to offer a place to put filters as wanted by the DP, and iris rods to hold and support accessories, such as zoom motors, lens lights, and lens support brackets. So we have the camera operator looking through the viewfinder at an upright image that shows what is being recorded on the film. "Wait a minute here, Jack. You said the operator looks through the viewfinder, right?" Right. "So he sees the picture." Yes. "Does the assistant have a viewfinder?" Get real. "So if he can't see the picture, how the hell does he focus it? How can he even know what's going on?"

Okay, here we leave the purely technical, and we have to get spiritual. I think of focus as a Zen exercise. No, wait, come back! It seems strange, but the practice arose in the early days. In fact, for years the operator didn't see the actual picture;

he looked through a finder attached to the side of the camera, a complex device that had to be adjusted for parallax and for the field of view of every lens.

We won't go too far into history, but here's a summary. The earliest cameras had a piece of ground glass inserted in the gate; the cameraperson would focus, take out the glass, load the film in the gate, close the camera, and crank. At some point there were borefinders (like low-power telescopes) set so the cameraperson could see through the lens by looking through the film (which, unlike today, did not have a jet-black antireflective coating). Film changed, you couldn't see through it, and side finders came in. In the 1930s, Arriflex in Germany developed a reflex mirror shutter, so the cameraperson could see through the lens. But the camera was noisy, so you couldn't record sound. And then there was that unpleasantness between Germany and the rest of the world. Quiet reflex cameras came in during the 1950s, first 16 mm and then 35 mm. The first production reflex cameras were built in the late 1960s. So at last a movie could be shot while sound was being recorded with the camera operator able to see the exact image being put on film. And still the assistant is standing by the side of the camera without any viewfinder. In the late 1980s, video cameras using a viewfinder system became practical, and today most assistants have an auxiliary video monitor so they can at last see the picture as it's being filmed.

VIDEO/ELECTRONIC: CCD, CMOS, CRT

How do the things I've said about film and the film camera apply to electronic photography? There are no loops, no magazines, no intermittent mechanisms. Hey, a video or electronic camera is still a black box with a hole in one end and a piece of glass in front of the hole. Inside the box is some material that stores the image. In video/electronic there is no film. Its place is taken by a sensor. These days it's a CCD (charge-coupled device) or a CMOS (complementary metal oxide semiconductor). You can find out a lot about them online. What you need to know is that they operate by allowing light to hit light-sensitive sensors. They convert the light to electrical currents of varying size. The amount of current equates to brightness/darkness, and the specific sensor is sensitive to a specific color (red, green, blue). Very complicated computations take place to make a digital record of the information acquired by the sensor. Then we have the equivalent of the camera's movement.

Again, it's complicated computing. The digital information is downloaded into a file so it knows where it belongs in the succession of individual frames, and it's stored in some device, usually tape or a card or a hard drive (external memory). This storage device is the equivalent of the film magazine that holds the exposed film awaiting processing. Neither digital nor tape requires processing as film does. Some cameras produce a record that needs electronic adjustment just to make the picture look normal,[2] but consumer and prosumer camcorders don't have that need.

[2]These top-of-the-line cameras produce a file that's analogous to a film negative. Work has to be done on it (printing the negative, processing the file) to make it a picture you want to see.

Sometimes the recording device, a tape recorder (VTR) or flash card or whatever, is the most easily damaged part of the camera. It gets a workout. Tape heads have to be cleaned periodically. And since tape is rust on plastic, the oxide surface of the tape will eventually wear down recording heads. One way to preserve your video camera's life is to play back only on a separate player; use the camera only for recording. Cards and hard drives don't suffer from mechanical wear; unless the camera uses a solid-state memory, you have to be careful about dropping the camera (never a good idea) or rough handling. The first problem with cards is their expense, but that's dropping rapidly, and less expensive forms of memory are appearing all the time. Because they're mostly costly, and certainly because they have a limited memory capacity, you have to transfer the data to something (usually an external memory), reformat the cards, and use them again. Now you're in the position of having destroyed your original. Of course, it's digital, so the theory says you've made a perfect duplicate. But because nothing is perfect, if you can, make two downloads of your original footage for safety. Remember that even the original card can be corrupted, so make your downloads as soon as possible after shooting. Digital movies can seem like magic, but, like magic, unexpected weirdness sometimes happens.

VIEWING SYSTEMS

The problem film cameras had for years with viewfinders doesn't exist with electronic cameras. Since the signal exists and can be amplified and sent anywhere, it's easy to have onboard monitors and electronic viewfinders. Be advised that these monitors and viewfinders suffer by comparison to the optical viewfinders found on film cameras. First, there's rarely room around the frame (there always is with optical viewfinders); you can't see if you're going off the set or, suddenly, shooting one of the grips at the side of the set. The electronic viewfinder, like any TV, can make your eyes tired (so can the optical, just not as fast). Almost any optical viewfinder allows the operator to see critical focus; electronic viewfinders never do (they're not big enough and there's not enough information; i.e., too few pixels). They have the advantage of adjustable brightness, so it's easier for the operator to see in low light or if there are a lot of filters stacked in front of the lens.

CONTROLS

Electronic cameras tend to have more controls than film cameras. There's a lot you can do to an electrical signal, and the engineers who design them try to give you every option. If you've ever seen a camcorder manual, you'll remember that it's maybe a half-inch thick, with dozens of menus and the ability to modify almost anything the camera can do. The menus alone tend to drive me crazy, and they'll annoy you, too. I'll get into this more in a future chapter, but just so you know: I try to figure out the best basic settings for any camera I'm using, and I make up a cheat sheet. I note any required or recommended settings for every item on the menu. That way I can get a picture that's not modified to a point beyond recognition, and I try to turn the camera into a point-and-shoot machine. Don't worry; I know you're going to fool around on your own. Good for you. It's important to break the rules, even this rule. Just don't break the equipment. Soon you'll know all you want to about the camera.

WHITE BALANCE

Every video camera has white balance (see Chapter 33). Basically, it's a way of telling the camera that the light source we're using is white (neutral) so the colors of all objects look the way we expect. The simplest way to white balance, outside of using presets (usually daylight and tungsten), is to hold a white card or paper in the light you consider neutral or white. You press the white balance button (it's in a different place on every camera, but the idea is basically the same). The camera will indicate in some way that it's white balanced, and you can shoot now with a natural or realistic look. It's possible to fool the camera, and this gives you creative latitude. If you put a bluish card in front of the camera while white balancing, the camera will register a slightly warm (orange) cast to the picture. This is great for emotional tone, but, again, beware of painting yourself into a corner. What's happening is that the camera sees blue, but it wants white, so it removes the blue, which is the same as adding the complementary color (yellow, but believe me it just looks warm). Of course, you can cool off the picture by the opposite tactic: Shoot a slightly orange card.

LENS

Ever since Daguerre, the lens has been the most important part of the camera to every photographer. Well, duh. It actually makes the image, and its quality will be the most important determinant in the look of your picture.

Technical and Aesthetic Considerations

Lenses are essentially prisms with curvature. The light that enters one surface of a lens slows down from its speed in the air. As a result, its path bends. The thicker the glass, the greater the angle from straight the light ray is bent. (We're getting into optical physics here. This is not a course in optical physics, so we'll make it very simple. You hardly need to know how a lens works to use it. But we're aiming at conscious control of our tools and techniques, so let's explain a few theories and bits of background information.) So if a lens has curvature, some light bends more than others. Smart guys design lenses so the bending of the light rays focuses at a point, and an image appears. Photographic lenses are made up of more than one element (each element is a simple lens itself), with different kinds of curves in very complicated forms and special glues to cement the elements together and with coatings to reduce flares—stray unwanted light that degrades the image.

Movie lenses are further set into carefully designed barrels. They tend to be made large enough to have many marks on them, showing focus points. You can imagine that if a lens has marks only at 12 feet, 25 feet, and infinity (as some lenses I have used have had), you might be hard pressed to focus at precisely 17½ feet (as indeed I was). So the best lenses have very long scales, at their lower (close) ends in inches, and with many foot markings until the depth of field (we'll talk later) renders more gradations superfluous. All lenses are constructed to focus at a specific point: the film plane. Movie lenses are built for a specific model of camera so not all lenses fit all cameras without modification (often a lens mount adapter). Some lens makers take pains to have the front of each lens the same size to facilitate working with them and even the same physical length no matter what the optical focal length is. All movie lenses have gears built into or attached to the focus ring; the gears engage the gears on the focus knob. They are also made with very expensive glass, with very expensive designs. It's no surprise that a good lens for a movie camera will cost $10,000 and up. (Way up.)

The remaining element in a lens is the aperture (the f-stop). It's the opening that controls the amount of light let in. The definition of an f-stop is the ratio of the focal length of the lens to the diameter of the opening. Thus, a 50 mm lens with a possible opening of 50 mm would be an f/1.0. A 25 mm opening in the same lens would be an f/2. You're not going to find too many lenses with a maximum opening of f/1.0, and it's *really* expensive to build them. But it's fairly common to have an aperture of f/1.4; that lets a lot of light in so you can shoot in low light conditions and get a good picture. One nice thing about a ratio: It means that an f/2 on any lens lets in the same amount of light as the f-stop on any other lens, irrespective of focal length. So once you determine the exposure, you don't have to calculate a new setting on the lens when you switch from a 50 mm lens to an 85 mm lens.

We see from the arithmetic in the previous paragraph that the larger the f/number, the smaller the opening. Everybody gets confused at this point. Most filmmakers—already scared out of their wits that they may have to remember fifth-grade arithmetic—think they're artists and freak. Just memorize it. There's no other way unless you want to carry around in your head a lot of physics and a computer. You may also have noticed that I mentioned a stop of f/1.4. Where the hell does that stupid number come from? Be prepared for a meltdown.

T-Stops, Exposure Relationships

Each f-stop in a standard series lets in half as much light as the previous stop. And the ratio of one stop to another is the square root of 2 (1.414). You're catatonic at this point, and you won't remember that this relationship makes it easy to remember (or to calculate) the series of f-stops: 1.0, 1.4, 2.0, 2.8, 4.0, 5.6, 8, 11, 16, 22. That's as far as most movie lenses go. It will be useful knowledge down the line.

At some point you may want to know how precise and sensitive stop settings are. The answer is, not very. As an assistant, I laughed when the "new" digital meters appeared, and the DP would say, "Put on a 2.8. No, wait, make that 2.8 and 1/10." So I'd put my hand up to the lens, do nothing—maybe blow gently at it—and say "2.8 and 1/10 on."

Stop rings are calibrated well and accurately to set the aperture precisely. But the divisions are small enough that it's impossible to be accurate and consistent in setting something as small as $1/10$ of a stop. It's also true that only robots can tell such small exposure differences when looking at the film; human beings are limited to a discrimination of $1/3$ of a stop, $1/4$ of a stop at best.

And it's time to bring up T-stops. You will encounter T-stops on lenses, often on zooms, and sometimes on expensive single-focal-length (prime) lenses. "T" stands for transmission. Since even the best-made, most expensively designed glass absorbs a little light, the amount getting through is slightly less than the amount calculated by the f-stop (a purely mathematical relationship, as we all recall). So for movies, which demand precise exposure (it's expensive or impossible to correct exposure errors in the lab, unlike the still darkroom), we want to know exactly how much light is getting to the film. Lens technicians calculate the precise amount of light exiting the lens, and calibrate the stop ring to reflect that. So at T/2, the lens is transmitting as much light as it is calculated to transmit at f/2. Oh, the weeping and wailing and gnashing of teeth. Oh, the humanity.

All good lenses are calibrated in T-stops, and most are so good that they're the same as f-stops—except on zooms. We'll keep that secret for later.

ISO, Amount of Light (D/X versus Int)

The most important classification for film is its speed: how sensitively it responds to exposure to light. Fast film is very sensitive to light; slow film is relatively insensitive. Why bother with slow film when we're trying to get pictures as easily as possible? There is a tradeoff involved. The faster the film, the grainier it is. Grain is in fact the image of the silver grains that make up the image. We'll talk more about that later. (By the way, the fact of grains means that film is actually a digital medium. The grains are either black or white, and therefore are sort of equivalent to 0s and 1s of digital language. I'm playing a little game here; the use of digital language involves a totally different language or philosophy of communicating information, and silver grains are possibly not just black or white but fade to grayish at their border. I just like to keep citizens from believing all the press releases—masquerading as fact—that mislead them about the wonders of digital.)

For our purposes right now, we want to know that slow films need more light and fast films need less. You need to know there are ISO numbers and what they mean. And you should memorize some information about the simple formula for the relationship among ISO numbers and stops. ISO classifications begin at, say, 10 (you can have lower speeds, but we're never going to confront them in cinematography). A sequence would be 10, 12, 16, 20, 25, 32, and so on. The sharper reader will have noticed that every third ISO number is approximately doubled. We can assume, and we are right, that this means that a film rated at 25 ISO is twice as fast as a film rated at 12 ISO. You may also remember that each stop lets in half as much light as the previous one. Therefore, exposure of f/2 with a film speed of ISO 12 is the same as an exposure of f/2.8 with a film speed of ISO 25.

Take a breath here. We're only talking about relationships of arbitrary scales (although they all do mean something precise for exposure), but you will have decided I'm selling you calculus, and you say it's spinach, and you say the hell with it. It amazes me that almost everyone fears and hates what they call "math," even when it's just simple, useful arithmetic.

But if you really want to become a good cinematographer, you're going to have to get over your phobias. So go slowly with this arithmetic, go over it again and again, and in fact repeat it until you become conversant with the concepts. I'm trying to get across concepts—some hardware, yes, and some specific routines— but mostly concepts to help you develop as a cinematographic artist.

Here are the useful concepts to remember:

1. ISO numbers denote film speed, and each doubling of an ISO number signifies a film that is twice as fast.
2. The ISO numbers run by ⅓ stops (ISO 250 is ⅓ of a stop faster than ISO 200).
3. The stops denote the amount of light entering the lens; the divisions of full stops signify twice or half as much light, so f/2.8 lets in half as much light as f/2.0.
4. Therefore (and I know you don't like syllogistic logic either), using a film stock of 100 ISO for which the exposure in a given situation is f/2.8 tells you that if you used an ISO 200 film in the same situation, you would have the same exposure at f/4.

All of these relationships are important for practical work. Every day cinematographers encounter situations that make them consider film speed and stop setting. For example, I've got tungsten-balanced film of ISO 200. I'm shooting in daylight, so I put on an 85 filter to balance the color (Kodak tells me so). I know an 85 cuts down ⅔ of a stop of light (the filter maker tells me this, or I measure how much light it cuts out with my exposure meter). So I can deduct ⅔ of a stop from every exposure meter reading to get the correct exposure, or I can reset my meter from ISO 200 to ISO 125, thus compensating for the stop loss due to the filter and allowing me to use direct readings from the meter. I read the exposure—it's noon on a sunny day in the desert in summer—and the meter indicates the proper exposure is f/32. But my lens stops down only to f/22 (it's a movie lens). And I don't want to go to f/22 anyway for aesthetic reasons (too much sharpness). I want to shoot at f/11, which is three stops down from f/32. So I put on a neutral density filter labeled .90. (By now I know that this filter cuts down three stops of light; you will learn this later, but I need it now for my example.) And now I adjust my meter's ISO setting to account for those three stops. One stop down from ISO 125 is ISO 64 (just cut it in half), two stops is ISO 32, and three stops is ISO 16. I set my meter to ISO 16, and now whatever I read off the meter is the correct exposure for that day, that film, and that stack of filters.

And this is a simple everyday occurrence. I haven't ventured into the dark forest of speed rate changes, polarizing filters, or other frequent situations. A cinematographer needs to know these facts and relationships reflexively, almost intuitively. The necessity for such adjustments arises every day on every show. He or she must be able to work quickly and accurately, must be able to synthesize the information usefully, and must be able to give the assistants accurate exposure information in a way that doesn't confuse them and leads to expensive mistakes.

Focus

While we're dealing with lenses, we have to introduce the concept of focus. I've talked about the Zen master concept. I may be going too far right now, but I've got to let you know about depth of field and how it's a major creative tool for you. We'll deal with the details later. Right now you need to know the theory of focus. The lens focuses the image at only one point: precisely where it's focused. Thank goodness, there's a characteristic called depth of field that saves us from having the actor's eyes in focus and her nose soft.

Depth of field is a phenomenon dependent on lens characteristics (focal length, stop, distance of the subject, and format) and exhibition characteristics. Depth of field can be thought of as the effect of apparent sharp focus for objects in front of and behind the actual point of focus. The lens issues we'll go into later; just remember the rule of thumb for these parameters: the shorter the lens and/or the deeper the stop and/or the further the subject and/or the smaller the format, the deeper the depth of field. Each element controls depth of field, and all the elements interact. Apparent focus—depth of field—divides itself so that $1/3$ of it falls in front of the focus point (closer to camera) and $2/3$ falls behind it.

Since depth of field refers to apparent focus, the way we see the picture determines largely how much depth of field there is. We've all seen small photographs that look in focus, but when they're blown up seem to be less sharp. Exhibition is like this. A movie on a TV screen (maybe 5 feet wide) or your iPhone (inches) looks overall more in focus than the same movie on IMax (up to 147 feet wide). The distance of the viewer from the screen also affects the apparent sharpness, so both factors come into play. We do tend to be more scrupulous about focus for movies than for TV, but with the advent of high-definition TV, this will probably change, and every job will demand "perfect" focus.

CHAPTER 29
Lenses

Let's start with prisms. We all know that Isaac Newton took a prism and used it to separate white light into bands of light of different colors (what we call a spectrum). And so had thousands of time-wasting fellows in the centuries since someone first picked up a piece of burned sand out of the campfire. But old Isaac did something unusual. He took a second prism and recombined the rainbow back into white light. And then he did something unprecedented: Instead of saying, "Oh, how pretty!," he contemplated, he observed, and he wrote about it.

So we owe lots of what we know about light to Newton. We know that light is composed of different wavelengths that can be spread and compressed. This characteristic allows us to make lenses (I've skipped a few steps here). We can bend light by directing it through glass. Light travels more slowly through glass than through air. So by directing light reflected off objects through a piece of glass whose thickness varies over its surface (curved), we can manipulate these rays to produce an image of an object onto a plane (another piece of glass, film, a digital target), albeit a fuzzy one.

Now, if the glass is ground so that only one side is curved and that curvature is precisely calculated, the glass will angle the light rays in a smoothly graduated pattern so some of the light rays will converge at the same point. And if we put together a couple of these ground pieces of glass—"elements"—we will be able to precisely control how the light bends in all kinds of ways.

Eventually, we've got something that consistently bends light rays from the same object to a common point on a plane. Voilà, focus! And if we put some film or a digital chip at that common point inside a box, we now have a device that can record a sharply focused image—a device otherwise known as a camera. Eureka!

It took a lot of people (some named Zeiss, Cooke, Leitz, and Angenieux) working hard over a long period of time to produce lenses that can give us an image that appears as a perfect two-dimensional representation of reality. One advance was figuring out that combining elements, arranged in a certain way, would enable the maker of the lens to correct certain deficiencies.

FIGURE 29.1
Simple lenses.

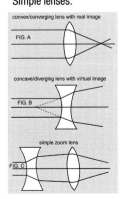

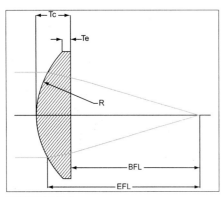

FIGURE 29.2
Plano-convex converging lens.

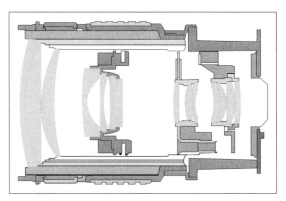

FIGURE 29.3
Lens with multiple elements.

Many unfortunate defects occur in simple lenses with few elements. One problem is that some lens shapes (say, a portion of a sphere) produce an image that is blurry at the edges. Another problem is that since glass spreads the colors of light, there can be fringes of color at points in the image; this reads as a softening of the edges in black-and-white and rainbow edges in color. If you're not annoyed enough by now, try this: The surfaces of the elements may reflect a small portion of the light. And keep reflecting and reflecting it in gradually diminishing quantities. Now we have a halo around bright points like headlights or bare lamps or a diffuse grayness where the subject should be dead black.

Rather than throw up their hands in disgust and go have a drink, optical engineers and lens designers kept working to eliminate these imperfections. So we have aspheric elements (ground so the cross section is curved subtly irregularly) to make sure all the rays converge at a common point. We have achromatic lenses to ensure all colors of a given light ray meet at a common point. And we have molecularly thin deposits of materials whose reflectivity is approximately ½ the wavelength of light so that the bouncing reflected light from the glass surfaces is canceled out, the image is crisp, and blacks are black.

You don't have to know about the characteristics of lenses to take a picture. Just buy a good (expensive) lens and use it. But knowledge is power, and the more you understand the technology you're working with, the more expressive and creative you can be in your work.

Lenses are precise, technically sophisticated instruments. Each top lens brand has its own special qualities and idiosyncrasies. I think, for example, that Zeiss lenses tend to be blazing sharp and a little cold. Calling them "cold" is a personal metaphor to try to express the feeling I get from them. Usually when we talk about "cold" in photography, we're talking about a bluish look to a picture. I don't mean that; the Zeiss lenses have no color bias to them.

Other makers give lenses different characteristics. The original Panavision lenses are all sharp and clean, with a soft fall-off in depth of field. That is, where the image stops being in focus, it's gradual with Panavision lenses as compared to a more sharply marked fall-off with Zeiss. That same gradual quality holds with Panavision's Primo lenses, arguably the sharpest lenses yet made and with the least amount of internal reflections.

There are other lens lines you may run into. Cooke, for years a major lens manufacturer but somewhat dormant through the 1970s, 1980s, and 1990s, has now come back in a big way. The major innovation is Cooke's new series of lenses that connect electrically with the camera and display lens information (stop, focus) on a monitor. With the right supporting equipment, you can retain that information as "metadata," data that provide information about other data. (In this case, it's the information about the f-stop and focus that's the data about the lens. You're probably familiar with this from working with digital photography; now it's available for film, too.)

Leica, renowned for its still-camera lenses, announced in 2010 that for the first time in the long history of the company, it would come out with a series of lenses for movie cameras. We'll have to wait to see how they work; they're barely in the rental houses.

Lens designers consistently improve the performance of lenses. We can look at movies made years ago, and we can see that some of their look—often what we see as their beauty—can come from "imperfections" in the old lenses. So if you're shooting a film and you want to have the look of an older movie (as Gordon Willis did for *Zelig*), it might pay to hunt up old lenses or modify modern lenses to mimic the qualities of the old ones. Stripping off the antireflection coating will give you the softness of the past. You can also use filters to soften the image, to diminish an actor's wrinkles, or to give the image a look that suggests memory. Here we are restoring the imperfections so painstakingly designed out of a lens, or as a friend of mine says, "Taking a $10,000 lens and putting $2 worth of cheap glass in front of it."

In talking about lenses you will encounter lots of specialized terminology used to describe all their varying characteristics. Let's start with how much a lens sees. You're probably vaguely familiar with the terms *wide angle* and *telephoto*. And for terms commonly used by folks who know nothing about optics, they're pretty useful. A wide-angle lens does indeed show a wide angle of view. And a telephoto lens does have something in common with a telescope. But as a professional you'll be referring to lenses by their focal lengths, a more precise way of talking about a particular lens's field of view.

So what is *focal length*? The focal length is the distance from the optical center of the lens (usually somewhere along the lens body) to the imaging point (the film plane or the chip). This distance determines the degree of magnification of a lens and gives the lens its unique "personality" (the interplay of field of view, depth of field, sharpness, and the presence or lack of internal reflections).

Lenses of a given focal length all have the same optical characteristics—let's confine ourselves to perspective relationships—no matter the make of the lens. But be aware, you'll get a different field of view using a 50 mm lens on a 35 mm film camera or top-of-the-line digital camera compared with using the same lens on a digital camera with a ⅔-inch sensor. With both cameras set up at the same distance from the subject, you'll see less in the frame—be "closer" to it—with the ⅔-inch sensor than you'll be with the 35 mm film.

Now you are probably saying, "This is crazy! You just said a lens is a lens—a 50 mm is a 50 mm, no matter what. And it shows the same perspective relationships. Were you lying to us, Jack?" Okay, cool your jets. Nothing is as simple as we would like it to be. Here's the situation: The *imaging* characteristics of the lenses are the same, but—and yes it's a big but—the sizes of the actual images recorded by different cameras are not the same. With a 35 mm frame you have a target area that is 0.866 inch by 0.630 inch (22 mm by 16 mm), but with ⅔-inch digital the target area is .346 inch by .230 inch (8.8 mm by 6.6 mm). Usually, the less expensive the camera, the smaller the target. But even some top-end cameras (Viper) have small targets compared to 35 mm film.

Now back to lenses. Lenses form images in a circle, called the image circle. No matter what else varies, a lens of a certain focal length makes a picture that looks like all the other pictures of lenses of that focal length. The lens can be designed—for economy—to make an image circle whose diameter is the same length as the diagonal of the frame. In fact, it has to be at least that big to cover the frame.

Let's say we have a 100 mm lens built to cover the VistaVision frame, which is the same size as a 35 mm still camera frame. It'll look like Figure 29.4. Of course, we could put the same lens on a standard 35 mm movie camera; the frame it would take is like the one in Figure 29.6. And the VistaVision frame takes as much of the image as shown in Figure 29.5.

And you'll notice right away that you see less of the picture formed by the lens. It looks as though we've zoomed in. And if the two pictures are projected on the same

FIGURE 29.4
An image circle covering a circle of diameter of about 1.785 inches or 45.33 mm.

FIGURE 29.5
VistaVision frame.

FIGURE 29.6
35 mm academy frame.

size screen, the one shot with a 35 mm camera would look like an enlarged part of the center of the VistaVision picture. And other formats are smaller, so the frame they cut from the picture formed by the lens seems to be comparably enlarged.

When we get to the smallest frame size, the picture, taken with the same focal length lens, has turned from a moderately wide shot to a "telephoto" shot. But what do we do if we want to see as much on the prosumer frame as we did on the VistaVision frame? We have to put on a wider lens—that is, one that covers a larger area. And since the frame is much smaller, the lens must be much wider. The picture in the frame is the size we want, but the characteristics of a wide lens—the exaggeration of perspective and the relatively long depth of field—are

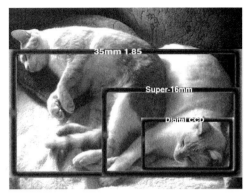

FIGURE 29.7
35mm, Super-16mm, and 1/3-inch (prosumer digital camera) frames.

pictorial artifacts. We may not want them, and in fact many cinematographers must go to great lengths to avoid the great depth of field. (Lessening depth of field makes the picture look and feel more like a conventional movie shot on 35 mm.) There's nothing they can do about the perspective relationships. It's a tradeoff for saving money. Figure 29.8 is a wonderful chart from Panavision that shows the relative sizes of fields for different formats.

Now if we superimpose these frames over a picture, we begin to see what the effect of the different cameras, specifically the target size (frame size), is on the shot (Figure 29.9). It becomes obvious that the size of the frame (in film; target in digital) radically affects the amount of the picture shown. And although we

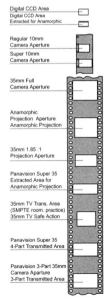

FIGURE 29.8
Panavision frame chart.

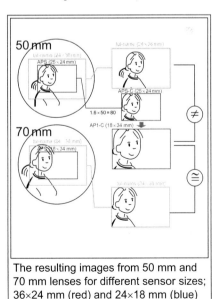

The resulting images from 50 mm and 70 mm lenses for different sensor sizes; 36×24 mm (red) and 24×18 mm (blue)

FIGURE 29.9
Target size versus focal length.

are showing a picture shot with a 50 mm lens, it will look different depending on which camera the lens is used.

You may have noticed (and if you haven't, you will) that a lens designed for one camera won't work on a camera with a different frame size. That's primarily because of the way the lens makes an image. (It is also often because the camera manufacturers demand different mounts for their cameras. But this is a trivial distinction.) The lens forms its image as a circle at a certain place (the film plane), and the lens designer can make this circle any size. In order to be economical, a specific lens will be designed to cover only the area of a specific frame. The standard is that the diameter of the image circle is the diagonal of the frame. That way the picture cut out of the circle by the frame is covered fully by the image.

The upshot of these lens characteristics is that you must know what camera you're using, you must have a lens built for that camera, and you must have a feel for the look of the picture a lens of a specific focal length gives you. You'll only get this feel by shooting a lot. And you'll probably shoot mostly with one kind of format. For me it was 35 mm movie format. So I'm used to the lenses used for 35 mm (and note I said "movies"—stills are different), and I've had to do a conversion in my head to know the look given by a specific focal length lens in a different format. Thank goodness there are tables everywhere (I would try the Internet), and there are rules of thumb. If you know 35 mm, for 16 mm a lens half the focal length will show about the same area of the scene. It's almost the same for $^2/_3$-inch digital—say, about 40%. And so on for other formats.

Now back to that question of "wide angle" and "telephoto." For 35 mm movies, wide angles generally are lenses of less than 30 mm focal length; "normal" lenses are 32 mm to 60 mm; and long lenses are 75 and up. You'll notice I brought in a new term—*normal*—and I said long instead of telephoto. Sorry. Normal lenses refer to the perspective relationship of the average person's visual field. It does *not* refer to the width of the area a person can see in his visual field—that's immense, about 180 degrees. And we rarely call a long lens telephoto because, strictly speaking, "telephoto" signifies a specific lens design and because "long" just means a lens that is usually physically longer and shows a significantly smaller area than normal lenses. As you use them, you will get used to how much a lens sees at 5 feet, 10 feet, 20 feet, and so on.

So a lens determines the field of vision that will be seen. And it also controls the amount of light that will be allowed to be transmitted to the target by controlling the size of the opening or "aperture." It does this with an iris diaphragm: that odd-looking thing with leaves that fold in and out, that you see when you look through a lens and turn the stop ring. The stop ring has numbers engraved on it, f-stop numbers. The iris itself opens and closes continuously, so theoretically you can set the opening anywhere you like. The stop ring, with its calibrations, allows you to determine the aperture setting with precision. The numbers are always the same: 1, 1.4, 2, 2.8, 4, 5.6, 8, 11, 16, and 22. Rarely does a movie lens stop down further than f/22, and essentially none opens wider than f/1. Each number in the series indicates an opening that lets in twice as much or half as much light as the next setting.

Now you may be looking at these strange numbers and wondering what kind of measurement of an opening they represent. You may have noticed a pattern where each stop is numerically half or close to half of every alternating number (1.4, 2.8, 5.6, 11, 22; 2, 4, 8, 16). That's because f-stops are defined as the focal length of the lens divided by the diameter of the aperture opening. Since the area of the aperture in relation to the diameter is calculated by the equation $A = \Pi(d/2)^2$, each time you double the diameter, you increase the size of the aperture by four. The relationship between one f-stop and the next is the square root of 2 (1.4…). That is, by multiplying or dividing a given f-stop by 1.4, you get the next stop, which admits twice as much or half as much light. (Take f/2. f/2 times 1.4 equals f/2.8, the next stop in the series, which lets in half as much light as f/2. Divided by 1.4, f/2 equals f/1.4, which lets in twice as much light as f/2.)

You will have noticed at some point that smaller numbers (f/2) mean larger openings and larger numbers (f/16) mean smaller openings. On behalf of all the photographic scientists who have ever lived, I apologize for the fact that this seems the reverse of what it should be. You see how this works: Since the focal length of the lens (the numerator in our fraction, the top number) stays the same for the lens we are using but the diameter of the opening—the denominator, the bottom number—can change (but is almost never larger than the focal length), as the size of the opening gets smaller, the value of the fraction, the f-stop, gets larger. Therefore, smaller opening = larger f-stop number, and larger opening = smaller f-stop number.

Here's an example: Take a 50 mm lens. If the diameter of the opening of the aperture is 25 mm (fairly large opening), then the equation

$$\text{f-stop} = \text{focal length/diameter of opening}$$

works out to

$$\text{f-stop} = 50\,\text{mm} / 25\,\text{mm} = \text{f/2}$$

and likewise if the diameter of the opening of the aperture is 3.12 mm (fairly small opening), then the equation

$$\text{f-stop} = \text{focal length/diameter of opening}$$

works out to

$$\text{f-stop} = 50\,\text{mm} / 3.12\,\text{mm} = \text{f/16}$$

And the only way to deal with this insult to common sense is to memorize it. Just remember: Small number, big opening, allows lots of light in; big number, small opening, cuts out light. So shooting in low light you will want to open up the lens (larger aperture, smaller f-stop number), and shooting in bright light you will want to close down the lens (smaller aperture, larger f-stop number).

Why in the world should you care about f-stops? Well, you're going to be dealing with them a lot. In fact, you could say that the DP's most important job is to tell the assistant what f-stop to put on the camera. The f-stop determines how much light is being allowed to reach the film or chip. You must choose the perfect f-stop to expose your picture so it carries the photographic range without being over- or underexposed and so you convey the mood or look you intend. To determine this, you will use an exposure meter (what almost everyone calls a light meter—me too—though it's properly an exposure meter because it meters the light and then computes the exposure setting, the f-stop). The more you understand about how f-stops work, the more control you have over exposure.

The divisions on the stop ring are in full stops, which you will recall denotes the doubling or halving of the light. Sometimes a difference of a full stop is too great an increment to accurately provide the precise setting you want. So you'll often be using $\frac{1}{3}$ stops as increments of change of exposure. This allows you to appreciate another neat relationship: ISO numbers (formerly ASA, so if you see film speed listed as ASA anywhere, you know it's the same as ISO) are the designation for film speed. The numbers begin at 10 and go up as high as you want. There's a regular progression: 10, 12, 16, 20, 25, 32, 40, 50, 64....

You can see that, just as with stops, there's an arithmetical relationship between the ISO numbers. Each is double the one that is two steps before it. By now we expect this means something, and by George it does. Each doubling of the ISO number indicates that the film so designated is twice as fast. So this means it needs half as much light to be exposed. And this strikes a chord: Each stop lets in half as much light as the stop before. So at the same shutter speed, a proper exposure of f/2.8 with an ISO 100 film would be equivalent to an f/4 with an ISO 200 film. Digital cameras are usually spoken of as having ISO equivalents, so you have a basis for exposing them accurately. But right now there is no official group setting a common standard for exposing digitally. These relationships are not arbitrary. Given these relationships and one meter reading, you can figure out the exposure for any speed film.

You may wonder about the ISO relationships. Since each is twice as fast as the one three steps before, and each full stop cuts in half the amount of light let in, we can see that each ISO represents a difference of $\frac{1}{3}$ stop. As it happens, and I don't think this is a coincidence, the finest gradation a human eye can tell in terms of exposure is $\frac{1}{3}$ stop. That means the way we designate sensitivity of films is just like the sensitivity of the eye.

And that tells us why you'll be working in $\frac{1}{3}$ stops. Warning: Almost everyone uses a digital meter these days. Digital meters are set up to read in full stops and $\frac{1}{10}$ of stops. I have worked with DPs who would call a stop as "2.8" and then say, "No make that 2.8 and two-tenths." I try not to laugh. There's no way anyone can tell the difference between those two exposure settings even if it were possible to find those gradations on the stop ring. So just call stops by thirds, and you'll be accurate enough and your wise-ass crew won't laugh at you.

Another thing a lens does is focus the image. This is kind of important. I have noticed that an audience will forgive almost anything—too dim a picture, a break in the film, a suddenly silent soundtrack—but if there's anything out of focus, the booing starts immediately. So pay attention because without focus the rest of your hard work is wasted. And, lucky you, the job and responsibility of focus are in the hands of your first assistant. It's a tough job that has to be executed perfectly every time a shot is made (see Chapter 30 for an in-depth discussion on how to focus).

About focus: In simplistic terms, inside your lens, one or more of the glass elements can move relative to all the other elements. This capability allows the reflected light from a specific object to be made to fall precisely at the film plane, rendering an image that's in sharp focus. To accomplish this you must have a mechanism that uses precise markings to allow you to know that you have moved the elements to the proper position.

On the barrel of your lens, in addition to the already familiar stop ring, you will find the focus ring. The focus ring allows you to accurately set the distance from the focal plane to your object of interest. There are numbers on the focus ring next to tiny hash marks that indicate when the lens is focused at a precise distance. You rotate the ring until your desired distance marking lines up with the "witness mark," a small stationary mark on the barrel, giving you perfect focus.

Now I'll bet you're thinking that all this sounds straightforward and simple. Remember, though, when the camera or the object/person moves during the shot, the distance setting has to be changed continuously as the action occurs. This is known as "follow focus." One heads-up is to realize that the measurements on the focus ring might be indicated in feet and inches, or they might be in meters and centimeters (or sometimes—groan—both). In any case, make sure you and your assistant know what units you're working with. Choose lenses that are calibrated in units you feel comfortable with. I know too many focus-pullers who thought they were working in feet and inches only to find out the lens was marked in meters and centimeters. Even NASA has made that mistake, but don't think anyone will be the least bit sympathetic if you screw up. The assistant will be fired immediately and the DP will look bad for having hired him or her.

The skill required to achieve consistently perfect focus is a complicated subject in and of itself. (Once again, refer to Chapter 30.) Earlier in this book I asked you to do some exercises on framing to see how shots look when you use lenses of different focal lengths. Think back to those exercises. Besides the sense of expansion of space you get with a wide lens and compression of space you get with a long lens, the focal length you choose affects the perceived sense of speed of camera movement and movement of actors on the screen.

With a wide lens the sense of speed is greatest when movement is along the axis of the lens—that is, when the camera is moving forward or backward or the actor is moving toward or away from the camera. With a long lens the sense of speed is greatest when the subject or the camera is moving sideways. Why do you think that is?

Okay, I realize you paid good money for this book, so I'll just tell you. A wide lens emphasizes depth by accentuating the size of objects close to the lens and by diminishing the size of objects in the distance. Therefore, movement to or from the lens means the subject enlarges or shrinks very quickly. This change of size in a short amount of time, over what seems to be a considerable distance, suggests speed. A long lens, in comparison, because of its compressive effect, doesn't show much change in size as the subject moves toward or away from the camera. So even though an actor may be running very fast directly at the camera, it seems as though there's hardly any movement at all, just bouncing up and down in place.

With horizontal movement, fast panning with a long lens causes the background to blur, creating an intensified sense of speed. A long lens shows a very small arc—just a sliver of the entire field of view. You must move it quickly to keep the subject in the frame. As a consequence, everything behind the actor appears to be whizzing past. The closer the shot (and the longer the lens), the faster the actor will appear to be moving. You remember how this works from the exercise in which you panned with an actor from one point to another and then panned at the same speed without the actor. I wanted you to see how even a moderately fast pan could cause strobing. You will always see strobing unless there's a foreground figure that mostly stays in the same position in the frame. In fact, this strobing of the background is part of what suggests extreme speed to the viewer.

Director Mike Nichols and DP Bob Surtees put these phenomena to brilliant use in the film *The Graduate*. When Ben (played by Dustin Hoffman) is trying to get to the church to stop Elaine from getting married, his car runs out of gas. He gets out of the car and starts running. Nichols has Surtees shoot Ben straight on with a very long lens so that as he's running toward us, he doesn't seem to be getting any closer. As Ben rounds the corner to the church, Surtees zooms out very wide. Now on a wide lens, if Ben were still running toward us, he would seem to pick up speed. But instead, since he turns and runs across the frame and we see a great deal of the landscape around him, the visual distance Ben has to cover is exaggerated, and it seems like he will never make it in time.

In a single shot, Nichols used the optical characteristics of lenses as a powerful storytelling device. Hoffman's acting is great. He brilliantly conveys the anxiety and determination of a man who's been racing against time since the night before. But at this point the audience might have begun to lose the sense of urgency. The unexpected but perfectly inspired use of the different qualities of long and wide lenses has us biting our nails right up to the climactic finale.

Understanding optics helps make sense out of the relationship between f-stops and *depth of field*. Depth of field refers to what range of objects will appear to be in focus even though they are in front of or behind the specific object/person on which you are focusing. Lenses show a greater area in focus than what is precisely at the point they're set to. It is a perceptual question, not a precise measurement.

To calculate depth of field, we use "circles of confusion." No, I'm not referring to all the people standing around the camera. I'm talking about the appearance of objects at distances further from or closer to the camera than the object you're focused on. Now a lens is in focus at only one position (the exact measurement to the object of interest—let's say 5 feet); a point 5 feet away shows up on the image plane as a sharp dot. At that setting a point at some other distance (say, 5 feet 6 inches) appears on the image plane as a fuzzy circle. This fuzzy circle is the circle of confusion. This fuzzy circle may be very small. If it is small enough, it will appear to the viewer to be a sharp point.

Now here's the tricky stuff: If you get close to the image, the circle looks fuzzy, but if you're far enough away, the circle looks sharp, like a point. What determines the acceptable fuzziness of the point is the size of the original format (35 mm, 16 mm, ²/₃-inch chip, etc.), the degree of magnification of the original (how big the screen is), and the distance of the observer from the projected image. Since all of these are variable, calculations need to be made so you ensure that you are working within the size circle of confusion that is acceptable for a given format and a given size of projection. Thus, for TV, the acceptable circle of confusion can be bigger than the acceptable circle of confusion for exhibition in a movie theater (a 4- or 5-foot-wide screen versus a 30- to 50-foot-wide screen).

Remember that everything that is not at the precise point of focus always creates a circle of confusion. The circles of confusion get bigger as we move away from the precise point of focus. (Either forward or back; that is, given the focus at five feet, from five and a half to six the circle of confusion gets bigger and from four and a half to four the circle of confusion gets bigger.)

Getting back to depth of field, you may sometimes hear it referred to as *depth of focus*, but *it is not depth of focus*. Depth of focus is another thing entirely. For now just understand that depth of focus refers to the infinitesimally small, but real, tolerance in the distance from the lens to the chip or film. Usually we act as though there is no tolerance, so we (or our friends the camera technicians) set the "flange focus distance" at a precise place. Flange = lens mount flange. For digital cameras, it's called "back focus," and it generally has to be adjusted very often, on the set. Things cause it to shift—mostly temperature, since digital cameras heat up. So you get to adjust the position of the lens with a dial on the front while you check focus on a focusing chart.

Because the f-stop increases or decreases the size of the aperture opening, the setting of the f-stop determines which part and how much of the surface area of the lens light rays will be allowed to pass through. A "shallow" f-stop (small number, large opening) admits light through a larger area of the glass of the lens than does a "deep" f-stop (large number, small opening). The smaller opening admits light only through the very center of the glass. (*Shallow* and *deep* are terms that also describe the depth of field, but that's not how I am using them here.) Interestingly, the center of the lens is the easiest to make and is the most free of distortions. Theoretically, then, a deep f-stop, small opening, will give us the sharpest, least distorted image. In practical terms, you will get a better, sharper image shooting at the higher f-stops. That is why, in the old days, no DPs wanted to shoot at a lens's maximum (widest) aperture; the image would be soft and distorted, and would not match shots made at a deeper (smaller opening, bigger number) stop.

That's with old lenses. Lens design today has pretty much eliminated the problem of lower quality at the outer edges of the lens. You can shoot wide open—f/1.4, even f/1.1—with confidence that the image quality will be as good as that at f/5.6 and that it will have very similar characteristics. There are exceptions, and that's a very advanced topic. It requires a trained eye, and it takes a few years to notice any differences. So you don't have to worry about any adverse effect on the perception of your average audience member, but perfectionist cinematographers know that there can be intangible differences in quality that may have a subtle impact on the emotions evoked by a shot.

Interestingly, or frustratingly, closing down the aperture a great deal can also have negative optical effects. The smaller the size of the aperture, the more diffraction defects become magnified. You can think of diffraction as the tendency of light rays to bend or scatter somewhat erratically as they hit the edges of the iris blades. (Note: Physicists, please don't get mad at me. I'm trying to get across some principles of optics but only so far as they have an immediate effect on photography. I know I'm not precise or complete. If I'm totally inaccurate, please let me know.)

Okay, the light hitting the blade edges bends and scatters. And just as with an imperfect piece of glass, the image will be soft, and the scattering of the light will reduce the saturation of colors and make the blacks look gray. Generally, we don't want that. So most DPs avoid closing down too much. Depending on the lens, this means never stopping down below f/8 or f/11. Again, with modern lenses, the effect is lessened, but it may still exist for a given lens, so you have to know your lens—test, test, test, and observe—in order to make the best decisions in choosing your f-stop.

You can see that any lens imperfection has the potential to lessen the depth of field by making the picture soft, blurry, or gray. You need to understand that although f/22 may offer infinite depth of field, the picture may be less pleasing than if you shot at f/11 with a slightly shallower depth of field. Remember that any filter placed in front of a lens will scatter light a little, causing some degradation of your image. Depth of field will appear to be greater with a "clean" lens (one that has no glass over it) than when you're using filtering.

Depth of field is incredibly important in any number of filming situations. One is when the camera assistant has to keep a moving actor or object in focus. Remember: No one "follows" focus. When focusing, you must be right with the actor, not following, so that the two of you are doing a kind of psychic dance. Anyway, it's not always possible to be perfect, no matter how skilled you are. So after the director calls "Cut!," you will often see the assistant run out with a tape measure, checking the exact distance between the camera and the subject. Then you'll see him or her frantically playing with a little disk called a "Kelly wheel" (or punching numbers into an iPhone app). After a minute with the wheel, the assistant will either look relieved or will call for another take.

What the assistant is doing is checking to see if depth of field will carry the apparent focus well enough that his imprecision in focus won't matter. We all have to learn what's "good enough" in many situations. This is a moment when it's important for the assistant to know if his work is acceptable; if it is, great, we move on; time, money, and creativity are saved. But if not, it's imperative to do the shot again, because—as you know—bad focus is unforgiveable.

The Kelly wheel is named for one of the men who invented it: Graham White "Skeets" Kelly, along with his buddy William Branch "Bill" Pollard. (It goes without saying that these guys were British.) It's basically a circular slide rule (a slide rule is a device engineers used to use to make calculations before the advent of electronic calculators). The Kelly wheel allows you to figure out depth of field for any lens at any focus and any stop very quickly. You may have seen, online or in reference works such as *The American Cinematographer Film Manual*, charts of depth of field for every focal length lens in existence. These are accurate and good to have, but they're cumbersome when you're on the set under the pressure of time. The Kelly wheel is fast and compact. These days, many, if not most, assistants use PDAs or smart phones loaded with one of the many programs available online, including some very good ones for figuring depth of field. As a DP, I don't care what device the assistant uses, just as long as it's fast and accurate.

Now even when you know you've got a lot of depth of field—you're on a 12 mm at f/11 and you're in focus from here to Brazil—it's still a good idea to "play it like it's a 250," meaning "Don't get sloppy." That's advice I got early on from an experienced assistant. Since the 10 to 1 (25 mm to 250 mm Angenieux) was the main long lens we used, and 250 was its long end, the advice meant "Always set focus as though you have no room for error." It's still good advice because you always want to keep your focus skills in top form so you'll be at the top of your game when it's really crucial. So when an actor decides to miss her mark, you'll be either ready to make the correction or you'll be saved by your depth of field.

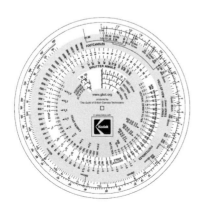

FIGURE 29.10
Guild Kelly wheel.
Reproduced by permission of The Guild of British Camera Technicians.

Depth of field can come into play in another way. Back when I was a camera assistant on the movie *Down By Law* (shot by Robby Müller and directed by Jim Jarmusch), I knew, because of Jim's style, that he would be doing long takes with multiple characters, each character equally important to the drama. And I also knew that because of Robby's style—and our locations, including a real jail and real swamps—I would not have a deep stop. Robby liked to shoot at f/1.4 or f/1.6. However, in this case I got lucky: He gave me an f/2.2 and sometimes even an f/2.5. Now, even with a 25 mm lens (90% of the movie was shot on a 25 mm), there's not a lot of depth of field when you're in confined spaces, as most of our interiors were. I didn't want the audience to be aware of shifts in focus from one character to another (that's almost as bad as leaving the focus on one actor and letting the other actors go soft), so I figured the thing to do would be to keep everybody in focus all the time. If you've gotten this far, you know that's optically impossible. It almost breaks a law of physics, and although I know how to manipulate the image with some arcane techniques, they would have been time consuming and expensive.[1]

I thought back to a job I did when I was a brand-new first assistant. It was a pilot for a TV series, and the director was coming off a big success with a miniseries, and he was feeling his oats. He called me in for an interview. (What a thrill! I hardly ever even had a director *talk* to me, never mind summon me for an audience.) I approached with trepidation. He said welcome to the show, and he only wanted one thing: "Keep everything in focus." Well, I sort of chuckled, and I said that was my job. "I don't think you're hearing me right. I want everything in the frame in focus all the time."

This time I didn't laugh, and I thought furiously how to explain physics to him. I started talking about different focal lengths of lenses and different f-stops and how the DP would decide how much stop to give me, and—in the midst of this very nice talk of mine, he said, "Everything. In the frame. In focus. All the time. See you tomorrow."

---

[1]Here are a couple of techniques:

You can shift the plane of focus of the lens so it's focusing on a slant. With the right setting, you could hold two people in focus who are not in focus with normal lenses. This is a nineteenth-century technique, developed for view cameras (the big things in old movies that the photographer disappears with under a block cloth). Movie cameras don't work that way, but Clairmont and Panavision make "tilt/shift" lenses that do the about the same thing. You can look up the principles involved. They're not complex, but they're way out of the zone of this book. You may have seen one of these lenses used in the rowing competition in *Social Network*, shot by Jeff Cronenweth, ASC.

You can use a split diopter. A diopter is what we call a magnifying lens that is used as a filter (optical corrections are measured in diopters). A diopter on the front of the lens is a way of getting closer to an object than the closest focus of the lens will let you. If you use a split diopter, you can focus simultaneously on something close and something far.

CAUTION: Both of these techniques rely on the subjects not moving. You get this situation sometimes, but there's a reason for the term *moving* pictures.

I went out thoroughly shaken, thinking, not for the first time, that I had made a horrible mistake in my career choice and wondering if I could get my old job back. But I really wanted to look good on this job. The Camera Department at Universal had gotten me this job, and if I did well, I could count on a lot of work from them. And if I did poorly, they'd just forget my name. The DP was a man I respected and sort of feared, a man for whom I had worked as a second on *Rockford Files*, and I didn't want to let him down. So I marched off and bought the fanciest depth of field calculator in the world (and had the company pay for it).

And I looked at that calculator every night, trying to get a sense of what lenses would help me and which ones would hang me out to dry. In thinking about the problem, I thought of one of the first things I learned about depth of field: You can use the edge of the depth of field as much as the precise point of focus. That is, if you've got one person at 5 feet and one at 15 feet, you probably can't keep them both in focus. And you don't want to throw the focus back and forth between 5 and 15 feet as the actors alternate speaking. It looks obvious, it calls attention to the fact that you're watching a movie, and it tends to push the audience right out of the picture. It surprises some people to know that such artistic concerns come from the technicians, but they do.

To deal with situations like this, I had been taught not to focus exactly at 5 and then throw the focus back to 15 as I switched focus from one actor to the other. (By the way, a lot of assistants and others call this "racking focus." I hate this term. *Racking* always means shifting the focus as fast as possible from one setting to another. I think it's obvious by now that I hate the obtrusive nature of such a move, and if you want the smoothest look to your work, you should, too. I like to think of the best way as "floating" focus. You're not slower, you just feather the start and end, and you feel a gentler movement than you would racking.) So I played the actor closer to the camera at the edge of his depth of field (say, 7 feet) and played the actress, further away, at the edge of her depth of field (say, 13 feet). That way, when I shifted focus from front to back, I moved the focus ring less. There was less of the image suddenly changing focus, and the shift happened faster because my hand had a shorter distance to traverse. On the pilot I made a point of playing my focus so that the maximum area of the shot was in focus; the speaker was always sharp, and if I had to shift to another actor, I played depth of field so the focus shift was almost unnoticeable. If you're careful and you shift focus in concert with the audience's shift of attention from one person to the other, the audience will never notice the change. The shift should occur just after the first character finishes speaking and just before the second one starts. The audience will look only at the actor who's talking and won't sense the fact that you've switched focus.

So this is the technique I used on *Down By Law*, and thank goodness I'd had the training on that pilot. Almost every interior scene—low light and wide-open aperture—had two or three characters among whom I had to play focus without anyone noticing. It worked well, and I'm very proud of it.

So when it comes to choosing lenses, you have decisions to make based on the many factors we just discussed. That's why it is so important to know what the practical and artistic needs of the production will be. Just be assured that over time, by testing lenses and by gaining experience from using various lines of lenses over and over, these choices will become easier and easier as you learn what works best for you and you become old friends with your favorite lenses.

CHAPTER 30
The Zen of Focusing

On the surface, focusing seems simple enough. During a blocking rehearsal, marks are laid to indicate the places on the set where the actors will be stopping and standing during a scene. The first camera assistant measures the distance from the focal plane (on the camera) to each actor's position using a cloth or fiberglass tape. The first makes notes or memorizes the distances that will need to be set when the scene is shot. The director calls "Action," and using the geared knob attached to the barrel of the lens, the first adjusts the focus as the scene proceeds to whatever distance the actor is from the camera. That's all there is to it!

Well, not so fast. The first thing that can go wrong is that actors often don't hit their marks, or they lean, or they move suddenly. You need to have a really good mental measuring tape in your head. You have to react to errors by actors and to erratic moves and to moves that were never rehearsed. You have to know which of several actors in the scene is most important and make sure you keep the focus on that actor. You have to try to keep several actors in a shot in acceptable focus all the time even though this is impossible according to the laws of physics.

All this time, you are standing next to the camera, eyes at the film plane (the precise place where the film is when it's exposed). One eye is on the actor, and the other eye is on the lens. This leaves no eyes to look at the video monitor. It's also tough to see both the scene and the lens. We all develop routines to deal with it. (I look at the corner of the matte box so the actor is in my left peripheral vision and the lens markings are in my right. It's tricky.)

You may have gotten the idea by now that the job of focusing is a hard job that takes a long time to learn. Yes. The first time on a set, I couldn't believe regular human beings did this job *without looking through the viewfinder!* And that's just as well because if you tried to focus through the viewfinder or by using a monitor, you'd always be lagging behind the movement of the actor. If you "follow" focus, you're late, out of focus, and fired. So you must be *with* the actor. There is a point when you will have entered the zone, a zone in which you, the assistant, react reflexively to the situation. You learn the actors' "clues" so you know when to anticipate their moves. As I progressed in the job, I began to think that I didn't do focus; I *was* focus. It's like a Zen practice. Read *Zen and the Art of Archery* to expose yourself to the method and philosophy. Yes, we're shooting movies, not arrows, but the same concepts are applicable. They both deal with very narrow limits of error, being on target, being focused. No pun intended.

Baby steps and incessant practice will make you a good focus puller. Wherever you are, try to guess distances to people or objects you see. Carry a tape measure with you (for this, use a steel one), and see how close you can come to actual distances. Let's say you feel a little weird doing that in public. Instead, go in your backyard with a friend, toss some rocks, then guess the distance from you to the rocks. Use your tape to measure the actual distances and compare them to what you guessed. After a lot of wrong guesses, you'll start to get a feel for what these distances will look like to you, and you'll develop an instinctive accuracy. When you get really good at it, you can amuse your friends and win some bets by showing off your ability to accurately guess distances just by looking.

Back on the set. There are some strategies you can use to help you with focus. Measure out ten feet, and memorize where that is on the set. This is an indispensable benchmark. It's good to know what five feet looks like, too. Always focus on the actor's eyes. Even if nothing else is in focus, this will look good. Always focus on #1. That's the first person listed on the call sheet, who will always be the star.

When you're shooting in a place with any regular divisions (tile, sidewalk spaces), measure the length of one division and use it to calculate the rough distance between you and the subject. When shooting in a room, measure the distances to furniture. Even when the actors miss their marks, you'll have a pretty good idea of where they are.

Remember that your arm span equals your height. If you're 5′10″ to 6′2″, you can figure you're span is six feet. So nose to fingertips is one yard. When you measure to actors, use a cloth tape. (A metal tape can get out of control and hurt people. You use a metal tape only when you can't leave the camera—for example, if you're on a crane 12 feet in the air.) Write the measurement on a piece of camera tape or a sticky note you've put on your tape. When you get back to the camera, put the note on your matte box as a reference.

Beware of getting more than three reference points for a shot. Too many measurements will confuse you. Remember that if you're shooting from the air, distances look different from the way they look on the ground. Measure more often and more carefully. On a crane or a platform (we call it a parallel), you can use a metal tape or, better, give your assistant the dumb end of the tape and have him take it out to the point to be measured. If you're flying, you're so high that pretty much everything is at infinity. Or ask your operator for eye focuses.

When you're on a long lens, it's tough; have your second go out with a slate and stand next to landmarks. Get a visual focus through the lens at each point. Number them. During the shot, have your assistant call off to you when the subject passes the landmarks you have measured.

To get an eye focus, have your second stand next to the actor or on the actor's mark. Have him hold up the slate at exactly the plane of the eyes. Focus on the printed lines on the slate (they're sharp and contrasty and easy to read). Backlight the slate, if you can, so you can see the lines more clearly. Refer to Chapter 28 for more about viewing systems.

CHAPTER 31
The Magic of Filters

There tends to be a lot of mysticism about filters. Filters and nets are given credit for every kind of great photography. I remember one time in college, a grad student friend of mine rushed into the film department all hot and bothered. "I've got it!" he yelled. "I know how Sven Nykvist gets those beautiful, crisp pictures for Bergman. I just saw a picture of his camera, and his matte box must be a foot long. Think of all the filters he can fit in there!" We were all duly impressed, with both my friend's sagacity and Nykvist's filtering genius. It was a number of years before I found out that the picture is at its sharpest when no filters are used; filters can change color, and can make the picture fuzzier. That's almost all. Then when I worked as an assistant to Robby Müller, I was besieged by other DPs and assistants wanting to know the secrets of Robby's "filter pack." Yes, I knew, and I give you the secret here: no filters. As Robby told me, "I prefer to light it."

When I started in the business, a few years before I worked with Robby, it was the fashion to use some sort of softening filter all the time. Back then we commonly used fogs, double fogs, and low-contrast filters. In the 1980s the fashion turned around to having a clean lens. I don't know why except to say fashion. You can see the effect of this fashion when you watch *Visions of Light*. In it Haskell Wexler talks about taking over for Nestor Almendros on *Days of Heaven*. Nestor has just said that filtering is cheating, and then Haskell admits to using some diffusion filtering on *Days of Heaven*—thus subverting Nestor. Why? My guess: It was the mid-1970s: fashion.

I've seen people get bent out of shape about filters the way they get crazy about using exposure meters. Calm down. You want to consider filters not as a mystery but as another tool, just as the meter is a tool, just as the camera is a tool. So what do you really need?

I never start a show without two specific filters. The first is an optical flat, which is, yes, a flat piece of glass—optical glass, so it has no imperfections and it's "water white"—that is, it's neutrally colored. The most common use you'll have for a flat is putting it in front of the lens as protection. You only need protection from projectiles—gunshots (yes, even blanks), explosions, gravel and dirt kicked up by vehicles. The flat is insurance; it's a lot cheaper than a lens, so it becomes expendable. If you're doing a show with lots of gunfire straight at the camera, you'll be returning several flats pitted with the wadding from blanks.

I also use flats to make homemade diffusion. An optical flat is what you use for the traditional Vaseline look. To do that, take a small amount of Vaseline, and put it on one side of the flat. Smear it around to get a thin, even film. Use a rag or a paper towel to wipe it down as thin as you can. Wipe in one direction. How thin do you want the Vaseline? You'll figure out after a few tries, but I recommend that you make it very thin; it has a bigger effect than you usually expect. And putting on a pattern by wiping in one direction will give you a different look for each direction. For example, I find wiping a horizontal pattern gives me a vertical smear to the picture. You'll discover your own preferred look.

Another traditional method, often as a last-minute emergency, is using hairspray from the hairdressers or dulling spray from the grips. Again, thinner is better. I've gotten my best effects not by spraying directly on the glass but by spraying a mist in the air and waving the flat through it. You can build up the thickness slowly when you do it that way.

Okay, you've got an optical flat as part of your standard order. The next indispensable item is a polarizing filter. In the business it's often called a Pola-screen; that's the name under which it was first marketed. The only time you won't want a polarizer is when you're shooting entirely indoors. It's really only useful outside because it reduces your exposure by about one and a half stops, and usually you can't afford that much inside. And its practical uses inside are limited. But outside it's a miracle worker. It will darken clear blue skies to a rich royal blue. It will eliminate reflections on water so you can see the fish swimming around. It will enhance reflections on windows to hide the activity inside. It will brighten sun reflections on the tips of breaking waves. Yes, it's a miracle worker. But wait, there's more! Everything it can do it can undo. It can leave skies pastel, kill or enhance reflections on glass and water, and eliminate the sun glints on waves. Of course, these effects are the result of the same action by the filter. Here's how it works. Rays of the light from the sun are (for all practical purposes) parallel, but they are vibrating in all configurations. If you could look at the sun and see individual light waves, you would see waves lined up at all 360 degrees of a circle, sort of like on the left of the filter in Figure 31.1.

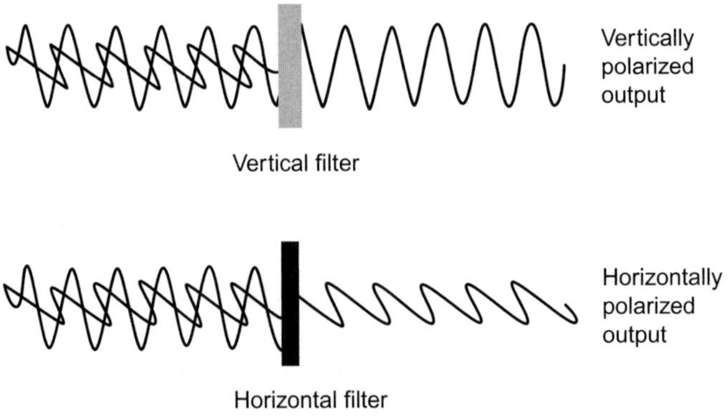

Vertically
polarized
output

Vertical filter

FIGURE 31.1
Light waves (diagram of polarized output showing vertical and horizontal filtration).

Horizontally
polarized
output

Horizontal filter

The polarizer cuts the amount of light in half (actually a little more than half) by letting through only the light waves that are parallel to scribings in the filter. We can choose which parallel rays to let through. Since all the light is now parallel, we can choose to see only the light that's not scattered (in the case of the sky), or only the light rays that show a reflection, in water or on glass, or the ones that don't show a reflection.

One of the nice things about a polarizer is that it returns to us a tool we had lost in the conversion from black-and-white to color. With monochrome film it was possible to use color filters to change the look of a scene. For example, we could use a yellow or a red filter to darken the sky a little or a lot. (They would darken the picture by letting through fewer blue rays than shooting unfiltered.) If we tried to use them with color film, of course, we'd just get an overall cast of yellow or red to our picture. Now, with the polarizer, we can darken the sky without changing color. Since the polarizer has an equal effect on all wavelengths of light, it has a neutral color.

Why do we want to darken the sky? Well, for art. Specifically, the sky is usually the brightest object in an exterior picture. It's usually so bright that it distracts from the action, or it stretches the density range of the film and begins to look overexposed. As you can imagine, it's worse with digital shooting, given its tendency to let white/overbright areas clip. The polarizer can help us both technically and artistically.

There may be occasions when the polarizer tends to make the frame "too pretty." The rich, clear, blue skies you sometimes get in the southwest can darken to look almost like a lake. In these cases you will want to back off the polarizer—to set it at, say, halfway.

This brings up how to use a polarizer. You rotate it. That's all there is to it. You either have a square filter to fit in a rotating filter slot in the matte box or a round filter that fits in a filter holder and can be oriented at any angle. The way to set it is to look at your subject through the polarizer. Rotate the polarizer, and at some point, you will decide you want the look you're getting. Let your assistant know this is the orientation for the polarizer. With a square filter, the assistant remembers the orientation. He can also take a look, remember what it looks like, and reset it while looking through the lens. With a round filter, your assistant marks "12 o'clock" on the filter holder. When attached to the matte box, he makes sure the filter is positioned with the mark straight up.

There are two other classes of filters you may want to carry as part of your regular package. If you're on an exterior, it is likely that the ISO of the film is too fast. Even with a film as slow as 50 ISO, you have to use a stop as deep as f/16 much of the time. For various reasons you may not want that deep a stop. If nothing else, you don't want to be forced into using it. Carry a set of neutral density filters. NDs, as they are universally referred to, come in full stop increments. Each .1 ND is one-third of a stop (corresponding to ISO gradations). Therefore, one stop is .3 ND, almost always written ND3 and called an ND3 or an N3 or a 30 neutral (30 from 0.30; i.e., .3). Two stops is ND6, and three stops is ND9. You can get filters darker than ND9, but they're uncommon. A "set of neutrals" is an ND3, an ND6, and an ND9.

Back in ancient times when I was an assistant, film came in only one type: 100 ASA, tungsten balanced. When we went outside, we needed the neutrals, but we also needed to compensate for the sensitivity to blue built into the emulsion. The standard conversion is a Wratten 85 filter. Wratten is a designation used by Kodak and others to refer to most color filters. Don't worry about it. Just call it an 85. (And Kodak says the true compensation for shooting tungsten-balanced film in sunlight is an 85B filter. This is probably scientifically correct, but no one ever uses an 85B in the business. We always use 85s. Don't worry about this either.) To make life easier, filter companies developed combination filters: 85N3, 85N6, 85N9. A standard 85 package is 85, 85N3, 85N6, 85N9. If you plan to use tungsten film for every situation, make sure you carry a set of 85s.

Why would you want to use tungsten film outdoors when Kodak and Fuji both make excellent daylight-balanced films? There might be a lot of reasons, but one that's powerful is money. No, the daylight films aren't more expensive, but if you have only a little to shoot outside, and you're not exactly sure how much to order, and you don't want a whole lot left over, you can order all tungsten and use 85s outside. In fact, you can use 500 ISO tungsten-balanced film for everything, the way Steve Poster, ASC, does because he loves the look of that particular emulsion. It's uncommon to use a very fast film outside, where you will have to filter it down so much, but it works perfectly well. I've done it a few times when I was caught by the necessity to shoot outside but I had no slow film. It looks fine. The only downside is that the operator will have a hard time looking through the camera when a lot of ND is in front of the lens. A wonderful alternative is to use gelatin filters and put them behind the lens or behind the gate. Some cameras (Panaflex, Arricam) have slots cut in the movement just in front of the film where a gelatin filter holder can be inserted.

A word about gelatin filters: Be careful. The great thing about gel filters, besides being able to go behind a lens (many lenses have a filter holder built in) or in a slot in front of the gate, is that there are many more kinds of filters available in gels than in glass. They cost anywhere from $20 to $70 (for a 3 × 3-inch size), depending on the specific filter. They are thus much less expensive than a glass filter, but they *are* fragile. Usually you use them once and throw them away. They have to be cut for use in holders. They are brittle, and it's difficult to cut them smoothly without practice. They acquire dust and dirt easily, and fingerprints are permanent—they get etched into the gelatin. It's easy to work with a 3 × 3-inch filter that usually gives you four pieces for filter holders and come out with zero filters because you've touched the gel or dropped it or somehow gotten dirt on it that you can't get off. Dirt tends to be more critical with gel filters; they are so close to the film plane that a spot might actually be seen as an image on the film, and fingerprints look like ugly diffusion.

Don't be scared. The advantages are so great that it's worth practicing until you can cut them accurately. The filters come in an envelope inside which is a piece of cardboard with lens tissue around the filter. Keep the lens tissue on the filter while you cut it. If the filter holder is a split holder with a friction fit for the gel, use a small piece of Scotch tape to hold the filter in the holder. The filter is held in the behind the lens holder by friction. Blow off any dust with a hurricane blower or Dust-Off, but be careful. These things go flying pretty easily.

Of course, you'll be thinking about the right size glass filter for your camera/lens setup. Avoid screw-on filters. You have to have a different one for each lens size, or you have to get filters for the largest diameter lens and step-down adapters to fit the filters on each other lens. It's a pain in the neck to change filters when you have to unscrew them, and it's horrible if you have more than one filter. That's why matte boxes have filter holders that slip in and out of slots in the matte box. The standard size for professional matte boxes is 4 × 5.65-inch; we call them "4 by 5s." There are also 4 × 4-inch filters, used for some older 16 mm cameras, and many aftermarket matte boxes for digital cameras. Since most digital camera manufacturers don't make matte boxes, you're facing the hell of many different makes of matte boxes, follow-focus, and rods, none of which will fit another. Good luck. Take your time prepping the camera, and make sure everything fits. You will also run into 6 × 6-inch filters, which were standard some 40 years ago. They've had a renaissance with the popularity of graduated filters.

For polarizers, you'll find it easier to use round filters. Usually, you'll use a 4½-inch round for primes and a 138 mm for zooms. I mentioned graduated filters, and I hate to do it, but I'll go over them here. *Don't use them.* I'd like to leave it at that, but you want to know why. Grads are filters with half clear and half the designated filter. They may have a sharp line at the division between the filter and the clear glass, a soft line, or a slow transition. Neutral grads are used to darken skies; grads in various colors are used to simulate sunsets or to put some color into a picture where it doesn't occur naturally. There's an overwhelming tendency for grads to look phony. The colors are artificial—that goes without saying. The neutral grads can work fine as long as there's a distinct horizon line and no part of your picture sticks up above it. If something is tall—say, a tree—the top of the tree will be darkened more than the bottom. The line on the grad will be obvious on the film, and any illusion is shattered. I have seen grads used well; of course, the definition of "used well" is that you can't see the grad. All too often there is a telltale object sticking up and being darkened unrealistically.

And now we come to diffusion. This is actually where we began. Some kind of diffusion has been used since the beginning of photography to blur reality and to soften hard edges. The most common use is to make actors look better. Mostly it's for women, but look at any recent films with Robert Redford—lots of extra softness in his close-ups.

By the way, we also call pieces of plastic that we put on lamps to soften the light diffusion. This shouldn't be confusing, since one is part of the camera department and the other is handled by grips and electricians. Someone must have run out of funny words to call things.

While there are dozens of kinds of diffusion, you can think of all of them falling into two classes: the ones that soften focus and the ones that spread light. The ones that soften focus have little lenses on the glass; they look clear but pebbled, like shower door glass. These tend to soften or eliminate facial lines without causing a halo effect. The ones spreading the light look like dirty pieces of glass. They quite distinctly cause more or less of a halo or sparkle effect around points of light. They are by far the largest class of diffusing filters. Also, diffusion, though not strictly filters, are nets. Traditionally DPs have gone to lingerie stores and bought extremely fine-mesh underwear. Then they have their assistants mount pieces of the lingerie into frames that go in front of or behind the lens. A few companies now make "net filters"—netting embedded between two pieces of glass—but most DPs who use nets do it the old-fashioned way.

Of course, I am simplifying the situation greatly. There are kinds (say, black-dot filters) that spread the light without causing a halo. There are many different gradations of these filters, designed to spread the light and soften the picture in different ways. It's impossible to deal with them except by going through every kind of diffusion made by every filter manufacturer. Even so, what you're interested in is how you feel about the filter's effect and how it looks to you. What you want to do is find a filter company or a camera rental house or a camera store. They'll have filters, and most places will let you borrow them for tests. Get a set and try them out. Almost all diffusion comes in different densities, usually 1 (hardly anything) through 5 (very heavy). Take some stills of friends. Better yet, do some little scenes with actors, light them, and see how the diffusion affects the photography. Shoot clean (no filter) shots, too, and keep records for yourself.

I think you'll find that any diffusion filter can work well for almost any circumstance. But eventually you will decide that you like one or two kinds best, and you'll stick with them. Test, test, test. That's the only way to know what you're doing and to be sure you're going to get the results you want.

CHAPTER 32
Film

Film is the basic stuff of films. Ha! Gotcha! Okay, it's really the reason for movies. Plenty of smart cookies tried to make pictures that move, and no one had any success until Eastman appropriated the technology to make tough, flexible, clear celluloid and made it commercially viable. Once flexible, transparent material to which photographic emulsion could be bonded was created, movies began almost immediately. Until then, although great progress had been made in making dry emulsions (Eastman's company was first called the Eastman Dry Plate company), attempts to make a continuous running series of pictures had been confined to glass plates and paper. You can probably figure out why they didn't work.

Today, digital formation and storage of images are practical, often excellent, and may supplant film as the preferred imaging method of the future. But not yet. So it is important for professional work to know something about film itself. It's not just a historical oddity.

Any photographic film is made up of several layers. The bottommost, and thickest, is the base. The first practical base was nitrocellulose, usually called nitrate. It had a composition similar to gunpowder; unfortunately, it would sometimes burn and explode just like gunpowder. This characteristic is responsible for the fortress-like building of projection booths (fireproofing) and for a still-prevalent notion that film is dangerous and causes fires.

Things are different today. The most common base for camera film (negative film used in cameras) is cellulose acetate (called safety film, a term not much used today). It allows a duller image than nitrate, but at least it doesn't burn under normal circumstances. Another substance, a polyester (often called Estar, a trademark of Kodak), is usually used for print films. It's enormously tough and dimensionally stable for long storage. It's so tough that if used as a camera film, a jam would likely tear the camera mechanism apart before the film ripped. So it's used for nonoriginal photography applications where it won't break a million-dollar camera, such as in labs and projectors.

I find it interesting that, partly because of the base, photographic film is now considered the best archival medium for movies. You may have seen pictures of decomposed film turning into goo. That's nitrate. Safety film, however, lasts at least 100 years, and maybe even 200 to 300. And it tends not to shrink or warp, although the polyester base is far more stable than acetate. All of this should help you understand why film itself is important. Digital archiving is seductive, but we don't know how long any digital storage will last. Tape can become brittle, and the oxide on tape tends to separate from its base. And we all know that digital coding seems to change (what seems like) overnight. Engineers are continually improving the amount of storage space, but they are also developing new—and improved—ways of encoding the information. We have all encountered the situation of a new operating system making the old one obsolete and even making it impossible to retrieve information stored with an outdated program. Those are the problems facing digital today.

But even color film, whose pictures are contaminated with residual chemicals and unstable dyes, can be separated into three archival black-and-white copies—one for each of the red, green, and blue layers—that offer longer life and the possibility of reconstituting the color picture accurately.

Okay, so film lasts a long time. What exactly is this stuff? On top of a base of $^4/_{1000}$ inch to $^7/_{1000}$ inch are layered a binder, the emulsion, often a protective surface on top, and a black antihalation layer on the back. The protective layer has little to do with photography. The antihalation layer keeps strong light from penetrating the film and bouncing off the pressure plate in the camera, thus causing halos around the bright light. You can see this effect in black-and-white movies from before the 1990s. Black-and-white film had no black backing, so car headlights always have a fuzzy glow around them—the halo. (By the way, modern black-and-white still has no antihalation layer. Most of the few black-and-white pictures made today are shot with color film and "decolorized" in postproduction. That's why you rarely see halos around lights in those movies.)

The emulsion layer is the most important for us because it gives us the picture. The chemical nature of film is a salt, a silver halide. This is a compound of silver and a halide (a gas), most often nitrogen. The emulsion is silver nitrate. All silver halides are sensitive to light; without adding other chemicals, they are sensitive only to light in the short end of the spectrum, blue (and ultraviolet). You may have seen old photographs—before 1900—in which the sky is blank or the eyes are unnaturally light. These circumstances exist because the film is extremely sensitive to blue; in order to get other colors to expose, the blue areas of the photograph are overexposed and therefore look white in the print.

Until at least 1910, you would have seen the strangest makeup on the actors on a movie set. Often their faces were chalky white, and their lips might be brown colored. All of this was to compensate for the characteristics of the film. That film is now called color blind, and it's still in use today, usually for graphic arts applications.

So the chemists working at the film manufacturers, in a tireless effort to make more money with new gimmicks, started adding chemicals. In effect, they added impurities to the emulsion. By the teens, a new type of emulsion called orthochromatic was common. The film was sensitive to green as well as blue, and it rendered colors in a gray scale more "realistically." (Can you call monochrome—black-and-white—realistic? It's always an abstraction. But this is not a philosophy book, so let's stick to practicalities.)

Photographers and cinematographers generally welcomed ortho as a great advance. But the emulsion was still insensitive to red light, so lips and traffic lights went black. It is interesting that *orthochromatic* means "true color" (roughly) from its Greek roots. And, of course, it wasn't true color. It wasn't color, and it wasn't true. But you have to sell the public some way.

In the 1920s, photographic chemists found new compounds that when added to the ortho emulsion would make the film sensitive to red. Now the emulsion was sensitive to all colors and would render them in an approximately equal way as shades of gray. Of course, the new film had a new name: *panchromatic*, meaning "all colors." And it was a real advance. Emulsions have undergone numerous improvements since the 1920s, but they're all now panchromatic (again, except for special applications).

You are probably thinking, "I just want to make movies. What do I care about all this history?" I'm glad you asked. Unless you're doing historic recreations (*Zelig*), you *don't* care. And you're not going to make black-and-white movies—they're not commercial—so let's stick to color. And this is where all this stuff comes into play. Color emulsions consist of three layers, one each sensitive to red light, green light, and blue light. (I am simplifying radically here. Kodak's website has a lot of helpful information about the structure of their films.) Each of the layers is a slightly different emulsion. The top layer is blue-sensitive. A yellow filter under it holds back blue and lets through red and green. The next layer is ortho—sensitive to blue and green. A red filter underneath holds back the green and lets through the red. And the bottom layer is panchromatic—sensitive to all colors.

All film works in basically the same way. A photon—the basic particle of light—guided by the lens hits the emulsion. It breaks off electrons, which causes the silver halide to become metal silver. At the moment, it's only potentially metal, but, again, we don't need to worry about that. It's enough to know that light changes the chemistry of the emulsion. Light makes the image, and we are in fact taking pictures of light—not things. Remembering this can be valuable. When you're composing, you want to think of the light; suddenly what we're doing becomes clear (after a lot of practice).

I want to emphasize that we're recording light; whether film or digital, the system is a way of making a permanent record of light rays—chemically for film, electronically for digital. And as my mentor Robby Müller once said when asked what he likes about light, "It makes things visible."

Of course, nothing is all that simple. We do not have an image on the film, nor do we have one on the chip. Digitally, the signal (light hits a sensor, causes an electric current) has to be recorded somehow and processed before it can be played back as an image. On the film there's eventually an actual picture, but right now it's a latent image. It holds potential. It must be processed in chemical baths to make the image visible. It's probably reductive to stress this. However, I want you, the budding cinematographer, to have an accurate foundation of knowledge for your creative endeavors.

An unusual aspect of film, not encountered in digital filmmaking, is the positive/negative process. The original camera film, when processed, is a negative; all the values of the scene are reversed. And all the colors are the complements of the colors in the scene. Before we have a picture, we must print the negative. In a controlled environment, we sandwich the negative and unexposed print film together, pass light through the negative to the positive, and we have another piece of film full of latent images, which gets processed just as the negative was.

Also, be aware that all high-end digital cameras give us a record that also does not look like the original scene. In this case the picture is generally gray-green and has very low contrast. It too must be processed, but this time electronically. That's all you need to know. The subject is really beyond the scope of this book. These cameras rent for upwards of $6,000 a day, so you probably aren't going to get your hands on one anytime soon.

Film demands careful handling. Even before the light strikes the emulsion, it's an unstable batch of chemicals. It will deteriorate with time, but careful handling can keep it fresh fairly long. Unexposed (and, by the way, exposed but unprocessed) film should always be kept cold. It is fine to freeze it for long-term storage. When I worked at Apogee, the late, great effects house, we used only maybe 100 feet of film a day. It came in 1,000-foot rolls, so we kept them in a deep freeze until we needed them. We did have to take them out of the freezer the night before shooting; it takes that long for the film to warm up. And you keep it in its can, well taped, so condensation doesn't form on the film.

In most cases, refrigeration is all you need. I keep my film in plastic storage bags so the can doesn't get rusty from condensation while it warms up. The rust won't hurt anything, but it's messy. Almost any size can of film will warm up after a few hours. You can usually pull it out of the fridge on the day of shooting, and it'll be usable by the time you start shooting. Kodak has an excellent page on storing and handling online. Download Technical Information Bulletin #Tib5202 May 2002, Storage and Handling of Unprocessed Film from Kodak's website at http://motion.kodak.com/US/en/motion/support/Technical_information/faq.htm#preprod16.

As well as age, ionizing radiation will cause film to deteriorate. We all know that x-rays will fog film, but even cosmic rays, given enough time, will do it. So eventually almost all unprocessed film, no matter how carefully it's treated, will become useless. Motion picture film, since it's a professional film, is made to higher standards than the stuff you stick in your snapshot camera. It gives better color rendition, but it also means it goes bad faster. So don't buy too much and try to hold on to it.

Electronic imaging is analogous to film imaging. The same basic action occurs: Electrons hit a sensitive place, a charge is formed, there is an accumulation of charges on a chip in a certain amount of time (like $\frac{1}{50}$ second), and then the record of these charges is dumped into a storage area. Either while shooting (tape) or afterward (data file) the information is stored where it is permanent and accessible. We know that the lasting power of digital information is still an open question.

Right now a friendly argument about digital acquisition is raging. Most cameras use CCDs (charge-coupled devices). Some now use CMOS (complementary metal–oxide–semiconductor). There are pros and cons to each, and again that's a matter for professionals. Novice filmmakers will generally be using CCD cameras.

CHAPTER 33
Color Temperature

Color temperature is a physics concept. The color temperature of any point in the spectrum is that temperature in degrees Kelvin (Celsius scale with zero as absolute zero) to which a black body (what's that, you ask? don't worry about it) must be heated to produce that color (wavelength). It's nice to know this, but the physics of it has no practical application in cinematography.

We must know about color temperature, however, since film does not respond to light the same way eyes do. It's the same way for electronic imagers (CCDs, CMOS, and whatever is new in the last month). Your eye-brain system "knows" what the color of most objects is supposed to be. The processing of nerve impulses in the brain from the optic nerve interprets whatever "actual" color (what the actual wavelength of light shows it to be) we see by approximating its "real" color (the one we know from experience) in our consciousness. You notice that this depends on our having seen the object in "white" (or neutral) light before. If you haven't, you accept the color as presented.

You are familiar with this at least from a sunset. Just before sunset, sunlight is very orange/yellow, and a white piece of paper looks orange in that light. We perceive it as white because we "know" that it's white. A few minutes later, when the sun actually sets, the skylight is strongly blue, and the paper is bluish; yet the paper still looks white. Or imagine that you are standing outside a house, looking through a window at a room in which an incandescent lamp is turned on. Compared to the sunlight, the lamp appears very orange. But go into the room and the lamp appears white.

Unfortunately, film does not have this built-in capability to compensate. Film sees color as the spectrum. Orange is orange and blue is blue. Manufacturers have gotten around this by making emulsions that read correct color in sunlight and other emulsions that read correct color in tungsten (incandescent) light. Daylight film in tungsten light looks very orange, and tungsten film in daylight looks very blue. So as cinematographers we adjust by using the film that is color-balanced for the lighting conditions we find ourselves in. Or we use a corrective color filter over the lens to remove the color that is too strong (an orangey filter for tungsten film in daylight, a bluish filter for daylight film in tungsten). Similarly, the electronic sensors in digital cameras respond to wavelengths, not to colors as humans perceive them. The method for color correction electronically is "white balancing," using a white paper placed in the dominant light of a scene. The camera learns that for this scene, this is white, and all other colors are rendered correspondingly.

Color temperature of sunlight is nominally 5500° K or 5600° K; this is in the shorter wavelength of the visible spectrum, and it tends to be blue. Nominally, again, tungsten is 3200° K into the red/orange area. Remember these numbers, but be warned that we will be playing some games with color temperature, and the tungsten, especially, is not what it seems. The story with tungsten is that 3200° K is an arbitrary number. (The sun is the sun, so its light is 5500° K or 5600° K—case closed. Of course, skylight may be a lot higher in degrees K.)

So while the sun is the sun, and it's always the same thing, not all tungsten light is created equal. What exactly is tungsten? It's the kind of lamp Thomas Edison invented: a tungsten filament inside a partial vacuum enclosed by a glass bulb. Electricity is put through the filament, the filament resists the electrical pressure, the resistance causes the filament to heat up, it gets very hot, and it glows. *Voilà*—light! But at 3200° K? Well, close, if you use movie lamps. Movie lamps have quartz-halogen bulbs that burn hotter even than household bulbs, and they maintain a pretty consistent color temperature. But they *do* get old, and the fixtures (the lenses, the reflectors) get dirty. So they regularly measure at 2900° K to 3000° K. The closest I've ever seen to 3200° K was a brand-new lamp in a brand-new fixture at the factory (Mole-Richardson, the first and still the best maker of movie lights). That lamp measured 3150° K.

It sounds as if it doesn't matter much, right? Well, your film—since it doesn't have your brain—is going to make the picture look a little warm. And you'll have to do things to compensate for that. And we're talking expensive movie lights here. Take a household bulb, and it probably measures 2700° K if it's new. If it's old, it could be down to 2500° K. So the color of your light sources may be all over the place. Are you getting nervous now? Well, take heart. There's a lot we can do with filters on the set and with printing adjustments in post. And the different shades of light become one of our best creative tools.

CHAPTER 34

Using and Handling Film Cameras and Lenses

Most of what you will need to know is conceptually the same for almost every make and model of film camera. Here are some questions you want to consider:

How do you open and close the camera? Let's hope this is fairly obvious. As a general rule, most 35 mm film cameras have a door on the left side that allows access to an internal chamber. (Just a note on direction: Left and right are from the operator's perspective looking through the viewfinder, with the lens in front, so left and right are the operator's left and right.) Inside the internal chamber you will find the pull-down mechanism, the device that intermittently feeds the film past the aperture and through the camera. On the other hand, most modern 16 mm cameras (Arriflex SR and 416, all Aatons) split the movement between the front of the camera (with the lens) and the magazine. There is no interior chamber, except the magazine itself. Half the gate (the aperture plate) is in the front, and half (the pressure plate) is in the magazine. Like 35s, older 16s (Bolex, Bell & Howell, Arriflex S and M) do have doors with internal compartments. Many of them have internal chambers that serve as places for the movement and for threading and accommodate 100-foot loads without the use of a magazine. In any case, care must be taken not to let dirt in; blowing out with Dust-Off is usually a good idea.

How do you get power to the camera (usually battery, maybe windup)? Most professional cameras work with batteries. Arri (16 mm cameras) and Aaton (both 35 mm and 16 mm cameras) have provisions for both onboard batteries and cable connections to separate batteries. Onboard batteries are usually small in size and capacity, but offer the convenience of mounting directly on the camera. And, of course, you can use block batteries (fairly large) or belt batteries (yes, a belt). And by the way, it's *belt batteries* (and block batteries, onboard batteries, etc.), not battery belts. That's just the way we talk, and you don't want to look like a greenhorn by saying "battery belts." Very old cameras are usually windup. No, I'm not kidding. And there are times this can be really useful: You're off the grid, and you can get shots when guys with dead batteries are sitting on their thumbs. It is possible to attach a battery-powered motor to Bolexes and the

Bell & Howells, but they're cumbersome and hard to find. The important thing for every camera—and you can see how vital it is for all electronic cameras—is to remember to keep your batteries well charged. There's nothing more pointless and more embarrassing than getting on a set and finding out all the batteries are dead. It's a sure ticket to the unemployment office. Also make sure you always have at least two batteries per camera. If one goes down, you'll have a spare. Having only one is the best way to make sure it dies on you. If you're using a spring-wound camera, wind it after every shot. The spring power only lasts a short time, so you want to be sure you're always ready with the maximum potential run time.

How do you attach the lens? Watch yourself here. I can't count the number of times I've seen beginners think they've mounted a lens correctly, only to have the lens fall off. Boom! A $1,000 repair. There are tricks to each kind of mount. The oldest kind, screw-threaded, isn't found much (again, older cameras). It offers a positive fit because once you get it threaded, the lens doesn't need any further lock, but the threads are always very fine. So be very careful that the lens goes on smoothly. Binding is bad, so don't force it. There is always a danger of cross-threading, which is forcing the threads against their design. The lens will seem to be welded to the camera, and you may not be able to detach it. Or if you can get it off, the threads will be damaged.

If you shoot with the lens badly mounted so that the elements are the wrong distance from the focal plane, you will end up with out-of-focus shots (and, of course, a pink slip). So make sure the threads are clean and in good shape before you try to mount the lens (the last guy to use it may have screwed up the threads and not bothered to tell anyone—it happens). Always store the lens with the lens caps on, and always clean the threads on both the lens and the camera periodically. My favorite trick is to take a long cotton swab (like a Q-tip, but with a long wooden stick; available at all film expendable supply houses) and put a little silicone lubricant on it. I like to use the silicone grease that Panavision sends out with its cameras for lubing the felt pads on the aperture plate. If that's not available, the next best thing is silicone spray (from a lot of manufacturers) you find at hardware stores. Spray a little on the cotton tip, and swab it around both the lens and camera threads. This will clean and lube the threads. The lens will go on so much more easily and without binding. I use the same technique with screw-on filters. (I hope you have a matte box for mounting filters; if not, screw-on is probably your only way to attach filters. You will need a lot of different-sized filters, and putting them on and taking them off takes too much time. A matte box lets you work with one size filter for every lens, and the filter is easily slipped into a holder in the matte box.)

Many other lenses are attached to the camera via a bayonet mount, with and without a twist-lock. Bayonet mount lenses are mostly found on the old Arri model S and model M cameras (both 16 mm). If your bayonet lens has no twist-lock, just push the lens into the lens mount on the camera, fitting it over the locating pin. Two spring-loaded ears on the outside of the mount (squeeze to open) control tabs that hold the lens (let go of the ears once you've seated the lens). Make sure the lens is all the way in and that the locks are working. The best way to test this is to try to pull the lens off the camera. Keep a good grip on the lens; if it's loose, you don't want to have it go flying across the room. With a twist-lock bayonet, insert the lens into the camera, then twist the lens to seat it. You'll hear a click. Again, try to pull the lens out. If it's locked in, you're good to go.

The most common modern lens mount is a variation on the PL mount. PL stands for positive lock, and it is. (Strictly speaking, only Arri and its licensees use PL mounts. They and the Panavision mount are both variations of the old Mitchell mount. Panavision's mount is proprietary, but Arri lets anyone use the PL mount. That's why there are plenty of PL mount lenses available, and it's why many high-end digital cameras have PL mounts.) A positive lock lens has three or four male flanges (cutouts of a donut-like piece of metal) on the back of the lens and a locating pin or hole. The flanges fit into corresponding female flanges on the camera; proper alignment is provided by the locating pin. The lens fits solidly with a lot of metal-to-metal contact, and there's a rotary ring on the mount that locks the lens into place. You'd think it would be impossible to screw up using such an elegant, precise system. *Au contraire.* It's very easy to cock the lens so it binds in the mount; you can miss the pin or try to seat the lens with the pin in the wrong place, or you can forget to hold the lock open when mounting and forget to close the lock when done. It's usually best to put the lens on from the front of the camera, not from the side, so you can see that it's aligning properly; this is especially true with long, heavy lenses. Use one finger to hold the lock open (there's a stop to keep it from going too far). Otherwise the lock may slip ever so slightly and prevent the lens from seating.

Use silicone spray on the flanges ("ears") of the lens (again, with the Q-tip; don't spray the lens; do I really have to tell you that?). It keeps the flanges clean, and it may make it slightly easier for you to fit the lens into the mount. Again, when you think the lens is locked (finger tight is enough; you don't need excessive force to get a solid lock), try pulling it off the camera. If the lens is cocked, or the lock is slightly misaligned, remove the lens and start over. Don't try to correct a mounting problem without completely removing the lens; you'll just get frustrated.

While we're handling lenses, let's talk about lens caps and cleaning. Novices universally have a fetish about both. They think the lens cap should go back on anytime the camera is not in use, and they'll try to put the front cap on between shots. This is crazy. First off, while you're shooting (the whole day), it's impractical to keep taking the caps off and on. Even in Los Angeles, the air's not that dirty. And you'll be really sorry when the director wants to check a shot and he or she can't see through the viewfinder because the lens cap is on. No matter how fast you remove it, the director will be annoyed and may raise holy hell with the whole camera crew. Lens caps should be taken off as soon as the lens comes out of the lens case. Pull them off and toss them back in the case. That way you know where they are. Don't try to handle a lens with the caps on. Never hold a lens by the cap. Most caps fit by pushing on, often loosely. It's not fun to think you have a firm grasp on the lens only to find yourself holding a cap, while the lens crashes to the pavement. Yes, I've seen it happen. Proper handling of lenses will keep both front and back elements clean, so get rid of those caps right away. Handle lenses with your hand around the barrel, not touching the ends. That way you've got a firm grip, and your hands are away from the glass. Pass lenses to another person by grabbing the barrel and putting the lens front down into the receiver's hand. They will grasp it and say "I've got it," or "OK," and then you can release your grip. Always communicate, or you'll be left with an empty hand and an expensive pile of broken glass on the floor.

No, you won't get a palm print on the lens. Almost all front elements are sufficiently recessed from the front ring so you are unlikely to touch the glass. And make sure the stop is open to its widest, the focus is on infinity, and a zoom lens is open to its widest (shortest) focal length. This keeps the lens in its most useful position. When you mount the lens, it's letting in the most light; the scene is likely to be in approximate focus; and with a zoom, you've got the biggest field of view. Set up this way, anyone looking through the eyepiece will see a wide-angle focused image instead of a close-in blurred one. Some lenses physically elongate at shorter focus settings, so setting this type of lens to infinity makes it shorter and more compact when you're putting the lens back in its case. Also, though rare, the leaves of the iris might stick together if stored in a closed position; the next time you use the lens, the blades won't move or may break, making the lens useless.

A little cautionary tale: Years ago, I was working on a film in Georgia in the summer. Georgia can be very humid; sometimes you could tell the difference between rain and the normal 99% humidity only by puddles on the ground. There were five cameras on this show, and there were at least eight assistants. You'd think that among us we would have caught any problem, but one of us left the stop set (to around f/11) on a 400 mm lens one night. And let me mention that we had an entire motel room for the camera department, air-conditioned and relatively not humid, where we kept equipment at night. Nonetheless, when one of us inspected the 400 mm the next morning, he saw that the stop was on and automatically opened the iris. And all those delicate, precise leaves stuck to each other and collapsed into the lens barrel. We had a special shipment from Panavision that day. Ever since, I've been fanatical about keeping the stop off when the lens isn't in use. (And I always have the production buy lots of silica gel to keep equipment dry in wet climates.)

And another thing about the lens cases: There are proper procedures for dealing with cases. These are not little pouches such as you might use for still lenses, and they are not canvas bags like still camera cases. We're talking about large—suitcase-sized—cases made of plywood and fiberglass, designed to take the worst that airline baggage handlers can do to them. Never close the lid of a case unless it's latched. Sure as shooting, if you don't close the latch, someone will come along and pick up the unlatched case, the lid will open, and your expensive lens will go crashing to the ground, instantly becoming expensive, useless trash. Let me repeat: *Always* latch the lid when it's closed; if for some reason you can't latch it, leave it open. That way everyone can see that there's equipment inside, and it's a clear sign to everyone not to pick up the case.

And about (shudder) cleaning lenses: For some reason novices think lenses must be cleaned every time they're put on or removed from the camera. This is way unnecessary. The lenses should only need cleaning on the first day of shooting, if even then. How can this be? Well, the people handling the lenses (primarily the camera assistants) know whether they've left their fingerprints on the glass. Lenses do not have some sort of magic quality that attracts dirt. Unless you've been shooting with dirt bikes, it's unlikely anything will ever get on the glass. So you clean the lens when you start the show. But you check both front and back elements religiously every time you mount the lens. You can't be too careful. Just don't wash the lens every five minutes.

When you do clean the lens, there's one way to do it: my way. Every other way is wrong. Okay, some great assistants may do it otherwise, but I know my way gets the lens clean and protects the coating.

1. Look at the glass. Is it really dirty? Most beginners clean lenses too often.
2. Then, get a large hand blower, like a Hurricane blower. (Don't use the kind with a brush. If your blower has a brush on it, throw the brush out. Brushes *do* attract dirt, and using them on a lens will scratch it.) Do not use Dust-Off. Any kind of compressed air has a propellant, and no matter how careful you are, some of the propellant will end up on the glass. This can only diminish the sharpness of the lens. And that air comes out pretty fast. If there are dust globs, you might drive them into the glass instead of blowing them away. So use a blower to blow away the surface dust.
3. Then look at the glass again. It may not need further cleaning. If it does, have lens tissue and lens cleaning fluid handy. First, bring the lens to your mouth

FIGURE 34.1
Hurricane blower.
Reproduced by permission of FilmTools®.

and blow on the lens. The water vapor from your breath will condense on the lens, giving it a lubricant. Then, using *photographic lens tissue* (anything else will scratch the surface), wad up a piece (to break the fibers, making the paper softer) and gently rub the glass with a circular motion. Then immediately *throw away* the lens tissue. (Never reuse lens tissue; grit gets into it. Don't worry, it's cheap.) So that's it for cleaning.

4. Unless you or some other idiot managed to get grease on the glass from his hands. If that's the case, you will discover that rubbing the glass with the lens tissue has just resulted in smearing it. So now, open the lens cleaning fluid. Take another piece of lens tissue, wad it up, put a drop or two on the tissue (never on the lens; the fluid is mostly alcohol, and it just might seep through the glue holding the glass and get on the inside of the lens), blow on the lens, and wipe with the wet tissue in a circular motion. Throw away the tissue. Then get another piece of tissue, wad it up, blow on the lens, wipe it circularly, and throw away the tissue. This last wipedown makes sure you've gotten all of the residue that might be left by the cleaning fluid. I know, it shouldn't happen, but do you want to take that chance?

Now the lens is clean, and the most you should have to do for the remainder of the show is to use the blower now and then to get rid of stray dust. You probably don't even need to do that, but it's fast, and it makes you look like you're taking really good care of your expensively rented equipment.

Why in the name of all that's holy am I so concerned about treating the lens gently? Well, the lens makes the image—remember that? And contrary to popular myth, glass is fragile and scratches easily. Besides that, remember the coating. Every modern lens (since, say, World War II) has a molecularly thin coating made by vaporizing various metals and allowing them to deposit on the surface of the lens. Because the thickness of this coating is approximately a fraction of the wavelength of visible light, it forms interference with scattered light that otherwise would tend to degrade the sharpness and contrast of the image. The coating is tough, but it is literally only a few molecules thick, so it demands careful treatment.

How is the film threaded through the camera mechanism? We return to opening and closing the camera. As I mentioned before, 35 mm and older 16 mm cameras have the pull-down movement inside the camera. Different cameras thread a little differently from each other (though all Panavision and Mitchell cameras are similar to each other and all Arri cameras are similar to other Arris). Newer 16 mm cameras and the Aaton 35 mm cameras have magazines in which a major part of the threading is inside the magazine.

In this case, half the gate—the pressure plate—is part of the magazine, and the other half—the aperture plate—is part of the camera. The Panaflex 16 has its threading inside the camera, similar to Panavision's 35 mm cameras. Even though there's always a threading diagram printed on the inside of the camera door, the only way to really learn to thread right is to have an experienced cameraperson demonstrate it for you and to practice it over and over.

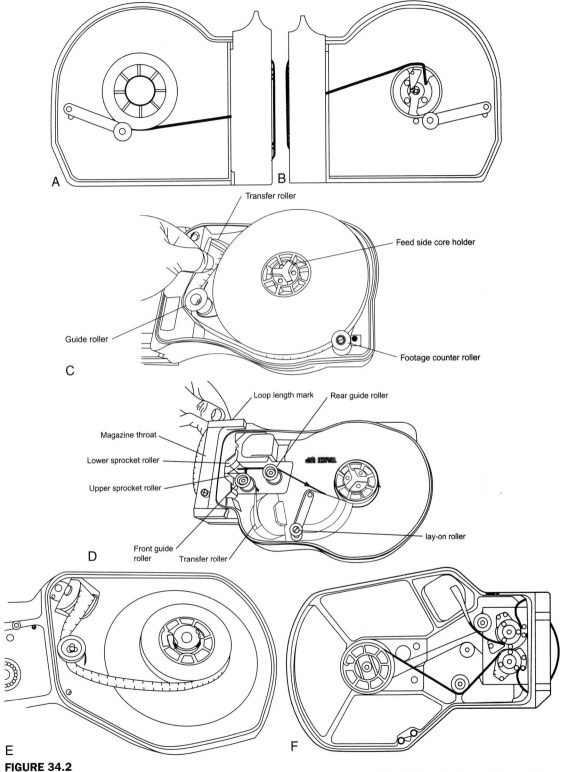

FIGURE 34.2

16 mm camera threading patterns. A) Arriflex 16SR feed. B) Arriflex 16SR takeup. C) Arri 416 feed. D) Arri 416 takeup. E) Aaton 16 feed. F) Aaton 16 takeup. *34.2A: Courtesy Arriflex, 34.2B: Courtesy Arriflex, 34.2C: Courtesy Arriflex, 34.2D: Courtesy Arriflex, 34.2E: Courtesy Aaton, 34.2F: Courtesy Aaton.*

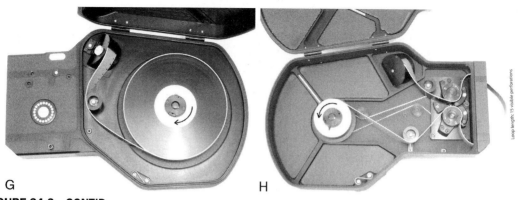

G   H

Loop length: 15 visible perforations

FIGURE 34.2—CONT'D
G) Aaton. H) Aaton. *34.2G: Courtesy Aaton, 34.2EH Courtesy Aaton.*

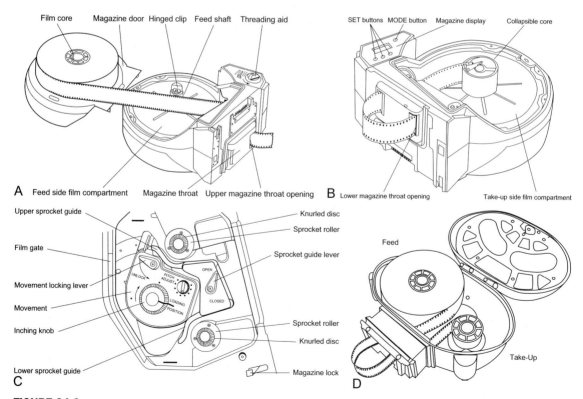

FIGURE 34.3
35 mm camera threading patterns. A) Arri 535B mag supply. B) Arri 535 mag takeup. C) Arricam Lite movement. D) Arri 535B mag.
34.3A: Courtesy Arriflex, 34.3B: Courtesy Arriflex, 34.3C: Courtesy Arriflex, 34.3D: Courtesy Arriflex.

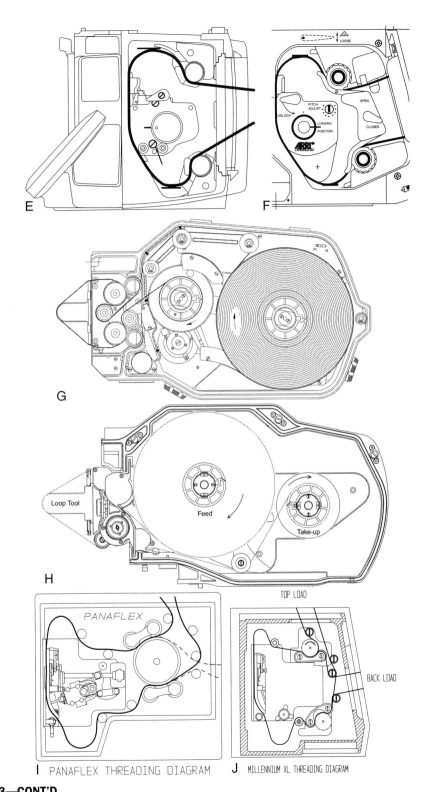

FIGURE 34.3—CONT'D

E) Arricam LT and ST. F) Arriflex 535 threading. G) Aton 35III. H) Aton Penelope. I) Panaflex. J) Panaflex Millenium.

34.3E: Courtesy Arriflex, 34.3F: Courtesy Arriflex, 34.3G: Courtesy Aaton, 34.3H: Courtesy Aaton, 34.3I: Image courtesy of Panavision Inc. 34.3J: Image courtesy of Panavision Inc.

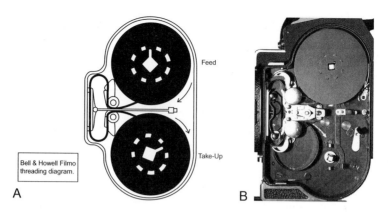

FIGURE 34.4
Older 16 mm camera
threading patterns.
A) Bell & Howell Filmo.
B) Bolex.

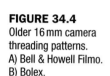

The older 16s, Bolex and Bell and Howell, also thread in the camera. Threading these is simple; the only trick is in forming the loop, which experience quickly teaches. If the loop is too big, you'll hear it (or see it, since you can load in the light). If it's too small, the camera will jam. A few mistakes, and you'll never get the loading wrong again.

What part of loading the film must be done in the dark, and what part can be done in light? Let's get acquainted with the changing bag. The changing bag is light-tight. Your hands enter the bag through light-tight sleeves so you can work inside the bag without being able to see what you're doing. Most beginners are scared to death by the idea of working blind. But you'll be surprised, with practice, how comfortable you will get doing this. Again, take time to learn how to use the bag. The proper way to handle a changing bag is to treat it with respect. Before you use a bag for the first time on a show, make sure you inspect and clean it carefully. First, it should be turned inside out and cleaned. Mostly just shaking out the dust is enough; also inspect it for film chips. Then you have to check the bag for light-tightness. Inspect the zippers; they must close easily and tightly. Any defect in the zipper will let light in. And then go into a darkroom and wait until your eyes have become accustomed to the darkness. Put the bag over your head, walk out into the light, and search for pinholes. Take about five minutes.

FIGURE 34.5
Harrison changing tent.
*Reproduced by permission
of Patti Harrison.*

(With a bag on my head, you ask? Yes. It's a pain in the neck, but once you do it and find leaks, you will understand the need to treat your changing bag with great care.)

Any type of changing bag will work—the larger the better, with lots of room for an open magazine and 1,000-foot roll of film. My strong preference is the Harrison Changing Tent. It was designed by Patty Harrison, a terrific camera assistant, along the lines of some modern camping tents. It has an external structure that keeps the fabric of the bag away from the loader's hands. It's more expensive than a conventional bag, but it's worth it.

Your bag should contain the film, in its can but with the tape unwrapped and thrown away; the magazine—open; and, if necessary, a pair of blunt scissors. The scissors are used to cut the end of the film when you've messed it up by bad loading or to clip ragged tears on short ends. Do not put tape in the bag. It's messy and unnecessary. (See the next topic.)

All film comes in a bag inside the film can and with a short length of tape to hold the end down. Save the bag (for recanning the exposed film) and pull the tape off. Put the tape on the inside of the can. This prevents it from getting into the magazine and jamming the film. It's a good routine because you know that you've removed the tape; it's also in the can for you to tape down the end of the exposed film when you unload it. Once the film is on the spindle and threaded, the magazine door can be closed, and the whole thing can come back out into the light.

The loader should have prepared a piece of camera tape about 6 inches long as an ID and put it on the supply side of the magazine. It looks like this:

LENGTH OF FILM	EMULSION NUMBER	MAGAZINE ID#
PROCESSING INSTRUCTIONS	NAME OF PRODUCTION DATE LOADED & LOADER'S INITIALS	

So it looks like this:

380 ft	5219-376-5848-29	mag #3
Dev Normal	Citizen Kane 2	2/12/14 JDA

The processing instructions go on after the film has been shot and unloaded (develop normal, push one stop, etc.). Note that we don't write, "Develop Normally." We're in show biz, so it's "Develop Normal." Also, by the way, night is "nite." The loader's initials are necessary, like the emulsion number, to identify who loaded the film and to follow up on any problems with the film that was used in this magazine.

Back to changing bags. Remember I told you to go into a darkroom to accommodate your eyes to darkness? If you have a darkroom, why are you using a changing bag? Well, Sparky, you will at some point be out of reach of the darkroom. And then the bag is a lifesaver. At most studios and in the better camera trucks you'll have a darkroom at hand. After using a bag, when you get a darkroom, you'll be in heaven. But before you get all excited, you have to check a darkroom that's new to you for light holes. It's the same thing. Stand in there five minutes (it'll seem like an hour; bring a radio or your iPod to keep you company) to let your eyes dilate. Then cover up every hole or gaping seam with photographic tape. Photographic tape is a special black masking tape that's actually opaque, unlike every other kind of tape.

At some point, you will probably use short ends. (Short ends are leftover unshot portions of rolls of film, carefully wrapped and canned for later use. To save money, producers will often buy short ends from film brokers who purchase studio leftovers. Short ends are perfectly safe to use as long as you have your lab do a snip test to make sure the film has not been fogged.) The downside of using short ends is that it limits the length of takes and it means a lot more time is spent loading and unloading film. This slows down things on the set. It may mean you'll need more magazines so they can be loaded ahead of time so the entire cast and crew doesn't stand around waiting for a reload. So using short ends can end up not saving as much money as you might think.

With many of the cameras you will be using, threading and loop formation will take place inside the magazine. Each camera is slightly different; following the directions in the manufacturer's manual (or in one of the reference books I've mentioned in the bibliography) is easy. Getting the threading right is not that difficult. First off, the film must be loaded in absolute darkness. In all of these magazines, this is fairly simple, involving pushing a length of film through a light trap, a light-tight opening through which the film passes out of the magazine (and through the camera), and back into the magazine. Then the threading in the camera can be done in the light. But it does require practice. And if you want to get a job as a second camera assistant, you will have to be a whiz at loading. On a professional shoot, any incompetence will show up fast on the set. Getting good at this takes a lot of practice.

How much of the camera/magazine must be wrapped with tape (every camera needs this)? We've got the tape out, so let's tape up the magazine. No, you're not doing this to make it light tight. If the magazine or camera leaks light, you're in bigger trouble than tape can fix. But taping serves other purposes. First, it lets you know that the magazine is loaded. No one will be grabbing an empty magazine. Second, if you use a different color of tape for each film stock being used, everyone will be able to tell instantly which film stock is in any particular magazine.

These days, with the profusion of film types, it's likely that you will be using more than one stock—at least, one for interiors and one for exteriors. Some shows will even mix Kodak and Fuji (the major manufacturers of film) on the same show. Each company's products have their own distinct visual quality, and will be chosen based on the look sought for the whole movie or for specific scenes in the movie. There was a time when there was only one emulsion available per manufacturer. Now, with the use of multiple film stocks, the person loading must arbitrarily assign a different color of tape to distinguish individual emulsions.

The third reason for taping the magazine is to prevent the accidental opening of a loaded magazine, not only by people but by ... speeding trains? Back when I was a first camera assistant, I worked on a show whose director was a lunatic. Yes, I know. That could be many shows. Anyway, this director, whom I'll call "Billy," wanted what he wanted when he wanted it, and reality had no effect on his desires. We were shooting in a railroad yard, and Billy wanted a shot of a train approaching from the point of view of a worm lying on the tracks. We carefully measured the height of the underside of the train from the ground, dug a shallow hole for the camera to allow clearance, and placed the camera in the hole with a remote switch attached. The placement was tricky, since the lens had to be high enough to see the train bearing down full frame but low enough not to get hit. We had an Arri 2C, then the current model of the original Arriflex.

Usually you would use a Bell and Howell Eyemo, a windup combat camera, in a crash box—¼ inch of steel plate—for something this risky. But since the shot was Billy's sudden inspiration and not planned beforehand, we didn't have an Eyemo on hand. To make the Arri as compact as possible, I used a 200-foot magazine. It's rarely used on professional productions (400 feet is a more useful length), but I had ordered three 200-foot magazines just in case we needed them. So we looked to be in good shape.

The camera was set up, and we rolled. The train sped over the camera. Everything went fine, except there was something wrong with the timing of the action, and we needed another take. I looked at the camera. About 60 feet of film had rolled. Given the initial 200-foot load, we still had enough film in the magazine for two more takes, with a margin of safety. But Billy wanted the magazine changed.

Why did Billy want that? Well, you always want to be careful with film exposed on a stunt. You never want to endanger the film because it might be the only time the stunt works. And although the situation was fairly well controlled and although the train had cleared the camera with no problems, it made some sense to reload and save the already exposed film from any possible disaster.

So we reloaded, checked the framing and the height of the camera, and shot take two. Fine. But now Billy wanted a third take, and we're down to our third and last 200-foot magazine. I slap it on the camera, and we shoot the train running over the camera again.

Now, remember, we're working in a railyard. There's no way to bring a camera truck into the yard—no road, lots of tracks, and the train company insistent on its rules of safety. So our camera truck had to be parked on a street about half a mile from where we were shooting. After each take, I had sent each 200-foot magazine containing the exposed film back to the truck, a half mile away, to be unloaded and reloaded in the darkroom. But Billy wanted to do yet another take even though take three was fine. Why? Who knows?

Of course, I told Billy we could certainly do take four, but the reloaded magazines were still on their way back from the truck, so it might be a short wait before we could shoot. Well, Billy went completely berserk. "I want that shot! Now! Why don't we have more magazines?" I gently explained about the three used 200-foot magazines, about having to download them, about the half mile of rails, rocks, and clinkers between us and the camera truck.

Billy is still going crazy. So I explained that of course we had more magazines, but they were 400-foot loads, which are, of course, bigger than 200-foot loads and couldn't be used because the train had just barely cleared the 200-footer. "I don't give a <bleep>!" screamed Billy. "Load the damn 400-foot magazine!"

By now I gathered that he didn't much care what could happen to the camera. So I pulled out a 400-footer. Just for the heck of it, before I loaded it on to the camera, I took two-inch gaffer tape—strong, cloth-backed, black—and wrapped the magazine with three layers of it. Then I loaded the camera, stood back, and we rolled.

Well, we got the shot, and Billy was actually happy. We all also got to see the unique spectacle of the train hitting the camera and throwing it 40 feet, where it landed lensdown in the yard. The lens, of course, was shattered—a mere $5,000 or $10,000. The camera was ruined, too (only about $30,000). And the magazine had a two-inch section peeled back as though a giant had used a can opener on an oversized can of beer. But the tape held! Despite the impact from the train, and despite its flight and rough landing, the tape had stretched, completely unbroken. And that's the shot in the film today, and that's why you tape up magazines. Now we get into using parts of the camera that will hold true for both film and digital cameras.

If it's a fully professional camera, how does the front—matte box, iris rods, follow focus mechanism—fit? To a professional camera assistant, the front of the camera is action central. Much of the assistant's job takes place here. "Iris" rods act as the support for almost any device you want to mount on the front of the camera. These rods are usually aluminum or carbon fiber tubes, 15 mm or 19 mm in diameter, that fit in a holder (on the side of the camera or in a mounting plate underneath the camera body). Apparently they're called iris rods because somewhere around 1910 a cameraman (very likely Billy Bitzer) took an iris diaphragm from a view camera and put in on the front of his movie camera so he could *iris in* or *out* of a shot by opening or closing the circle of the iris while the camera was running. Because it came from a camera with a 4 × 5-inch or 8 × 10-inch negative, the still-camera iris mechanism was much larger than that found inside a movie camera lens. This effect of a circle opening or closing on screen is probably familiar to you from silent movies or from seeing more modern movies imitating the effect (as in *Shoot the Piano Player*). Of course, there needed to be a way of attaching the iris diaphragm to the camera. I give you—ta-da—iris rods! And we've called them that ever since.

FIGURE 34.6

Matte box and iris rods.
Reproduced by permission of
O'Connor. www.ocon.com.

Perhaps the most important device that attaches by means of the iris rods is the follow focus mechanism; it's designed to engage the gears on the lens's focus ring. This is how you get the picture in focus. Believe me, an audience will forgive a lot—stupid plot, bad acting—but they will never forgive an out-of-focus picture. If you're assisting, your minimal required job is perfect focus. Any lens support (almost always for zooms) also fits on the rods. Zooms and other large, heavy lenses have to be kept from having their weight strain the connection to the camera, compromising focus and even bending and damaging the lens mount.

Also in front of the lens, attached to the iris rods, is a matte box that functions both as a sunshade and as a filter holder. The name "matte box" also has a story behind it that I'll get to in a second. The shape of the matte box is like that of a four-sided Egyptian pyramid turned on its side with the pointed end cut off. The smaller end fits up around the front of the lens, and the wider end flares out at the very front of the entire camera assembly. All matte boxes have slots to slide filter holders in and out. Professionally, we rarely use filters that screw directly onto lenses. Those filters take forever to change, and you'd have to have dozens of them to fit every possible size lens. Instead, we use a single size filter (usually 4 × 5.565-inch, sometimes 4 × 4-inch or 6 × 6-inch) that slides easily into the slot in the matte box. That way you need only one set of filters because the matte box works with any kind of lens you might use.

FIGURE 34.7
Fluid head.
Reproduced by permission of O'Connor. www.ocon.com.

Usually the matte box has screws on it to attach an extension sunshade, which we always call an eyebrow (for obvious reasons). Not so obvious: Why is this sunshade filter-holding device called a matte box? Well, you must have seen movies with "binocular" or "keyhole" cutouts defining the frame, used to suggest that someone is looking through binoculars or spying through a keyhole. (Have you ever been able to see through a keyhole? Me neither. But what would a melodrama be without keyhole peepers?) Back when everything was done in camera, a rigid piece of board or cardboard with the proper hole cut in it—called a matte—was placed in front of the lens. And to hold it securely in front of the lens and to keep the placement consistent—say, for double exposures—someone devised a box to hold the matte, thus matte box. High-end digital cameras (like the Panavision Genesis) are also equipped with a full complement of accessories, including matte boxes, or (like the Red) they have a large number of aftermarket accessories available.

How does the camera mount to the head and the head to the tripod? Before you do anything with your camera, you'll want to fasten the head you'll be using onto the tripod. The head is what we call the device that allows the camera to pan and tilt, be leveled, and not fall to the ground. There are various types like gear heads, friction heads, and so on. You can learn more about these in Chapter 11.

FIGURE 34.8
Keyways on Mitchell base.
Reproduced by permission of O'Connor. www.ocon.com.

Once fastened to the tripod, the head is there ready to allow the camera to be quickly attached. So you've got three pieces of equipment you always use on a job: cameras, heads, and the tripods or dollies or cranes. If you're on a professional film, you're going to have tripods (and dollies and cranes) with a Mitchell top (Mitchell mount). The name and the design come from the old Mitchell Camera Company, Hollywood's standard from 1920 through 1970. It's a flat top with a concentric cutout to center the head and a keyway to position the head precisely and positively.

FIGURE 34.9
100 mm ball mount on top of Fisher dolly.
Photos courtesy of J.L. Fisher, Inc.

The design is elegant, strong, and mostly foolproof. You may have had experience with ball mounts, which have a section of a sphere on the top of the tripod, into which a head with the matching size spherical section fits.

Most ball mounts are strictly amateur for a good reason: Professional cameras are heavy, and tend to fall over when you're trying to adjust the camera's level. I have rarely seen ball mounts on professional sets. Only once was I in a situation where a ball mount came in handy. I had to mount a camera in a steel-floored bus. All I had was a ball mount tripod and head and some grip chain. The grips and I chained the tripod rigidly to the bus, but the top of the head was all off level, no matter how we lengthened or shortened the legs to level it. With the ball head, it was easy to level the camera.

The head attaches to the top of the tripod (or dolly, crane; I'm not going to say this anymore) and is secured with a bolt, usually $^3/_8$-inch, and a washer. It needs to be tied down tightly. You really don't want the head to be loose and rattle; the operator will reeducate the AC in an unpleasant manner if it does. And you *really* don't want the camera to fall off; the AC can just go on home if that happens. There's usually some kind of quick-release mechanism to mount the camera on the head. Professional cameras come with their own mounting plates, usually a variation of a dovetail. Smaller and amateur cameras rely on the mounting plate that is part of the tripod head. Now hear this: *Do not* leave the quick-release plate on the camera. Leave it on the head. It's part of the head, and every head should keep its parts together. At some point it will be separated from the tripod, and it will be lost forever. Of course, you wouldn't want to do that. So watch out for your assistant, who may be in a hurry and forget to separate the quick-release plate from the camera. Of course, digital cameras use the same heads, tripods, dollies, and so on.

FIGURE 34.10
Tripod and spreaders.
Reproduced by permission of O'Connor. www.ocon.com.

Almost every tripod comes with spreaders. Spreaders exist to keep tripod legs from slipping and splaying and dumping the camera onto the asphalt. Small tripods have them built in; for larger tripods the spreader attaches to the bottom (points) of the sticks. (That's what movie people call tripods. It's also what movie people call the slate—the clapper board. Go figure.) I hate spreaders. They get in the way, tend to pinch fingers, and they're one more thing you have to futz with when you're adjusting the tripod. Here's a hot tip for you: Get a piece of old or scrap carpet about 5 × 5 feet square. Anything is okay as long as it's got a sturdy backing. You can get remnants from carpet stores, or you can cut up an old carpet that someone is throwing out. Cut a small hole in the center of one edge to put a rope through, and you can roll up the carpet, tie it up, and store it and carry it easily. It's Hollywood standard. Not only will you look professional, you'll have a much easier time dealing with the tripod.

You will put the tripod points down on the carpet; they will stick there, and the tripod legs will not slip. It's simple to do; the carpet protects delicate surfaces like wooden floors, and you can easily move the legs to adjust the level of the camera. The camera always needs to be level except when it's tilted for effect. (Any decent head will have a bull's-eye level so you—again, your assistant—can level the camera. For quick looks, I get the camera to a "cowboy level": I put my eye at the height of the top of the tripod and get an approximate level to the horizon. And we all have horizons in our head. Mother Nature is fantastic.) So your magazines are now loaded, and your camera is set up and ready to shoot.

FIGURE 34.11
Bull's-eye surface levels.
Reproduced by permission of Kraft Tool Co.®

CHAPTER 35

Using a Tripod and Head

I want you to use a tripod—*all the time*. And let's get this out of the way: When I speak in general about a tripod, I mean a firm mount for the camera: a tripod, a dolly, a crane. A tripod makes shots better. Still photographers have known this forever. But ever since Brownies were invented, most folks never think of using a tripod; it's so much easier to hand-hold the camera.

When movies were young and cameras were big and heavy, no one would have tried to hand-hold a camera. You couldn't do it without straining something important. And anyway, how would you crank it? So tripods were the way you put a movie camera in place. Home movie cameras—16 mm at first, then 8 mm, super-8, video, and now digital—existed since the 1920s, and whoever shot the birthday party just hand-held the camera; tripods were expensive, bulky, clumsy, and unnecessary. I'll grant you that snapshots or home movies don't need tripods. But almost no one would have thought for years of making a professional movie entirely handheld—until the digital revolution.

Now cameras capable of giving a remarkably good picture—in color, with sound— are available to even the smallest budget. Anyone can make a "feature." And you can hold the camera in your hand all day and not get tired. So, of course, that's what happens. But I beg you: Don't do it. I like to operate the camera handheld, and I'm good at it. I learned from pros, and I learned with a 35 mm Panaflex. It's a lightweight camera at 24 pounds. You don't casually sling it on your shoulder, and you move carefully, respecting the camera's weight and momentum.

There's something else about hand-holding: It really is a special effect. That is, most audiences think of a steady camera as normal; when they see handheld, although they're getting more used to it every day, they see it as abnormal. I've found that even many movie reviewers have begun mentioning the abundant use of handheld when they talk about some movies. They don't like it, and neither do the average citizens I discuss movies with. What I want to do is to preserve hand-holding as one of the tools in the DP's kit. When it's not used indiscriminately, the handheld look says something to an audience: This is something that came up too fast for us to use a tripod, this is news, this is exciting and maybe dangerous, this is real. Any and all of these messages come across. But not when an entire film is handheld. Then the technique reads as sloppiness. And you want the audience to watch the story without getting dizzy and nauseated.

I doubt that you'll encounter wooden tripods. If you do, check them carefully to make sure they're not broken. They're probably old and have been treated badly. The connection of the legs to the mount is usually by a long bolt with nuts at each end. You'll probably find a tightening nut and a lock nut. To tighten the sticks to your specification, take off the lock nut and loosen or tighten the other nut, then replace the locknut. *Tightly.* I like to have it tight enough that the leg won't move just from gravity and loose enough that I can move it with one arm slightly extended.

Very often these nuts are lost or frozen, and the threads of the bolt may be stripped. Carry some spare nuts in your toolbox. And carry some penetrating oil and WD-40 (the industry's universal solvent and lube). To work with the bolt without having it twist without loosening, you'll need a couple of medium-sized crescent wrenches, one for each side of the bolt. I hope you don't run into rusty or mistreated bolts, but you will.

At the bottom of the legs will be points for securing the tripod in soft ground. Some tripods will have a mechanism for retracting the sharp point into the leg so the tripod is standing on rubber tips. Other tripods need you to attach rubber tips—like crutch tips—to the points. Of course, if you use a carpet as I suggest (Chapter 34—when are you going to get the idea?), you will already have taken care of the points doing damage, and you don't need no stinkin' rubber tips.

You'll notice that the lock for extending the legs is different on the wooden and the Ronford sticks. The Ronford style is simple and positive. I've never seen one go bad, but the old style for the wooden sticks often has issues.

FIGURE 35.1
Wooden tripod locks.
Reproduced by permission of www.VisualProducts.com.

You'll notice two kinds, one with a single wheel and one with a double. The wheels surround nuts, and they are there to make it possible to grip them. On either kind, down (from the outside) is tighten, and up is loosen. Don't forget this. You can actually tighten going the wrong way, but at some point the tripod will collapse. The locks work by traveling along a threaded shaft (like a bolt without a head) to pull together the two wooden parts of each shaft of each leg. The metal collars that hold the lock to the wood have two or three screws. They're going to be loose—tighten them—or lost—carry an assortment. The locks will need lubrication—again, WD-40. Keep the WD-40 off the wood, and don't use anything else slippery (like silicone spray) on any legs. You'll just be setting yourself up to drop them. You may have to clean off the legs; as they get dirty, they tend to stick. Just use some mild household cleaner so you get the junk off without making the legs slippery.

When you work with a hi-hat, you'll place it so you've got the approximate shot. Then the grips, standing by in readiness, will have a furniture blanket for you to sit on, wedges to level the hi-hat platform, and sandbags to weigh it down. When that's taken care of, you'll have to reframe the shot, but it will be more comfortable.

As I said back in Chapter 11, your big choice is between a geared head and a fluid head. And, no kidding, a geared head is weird at first. I remember my first day on a set thinking, "How in the world am I ever going to learn this?" and praying that maybe I could get by with a fluid head. After a few years of assisting and of necessity working with the gears—just to be able to see the lens or to open the door for loading—the head became less alien and at least a part of my world. And I practiced with it every free moment, following people—grips, electricians, prop people —around the set. When I finally got the chance to operate, I was still petrified with fear and covered with sweat. But I kind of knew what I was doing, and with practice it slowly came to me. Of course, for the first year, before every shot, I would silently move my hands and chant the direction I was moving so I knew what was left/right and what was up/down. But I could do the work, and eventually one day it all clicked.

Once you're feeling comfortable with the wheels, you'll probably figure out your own way of working with the head. I like to work in as low a gear as possible (modern heads have three gears; the old Worrall head, the prototype, had two) for the control it gives me.

It's important to have the camera balanced on the head so it doesn't want to tilt down or up on its own. This is easy to do by sliding the camera back and forth on the sliding base plate. It's also the assistant's work. I hope you find an assistant who'll do this, but don't depend on it.

I've adapted the spinning pan (a whip pan done by spinning the pan wheel) from seeing other operators use it. What I'll do, on a fast move, is to start panning in gear, then throw the pan wheel forward and pull the camera with the tilt handle. I can slow down the pan gradually by resting the palm of my left hand on the wheel. This way I can achieve a very fast pan without having to put my head in a higher gear.

Most operators hold the handles on the wheels between the thumb and forefinger. Everyone's first instinct is to grab the handles like the handlebars of a bike. Don't. It's awkward to work, and you have too little finesse. Holding with the thumb and forefinger allows you to use your wrist and elbow instead of just your elbow (with the bike grip). I'll tell you how I work the wheels. A while ago, I hurt my thumb, and I couldn't use it at all. I'd seen other operators put the handle between the first two fingers, so I tried that out of desperation. To my surprise, it worked well almost instantly. I find that I prefer that grip now, and I have even more control with it.

All fluid heads have adjustments to the drag—the resistance—on the pan and tilt. It's again a matter of individual preference. Most heads have a method of setting the counterbalance weight. This will neutralize the weight of the camera; you won't have to fight a heavy spring in the head that gives it its resistance to the camera's weight. The inertial weight of the camera is essentially eliminated so you don't have to fight it when operating.

You (that is, your assistant) will want to adjust the counterbalance so the camera doesn't tend to spring back to the neutral position when tilted down and doesn't tend to tilt down too easily on its own. Which brings up an important law: Always lock off the tilt of the camera when you're not operating. And the corollary: No operator ever locks off the tilt. So the assistant has to be alert and always ready to lock the tilt when the operator turns off the camera. This is absolutely true. As an assistant, I was scrupulous about locking the tilt. I never expected my operators to lock it, and I was rarely disappointed. And the first day I moved up and worked as an operator, I turned off the camera at "Cut!" and walked away without tightening the tilt lock. It's apparently a built-in response.

CHAPTER 36
The Dolly Grip

The dolly grip is a kind of strange position. Originally the job was a sort of simple, physical one: Take care of this big, heavy piece of equipment (the dolly, which used to be huge) and push it if necessary from one position to another during the take. That meant pushing it along tracks, so the only finesse required was a sensitivity to the start moment, the ending, and the speed of the dolly. With the invention of the crab dolly, the dolly grip could move on any smooth surface without track. Quickly directors developed complex shots that involved two or three or more distinct moves, usually in different directions. Now the dolly grip had to have cues for every start, had to nuance (we say "feather") her starts and stops, had to adjust her speed to the speed of the actors, had to be ready to change the height of the hydraulic arm on the dolly, and had to remember several moves and start and stop points that might be invisible from where she's working. All this while pushing around a 400- to 1,000-pound wheeled cart with a 50-pound camera and a 200-pound operator on it.

I think it's a demanding job, and I know that the dolly grip is as much a camera operator as the camera operator. I'd like to see the dolly grip put officially within the camera department; this would mean more money and more respect (that's sad but true), and formally acknowledge what is a de facto truth now.

CHAPTER 37

Laboratory and Postproduction Processes

303

"The relationship between a cinematographer and the laboratory processing his or her film can mean the difference between the revelation of seeing exactly the images conceived upon exposing the film or a defensive frustrating time spent constantly seeking to achieve the right look."

—**Rob Hummel,** *ASC Handbook*

Today, "lab" (by which I mean all motion picture postproduction processes) may be seen to play a bigger part in cinematography than in the past. I offer this quote from the *ASC Handbook* because, although it dates from the days of purely photochemical procedures, the lab has always been a vital element of cinematography.

Ansel Adams conceived of the negative as sheet music or a musical score, with the print being the performance. This is a valuable way to look at our work as cinematographers. Whether the photography yields an actual negative or a digital record, it is only the first step in cinematography. The performance is in post, especially in timing the answer print. It is vital to understand the entire process. It's all too easy to imagine that our work is done when principal photography is finished. Whether it's professional feature work or the first little digital films, the DP is responsible for—and entitled to control of—the final look.

Let's start with the old standard: film processing. When you're shooting with film, you need to know how to deal with the lab. Let's remind ourselves that we are working with a negative/positive process; the exposed, unprocessed film you send to the lab will become the negative, and then there will be either a film print made (dailies, which become workprint) or a telecine version on tape.

The camera negative is a low-contrast, high-speed emulsion with wide latitude (able to register a contrast range from very dark to very bright). Today's negatives can register a useful range of around 13 stops, far more than even 15 years ago, and far more than most digital processes. The only digital cameras with a range this large are the high-end professional cameras such as the Panavision Genesis or the Arri Alexa. In choosing between film and digital, consider that on a limited budget you can afford to purchase fully professional film if you have 16 mm cameras available, but you probably cannot afford to rent prohibitively expensive professional digital cameras. For that, and other reasons, film will still be around for a while.

So here we are. We have an exposed roll of film, we turn it into the lab, the lab develops it, and the processed negative is returned to us. Are we done? Well, there're a few more steps to consider.

Remember, we've got a negative, and we want to look at a positive. The lab will take the negative, sandwich it with print stock, and run it through a machine. This machine, the printer, sends light through the negative, thus exposing the print film, giving us another latent image. Since it's a neg/pos process, the image on the print film is the reverse in tones and complementary in color to the camera negative. *Voilà!* We have a positive we can look at. And let me remind you that the print stock is in a sense the opposite of camera negative in all respects: It is fine grain, low speed, high contrast, and high saturation.

Here's why: It needs to be fine grain so there is little or no added grain, which would appear as noise on the print. It is high contrast and high saturation in order to register as much of the negative's contrast range as possible and to return the image to the contrast of the original. It is low speed because a small, controlled amount of light can expose it. Thankfully, these characteristics tend to reinforce each other, and print film can be made to give a beautiful picture fairly easily.

Of course, all of this work is done in the dark, on machines that are carefully set up to give precise exposure times and precise registration of negative and positive films. Interestingly, these days, all color films, no matter who makes them (and almost all professional work is done in color), are processed with chemicals, at temperatures and times carefully regulated, specified by Eastman Kodak as ECN2 processing.

No matter what medium the budding cinematographer will use when he or she becomes a professional, he or she needs to follow certain procedures. Probably the most important is communication with the lab. It's vital to be able to talk to the person handling your precious original material to make sure nothing is damaged and to retain the look you've worked so hard to achieve. The cinematographer needs to have a contact person at the lab to inform her of the status of the film and to keep track of any damage in shooting (scratches, torn film) or in processing (bad chemicals, lost film). Equally important is a good relationship with the timer or colorist. This is the person who will determine how the daily prints will look; he can save you or destroy your career. No producer or director knows the technical work that goes into cinematography. They just want it to look good. So to preserve the integrity of your vision, it behooves you as DP to talk with the timer, to establish guidelines for printing, and to set up a reliable system of communication.

In both photochemical and electronic printing, the light passing through the negative is adjusted, varying intensity and color balance. Traditionally, the printer has three lights (red, green, and blue) or a single light with color controlled by filters. The timer sets up these lights for each scene based on his estimation of what the DP wants (hence, the paramount importance of communication). In a conventional lab, the lights have 50 points, with 0 the lowest intensity and 50 the brightest, so 25 is theoretically the middle, and it would indicate a perfectly exposed negative. In practice, most DPs shoot for a printer light around 30 to 35. That is, each light (R, G, B) should fall in that range. Unfortunately, there is as yet no agreed upon printer exposure scale for telecine, although some industry organizations are working on it.

First off, the DP needs to know how the film responds. Kodak and Fuji give very accurate speeds for their negatives, and their figures should be a starting point. But every lab is different (although good ones are consistent and identical in their processing), primarily in their printing. Every timer/colorist is different. Every DP meters and lights differently. So there is a combination of factors. In dealing with the lab, the DP should talk with the timer: What does the timer consider normal, and what kind of chart does the timer like as a reference? (See Chapter 26.)

For this purpose use some sort of gray card or color chart, exposed in the light that the scene will be shot in. The timer will use this "test" as a neutral reference to set timing lights. Your tests will tell you whether you like the standard ISO rating or want to modify it. Then you know how the lab and your timer work, and you can use your chart as a reference for every scene you shoot.

Exposed film must be prepped for the lab. There will be a camera report, and it must be neat, accurate, and complete. The camera assistant fills out the report and must check with the DP to make sure instructions are accurate. The most important points are length of the film, type of processing (normal, push or pull), and indications of the look. (Is it a night scene? Print for darkness, low-key. Is it a sunset scene? Retain the orange look.)

The film will be in a black bag, inside a light-tight can, sealed with camera tape. Every can, and the report, must have some identification. Suppose the report gets lost? Well, you're screwed. But if you've remembered to put an ID tape on the can after you download it, you will probably be saved. (See Chapter 34.) The tape needs to have the emulsion number, the name of the film, the date exposed, basic lab directions (develop normal or push), and the name of the production company. Any lab, seeing a can without a report, will look for that tape. Since it's the same information that's on the ID tape on the camera magazine, most assistants just pull the tape off the mag and slap it on the can.

When working with videotape or digitally, there will be no processing, and the medium is not affected by visible light. Nonetheless, every tape, card, or drive must have a report listing the production, DP and director, and all the shots made, with an indication of which are "print" takes (the director's preferences). It is just as important with digital as it is with film to include a gray card/color chart at the head of every scene. At some point there will be color correction, and besides it's good to have a reference (checked on the on-set monitor) to judge the accuracy of your playback or projection system. Monitors and projectors for digital and video tend to be wildly inaccurate outside of a lab, and for self-protection alone, the DP needs to have an unimpeachable reference.

A lot of what we're talking about is conventional film processing and printing for film dailies. These days, by far the majority of movies have electronic dailies. These are produced by telecine, confusingly both the name of the process and the machine used in the process. The telecine process produces an electronic print of the negative, basically by shining light through the negative on to an electronic sensor, which then acts as a digital camera does to create a digital record. Most of your work, of course, will be transferred rather than printed. The price for printing and for transfer is about the same, but a telecine transfer gives the filmmaker a digital "workprint" that can be easily edited through computer techniques. And in editing, digital has totally replaced traditional film editing (with the exception of a very few holdouts, like Stephen Spielberg).

Television in the United States has 30 frames per second, and film runs at 24 frames per second. In the telecine process, this disparity is resolved by taking advantage of TV's characteristic that each frame is made up of two fields. The electron tube scans the picture in lines, in the NTSC system, 525 lines per frame. Half of the picture is scanned for each frame, first odd lines and then even (1, 3, 5, . . . 525, and 2, 4, 6, etc.) so that every four frames of film are transferred to five frames of video, as shown in Figure 37.1.

Of course, there will be some strange things happening in the video frames that consist of fields from two different film frames. Most of the time there is no problem. However, tight patterns can move slightly between film frames, and cause a moiré pattern on the screen. To avoid this artifact, the DP must work with the wardrobe department to avoid, say, narrow stripes. Thank goodness, the era of 30 interlaced frames is coming to an end as the world's TV converts to digital broadcasting, high-definition broadcasting, and progressive scan screens. And even now, all high-end work is done with progressive scan (1 frame = 1 field) so video artifacts are eliminated.

FIGURE 37.1
3:2 pull down.
Reproduced by permission of www.VisualProducts.com.

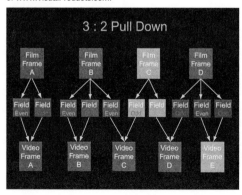

This brings us to the current cutting edge of electronic finishing. Many films (approaching most) have their postproduction done electronically, with a digital intermediate (DI). With a DI the processed negative is scanned—progressively—into digital files at 24 frames per second. The scanning time is much slower than with telecine; this allows much more information to be gathered and stored electronically than in a standard telecine transfer. The resulting digital files can be manipulated easily. Color timing and effects can be integrated into the movie. Unlike the photochemical process, there is little or no loss in quality, since digital files can be duplicated indefinitely. When the movie is finished, the lab will make elements for distribution. These elements can be negatives from which conventional release prints are made or digital records for digital projection. Any other digital form (DVD, etc.) can be made from the original file. It is also easy to make protection masters on film. The negative is printed through precise (color separation) filters to make red, green, and blue masters on black-and-white film. Although the digital file is theoretically perfect and could be stored indefinitely, film is still the preferred archival material. No digital medium (tape, hard drive, solid-state memory) has demonstrated its lifetime beyond a decade or two. And there will always be the problem of new electronic coding and media. Try to find a machine that can run two-inch tape today, which was the broadcast standard only 30 years ago. The machines have mostly been scrapped, and the oxide is continually separating from the tape. But film processed to archival standards and stored in climate-controlled vaults has been shown to have at least a 100-year life, maybe 200 years.

Some of these matters may seem way beyond your immediate concerns, but you will run into these issues as you advance in your career. You need to become familiar with all the issues so you can make intelligent decisions and give good advice to producers about the original shooting medium and the safeguarding of their movie against deterioration.

APPENDIX 1
Cheat Sheets

INTRODUCTION • NONFILM CAMERA CHECKLISTS AND CHEAT SHEETS

In this section you will find a checklist/cheat sheet for a few nonfilm cameras. I've used these cameras a lot. You may well have other cameras; these cameras are around ten years old or more and are completely out of date. I would love to give you cheat sheets for new cameras, but digital cameras come out so often that I would be behind the times as soon as I wrote something.

So use these as guides to make your own cheat sheet. Go through the manual for your camera, and use the most common settings with the least processing of the picture data. You can manipulate the settings and play around with the picture during editing and postproduction. Minimal processing in the camera will allow you the most options later. Also, make sure settings that affect your editing program (like drop frame or nondrop frame) are correct. Check with your editing program.

SIMPLE STEPS FOR OPERATING A VIDEO CAMERA

Here are things you have to know.

THE LOCATION OF THE "ON" SWITCH

Re: STANDBY There will be a button, usually on the back of the camera. There's a switch that goes one way to standby or cam, and in the other direction to VCR or playback (usually you put the camera on standby and then hit a little red button to start filming; the other way lets you look at your work).

OPENING THE LCD SCREEN

It's probably a matter of flipping it out from the body. Half the time you'll be using it as a viewfinder. See if you can use the viewfinder and the LCD at the same time or if one disables the other. Find the diopter correction—for your eyes—on the viewfinder. It's usually a ring or a lever near the end of the eyepiece.

WHERE IS THE "MENU" BUTTON?

You are going to use this to set up your camera so it does what you want. As I said, this is important. If it's not obvious, look in the index of the manual, and look for a section on parts of the camera—a drawing that will show you where every button, slide, and switch is. Then, look for the section (probably under "menu") that will instruct you how to set up the camera using the menu. We'll go through the most important parts of the menu and suggest the best settings.

And now, here are some things you should do and should *not* do.

MANUAL VERSUS AUTO

You have to be concerned with autofocus and autoexposure. Auto will work, but it's a giveaway to the audience that you're treating this like a snapshot camera. Autofocus will suddenly shift focus to whatever is big or prominent in the frame. You probably don't want this, especially if it's an extra just walking past to give you a little bit of foreground composition. Autoexposure is even worse; if someone in a white shirt walks into frame, the picture suddenly darkens and vice versa. This is ugly and looks amateurish.

ZOOM IN AND OUT

Is it working? Is there more than one location for the control (it's often on the handle and on the top of the camera). How fast and how slow can you go? Can you make a gentle start and stop, or—like most prosumer camcorders—does it have a very hard start and stop? You won't have any control over the zoom speed or the start and stop in most prosumer cameras, so let's here and now decide to use the zoom sparingly.

EXPOSURE

Well, right now you're going to use the autoexposure feature. I know I said not to, but here's how: Once you're ready to shoot, put the camera on autoexposure. It'll give you what the camera thinks is the best exposure for the shot. Most of the cameras have a really good metering system, so you can trust it for a good average exposure. Then turn off the autoexposure function. The stop it has set will stay on the camera. You'll have a good exposure for your shot, and you won't have the exposure fluctuating every time someone in a bright or dark shirt walks by.

And there's a setting for GAIN, which is boosting or lowering the exposure sensitivity. Set it at 0db! Any other setting degrades your picture. Boosting gain lets you shoot in very low light but at the expense of a great deal of video noise, what looks like a coarse pattern over the picture. Experiment. Don't just take my word for these things. I am trying to save you some trouble, but if you want to play around, do it. This is supposed to be fun, right?

WHITE BALANCE: AUTO LOCK OFF

As you have seen—most auto controls are off.

- Color temp (look at Chapter 33).
- Presets: You will usually use these for white balance—primarily settings for sun or for tungsten light).
- Zebra: Set it at 100% for only the brightest thing in the picture.

Some cameras will allow you to have two zebra settings. If you have only one, it's usually most useful to set it to 100% so you don't have clipped areas in your frame. "Clipped" means overexposed beyond the ability of the sensor to handle it. Here's a major place where digital and film differ. Film can handle overexposure. True, there's a point at which any film will be so overexposed that there's no detail and the picture just has blank white areas. But since film responds in a nonlinear way, there is almost always some detail in the overexposed areas; there's no such thing as totally blank white. But digital responds in a strict linear way. When you overexpose, the sensor cannot make sense of it, and the result is an absence of signal on the record (the tape, memory stick, whatever). Instead of a bright white place (film), it looks like a hole in the screen. It's very unattractive, and tends to throw the audience out of the picture. Now if I have a camera with multiple settings for the zebra, I set one at 100% and the other where I want skin tones to expose. Caucasian skintones are one stop above middle gray. So you could set your skintone zebra at 50%, which is middle gray, or you could set it at 60%. This will make sure you have a well-exposed picture, and will help to keep your highlights from clipping.

YOUR CAMERA CAN'T HANDLE TAKING A PICTURE INSIDE AND OUTSIDE SIMULTANEOUSLY

Almost no picture-taking medium can; the difference in light level is too great. You can try it if you want to see for yourself. But plan your filming so a shot is *either* inside or outside.

KEEP RECORDS

When you're in the throes of production, nothing seems less important than records. "C'mon, we're making a movie here! We're losing the light! Write that stuff later!" Well, no. You have to know what you have and where it is for editing. When you shoot film, you have to give information to the lab so they process and print your film correctly. On the most basic level, you have to know which roll is exposed and which is fresh; you don't want to ruin part of your masterpiece by shooting over it. Through your career, as you become more professional, you will find that accurate records are vitally important. After a while, you'll have people to keep records for you. But right now, it's all about *you*. Develop good habits now; they'll pay off in future jobs, and you'll always know at a glance if your crew is doing things right. You might get away with sloppiness now, but you'll be slapped down hard in the real world, and you'll lose jobs if you aren't scrupulous about your records.

- Label your tapes: date, #, your name, project.
- Keep script notes: shot #, # of takes, good takes, and a short description.

SLATE

Always use one and keep it simple: project, director, DP, scene, take, date.

MEDIA

You'll be buying tape for the films. That seems contradictory, but let's not get into any simpleminded semantics. You're making movies—films, no matter what the medium. I suggest a fairly high-end tape, since you'll be using it repeatedly for editing and because I don't want any camera damage or tape dropouts.

If your camera uses cards, buy the best you can find. It will never pay to skimp on recording the results of all your hard work.

PD 100 CHEAT SHEET

THE NIGHT BEFORE
Charge the batteries.
Prestripe tapes.

ON THE SET
Set up tripod.
Put camera on tripod.
Turn it on.
Set diopter.
Open LCD screen.
Find menu button.
Find menu wheel.
Push menu button.
Set or check menus.
Load tape.

MENU SETTINGS
MANUAL SET
    Auto shutter: Off
    Progressive scan: Off

CAMERA SET
    Digital zoom: Off
    16:9 wide: Off
    Steady shot: On
    AE shift: Skip
    Gain shift: 0dB
    Frame rec: Off
    Int. rec: Off

SKIP VTR SET

LCD/VF SET
    LCD F.L.: Brt norm
    LCD color: Center bar
    Viewfinder B.L.: Normal

SKIP MEMORY SET

SKIP CM SET

TAPE SET
   Audio mode: FS48k
   Mic level: Manual
   Remain: Auto
   Data code: ? (This doesn't concern us now.) Date/cam or date
   Time code: NDF

SETUP MENU
   Clock set: Local time
   Ltr size: Normal

OTHERS
   World time: Skip
   Beep: Off
Commander: Off
Display: LCD
   Rec lamp on/off, your choice
   Color bars: Record only at head of roll
   DV editing: Do not select

EXIT

Exposure button:
   Hit wheel once to access Manual.
   Set exposure.
   Hit again for Auto.

Use manual focus: Press focus button.
   Set focus manually with lens ring.

When finished shooting, make sure the camera is off (power switch set to OFF, not to VCR).

DCR-TRV15/17 CHECKLIST/CHEAT SHEET

THE NIGHT BEFORE THE SHOOT

Charge the batteries!

ON THE SET

Set up tripod.
Put camera on tripod.
Turn it on.
Set diopter on viewfinder.
Open LCD screen.
Find menu button (bottom left).
Find menu wheel.
Push menu button.
Set or check menus.
Load tape.

MENU SETTINGS

MANUAL SET
    Program AE:
    P effect: Off
    D effect: Off
    Wht bal: Auto
    Auto shutter: Off

CAMERA SET
    Self-timer: Off
    Digital zoom: Off
    16:9 wide: Off
    Steady shot: On
    NS light: On
    Frame rec: Off
    Int. rec: Off

SKIP VTR SET

LCD/VF SET
    LCD bright middle (center bar)
    LCD color: Center bar
    Viewfinder B.L.: Bright normal

SKIP CM SET

TAPE SET
    Rec mode: SP
    Audio mode: 16 bit
    Remain: Auto

SETUP MENU
    Clock set: Local time
    Auto TV: Off
    TV input: Video
    Ltr size: Normal
    Demo mode: Off

OTHERS
    World time: Skip
    Beep: Off
    Commander: Off
    Display: LCD
    Rec lamp: On/off, your choice

EXIT
On lens right: Nightshot: Off
Exposure button:
    Hit wheel once to access Manual.
    Set exposure.
    Hit again for Auto.
Use Manual focus: Press Focus button.
    Set focus manually with lens ring.

When finished shooting, make sure the camera is off (power switch set to OFF, not to VCR).

PREPARATION FOR IN-CAMERA-EDITED SHOOTS

Let's talk about prep. I'm a DP; I spent all of my professional career in the camera department. I know camera prep, but I know grip/electric and sound only by observation and common sense. Probably at one point or another in your career, you will do everything, so you'll want to know the condition of all your equipment.

Camera prep at this stage is pretty much picking up a video camera and turning it on. Did it work? We're good to go! But let's begin a system that will pay off now and every time you decide to use a camera.

First, turn it on. Does it work? If not, check for the battery, replace the battery, or get another camera. Look through the viewfinder. Is it bright? Can you focus and zoom? Can you bring up the menu? (Every camera is a little different, so check out the manual.) Do you have a carrying case? A spare battery? A battery charger? You want some kind of carrying case. It protects the camera, makes traveling more convenient, and gives you a place to store some small tools there's no other place for.

Always have at least two batteries. Something could go wrong. If you don't have multiple batteries, what goes wrong will be the battery. And remember the most important rule: *Charge every battery every night*. The assistant (again, on a professional shoot, it's always the responsibility of the camera assistants) who forgets to do this is an idiot. He prevents shooting, he inconveniences a lot of people, and very soon he finds himself trying to get a job selling shoes. Some people may have had a bad experience with rechargeable batteries: Some have a "memory," and after many partial rechargings, they'll take only a partial charge. This is likely in NiCd batteries and possible in lithium batteries. There are a million articles online that explain this effect better and at greater length than I can. But still, the worst thing is to have an uncharged battery. I have maybe once or twice had a problem with a battery that had a "memory" and therefore thought it had a full charge when it was only partially charged. But I have had several experiences of an assistant showing up with uncharged batteries.

It's okay to charge a battery even if it's had slight or no use. Actually, it's always a good idea. You want to arrive on the set with at least two fully charged batteries. Any other procedure risks disaster.

Prepping professional film cameras, a lengthy job with exacting standards, is discussed in Chapter 34. Right now, it's enough to make sure that you check every piece of your equipment for completeness and working condition before every job.

At last we're ready to do some filming! (Okay, here it's taping, but let's pretend.) I'm going to send you out into the big, wide world to shoot. Gather some friends to "act" for you, and have fun.

TIPS FOR IN-CAMERA-EDITED SHOOTS

Before you start, visualize your movie. You're going to try to shoot exactly what you've pictured in your mind. You may find a simple storyboard or a shot list helpful. Don't get bogged down by it. Preplanning is always important and always good, but it's not the whole point.

At one time I was shooting low-budget karaoke music videos. Everything had to be done as simply and cheaply as possible in the least amount of time. At the same time, the result was expected to be very dynamic, very visual and entertaining. Sure.

The scenario for one particular video had two attractive young women in a flashy convertible pulling up to an isolated desert gas station. They beguile the gas station attendant in a sexually provocative manner, then pull a lesbian liplock, and speed off without paying for the gas, leaving the poor fellow feeling cheated out of more than just money. This was all with no dialogue, of course. Remember, this was for karaoke.

All well and good, but the preceding scenario was all I'd been told about the piece right up to the morning of the shoot. Fortunately, the gas station set was about a two-hour drive away, so on the drive to the location the director and I were able to work up a "shot list." A shot list is a plan for the day's work. The scene is broken down into shots, and the shots are arranged in an order that's most efficient to shoot. The director and DP work up the shot list, and the AD usually is responsible for making sure we shoot everything on the list in a timely manner.

I can't say whether the video would have been better if we had spent more time planning it and drawing storyboards (the client was pretty happy with it). But here are two things to consider: We *did* have a plan, even though we worked it out the morning of the shoot, *and* we couldn't have shot it as fast if we hadn't by then had a lot of experience making movies—experience we could draw on for ideas and know-how. To ensure the best results with your exercise, let me suggest a few concepts for in-camera shoots that you might not have thought about.

1. Control the screen direction: Keep the action moving either left to right or right to left, unless you want an effect of disorientation.
2. Follow eyelines: If your actor looks toward something just before you cut, and you cut to the thing at which he is looking, use *his* point of view.

3. **Change subject image size moderately:** When you cut during continuous action (for example, a person starting to sit down in a chair), move either closer or further away—enough so that the person changes size in the frame but not so far that it's a jolt.

4. **Change your angle:** When you cut during action, move your camera location enough so the change is noticeable.

5. **Entrances:** Try to avoid a long stall at the head of a shot, especially where we see the actor waiting for you to call "Action!"

TIPS ON SHOOTING WHEN SCOUTING LOCATIONS

1. Take stills. If you like the place, you want to have something you can sit down and discuss.
2. You're also going to use videotape. Okay. Think!
3. Don't pan quickly. If you pan, let the shot rest on something, then pan to the next pertinent thing, and so on. Pan slowly to avoid strobing.
4. Occasional close-ups are interesting, but mostly we're looking for wide shots.
5. Use a tripod. Get a small, lightweight tripod.
6. Okay, I'll be honest: Tripods are a pain in the ass. So use a monopod. It's a great tool to have, and you can get them fairly cheaply. They're small, light, don't have a head (just a bolt to attach to the camera), you can carry them like an umbrella, you can use them as a walking stick or a weapon, and mainly they will allow you to get shots that are generally not shaky.
7. Again, think. Don't shoot too much—although too much is better than too little. *Do* reprise areas; take us back to the first areas so we have our memories refreshed.
8. Give us a sense of the geographical situation—other buildings, streets, the general area.
9. Pay attention to windows and others sources of daylight; existing lighting (fluorescent, incandescent, mercury vapor, sodium, neon, other); and practical lights (e.g., desk lamps; size, possibility of moving, possibility of relamping).
10. Make sure you know the compass directions for each location. Note them as metadata on stills if you can; make a sound note on video.
11. We need to know parking areas and what floor any location is on, and when you get serious about the location, take a picture of the circuit breaker/fuse box for the building, and note its location.
12. Make notes of any special problems or circumstances you notice.

APPENDIX 2
Checklists

DP LOCATION CHECKLIST

1. ☐ Take location stills (see Cheat Sheet 1.7).
2. ☐ Note all sources of daylight.
3. ☐ Make note of permanent existing lighting.
4. ☐ Note all practical lights and the feasibility of adding practicals.
5. ☐ Take note of the number and size (in amps) of circuits.
6. ☐ Note the location of the breaker box (or, if you're really unlucky, the fuse box).
7. ☐ On what floor of the building is your location situated? If it's not the ground floor, get a new location.
8. ☐ Is the floor smooth and level?
9. ☐ Measure the dimensions (in square feet, length and width) of the interior space and exterior spaces if necessary.
10. ☐ How long you would have to make a cable run from a generator?
11. ☐ Where can you put the generator to shield the sound?
12. ☐ How close to the site can you park equipment trucks?
13. ☐ Note the availability and safety of parking for the cast and crew.
14. ☐ Note the availability of bathroom facilities for the cast and crew.
15. ☐ Note how far the cast and crew will have to travel to get to the location.
16. ☐ Determine the compass orientation of the exterior of the structure.
17. ☐ Determine the compass point location of windows on the interior for exterior lighting sources.
18. ☐ Note any changes to the set you will need the Art Department to take care of.
19. ☐ Determine the need for any permits.
20. ☐ Take note of any other special problems or circumstances.

CHECKLIST FOR MOVIE ON FILM

Item	Good	Bad	Jerky/smooth	Consistent	Speed
Assisting					
Focus					
Zoom					
Lighting					
Exposure					
Contrast					
Shadows					
Operating					
Head room					
Lead room					
Pans/tilts					
Composition					
Off set					
Dolly					
Dolly start					
Stop					
Art					
Emotion					
Coverage					
Actor's face					

CAMERA ASSISTANT CHECKLISTS

The camera assistants have sole responsibility for everything that happens with the camera, the lenses, the film stock, and the magazines. They are responsible for the overall care and operation of all camera equipment during production.

RESPONSIBILITIES

The *first assistant*:

- Orders, tests, and preps all camera equipment and lenses
- Directs the organization of all camera equipment on the camera truck and on the set
- Builds and mounts the camera
- Places the camera on the set
- Maintains and mounts the lenses
- Focuses
- Zooms
- Checks and cleans the film gate
- Supervises the second assistant

The first assistant has to be by the camera at all times and does not help with any other functions such as lighting. The first must always have tape, the ASC manual, measuring tape, and a small flashlight close at hand, which is to say that the ditty box is always by you and the camera. (See Elkins, *The Camera Assistant's Manual.* This is the best, most complete book on working as an assistant. Besides data on every camera in common use, there are lists of tools, expendable supplies, and accessories. There are forms for inventory, camera reports, and more. It's an invaluable asset for every assistant.)

The *second assistant*:

- Inventories film stock
- Loads and unloads magazines
- Hands the magazine to the first
- Lays marks
- Bangs slate
- Prepares camera and lab reports
- Transports camera equipment
- Runs for anything the first needs
- Manages all other paperwork

The second assistant must be in constant communication with the first assistant and be ready to instantly carry out any orders given by the DP, the operator, and the first. He runs for equipment or errands as directed by the first, the DP, or the operator.

The key to being a good assistant is always remaining calm and always having everything you need right beside you. Also, remember the following before every take, and you will stay out of trouble. Let your mantra be **B-FLAT**:

> B = Battery
> F = Focus
> L = Level (always level the camera)
> A = Aperture (f-stop)
> T = Tachometer (speed of camera)

CAMERA EQUIPMENT INVENTORY

Refer to Elkins, *The Camera Assistant's Manual.*

CAMERA AND LENS TESTS

Refer to Chapter 8: Selecting a Camera, and Chapter 34: Using and Handling Cameras and Lenses.

THE NIGHT BEFORE THE SHOOT

First assistant:

- Check your call time and be prepared to be early
- Be ready for any special effects or inclement weather (pack protective apparel)
- Check with the second to be sure she's got everything under control
- Check with the DP for last-minute instructions

Second assistant:

- Check your call time and be prepared to be early
- Be ready for any special effects or inclement weather (pack protective apparel)
- Charge batteries
- Make sure all lenses and filters are clean
- Check the changing bag for dirt and holes (before the first day)
- Clean the magazines and load them with film (tape entire perimeter of mag with camera tape of the color you have designated for the type of emulsion)
- Assign every magazine a number and label each with a piece of white tape with the # on it
- Prepare a label on white camera tape for each can of film (enough to start the day) with this information:

> Emulsion #
> Footage
> Date
> Title of film

Roll #
Mag #
Loader's initials

- Put this tape label on the can. When you load the mag, transfer the label to the supply side of the mag. Later, after you have downloaded the mag, you can transfer the label to the film can before it goes to the lab.
- Prepare a camera report for each can of film and tape it to the can. It's a good idea to take some downtime to make a camera report for every can of film. That way, when you load, all you have to do is put the date and magazine number on the report, and you're good to go.

ON THE SET—THE FIRST ASSISTANT

- Unpack, assemble, and warm up the camera and all components at the start of each shooting day
- Do not leave the camera unattended; have the second stand by if you must leave
- Load and unload proper film into camera
- Reset footage counter to zero after each reload
- Keep all parts of the camera, including camera body, lenses, filters, and magazines free from dirt, dust, and moisture
- Set and mark diopter adjustment on viewfinder eyepiece for each key person looking through the camera
- Check that the camera is balanced and level before each shot. If the camera is on a tripod, the tripod *must* be securely positioned and leveled
- Check to be sure that no lights are kicking into the lens, causing flares; work with the grips to kill flares
- Place proper lens, filters, and other accessories as instructed by the DP or camera operator
- Check that the lenses and filters are clean before filming
- Set T-stop as instructed by the DP
- Measure distance to subjects during rehearsals
- Mark lenses for focus if necessary
- Check depth of field for each shot *as needed*. Use your Kelly wheel or an app on your iPhone or PDA
- Check that the camera is set at correct speed during filming
- After each printed take or when instructed by the DP, check the gate for hairs (emulsion buildup) and request another take if necessary
- Keep the DP, AD, and director or script supervisor updated on how much footage is left in the magazine (if you have a script supervisor, check with him/her first to see if you have enough footage to shoot the scene)

ON THE SET—THE SECOND ASSISTANT

- Keep lenses, filters, at least one magazine, and a spare battery near the camera
- Download film inside changing bag, changing tent, or darkroom
- Tape exposed film can with black tape (black = exposed)

- Any remaining film not yet exposed should be recanned with white (or the color designated for that emulsion) tape and labeled as "short end" with the following information:

  Emulsion #
  Footage
  Date
  Loader's initials

- At the end of the day, exposed film must be given to the AD or to the person she designates
- At the end of filming, all film must be given to the AD or to the producer

CINEMATOGRAPHY TEXTS, GUIDEBOOKS, "STANDARD WORKS"

Bare Bones Camera Course for Film and Video by Tom Schroeppel. Tom Schroeppel. (2000) Paper. 89 pages.
    A brief text that whittles the theory down to the essentials. It gives several good exercises and a number of rules-of-thumb to hold on to as a beginner. It addresses basic camera handling and the analysis and reconstruction of scenes. It is very good, very short, but limited to absolute beginners.

The Negative by Ansel Adams. Ansel Adams. (1995) 288 pages.
    Indispensable. Although Adams is a still photographer, in this book he put all of his hard-won knowledge about his Zone System. It's still the best way to begin thinking about exposure.

BY AND ABOUT CINEMATOGRAPHERS
Interviews

New Cinematographers by Alex Ballinger. Collins Design; annotated edition (2004). Paper, 192 pages.

Cinematographer Style Special Edition DVD & Book by Jon Fauer (2008). DVD: 86 minutes. BOOK: American Cinematographer (2008). 384 pages.

Visions of Light: The Art of Cinematography DVD (2000). 92 minutes.
    A classic. You must see it for inspiration if nothing else.

Masters of Light by Schaefer & Salvato. University of California Press (1986). 368 pages.

Contemporary Cinematographers by Pauline B. Rogers. Focal Press (1998). 240 pages.

Art of the Cinematographer by Leonard Maltin. Dover Publications; Rev. Edition (1978). 144 pages.

Memoirs

Every Frame a Rembrandt: Art and Practice of Cinematography by Andrew Laszlo. Focal Press (2000). 272 pages.

Vittorio Storaro: Writing with Light: Volume 1: The Light by Vittorio Storaro. Aperture; Bilingual edition (2002). 312 pages.

A Man With A Camera by Nestor Almendros. Farrar, Straus and Giroux (1986).
322 pages.
Almendros's book is the only one I know in which a cinematographer takes the reader one by one through the thought processes and lighting techniques for each of his movies. All of the movies he shot are worth seeing. Unfortunately, the book is out of print, but it's widely available at libraries.

History

Making Pictures: A Century of European Cinematography by Sven Nykvist. Harry
N. Abrams (2003). 482 pages.
All of the above are interviews, either general or directed to the professional community, memoirs, or history.

VISUAL EXPRESSION

Picture Composition for Film and Television, Second Edition by Peter Ward. (2002)
Focal Press. 288 pages.
A very nicely written theoretical and historical survey of composition with some attention paid to lighting and staging. It deals only in the abstract with on-set cinematography.

The Visual Story by Bruce Block. Focal Press; 2nd edition (2007). 312 pages.
Again, this is not a work specifically about cinematography. It is a philosophical and aesthetic essay that elaborates the theories of two great teachers, Sergei Eisenstein and Slavko Vorkapich. Excellent for its kind, but without practical references.

LIGHTING BOOKS

Set Lighting Technician's Handbook, Fourth Edition: Film Lighting Equipment, Practice, and Electrical Distribution by Harry Box. Focal Press (2011). 556 pages.
Box is mostly a comprehensive reference.

Reflections, First Edition by Benjamin Bergery. A S C Holding Corp. (2002). 268
pages.
Limited to a few specific lighting setups, Reflections *is excellent for what it covers. It is a collection of articles that originally appeared in* American Cinematographer *magazine. Most of them are accounts of a noted cinematographer lighting a small scene as a demonstration for students. I enjoy and appreciate this book, but it is clearly aimed toward cinematographers who have spent a year or more learning the simplest aspects of cinematography are now ready to experiment on their own by imitating masters.*

SPECIALIZED TECHNICAL WORKS AND MANUALS

Operating Cinematography for Film and Video: A Professional and Practical Guide by
William E. Hines, SOC. Ed-Venture Films/Books (1997). 254 pages.
Hines writes from the point of view of a professional, but his book is generally directed at those already in the profession.

Image Control: Motion Picture and Video Camera Filters and Lab Techniques by Gerald Hirschfeld. ASC Press (2005). 172 pages.
Hirschfeld is brilliant. This work on filters and laboratory work is indispensable. Again, it is directed to professional cinematographers, not beginners, but it's a book to read and reread, redoing the exercises Hirschfeld has done.

The Hand Exposure Meter Book, Martin S. Silverman, Jim Zuckerman, Bob Shell, Minolta (2001). 92 pages Out of Print
It's a crying shame that this book is out of print. I think it's the best book on exposure and on using light meters I've ever read. It's almost the only one. Good luck finding a copy.

MANUALS

American Cinematographer Manual, Ninth Edition by Stephen Burum. American Society Of Cinematographers. (2004). 887 pages.

The Camera Assistant's Manual, Sixth Edition by David E. Elkins. Focal Press. (2011). 544 pages.

Arricam Book, Second Edition by Jon Fauer. ASC Press (2005). 408 pages.

Panaflex User's Manual, Second Edition by David Samuelson. Focal Press (1996). 300 pages.

Jumpstart Cinematography Calculator by American Society of Cinematographers. ASC. No date. One card.

American Cinematographer Video Manual from the American Society of Cinematographers. American Cinematographer (2005). 468 pages.

Anton Wilson's Cinema Workshop 4th Edition by Anton Wilson. American Cinematographer (2004). 308 pages.

Professional Cameraman's Handbook, Fourth Edition by Verne and Sylvia Carlson. Focal Press (1994). 576 pages.

David Samuelson's "Hands On" Manual for Cinematographers by David Samuelson. Focal Press (1994). 344 pages.
The title of Samuelson's book suggests that his book is a practical set of instructions. It is, rather, a British version of the American Cinematographer Manual. *It is mostly charts, lists, and tables for reference, with a few essays directed to the professional working cameraman.*

All of these manuals are of greater or less use. All except the Jumpstart Cinematography Calculator *are designed for the professional camera assistant or Director of Photography. The* Jumpstart Cinematography Calculator *is a collection of tables and lens and camera information culled from the* American Cinematographer Manual, *priced affordably. It is for advanced students, those in their second or third year of studying cinematography.*

Many of these manuals refer to a specific professional camera (Arriflex, Arri, or Panaflex) or are for a specific job classification. They are all directed to working professionals.

OF HISTORIC INTEREST

Painting With Light, Fourth Edition by John Alton. University of California Press. (1995). 191 pages.
  Written in the early 1950s, this is an idiosyncratic account of a maverick cinematographer's style from the 1940s.

Professional Cinematography by Charles Clarke. ASC Holding Corp. (2002). 206 pages.
  Published in the early 1960s, Clarke's book is a snapshot of film photography at the end of the black-and-white era, before Hollywood's massive conversion to all-color production.

History of Movie Photography by Brian Coe (OP). Eastview Editions (1982). 176 pages.
  Published in 1982 and now out of print, Coe's book is only a history and offers no information about the work of a cinematographer.

Principles of Cinematography, Leslie J. Wheeler (OP). Fountain Press/Argus (1977). 440 pages.
  Last revised in 1969, Wheeler has a very nice discussion of motion picture technology as it existed before the 1970s, before the advent of lightweight cameras like the Panaflex and the Arriflex, and before Steadicam®. Although many principles are timeless, the specifics are superannuated.
    All of these books are good but dated.

GRIP BOOKS

Uva's Basic Grip Book by Michael Uva. Focal Press (2001). 240 pages.

Uva's Guide To Cranes, Dollies, and Remote Heads by Michael Uva. Focal Press (2002). 368 pages.

Uva's Rigging Guide for Studio and Location by Michael Uva. Focal Press (2000). 320 pages.
  I admire Mike Uva's grip books. His books are all for the somewhat experienced professional who wants to fine tune his or her skills. They are not meant for beginners, and are peripheral to learning cinematography.

MAGAZINES
American cinematographer

The standard journal for the technical end of the industry. Interviews with cinematographers about current films, technical and equipment news, historical articles.

ICG

The Union (IATSE #600) magazine, originally International Photographer. It has changed and improved over the last ten years, and can compete with *American Cinematographer*. More articles directed toward the camera crew.

Student filmmakers

A fairly new publication, the many articles cover the panoply of filmmaking. Everything is directed to the student or beginning filmmaker. As such, it fills a void, and presents practical information of immediate use to low-budget but aspiring filmmakers.

Index

Note: Page numbers followed by *b* indicate boxes and *f* indicate figures.

A

Aaton cameras, 57, 62, 215–216, 285*f*, 286*f*
achromatic lenses, 246
action safe lines, 62–63, 63*f*, 145*f*, 146
action scenes, planning for, 27, 28
actors and actresses. *See* cast; children, working with
Adams, Ansel, 209, 303
ADs. *See* assistant directors
All the President's Men, 15, 189
Allen, Woody, 119, 126–128
Almendros, Nestor, 73–74, 265
Altman, 133–134
American Beauty, 191, 192*f*
American Friend, The, 199
American Society of Cinematographers, 1
amps (amperes), 47
AMTP (Association of Motion Picture and Television Producers), 2
anamorphic lenses, 67
Angenieux lenses, 69
animals, working with, 22, 23, 24
answer prints, 227
antihalation backing, 79–80, 272
aperture (f-stops), 208, 241–244, 250, 251–252, 255–256
apple boxes (man-makers), 12, 146–147, 164
Arnaz, Desi, 60
Aronofsky, Darren, 56
Arri cameras, 57, 62, 80–81, 215–216, 285*f*, 286*f*
arriving early, 103
art directors, 51
aspheric elements, 246
assistant directors (ADs)
    coverage, 120–121
    first day of shooting, 109, 112, 113–114, 115, 116
    production meetings, 93–94
    shot lists, 35

Association of Motion Picture and Television Producers (AMTP), 2

B

back cross lighting, 179, 180–181, 184
backlighting, 179, 179*f*, 183
ball mounts, 85, 294, 294*f*
Barney Miller, 180–181
batteries, 279–280, 313
bayonet mounts, 280–281
behavior, 107–108
Bell and Howell cameras, 216, 286*f*, 288*f*
belt batteries, 279–280
Bening, Annette, 192*f*
best boys
    hardware kits, 92
    hiring, 37, 38
    pre-production, 92
    trucks, 95
Biograph, 1
Bird, 87
Birtch, Thora, 192*f*
Bitzer, G. W., 1–2
Black Swan, 56, 80
black-and-white film, 20, 79–80, 272
blocking, 110, 119–120
Bolex cameras, 216, 286*f*, 288*f*
boom operators, 112–113, 115
bounce light, 183, 193, 197
Bound for Glory, 123
Bracco, Lorraine, 123
Brakhage, Stan, 39
Breathless, 132
Brown, Garrett, 90, 90*f*
Brown, Karl, 1–2
budgets
    camera choice, 55, 56
    pre-production considerations, 25
    telecine, 227
bull's-eye levels, 295, 295*f*

C

call sheets, 97–100, 98*f*, 104
call times, 97–100, 104–105
Camera Assistant Training Program, 2–3
camera assistants. *See* first camera assistants; second camera assistants
camera lucida, 235
camera obscura, 235
camera operators
    call time, 105
    first day of shooting, 111, 112–113, 114, 115
    hiring and experience with, 37, 38
cameras, 235–244
    accessories, 65
    backup, 64
    controls, 239–240
    film versus digital, 55–60
    first day of shooting, 109
    follow focus, 237–238
    gate, 236–237
    height, 161
    iris rods, 237–238
    leveling, 143
    matte boxes, 237–238
    movement, 161, 162, 236–237
    opening and closing, 279
    operating, 141–157
    overheating, 59
    overview, 235–236
    power sources, 279–280, 313
    selecting, 55–65
    sensors, 238–239
    shutter, 236–237
    taping magazines, 290–291
    testing, 61–62, 64, 94
    using and handling, 279–295
    viewing systems, 237, 239
    viewpoint and position of, 20
    white balance, 240

Cameron, James, 55

Canon cameras, 57, 216–217

carbon fiber tripods, 84

Carlson, Verne and Sylvia, 216–217

cast

    camera operation, 147–149

    considering during script reading, 10–11

    cosmetic diffusion, 13

    first day of shooting, 110, 112–113

    height differences, 12

    pregnancies, 12

    skin tones, 12–13

    symmetry of face, 11–12

    testing lenses with, 72

Cat from Outer Space, The, 22

Cat People, 23

CCD (charge-coupled device) sensors, 238–239

changing bags, 288, 289

Chapman dollies, 51, 92*f*, 147*f*

charge-coupled device (CCD) sensors, 238–239

children, working with, 22, 23–24

chokers, 129, 129*f*

cinematographers. *See* directors of photography

circles of confusion, 255

Citizen Kane, 50, 118, 133–134

clipping, 196–197, 227, 267, 314–315

close-ups, 119–120, 125–140, 171*f*, 172*f*, 173, 173*f*

CMOS (complementary metal oxide semiconductor) sensors, 238–239

Colbert, Claudette, 12

collar points, 129, 129*f*

color blind film, 272

color charts, 71–72

color correction (Wratten 85) filters, 72, 79, 201, 268

color separation filters, 199

color temperature, 19–20, 197–199, 277–278

color temperature blue (CTB) gels, 199–200

color temperature meters, 198–199, 200, 201

color temperature orange (CTO) gels, 199–200

colored light, 193

colorists, 225–227, 304

compasses, 42, 43

complementary metal oxide semiconductor (CMOS) sensors, 238–239

composition

    balanced and unbalanced, 146–147, 146*f*

    following the actor, 162

    overview, 159–168

    showing the actor, 152, 159, 160–161

continuous spectra, 200*f*

contrast, 20

contrast filters, 190

Cooke lenses, 247

Cornell, 4

Cosentino, Cos, 103

Coutard, Raoul, 50

coverage, 118–119, 125–140

cowboy shots (cowboy close-ups), 129–130, 132*f*

crab dollies, 91, 120, 162, 163, 165, 301

Craft Service, 103–104

cranes, 3, 4

crew

    See also specific job titles

    hierarchy, 105–106, 106*f*, 107

    hiring, 217, 218

    overview, 37–40

    pre-production preparation, 89–95

    specific job assignments, 40

cribbing, 146–147, 163, 164*f*

cross lighting, 179

crossing the line (180-degree rule), 126–128, 160–161, 169–175

crushing blacks, 227

C-stands, 187*f*

CTB (color temperature blue) gels, 199–200

CTO (color temperature orange) gels, 199–200

D

dailies, 56, 190, 306

darkrooms, 289

daylight-balanced film, 78, 79, 268, 277–278

Days of Heaven, 265

Deakins, Roger, 183–184, 201

demo reels, 229–232

depth, illusion of, 133–134

depth of field, 244, 254, 255, 256–257, 258, 259

designed (planned) masters, 120

DI (digital intermediates), 306–307

dialogue scenes, planning for, 10, 24, 25

Dibie, George Spiro, 74, 180–181

Dickson, W.K.L., 1

diffraction, 256

diffusion, 16, 269–270

diffusion filters, 73–74

digital imaging technicians (DITs), 37, 58, 178

digital intermediates (DI), 306–307

digital media

    choice of, 80–81

    duration of, 272

    exposure, 196

    film versus, 55–60

    pros and cons of, 239

diplomacy, 32–33, 34–35, 93–94, 108, 140, 152

directors

    camera operators and, 142–143, 151, 152

    coverage, 118–119

    first day of shooting, 110, 112–114, 115

    paranoia of, 33–34

    production meetings, 93–94

    reading mind of, 33, 141

    talking through script with, 32

    vision of film, 10, 32–33

directors of photography (DPs; cinematographers)

    apprenticeship, 1–3, 4

    camera operators versus, 142

    college courses, 4–5

    replacement, 39

    women as, 1

discontinuous spectra, 200*f*

DITs (digital imaging technicians), 37, 58, 178

diving boards, 147*f*

dollies

    advantages of, 51

    camera operation, 146–147

    crab, 91, 120, 162, 163, 165, 301

    doorway, 91, 91*f*, 92, 162, 162*f*

    first day of shooting, 109

    following the actor, 162

    marks, 167

    operating, 165–166

    planning shots, 163

    tracking shots, 121–122

    western, 91, 91*f*, 92

dolly grips

    first day of shooting, 112–113, 115

    hiring, 37

overview, 301–301
responsibilities of, 165–166,
167–168
donuts, 76
doorway dollies, 91, 91*f*, 92, 162,
162*f*
Down By Law, 258, 259
DPs. *See* directors of photography
Dylan, Bob, 231

E

Eastwood, Clint, 39
eating on own time, 103–104
Éclair cameras, 216
Edison, Thomas, 1, 178, 278
Edison plugs, 187, 187*f*
EDLs (edit decision lists), 227
effects, considering during script
reading, 27–30
8½, 162
electrical power
cameras, 279–280, 313
long cables and voltage drop, 44
using existing supply on location,
46–48
W = VA formula, 47, 49
Elkins, David, 216–217
Elswit, Robert, 79–80
Emshwiller, Ed, 4
emulsion tests, 210*b*
equipment
See also specific types of equipment
on location, 51
overview, 185–187
planning for needs, 28, 29
ER, 123
etiquette, 107–108
existing light, 45–46, 189
exposure
overview, 195–214
video camera operation, 314
exposure meters, 195, 203–204, 205,
205*f*, 207
exteriors
film choice, 78
lighting, 17, 181–182
ordering film stock, 16–17
eyebrows (sunshades), 76, 293
eyeline, 125, 147–148, 323

F

facing camera, 159, 160
fatigue tilt, 149
Fellini, Federico, 162
Figgis, Mike, 56

film
chemical composition of, 271,
272, 273
digital versus, 55–60
exposure, 196
grain, 78–79
keeping cool, 274
layers of, 272, 273
loading in darkness, 288, 289
ordering stock, 16–17
processing, 274, 303, 304, 305
selecting, 77–81, 217
sensitivity of, 242–244
shooting for slow motion, 79
technicalities, 271–275
testing, 94
threading, 284, 286*f*, 288, 288*f*,
290
film speeds (ISOs), 64, 208–209,
242–244, 252
filters
color correction, 72, 79, 201, 268
color separation, 199
compensating for, 208
contrast, 190
diffusion, 73–74
on digital cameras, 74
donuts, 76
gelatin, 268, 269
graduated, 196–197, 269
netting, 74, 270
neutral density, 72, 73, 202–203,
208, 267–268
number of, 75
optical flats, 73, 265–266
polarizing, 73, 75–76, 196–197,
266, 266*f*, 267, 269
screw-on, 269
size of, 75
skin variations, 13
technicalities, 265–270
testing, 74, 94
first camera assistants
call time, 104–105
feedback on directions, 106
first day of shooting, 109, 111,
112–113, 115
hiring and experience with, 37, 38
night before shooting, 334
pre-production, 89
responsibilities of, 333
on set, 335
smart side of camera, 166
first day/first shot, 109–116
Fisher dollies, 51, 92*f*, 147*f*, 165

fixing in post, 201
flags, 144–145
flat (spherical) lenses, 67–68
Flickering Blue, 53*f*
float, 90
floating focus, 259
floors, 51, 52
fluid heads, 85, 86*f*, 293*f*, 299
fluorescents, 197–198
focal length, 247, 248, 249*f*, 251
Foch, Nina, 103
focus
floating versus racking, 259
follow, 237–238, 253, 261–262,
292
lenses, 252–253
overview, 244
technicalities, 261–263
focus markings, 71
follow focus, 237–238, 253,
261–262, 292
foot-candle meters, 195
foot-candle/stop table, 196*f*
forcing the master, 119–120
Ford, John, 134
foreground objects, 133–134
48-Hour Film Project, 218
Fraker, William, 76
frame chart tests, 62–63, 63*f*
frame lines, 143–144
frame store, 227
frame within a frame, 134, 134*f*
Freezer Jesus, The, 50*f*
Fresnel spotlights, 186, 186*f*, 193
friction heads, 85
frontlighting, 177, 178–179
f-stops (aperture), 208, 241–244,
250, 251–252, 255–256
Fuji film, 77, 78
full frame lines, 62–63, 63*f*, 145,
145*f*, 146
full shots, 132*f*

G

gaffers
first day of shooting, 110
hiring and experience with, 37, 38
pre-production, 89, 92
gaffer's glass, 206np, 206
gain setting, 314
gamma, 227
gates, 236–237
geared heads, 85–87, 86*f*, 87*f*, 299
gelatin filters, 268, 269
gels, 199–200

generators
    locating, 48
    long cables and voltage drop, 44
    loss of, 48, 49, 50
    overview, 92, 93
genres, considering during script
        reading, 21
Girl With A Pearl Earring, 15, 16
Gladwell, Malcolm, 6
glossies, 10–11
gloves, 186
gobo arms, 187*f*
Godard, Jean Luc, 50, 132*f*
Good Night and Good Luck, 79–80
Goodfellas, 123
Gossen incident meters, 205–206
grading (timing), 225–227
Graduate, The, 254
graduated filters (grads), 196–197,
        269
grain, 78–79, 242
Grand Valley State University, 4
gray cards, 61, 64, 190–191, 201, 204
Greer, Jane, 191*f*
Griffith, D. W., 1
Griffolyn, 197, 197*f*
grip wedges, 163, 164*f*
grips, 4, 37. *See also* dolly grips; key
        grips
Groucho shots, 148

H

hairspray, 73, 266
Hall, Conrad, 21
handheld work, 149, 150–151, 151*f*,
        297–298
Hard Day's Night, A, 132
hard light, 191, 191*f*
Harrison, Patty, 288*f*
Harrison Changing Tent, 288, 288*f*
headroom, 126, 127*f*
heads
    adjusting, 143
    balancing camera on, 299
    fluid, 85, 86*f*, 293*f*, 299
    friction, 85
    geared, 85–87, 86*f*, 87*f*, 299
    mounting cameras to, 293, 294
    using, 297–300
    weight of, 88
hierarchy, crew, 105–106, 106*f*, 107
hi-hats, 84–85, 85*f*, 86*f*, 298–299
historical periods, considering during
        script reading, 14–15, 16
Hitchcock, Alfred, 9, 133–134

HMI units, 16, 79, 93
Hochheim, Frieder, 192*f*
Hoffman, Dustin, 254
Hollywood Ending, 126–128
Horse Whisperer, The, 43–44
House, 57
How the West Was Won, 3
Howe, James Wong, 180–181
Hummel, Rob, 303
Hurricane blower, 283

I

I Love Lucy, 60
illumination, 177–178
image circle, 248, 248*f*, 250
in-camera editing
        preparation for, 321–322
        tips for, 323–324
incident meters, 204, 205, 205*f*
infrared light (IR), 203
interiors
        film choice, 16–17, 78, 79
        planning lighting, 17
International Cinematographers
        Guild, 2
IR (infrared light), 203
iris rods, 237–238, 292, 292*f*
irises, 134
Irwin, Matt, 203
ISO tests, 64
ISOs (film speeds), 64, 208–209,
        242–244, 252
Itoya Profolio, 13–14

J

Jarmusch, Jim, 118, 258

K

Kawin, Bruce, 240
Kelly, Graham White, 257
Kelly wheel, 256–257
Kenko incident meters, 205–206
key grips
        first day of shooting, 110
        hardware kits, 92
        hiring and experience with, 37,
            38
        pre-production, 89
key light, 190–191, 196, 206
kick angle, 182*f*, 183
Kinoflo units, 93, 192, 192*f*
knees, 131*f*
Kodak film, 77, 78, 79–80, 274
Kovacs, Laszlo, 206
Kubrick, Stanley, 90*f*

L

laboratory processes, 303–307
lamp operators (secondary
        electricians), 37
Landis, John, 24
lazy Susan seats, 143, 167–168
Leaving Las Vegas, 56, 80
LED units, 93
Leica lenses, 247
Lemmon, Jack, 225
lens caps, 281–282
lens cases, 282–283
lens flares, 144–145, 145*f*
lenses
    achromatic, 246
    anamorphic, 67
    attaching, 280–281, 282
    cleaning, 282–283, 284
    for digital cameras, 70, 72
    exposure relationships, 241–242
    film sensitivity, 242–244
    first day of shooting, 109
    flat (spherical), 67–68
    focus, 244
    focus markings, 71
    ISO, 242–244
    long, 250, 254
    normal, 250
    removing reflections, 76
    selecting, 67–76, 216
    simple, 245*f*, 246
    sunshades (eyebrows), 76, 293
    technical and aesthetic
        considerations, 240–241,
        245–260
    telephoto, 247
    testing, 71, 72, 94
    tilt/shift, 258
    T-stops, 241–242
    using and handling, 279–295
    wide-angle, 247, 250, 253, 254
    zoom, 68, 69
Levitin, Daniel, 6
Libatique, Matty, 80
lifting blacks, 227
lighting
access to, 217
    dialogue scenes with multiple
        characters, 24, 25
    direction exercise, 212*b*
    early pre-production
        considerations, 10–11
    existing, 45–46
    faces, 214*b*
    historical periods, 15, 16

interiors and exteriors, 17
location, 43–46
loss of generator, 48, 49, 50
overview, 177–184, 189–193
packages, 93
quality exercise, 213*b*
skin tones, 12–13
studio, 50, 51
time estimates, 110–111
W = VA formula, 47, 49
working with children, 23–24
Liotta, Ray, 123
loaders, 37
location managers, 41
locations
    checklist, 52*b*, 329
    considering during script reading,
        14–18
    overview, 41–54
    scouting, 52–53, 54, 325
lo-hats, 85*f*
long lenses, 250, 254
look room (nose room), 132–133,
    169, 174
Lucas, George, 55
Lumiére, 178

M

Mad About You, 164
makeup
    early pre-production
        considerations, 10–11
    first day of shooting, 114
man-makers (apple boxes), 12,
    146–147, 164
Mann, Michael, 55
marks
    actor, 110, 113
    dolly, 167
masters, 117–123
matte boxes, 75–76, 150, 237–238,
    269, 280, 292–293, 292*f*
Matthews doorway dollies, 162*f*
Matthpoles, 179, 179*f*
McConkey, Larry, 123
mechanical effects, planning for, 28
mercury vapor lights, 178
metadata, 247
Mitchell tops, 85, 85*f*, 293, 293*f*
Mitchell Vitesse heads, 87, 87*f*
Mitchum, Robert, 191*f*
moiré pattern, 306
Mole-Richardson 2K, 186*f*
Moment of Grace, A, 171*f*, 172*f*
monitors, 239

monopods, 42–43, 325
Montana shots (two tees), 129, 130*f*
Müller, Robby, 73–74, 199, 258,
    265, 273
Murphy, Brianne, 1
Musco lights, 93
Musuraca, Nick, 21–22

N

ND (neutral density) filters, 72, 73,
    202–203, 208, 267–268
netting, using as filter, 74, 270
networking, 229
neutral density (ND) filters, 72, 73,
    202–203, 208, 267–268
Newton, Isaac, 245
Nichols, Mike, 254
noise on set, 105
Noises Off, 111–112
normal lenses, 250
nose room (look room), 132–133,
    169, 174
note taking
    during script reading, 13–14
    video camera operation, 315
Nykvist, Sven, 265

O

O'Connor 2575D fluid heads, 86*f*
180-degree rule (crossing the line),
    126–128, 160–161, 169–175
one-quarter shots, 160
optical flats, 73, 265–266
orthochromatic emulsion, 273
OTS (over-the-shoulders), 130, 133*f*,
    135, 137–138
Out of the Past, 21–22, 191, 191*f*
over lighting, 181–182
over-the-shoulders (OTS), 130, 133*f*,
    135, 137–138

P

painting (over lighting), 181
Panaflex cameras
    digital, 57
    lenses, 67
    mounted, 86*f*
    movement, 236, 236*f*
    threading, 284
Panahead geared heads, 86*f*
Panavision cameras, 2, 57, 62, 67
Panavision frame chart, 249*f*
Panavision lenses, 247
panchromatic emulsion, 273
pans, 136, 139, 254, 299

Parker, Larry, 197–198
parking, 43, 51
persistence of vision, 240
photographic lens tissue, 283–284
pinhole cameras, 235
PL (positive lock) mounts, 281
planned (designed) masters, 120
polarizing filters (Pola-screen), 73,
    75–76, 196–197, 266, 266*f*,
    267, 269
Polaroid 110A camera, 190, 190*f*
Pollard, William Branch, 257
pork chops, 147*f*
positive attitude, 25, 26
positive lock (PL) mounts, 281
Poster, Steve, 268
postproduction
    demo reels, 229–232
    processes, 303–307
    timing and transferring, 225–227
pre-production
    cameras, selecting, 55–65
    crew, 37–40, 89–95
    film stock, selecting, 77–81
    lenses, selecting, 67–76
    location, 41–54
    night before, 97–100
    script reading, 9–20
    shot lists, 31–35
    tripods and heads, selecting, 83–88
printing lights, 198–199
prints, 18–19
production
    cameras, operating, 141–157
    composition, 159–168
    equipment, 185–187
    exposure, 195–214
    lighting, 177–184, 189–193
    180-degree line, 169–175
    shooting, 103–108
production designers, 51
production meetings, 93–94
production schedule, 24, 25
prosumer cameras, 57, 64, 150–151,
    249, 249*f*
punctuality, 103

Q

Quality Light-Metric, 204
quiet on set, 105
Quinn, Declan, 80

R

racking focus, 259
Redford, Robert, 43–44, 269

reflected meters, 204
reflectors, 197
reflex viewing system, 237, 238
registration tests, 61–62
rehearsals, 112–114, 121, 144
retakes, 151–152
reversal film, 80
reverse masters, 120–121
Revolutionary Road, 183–184
rimlighting, 183
Ronford tripods, 84–85, 84*f*, 298

S

Scorsese, Martin, 123
screening room etiquette, 140
screw-on filters, 269
scripts
 action/stunt scenes, 27, 28
 animals, 22, 23, 24
 cast, 10–11
 children, 22, 23–24
 dialogue scenes, 10, 24, 25
 effects, 27–30
 equipment needs, 28, 29
 genres, 21
 historical periods, 14–15, 16
 locations, 14–18
 note taking during reading of,
  13–14
 overview, 9, 10
 positive attitude about, 25, 26
 shot lists, 27–30
 talking through with directors, 32
Searchers, The, 134
seasonal considerations, 17–18
second button, 129, 130*f*
second camera assistants
 call time, 104–105, 106
 first day of shooting, 109, 110,
  112–113, 114
 hiring, 37, 38
 night before shooting, 334–335, 334
 responsibilities of, 333, 334
 on set, 335–336
secondary electricians (lamp
  operators), 37
Sekonic incident meters, 205–206, 205*f*
sensors, 238–239
Serling, Rod, 231
Serra, Eduardo, 15, 16
set call, 104
Shining, The, 90*f*
shoes, 186
shoot call, 104
short ends, 289–290

shot lists
 considering during script reading,
  27–30
 first day of shooting, 110
 in-camera editing, 323
 overview, 31–35
 preparing, 29–30
 storyboards versus, 31
shutter tests, 61
shutters, 236–237
simple lenses, 245*f*, 246
16 mm format
 cameras, 215–216, 279
 focal length, 250
 perforations, 236
 registration tests, 61–62
 35 mm versus, 80
slates, 114
slop, 85
slow-motion speed, 79, 87
small masters, 120
Society of Motion Picture and
  Television Engineers (SMPTE),
  209
soft light, 191, 192, 192*f*
Sony cameras, 57, 59
sound mixers, 114, 115
soundtracks, demo reel, 231
Spacey, Kevin, 192*f*
Spectra incident meters, 205–206,
  209
spherical (flat) lenses, 67–68
Spielberg, Steven, 55
split diopters, 258
spot meters, 204, 209–210
spreaders
 tripod, 83, 84*f*, 294–295, 294*f*
 wall, 179–180, 180*f*
stacking, 112
stage line, 170–171, 171*f*
standard coverage, 118–119
stand-by camera operators, 141–142
stand-ins, 110, 111–112
Steadicam Operators' Association, 90
Steadicams, 89, 90–91, 90*f*, 122, 123
stills
 location, 42
 printing, 18–19
stingers, 187
Storaro, Vittorio, 9
storyboards, 31, 32*f*
Stranger Than Paradise, 118
stunt coordinators, 27
stunts, planning for, 27, 28
sunshades (eyebrows), 76, 293

super-16 format, 56, 61–62, 80,
  215–216, 249*f*
super-35 format, 69–70
Surtees, Bob, 254
Suspicion, 133–134

T

tape measures, 262
Taylor, Rodney, 13–14
telecine, 225–227, 306
telephoto lenses, 247
28 Days Later, 57
35 mm format
 cameras, 279
 focal length, 250
 frame, 248–249, 248*f*, 249*f*
 perforations, 236
 16 mm versus, 80
Thomas, Kristin Scott, 43–44
3:2 pull down, 306*f*
three-person setup, 172*f*, 174
three-point lighting, 184
three-quarter shots, 160–161
tilt/shift lenses, 258
time of day, 15
timers, 225–227, 304–305
timing (grading), 225–227
Titan cranes, 3, 3*f*
title safe lines, 62–63
Touch of Evil, 118, 160
tracking shots, 121–122, 163,
  164–165
tripods
 carbon fiber, 84
 disadvantages of, 51
 locks, 298, 298*f*
 mounting cameras to, 293,
  294–295, 294*f*
 selecting, 83–88
 spreaders, 83, 84*f*, 294–295,
  294*f*
 using, 297–300
 wooden, 84–85, 84*f*, 298, 298*f*
trucks
 loading, 95
 preparing, 94, 95
truss system, 179–180, 180*f*
tungsten light, 197–198, 278
tungsten-balanced film, 78, 79, 268,
  277–278
Twilight Zone, The, 24, 231
two tees (Montana shots), 129, 130*f*
two-person setup, 170–171, 171*f*,
  172*f*, 174*f*
two-shots, 135, 138

U

under lighting, 182
Usual Suspects, The, 133–134
Uva, Mike, 29

V

Vaseline look, 73, 266
video cameras
    DCR-TRV15/17 checklist/cheat
        sheet, 319–320
    PD 100 cheat sheet, 317–318
    tips for operating, 313–315
viewfinders, 144, 145, 237–238,
    239
viewing systems, 237, 239
Visions of Light, 265
VistaVision frame, 248–249,
    248*f*

volts, 47
Vortex Media, 202

W

waist shots, 131*f*
wall spreaders, 179–180, 180*f*
warm cards, 202
watts, 47
Wayne, John, 134
weather considerations, 17, 18
websites, 232, 240
Welles, Orson, 118, 133–134,
    160
West Wing, 123
western dollies, 91, 91*f*, 92
Wexler, Haskell, 265
white balance, 19–20, 201, 202, 240,
    277–278, 314–315

wide shots, 126, 130–132, 135–136,
    138
wide-angle lenses, 247, 250, 253,
    254
Willis, Gordon, 15, 247
women as cinematographers, 1
Wooden, John, 9
wooden tripods, 84–85, 84*f*, 298,
    298*f*
Wratten 85 (color correction) filters,
    72, 79, 201, 268

Z

zebras, 196, 197*f*, 314
Zeiss lenses, 71, 246
Zelig, 247, 273
zoom lenses, 68, 69
zooms, 136, 139, 167, 314